Health Service Marketing Management in Africa

Health Service Marketing Management in Africa

Edited by
Robert Ebo Hinson, Kofi Osei-Frimpong,
Ogechi Adeola, and Lydia Aziato

Routledge
Taylor & Francis Group

A PRODUCTIVITY PRESS BOOK

First edition published in 2020
by Routledge/Productivity Press
52 Vanderbilt Avenue, 11th Floor New York, NY 10017

2 Park Square, Milton Park, Abingdon, Oxon OX14 4RN, UK

Routledge/Productivity Press is an imprint of Taylor & Francis Group, an Informa business

No claim to original U.S. Government works

Printed on acid-free paper

International Standard Book Number-13: 978-0-367-00193-3 (Hardback)
International Standard Book Number-13: 978-0-429-40085-8 (eBook)

Library of Congress Cataloging-in-Publication Data
Names: Hinson, Robert (Robert Ebo), editor, author. | Aziato, Lydia, editor, author. | Adeola, Ogechi, editor, author. | Osei-Frimpong, Kofi, editor, author.
Title: Health service marketing management in Africa / editors: Robert Hinson, Lydia Aziato, Ogechi Adeola, and Kofi Osei-Frimpong.
Description: New York : Routledge, 2020. | Includes bibliographical references and index.
Identifiers: LCCN 2019035257 (print) | LCCN 2019035258 (ebook) | ISBN 9780367001933 (hardback) | ISBN 9780429400858 (ebook)
Subjects: LCSH: Medical care–Africa–Marketing. | Health services administration–Africa.
Classification: LCC RA410.55.A35 H437 2020 (print) | LCC RA410.55.A35 (ebook) | DDC 338.473621096–dc23 LC record available at https://lccn.loc.gov/2019035257
LC ebook record available at https://lccn.loc.gov/2019035258

Visit the Taylor & Francis Web site at
www.taylorandfrancis.com

Contents

About the Editors and Contributors

George Acheampong holds a PhD from the University of Ghana after completing coursework at the University of Copenhagen. His research interests focus on how businesses can influence African development through market led approaches. These specifically focus on entrepreneurship and internationalization issues. Some of his contributions have appeared in the *International Marketing Review* and *Journal of Small Business and Enterprise Development*. He is a member/fellow of the Academy of Management, Development Economics Research Group (Copenhagen) and Academy of African Business and Development. He is currently a lecturer at the University of Ghana Business School.

Ogechi Adeola is an Associate Professor of Marketing at the Lagos Business School (LBS), Pan-Atlantic University, Nigeria. She is also the Academic Director, LBS Sales & Marketing Academy. Her research interests include tourism and hospitality marketing, strategic marketing, healthcare services, and digital marketing strategies in sub-Saharan Africa. She has published academic papers in top-ranking scholarly journals. Her co-authored papers won Best Paper Awards at conferences in 2016, 2017, and 2018. She holds a Doctorate in Business Administration (DBA) from Manchester Business School, United Kingdom.

Isaiah Adisa is a private researcher working with a faculty member at the Lagos Business School, Pan-Atlantic University, Lagos, Nigeria. He studied Industrial Relations and Human Resources Management at the Olabisi Onabanjo University (formerly Ogun State University), Ago-Iwoye, Ogun State, Nigeria. He graduated with second class honours (upper division) and distinction, respectively, from undergraduate and postgraduate studies at the same university. He is an astute researcher whose interests focus on, but are not limited to, industrial relations and human resources management, organisations strategy, marketing, and gender-related studies.

Charles Ampong Adjei is an Assistant Lecturer in the Department of Community Health Nursing, School of Nursing and Midwifery, University of Ghana. He holds a Master of Public Health and Master of Philosophy in Nursing from the University of Vrije/KIT in the Netherlands and the University of Ghana respectively. He is currently a final PhD candidate at Maastricht University, the Netherlands. Charles is an experienced teacher and a researcher. His research focuses primarily on communicable diseases, sexual and reproductive health, and preceptorship in nursing. He is a consultant to several firms including PPAG, Nurses-CPD Consult, and Hepatitis Alliance of Ghana.

Douglas Opoku Agyeman holds an MPhil in Marketing and is a teaching assistant in the Department of Marketing and Entrepreneurship at the University of Ghana Business School. He currently directs a community-based human trafficking prevention project and a youth leadership project in Ghana through the Cheerful Hearts Foundation and Patriots Ghana respectively. His research interests are in the areas of SME growth, social entrepreneurship, and sustainable socio-economic developments in sub-Saharan African countries. He has published in the *Journal of Entrepreneurship and Innovation in Emerging Economies*.

Solomon Yaw Agyeman-Boaten holds an MPhil in Economics from the University of Ghana. His research spans the interface of development economics and institutional environments of business and their implications for the welfare of Ghanaian households. He is currently a research assistant at the University of Ghana Business School.

Golda Anambane is a lecturer in the Department of Marketing, Wisconsin International University College, Ghana. She holds a Master of Philosophy Degree in Marketing from the University of Ghana and has taught a number of undergraduate courses since becoming an academic. Aside her experience in teaching, Golda has a profound interest in research and has had papers published in recognized peer-reviewed journals. She emerged as the Valedictorian of her Master's degree graduating class (College of Humanities, University of Ghana – July 2018). She was also the proud recipient of the Best Marketing Student award during her graduation for a Bachelor's degree (All Nations University College, Ghana – November 2012).

Thomas Anning-Dorson is a Senior Lecturer at the Wits Business School of the University of Witwatersrand, Johannesburg, South Africa. He holds a PhD in Marketing from the University of Ghana Business School. His research interest spans innovation, service management, strategy, and emerging markets.

Kenneth Appiah is a Lecturer in Marketing, Entrepreneurship, Small Business Management, and International Business at Cumbria Business School, University of Cumbria. He holds a PhD in Marketing/International Business from the University of Bedfordshire, UK. His research focuses on market entry strategies, internationalisation and competitiveness of SMEs, particularly emerging SMEs, and technology transfer; innovation, technology, and development; and influences on marketing and SMEs. Kenneth has published articles in a number of journals such as the *Journal of Critical Perspective in International Business*, *Journal of Business and Retail Management* and several other outlets.

Kumiwaa Asante is a graduate assistant at the Ghana Institute of Management and Public Administration (GIMPA) Business School. She holds an MSc in Business Administration (Marketing option) and is working towards her PhD in Marketing at the University of Stellenbosch. Her research interests include marketing, consumer behavior, social marketing, marijuana research, mental health, and health marketing.

Lydia Aziato is an Associate Professor and the Dean of the School of Nursing and Midwifery, University of Ghana. She has been a nurse since 1997. She had her Bachelor's degree in Nursing and Psychology and an MPhil in Nursing from the University of Ghana. She had her specialty training in Oncology Nursing from the Cross Cancer Institute in Edmonton, Canada in 2006 and a PhD in Nursing from the University of the Western Cape, in 2013. She has published over 50 papers in credible peer-reviewed journals. Her research interests are pain, cancer, women's health, and surgical nursing. She has advanced skills in qualitative research.

Anita Asiwome Adzo Baku is a lecturer in the Department of Public Administration and Health Services Management of the University of Ghana Business School. She has a PhD in Management from the Putra Business School, Universiti Putra Malaysia. She lectures on courses in insurance and health services management at the University of Ghana Business School. Her research interests cover healthcare financing and health insurance, occupational safety and health management, health policy, and management. She has produced various publications and is a reviewer for journals such as the *International Journal of Sociology and Social Policy* and the *International Journal of Workplace Health Management*.

David Ehira is a graduate student of Interactive Media at the University of Westminster. He has been involved in transdisciplinary research efforts in cognitive technologies, marketing, and the use of artificial intelligence (AI) expert systems. Known for his creativity and meticulousness in putting ideas into motion, he is interested in the application of emerging technologies to creating user-centred innovations for optimising business processes and enhancing service delivery systems. His current research interest lies in the use of artificial intelligence systems for promoting sound mental health among employees in the UK.

Jimoh G. Fatoki is a Research Assistant in the Department of Operations Management at Lagos Business School, Nigeria. He graduated from the Department of Agricultural and Environmental Engineering, University of Ibadan, Nigeria with first-class honours; and he won the Association of African Universities (AAU) graduate internship award in 2015 after bagging a Master's degree with distinction from the same university. Mr Fatoki has co-authored five peer-reviewed research articles in academic journals and he is currently embarking on a PhD study in the Department of Business Administration and Management at New Mexico State University in the United States.

Ama Pokuaa Fenny is a Research Fellow with the Institute of Statistical, Social and Economics Research (ISSER) at the University of Ghana. Since 2005, she has researched and published in the area of developmental issues in health financing, health service delivery, and social protection. Her current research areas include finding synergies to integrate governmental policies into service delivery systems in Ghana. She has a PhD in Health Economics from the Department of Public Health, Aarhus University, Denmark and an MSc in Health, Population and Society from the London School of Economics and Political Science (UK).

Deli Dotse Gli is a Teaching Assistant in the Department of Marketing and Entrepreneurship at the University of Ghana Business School. Deli Dotse Gli obtained his Master of Philosophy (MPhil) degree from University of Ghana Business School. Deli Dotse Gli is passionate about research and teaching, with research interests in corporate marketing, health marketing, sustainable marketing, and consumer engagement.

Robert Ebo Hinson is an Extraordinary Professor at the North West University Business School in South Africa and Head of Department of Marketing and Entrepreneurship at the University of Ghana Business School. He has also served as Rector of the Perez University College in Ghana and holds two doctorate degrees; one in International Business from the Aalborg University in Denmark and the other in Marketing from the University of Ghana.

Abel Kinoti Meru is a Professor and Dean, Riara University School of Business, Kenya, and the founding Chair of the Academy of International Business – Africa Chapter. He is a seasoned innovation and business incubation consultant. He holds a Doctorate Degree in Commerce from Nelson Mandela Metropolitan University, South Africa, an MBA (Marketing) and a Bachelor of Commerce (Accounting) degree. He also holds a Post Graduate Certificate in Academic Practice from York St. John University (UK) and an International Faculty Programme Certificate from IESE Business School, University of Navarra-Barcelona (Spain). He also has extensive training in case writing and the use of case teaching methods from Lagos Business School, Pan-Atlantic University, Nigeria and Gordon Institute of Business Science, University of Pretoria, South Africa. He is a renowned author.

Mary Wanjiru Kinoti is a Professor and a certified behavioral scientist and axiologist from the United States of America, and is Associate Dean at the School of Business, University of Nairobi, Kenya. She holds a PhD Degree in Business Administration from the University of Nairobi, Kenya, and an MBA-Marketing and BCom Finance and Economics from India. She has co-authored other book chapters, among them "Women Empowerment through Government Loaned Entrepreneurship Teams in Kenya" in *Research Handbook on Entrepreneurial Teams: Theory and Practice*, Edward Elgar Publishing, and *The Business Case for Climate Change: The Impact of Environmental forces on Kenya's Public Listed Companies*, Emerald Group Publishing Limited.

Philip Afeti Korto is a seasoned Ghanaian Health Service Administrator who has been working in the Ghana Health Service for over a decade. He holds a BSc Administration (Health Service Administration option) from University of Ghana Business School (UGBS). He also holds a Master of Public Administration from the Ghana Institute of Management and Public Administration (GIMPA). He has worked as the Head of Administration and Support Services at three different hospitals and he currently works in the same capacity at Achimota Hospital. He once worked at Ridge Hospital as a junior Administrator. He has some publications to his credit and is currently writing a text book on Hospital Administration in Ghana. He occasionally gives practical lectures at UGBS. He is an active member of the Association of Health Service Administrators, Ghana (AHSAG).

Mahmoud Abdulai Mahmoud is a Senior Lecturer in the Department of Marketing and Entrepreneurship, University of Ghana Business School. He is also a Senior Research Fellow in the Department of Marketing Management, University of Johannesburg, South Africa. Mahmoud holds a Doctorate Degree from the University of Ghana. He has a number of peer review journal publications to his credit. He has consulted and trained several institutions in the areas of marketing, sales, and customer service.

Gwendolyn Mensah is a Lecturer in the Adult Health Department, School of Nursing and Midwifery, College of Health Sciences, University of Ghana. She took her PhD at the then Nelson Mandela Metropolitan University, now Nelson Mandela University, from 2014 to 2017. She enrolled onto the MPhil program in 2010, completing it in 2012, and the BA Nursing with Psychology in 2004, completing in 2007, all at the University of Ghana. She was trained as a State Registered Nurse and a Registered Midwife in 1992 and 1996 respectively. She has been a nurse/midwife for 27 years and a Deputy Director of Nursing Services.

Obinna S. Muogboh is Faculty Member and Head of the Operations Management Department, Lagos Business School (LBS), Pan-Atlantic University, Lagos. He was Director of the Doctorate program and served as Managing Editor of *LBS Management Review*. Dr Muogboh also served as the Chief Executive Officer of Jess-NP limited, a Nigeria-based manufacturing firm. He also worked as Researcher at the Automation and Robotics Laboratory, and the Center for e-Design and Realization, University of Pittsburgh, USA. He was an International Fellow at INSEAD, France, and in the Open University, UK. He has consulted for various organisations, including multilateral agencies such as UNIDO. His research is in the area of manufacturing management, logistics, and operations strategy. His work has been published in many international journals. He received his MSc and PhD in Industrial Engineering from the University of Pittsburgh, USA. He received his BEng in Electronic Engineering from the University of Nigeria, Nsukka.

John Muriithi is currently Deputy Vice Chancellor at Riara University, Nairobi, Kenya. Dr. Muriithi is a proven leader in the corporate world and also has impressive teaching and management credentials at various universities. John was CEO of the Mater Hospital, Nairobi, Kenya (2008–2015). Between 2001 and 2004, John served as Chief Executive of SC Johnson East Africa as well as on the management board of SC Johnson sub-Saharan Africa. John has taught marketing and strategic change management in executive education and MBA programs at Strathmore Business School since 2009. Dr. Muriithi holds a Doctorate in Business Administration from the California School of Business and Organizational Studies, an MBA from USIU, Nairobi, and a BEd (Chemistry) from the University of Nairobi.

Michael Nkrumah holds an MSc Marketing and a Postgraduate Certificate in Business Administration from Ghana Institute of Management and Public Administration. He is an adjunct lecturer in marketing with the same institute. He manages a startup called SnooCODE, a fit-for-purpose addressing system for individuals and businesses across the developing world. Michael

Nkrumah also has experience in the advertising field, planning media campaigns for consumer brands such as McVities, Beiersdoff (Nivea), GlaxoSmithKline (Lucozade, Panadol, Sensodyne, Colart), and Merck SevenSeas. Michael's research interests include both qualitative and quantitative approaches in exploring positioning strategies for service brands and B2B firms, issues pertaining to religious influence on customer orientation and perceptions of value, conceptualizing brand love for service brands, and the relationship between corporate reputation and brand crisis. Michael has published in international peer-reviewed journals.

Adaeze Nworie is a Registered Nurse with over 20 years of experience in Healthcare. She also has an MBA in Marketing and Supply Chain from Penn State University, USA. Based in the United States, she started Protem Homecare, a Medicare-certified homecare agency, in 2006, Protem Hospice in 2014 and, more recently, Alliant Treatment Center in 2017. She is currently enrolled in a Doctor of Nursing Practice (DNP) program at the Ohio University in Athens, Ohio.

Michael Boadi Nyamekye (PhD) is a Lecturer at the University of Professional Studies, Accra, Ghana. The focus of his research is in the area of innovation, nonprofit marketing, service marketing, and strategy.

Raphael Odoom (PhD) is a research associate in the Department of Marketing Management, University of Johannesburg, and is currently with the Department of Marketing and Entrepreneurship at the University of Ghana Business School. His research interests are in the areas of branding, digital marketing, and small business management. He has published in the *International Journal of Contemporary Hospitality Management, Journal of Enterprise Information Management, Journal of Product and Brand Management, Qualitative Market Research: An International Journal* and *Marketing Intelligence and Planning*, among others.

Lillian Akorfa Ohene is a registered nurse with several years of teaching experience in basic and advanced nursing. As a lecturer in the Department of Community Health Nursing, University of Ghana, Lilian holds a Bachelor of Science, Master of Philosophy and a PhD, all in Nursing. She specialized in the field of paediatric nursing and was a beneficiary of a Queen Elizabeth II Scholarship. Dr Ohene is the Faculty Counsellor, Sigma Theta Tau, Chi Omicron Chapter at the University of Ghana, a Foundation Fellow, Ghana College of Nurses and Midwives, and a member of the West African College of Nurses and Midwives.

Emmanuel Okunga Wandera is a medical doctor with a specialization in Applied Epidemiology. He currently serves in the Division of Disease Surveillance and Epidemic Response as Head of Epidemic Preparedness and Response and also Public Health Emergency Operations Centre Manager in Kenya.

Oluwayemisi Olomo is a doctoral candidate in Marketing at Lagos Business School, Nigeria and an Adjunct Lecturer at Pan-Atlantic University, Nigeria, where she teaches marketing to undergraduate students. Her research interests include health branding, corporate branding, corporate communications, and social media marketing.

Ellis L.C. Osabutey is a Reader in International Business, Strategy and Technology Transfer at Roehampton Business School, University of Roehampton. His research interests include Foreign Direct Investment and Technology Transfer; Innovation, Technology, and Development; and Institutional Influences on International HRM/D and Marketing. His current research aims to produce critical and unique research outputs that can, distinctly, bring out nuanced African and non-African contexts to promote evidence-based policy-making in developing countries and Africa. Ellis has published articles in journals such as the *Journal of World Business, Journal of Business Research, International Journal of Contemporary Hospitality Management, Technological Forecasting and Social Change*, etc.

Kofi Osei-Frimpong is a Senior Lecturer in Marketing at the Ghana Institute of Management and Public Administration (GIMPA) Business School, Accra, Ghana. He received his PhD from the University of Strathclyde, Glasgow, UK. Kofi is also a Research Fellow at the Vlerick Business School, Belgium. His research interests include value co-creation in healthcare service delivery, customer engagement practices, social media use, online live chat, and artificial intelligence. He is published in high impact journals such as *Computers in Human Behavior*, *Journal of Business Research*, *Technological Forecasting and Social Change*, the *International Journal of Retail & Distribution Management*, *Journal of Marketing Theory and Practice*, *Journal of Service Theory and Practice*, and *Journal of Nonprofit and Public Sector Marketing*, and he has also presented papers at international service research conferences.

Olutayo Otubanjo is a Senior Lecturer at The Lagos Business School, where he teaches full time and presents executive MBA modules in marketing management. He was a Visiting Research Fellow at The Warwick Business School, University of Warwick (UK) and was in a similar capacity at The Spears School of Business, Oklahoma State University, USA. He holds a PhD in Marketing with an emphasis on corporate identity. Otubanjo attended the University of Hull (UK) and Brunel University, London. He has published in the *Academy of Marketing Science Review*; *Tourist Studies*; *Management Decisions*; *Marketing Review*; *Journal of Product and Brand Management*; *Corporate Reputation Review*; *Corporate Communications: An International Journal* etc. His research interests sit at the interface between *social constructionism*, on the one hand, and the elements of corporate marketing including *corporate branding*, *corporate identity*, *corporate reputation*, *corporate communications cum corporate PR*, on the other. He was at one time in his practitioner career, Director of Strategy and Account Planning at FCB Nigeria.

Nana Owusu-Frimpong is a Professor of Marketing at the Ghana Institute of Management and Public Administration (GIMPA) Business School, Accra, Ghana. He received his PhD in Marketing from Durham University, UK. He has published extensively in leading academic journals such as the *Journal of Business Research*, *International Business Review*, *Technological Forecasting and Social Change*, *Journal of Services Marketing*, the *Services Industry Journal*, *Journal of Retailing and Consumer Services*, and *Thunderbird International Business Review*. He has published in the areas of financial/services marketing, consumer behavior, international marketing, foreign direct investment in emerging markets, and customer relations management.

Gideon L. Puplampu holds a PhD in Nursing Education and Research from the University of Alberta, Canada. His interest in global health trends and healthcare consumerism makes him an interesting author on the subject. Gideon received a lifetime international award in 2013 from Golden Key International as an outstanding scholar. Gideon is currently a lecturer at the School of Nursing and Midwifery, University of Ghana, Legon. His specialty area is in mental health nursing with a focus on HIV, hope, and healthcare consumers' behaviors. Gideon has authored several peer review articles.

Ibelema Sam-Epelle is currently a Doctorate of Business Administration (DBA) candidate at the University of Gloucestershire. His current research interest involves the behavioral aspects of individualised information systems. In fulfilment of an MSc in International Business, he independently developed a social media marketing strategy for a carpooling startup in the United Kingdom and has since co-authored a book chapter on smartphones. Over the years, Ibelema has also contributed at Mobility Arena, one of West Africa's revered technology-oriented online resources.

Nii Norkwei Tackie is Research Assistant at the Marketing and Entrepreneurship Department of the University of Ghana Business School. His research interests include consumer behavior, social media, marketing analytics, and big data.

Ernest Yaw Tweneboah-Koduah is a senior lecturer at the University of Ghana Business School. He obtained his Doctor of Philosophy (PhD) degree from London Metropolitan University, UK. His teaching and research interests include social marketing, health marketing, services marketing and political marketing. He has published in peer-reviewed international journals including the *Journal of Social Marketing*; *African Journal of Economics and Management Studies*; *Journal of Hospitality Marketing and Management*; *Journal of Small Business and Enterprise Development*; *Journal of African Business*; *Journal of Nonprofit and Public Sector Marketing;* and *Health Marketing Quarterly*.

Andrews Agya Yalley is a marketing lecturer at the University of Cape Coast, Ghana. He received his PhD in Marketing from the University of Coventry, United Kingdom. His research focuses on service marketing, co-production, political and religious marketing, and sustainability marketing. His research has been published in refereed journals and other international marketing conference proceedings.

Acknowledgments

The authors acknowledge the support of all the reviewers who gave constructive feedback to the chapter authors. The authors also acknowledge the Development Policy Poverty Monitoring and Evaluation Centre of Research Excellence at the University of Ghana and the Skills Development Fund as well.

1 Introduction to Healthcare Service Marketing Management

Building Customer-Driven Health Organisations

Robert Ebo Hinson, Kofi Osei-Frimpong, Ogechi Adeola, Lydia Aziato

INTRODUCTION

Healthcare services are considered the backbone of society and human wellness. The recent institutional transformations in the healthcare services have enormous potential for research and the sector is fast becoming an exciting field of inquiry for marketing and management scholars. Given that marketers are concerned about the creation of value for customers, one of the latest trends in the healthcare sector in Africa is the application of tested and established principles of value creation in mainstream marketing to the healthcare sector. However, this remains a grey area which requires a comprehensive understanding and application of mainstream marketing and management principles. As a result, this book presents contemporary and thoughtful insights to address marketing and management related principles in healthcare delivery within the African context.

Healthcare services are considered the backbone of society and human wellness. In recent times, these services have undergone extensive institutional transformation (Danaher and Gallan, 2016). Within the context of this transformation, marketing, service quality and value creation enhance the service experience of healthcare customers (Osei-Frimpong, 2016). For example, Sahoo and Ghosh (2016) identified service delivery, amongst others, as a significant contributor to enhancing customer satisfaction in private healthcare delivery. It is notable that the healthcare industry has enormous potential and is fast becoming an exciting field of endeavour for marketing practitioners. Given that marketers are concerned about the creation of value for customers, one of the latest trends in the healthcare sector is the application of tested and established principles of value creation in mainstream marketing to the healthcare sector.

Stremersch (2008) notes that the application of marketing to healthcare is a fascinating field that will likely have more impact on society than any field of marketing. He further states that an intrinsically unstable environment characterises this very relevant emerging field, hence raising new questions. Changing regulations, discoveries and new health treatments continuously appear and give rise to these questions. Furthermore, advancements in technology not only improve the healthcare delivery systems but also provide avenues for customers to seek information regarding their health conditions and influence their participatory behaviours or changing roles in the service delivery (Osei-Frimpong, Wilson and Lemke, 2018). Increasingly, there is a shift from the doctor-led approach to a more patient-centred approach. About a decade ago, Kay (2007) argued that healthcare organisations need to utilise marketing tools more effectively for customer information and assistance in their healthcare decisions. This effort can only be achieved by healthcare organisations that promote increased accessibility of care and improved quality of service. Kay (2007) argued these points from the perspective of the US-based healthcare system described as "market-based".

In Africa, the importance of marketing-driven practices in improving the delivery of healthcare services cannot be overemphasised. The issue of healthcare delivery and management is significant for policymakers, private sector players and consumers of health-related services in developing economy contexts. Scholars have strongly argued in favour of marketing and value creation in healthcare service delivery in Africa (i.e. Wanjau, Muiruri and Ayodo, 2012; Mahmoud, 2016; Osei-Frimpong 2016). For instance, in Ghana, Osei-Frimpong (2016) advocated for healthcare service providers to understand patient needs or goals and adopt a holistic engagement approach that would result in positive experiences. Customer experience affects the perception of service quality and acceptability of healthcare services. In South Africa, Hasumi and Jacobsen (2014) found that long waiting times, unavailable medications and staff who are perceived as being unfriendly affected the acceptability of healthcare services. In Egypt, Shafei, Walburg and Taher (2015) identified areas of shortfall in service quality as including physician reliability, physician assurance, nursing reliability and nursing assurance. In the Nigerian context, Adepoju, Opafunso and Ajayi (2018) found that patients were not satisfied with the quality of service in most of the dimensions assessed (i.e. assurance, reliability, tangibles, empathy and responsiveness). In a study on factors affecting service quality in the public health sector in Kenya, Wanjau, Muiruri and Ayodo (2012) found that low employee capacity, low technology adoption, ineffective communication channels and insufficient funding affect service quality delivery to patients, thus influencing healthcare service quality perceptions, patient satisfaction and loyalty. These examples of healthcare service marketing research, in the present contexts, highlight the need to utilise marketing and value creation tools in the delivery of healthcare services. Furthermore, there is a need for the integration of service marketing and management principles to enhance the delivery of quality healthcare across Africa and other developing economies. Therein lies the critical importance of this book.

Drawing on the above discussions, this new book on Health Service Marketing Management responds to calls for quality healthcare service management practices or processes from developing economy perspectives. Focusing primarily on Africa, this book covers seven thematic areas, namely: Strategy in Healthcare; Marketing Imperatives in Healthcare Management; Product and Pricing Management in Healthcare; Distribution, Marketing Communications and Branding in Healthcare; People, Physical Evidence and Service Quality Management in Healthcare; Process Management in Healthcare; and Technology in Healthcare.

BOOK THEMATIC AREAS

This book takes a holistic view of the healthcare service delivery by integrating key concepts that could enhance the performance of the sector from the perspective of the healthcare organisation, professionals and customers. In particular, the book advocates for a need for healthcare organisations and professionals to reorient to understand the changing customer better. This also suggests a need for healthcare organisations to improve on their engagement with customers to ensure a holistic experience. In contributing to the growth and development of the healthcare industry in Africa, this book offers a comprehensive understanding of how the healthcare service sector could be managed to ensure sustainability, competitiveness and overall value creation.

The book is divided into seven parts as summarised in the following sections:

STRATEGY IN HEALTHCARE

The first part of this book discusses two important topics, namely, the societal and healthcare context, and strategic planning and healthcare services. In Chapter 2, Aziato, Ohene and Adjei discuss the societal and healthcare context. This chapter sheds light on the integrated literature of healthcare and positions healthcare in the context of changing societal factors such as globalisation, economic factors, technological factors, cultural revolution, the consumerist customer and some key healthcare developments. The authors argue that despite the milieu of challenges in African healthcare, healthcare professionals should improve their orientation toward the changing societal context, in particular the cultural diversity within the continent, and promote services that will enhance customer satisfaction. Chapter 3, by Adeola and Adisa, addresses the issue of strategic planning and healthcare services. This chapter examines the nature of the market and how a strategic planning process can be used to solve the challenges associated with marketing healthcare delivery in Africa. The authors affirm the importance of strategic plans in improving healthcare delivery and call for a need for healthcare organisations to develop strategic plans that respond to the changing dynamics of the environment in order to create a healthcare sector that understands the needs of the people. The chapter further sheds light on the relevance of integrating intensive research in assessing the internal/external environments of the healthcare organisation to guide the development of strategic plans and their effective implementation.

Marketing Imperatives in Healthcare Management

The second part of the book addresses some key marketing concepts as applied in healthcare management. Anning-Dorson, Tackie and Nyamekye explore marketing in healthcare management in Chapter 4. They explain the critical role of marketing in healthcare management and offer some considerations of the strategic value of marketing to healthcare and how it could be adopted by entities operating in the healthcare space. The chapter argues that while the marketing concept was not a priority of healthcare organisations in the past, the changing market conditions and growing competition have made the adoption of marketing principles and philosophies relevant in today's healthcare environment. Chapter 5, by Adeola, Ehira and Nworie, discusses segmentation, targeting and positioning (STP) in the healthcare sector by clearly explaining the approaches to the market segmentation process for healthcare services and the factors to be considered in selecting a healthcare target market. The chapter contends that STP informs the identification of needed healthcare niches and as a result contributes to the proper management of expectations, increased patient satisfaction and proper allocation of limited resources. The final section of this chapter discusses consumers and consumer behaviour in healthcare services management. Hence, Chapter 6, by Puplampu, Fenny and Mensah, describes the major features of consumers and consumer behaviour in healthcare delivery and the factors and models associated with consumers and consumer behaviour. They argue that while consumers' behaviour is influenced by a number of factors, the decision to purchase healthcare services or equipment is becoming a complex phenomenon due to the changing nature of healthcare consumers as they become more knowledgeable and enlightened and have increased expectations. In light of this, the chapter offers some recommendations to guide healthcare professionals in the discharge of their duties.

Product and Pricing Management in Healthcare

The third part of the book discusses healthcare products and pricing management. Muriithi, Kinoti, Okunga and Kinoti discuss healthcare product management in Chapter 7. The chapter explicates the complex nature of the healthcare product and evaluates related marketing issues. The chapter addresses two broad categories of the healthcare product: (1) pharmaceutical products as well as medical technology devices; (2) marketing of healthcare services by hospitals and healthcare providers. In Chapter 8, Acheampong and Agyeman-Boaten provide an in-depth discussion on the utilisation and pricing of healthcare services. This chapter deliberates on the demand for healthcare services, its prediction and factors that influence this demand, and explores the various pricing strategies being used in healthcare services. The authors acknowledge the significant improvements in healthcare demand and supply in recent years in developing countries, but stress that more work needs to be done to improve upon all aspects of healthcare in developing countries.

DISTRIBUTION, MARKETING COMMUNICATIONS AND BRANDING IN HEALTHCARE

This part of the book also focuses on the distribution of healthcare products, marketing communications strategies in healthcare services and branding strategies in healthcare management. Chapter 9, by Mahmoud, presents an extensive literature review on distribution in healthcare markets. The chapter reveals multiple healthcare distribution systems in the healthcare markets. Among the different distribution systems are centralised and decentralised systems, supply chain arrangements, public and private participation arrangements, producers, purchasers and providers. The chapter also highlights a number of recommendations to improve the efficient and effective distribution of healthcare markets in Africa. Application of integrated marketing communications in the healthcare sector, with insights from sub-Saharan Africa (SSA), is the focus of Anambane and Hinson's contribution in Chapter 10. The chapter explores how healthcare providers, particularly hospitals in SSA, use the various marketing communication mixes of advertising, public relations, sales promotion, direct/digital marketing and personal selling. The chapter argues that while marketing communication tools like public relations, direct/digital marketing and advertising have been fairly well used by hospitals in the context under consideration, sales promotion and personal selling are yet to be widely embraced in the sector. The authors provide insights into the application of the marketing communication mix elements as a strategic tool in healthcare management. The effectiveness of the communication of healthcare institutions is likely to contribute to the branding of healthcare organisations. Following this, Chapter 11 by Olomo and Otubanjo sheds light on the concept of healthcare branding, which is increasingly becoming important in the light of competing health choices for consumers and emerging socio-economic trends across the African continent. The chapter adopts the theoretical perspective of social constructionism and provides detailed insights into how co-creation of knowledge occurs between various parties in the health brand promise. Effectively, the authors explicate the brand-building process, the benefits of branding and its relevance to sub-Saharan Africa healthcare. Further, Chapter 12 examines the importance of branding in small and medium-sized healthcare institutions. In this chapter, Odoom and Agyeman contend that branding is not an exclusive preserve of large healthcare institutions only, but also a crucial function for small healthcare service providers, especially in sub-Saharan Africa, to build their brand and boost their market performance. The authors focus on Gelb's brand trust model and present four brand-building strategies for small healthcare organisations to include consistent experience, competitive differences, customer value and familiarity.

PEOPLE, PHYSICAL EVIDENCE AND SERVICE QUALITY MANAGEMENT IN HEALTHCARE

The fifth part of the book discusses in detail both the healthcare employee and management of the physical evidence and service quality in healthcare to create a unique customer experience. Chapter 13, by Yalley, discusses a need to consider managing healthcare employees as a strategic tool for healthcare organisations in building customer-driven service. The chapter highlights managing healthcare employees as a key challenge for African healthcare organisations. A number of human resource management (HRM) challenges facing African healthcare organisations, as well as some strategic interventions, are discussed in detail. Further, Hinson and Nkrumah discuss the physical evidence and healthcare service quality management in Chapter 14. The chapter brings to the fore the importance of service quality in healthcare through the lenses of healthcare customers by drawing on its effect in improving overall service quality for customers and success for healthcare organisations. This chapter also elaborates on the need to give attention to customer perception variables as well as leverage their rich insights to create models of continuous improvement in quality healthcare delivery. Chapter 15, by Osei-Frimpong,

Asante, Nkrumah and Owusu-Frimpong, discusses how healthcare organisations could develop customer loyalty in the healthcare sector. The chapter seeks to deepen our understanding of customer relationship management techniques and practices in healthcare, with particular interest in outlining strategies to be adopted by healthcare providers to enhance customer participation and improve customer satisfaction, experience and loyalty. The authors bring to light the changing roles of the healthcare customer and discuss how care should be delivered to promote customer loyalty. The chapter also advocates for cooperation between the healthcare professional and the customer in co-creating healthcare, and for a holistic service delivery that could result in overall positive experiences.

Process Management in Healthcare

The sixth part of the book discusses issues relating to healthcare financing and insurance, healthcare logistics management and policies and procedures in healthcare management. In Chapter 16, Baku discusses financing healthcare and health insurance. This chapter sheds light on the tools and skills needed to effectively manage the finances of a healthcare organisation and understand the operations of health insurance schemes. Given the increasing cost of financing healthcare, it becomes imperative to understand the strategic and sustainable management of the financial resources in healthcare organisations. The author argues that the method of financing healthcare has implications for the marketing of the service as well as the satisfaction healthcare customers derive from the service. Further, Muogboh and Fatoki shed light on managing healthcare logistics in Chapter 17. This chapter provides details of how healthcare service providers in sub-Saharan Africa utilise and integrate human resources, facilities and equipment in the best possible way to meet their need to achieve the physical, mental, emotional and social wellbeing of their customers. It explicates the critical importance of logistics management activities in sub-Saharan African healthcare industries as well as the organisation and maintenance of healthcare facilities and equipment. The authors argue that improving the efficiency and effectiveness of the healthcare industry requires the harnessing of resources to ensure fragmented activities are efficiently linked in a proactive and dynamic manner through the use of innovative logistics practices to address the peculiar challenges of healthcare delivery in sub-Saharan Africa. The final chapter of this section, Chapter 18, authored by Korto, deepens healthcare management scholars' and practitioners' understanding of health policy procedures with regard to their day-to-day operations and will serve as reference material for them. The chapter asserts with a significant margin of certainty that regardless of how comprehensive, well-articulated, sound or good an adopted public policy may appear on paper, it is of no use unless the policy is effectively implemented by street-level bureaucrats to solve the societal problem(s) identified. Emphasis is placed on important topics such as policy articulation and healthcare delivery; characteristics of effective policy; ways of stating policy; and compiling and communicating policy.

Technology in Healthcare

Advancements in technology not only improve the healthcare delivery systems but also provide avenues for customers to seek information regarding their health conditions and influence their participatory behaviours or changing roles in service delivery. As a result, this part of the book is dedicated to addressing technological issues and related applications in healthcare delivery. Chapter 19, by Appiah, Sam-Epelle and Osabutey, discusses technology and health services marketing in Africa. In this chapter, the authors explore how technology is impacting developments in the African healthcare sector – with a keen focus on health service quality. The chapter also highlights some current challenges facing the healthcare sector in Africa, and how entrepreneurs in some of these countries are innovatively overcoming some of these obstacles, mainly with low-cost solutions and strategies. Relatedly, Chapter 20 discusses the application of technology in healthcare delivery in Africa. Tweneboah-Koduah and Gli present an overview of the role of technology in the delivery of healthcare in sub-Saharan Africa. The chapter clearly highlights opportunities which information technology presents for improving quality of life on a continent that is geographically dispersed and coupled with high rate of poverty. Furthermore, the chapter captures some top technological trends advancing efficient healthcare delivery in Africa such as telemedicine, virtual reality, mobile financial services, and cloud technology, internet of things, drone technology, counterfeit detectors, artificial intelligence (AI) and digital communication tools. Chapter 21, the final chapter of the book, by Odoom and Agyeman, touches on technology and social media in healthcare delivery. This chapter discusses the role or opportunities that social media and healthcare technology can offer to the healthcare system, innovation and improvement. It highlights some types of healthcare technologies that will guide research and development, along with some current examples. Some action steps are also suggested to influence the adoption of technology into routine health practices in sub-Saharan Africa.

CONCLUSION

This book presents significant insights into healthcare service delivery by applying key marketing and management principles to enhance performance, sustenance and wellbeing. The book showcases a number of illustrations of best practices and also highlights some challenges within the African healthcare sector. One unique aspect of this book lies in the discussion of forward-looking recommendations and strategies that seek to transform the healthcare service sector. Overall, this contemporary book seeks to serve as a reference resource to practitioners of a sector that has been largely neglected within the developing country contexts.

REFERENCES

Adepoju, O. O., Opafunso, Z., and Ajayi, M. (2018). Primary health care in South West Nigeria: evaluating service quality and patients' satisfaction. *African Journal of Science, Technology, Innovation and Development*, *10*(1), 13–19.

Danaher, T. S., and Gallan, A. S. (2016). Service research in health care: positively impacting lives. *Journal of Service Research*, *19*(4), 433–437.

Hasumi, T., and Jacobsen, K. H. (2014). Healthcare service problems reported in a national survey of South Africans. *International Journal for Quality in Health Care*, *26*(4), 482–489.

Kay, M. J. (2007). Healthcare marketing: what is salient? *International Journal of Pharmaceutical and Healthcare Marketing*, *1*(3), 247–263.

Mahmoud, A. M. (2016). Consumer trust and physician prescription of branded medicines: an exploratory study. *International Journal of Pharmaceutical and Healthcare Marketing*, *10*(3), 285–301.

Osei-Frimpong, K. (2016). Examining the effects of patient characteristics and prior value needs on the patient-doctor encounter process in healthcare service delivery. *International Journal of Pharmaceutical and Healthcare Marketing*, *10*(2), 192–213.

Osei-Frimpong, K., Wilson, A., and Lemke, F. (2018). Patient co-creation activities in healthcare service delivery at the micro level: the influence of online access to healthcare information. *Technological Forecasting & Social Change*, *126*(January), 14–27.

Sahoo, D., and Ghosh, T. (2016). Healthscape role towards customer satisfaction in private healthcare. *International Journal of Health Care Quality Assurance*, *29*(6), 600–613.

Shafei, I., Walburg, J. A., and Taher, A. F. (2015). Healthcare service quality: what really matters to the female patient? *International Journal of Pharmaceutical and Healthcare Marketing*, *9*(4), 369–391.

Stremersch, S. (2008). Health and marketing: the emergence of a new field of research. *International Journal of Research in Marketing*, *25*(4), 229–233.

Wanjau, K. N., Muiruri, B. W., and Ayodo, E. (2012). Factors affecting provision of service quality in the public health sector: a case of Kenyatta national hospital. *International Journal of Humanities and Social Science*, *2*(13): 114–125.

2 The Societal and Healthcare Context

Lydia Aziato, Lillian Akorfa Ohene, Charles Ampong Adjei

2.1 INTRODUCTION

Healthcare has a globally understood definition of being aimed at achieving optimal health for all individuals across the life span. There are cultural variations across each society that influence the healthcare choices and practices used in that specific area. The cultural variations in the African context have led to a lot of disparities in healthcare services. For example, religiosity and use of unsafe traditional medicine have negatively impacted access to healthcare services in many African communities. Healthcare is dynamic and modern technology has led to many innovations and advanced techniques in health. This requires that healthcare institutions in Africa should improve and develop their infrastructure and equipment to meet global standards as well as provide high-level training of healthcare professionals. The explosion of information made available by medical research and the worldwide web has created highly informed clients even within the African context. Thus, the dynamics and competition in healthcare demand a closer discourse and understanding of the societal factors that influence healthcare.

2.2 THE EMERGENCE OF HEALTHCARE AS AN INSTITUTION

Over the decades, healthcare institutions evolved from charitable guesthouses to hospitals, some of which are now huge scientific centres of excellence. The changes in health institutions were influenced by factors such as the evolving meaning of diseases, economic and geographic related factors, religion and race, living conditions of individuals, technological growth, and the perceived needs of societies (Risse, 1999). In the eighteenth century, medical and surgical interventions expanded in such a way that hospitals took over the physical spaces of churches (Andrews, 2011). By the nineteenth century, hospitals became so widely known and commonly frequented by patients that they began to be constructed with industrial proportions, able to have thousand-bed capacities. France, for example, in the early 1800s was noted for the large bed capacity of its hospitals, which housed wounded soldiers from the frequently occurring European wars fought in and around French territory. It was reported that such hospitals were the first teaching institutions of medical science for the training of physicians. The Florence Nightingale model School of Nursing which influenced the training of nurses globally was established within King's College, London, England in 1860 (Karimi & Masoudi Alavi, 2015). Nursing is one of the oldest professions in healthcare and has its values and practice linked to Christianity, in which care and help for the vulnerable is a practice of the faith (Bullough, 1994). In the early years, communities began establishing health institutions to manage communicable diseases such as leprosy. The formal training of health professionals arose during the medieval and early renaissance eras (Weakland, 1992), replacing the initially dominant extremely superstitious practices of the Roman Catholic Church. Historically, it was believed that highly skilled Muslim doctors from the Middle East drove the training and education of contemporary health professionals, which increased the hope of recovery for the sick (Weakland, 1992).

For the greater part of the nineteenth century, it was common practice for physicians to attend to middle-to-upper-income patients in their homes, rendering institutional care mostly for the socially marginalised and the poor (Wall, 2013). However, during the latter part of the century, societies became increasingly more industrialised and mobile. Medical practice also continued to evolve in a more sophisticated and complex manner (Sather, 1992; Stone, 1984). The introduction of industrial medical equipment and intricate procedures thus gave rise to the wider patronage of hospitals across classes, as complex care could not be given in the home. This resulted in the gradual shift towards professionalism of healthcare services and then a competitive care environment which contributed to the development of modernised hospitals (Bullough, 1994; Risse, 1999).

Fast forwarding to the early twentieth century, the power of science has impacted heavily on decisions and practices of hospitals (D'Antonio, Connolly, Wall, Whelan, & Fairman, 2010). In the contemporary twenty-first century, economic factors continue to dominate and direct the establishment and operations of healthcare institutions (Swain, 2016). The economic variations between regions have reinforced disparities in the establishment and practices of health institutions. Therefore there is the need to look at globalisation as a key player in healthcare delivery.

2.3 GLOBALISATION

In recent times, healthcare industries have been increasingly challenged by globalisation. The demand for good health for all populations and the progressive interconnectedness of countries around the globe (Huynen, Martens, & Hilderink, 2005) appear to account for some of these changing global trends. Given the effect of globalisation on every aspect of society (Mittleman & Hanaway, 2012; Segouin, Hodges, & Brechat, 2005; Walpole et al., 2016), this section describes the implications of globalisation, particularly for the healthcare industries, and how healthcare organisations could derive maximum benefits from this global transformation occurring at an unprecedented rate over the past decades. Various scholars have tried to delineate the concept of globalisation which has informed the development of several frameworks (Huynen et al., 2005; Woodward, Drager, Beaglehole, & Lipson, 2001). Some of the scholars tried to explain the linkages between globalisation and health (Woodward et al., 2001) and others sought to identify the features of globalisation (Huynen et al., 2005). Nevertheless, globalisation remains a complex phenomenon which has attracted different opinions in the past century, particularly as to how it happens, its main drivers, and its actual timeframe (Lee, 2004).

The most critical discussion in the academic and policy circles centres on whether globalisation is good or bad for human health (Lee, 2004). From the perspective of the World Health Organisation (WHO, 2019a), globalisation presents both positive and negative effects on health. In fact, the frequently changing trend of disease occurrence places much emphasis on the global unification, integration, and cooperation which are key benefits of globalisation (Ergin & Akin, 2017). In the healthcare environment, globalisation has led to improved medical care in many countries (Murphy, 2007). For example, the development of new medicines, advancements in medical investigations, and adoption of equipment which influences the care of patients have all occurred due to globalisation. Now, medical inventions such as the computerised tomography (CT) scan and less invasive surgical interventions are becoming common in most locales including Africa. Although the CT scan was invented in 1972 by engineer Godfrey Hounfield in England and a physicist Allan Cormack in the United States, due to globalisation it has spread worldwide (Castillo, 2012).

Globalisation can also have negative effects on economies and societies, especially those of low-income countries (Aluttis, Bishaw, & Frank, 2014; Kalipeni, Semu, & Mbilizi, 2012; Kasper & Bajunirwe, 2012). A typical negative consequence of globalisation is the migration of healthcare providers from low-income countries with poorer economic conditions to high-income countries (Kalipeni et al., 2012; Kasper & Bajunirwe, 2012; WHO, 2019a). In many countries, the migration phenomenon deprived these poorly resourced countries of their critical health staff, which to date appears to have had adverse effects on their health systems. It is estimated that 56 per cent of Ghanaian trained doctors and 24 per cent of nurses are working in high-income countries within Europe and North America (International Organisation for Migration, 2009). These and other factors might be accounting for the reduced competitive advantage of African countries in the international market within the healthcare industry. It is therefore crucial that these countries explore more proactive interventions to build customer-driven health organisations paying particular attention to the societal and the healthcare context.

Establishing attractive markets in today's healthcare industry requires the provision of top-notch services that meet the needs and demands of consumers irrespective of their geographical location. This opinion has previously been expressed by Segouin et al. (2005) who believed that the provision of quality healthcare at a lower cost could be to the benefit of low- and middle-income countries. Countries in Africa ought to commit more resources to research to validate the effectiveness of the available indigenous medicinal plants by drawing lessons from China where herbal medicines are integrated into the formal health system and remain attractive to the global communities. Lessons can also be drawn from countries such as Iran and India that are known to provide affordable and quality medical services that attract diverse healthcare consumers from different parts of the world. However, the realisation of these benefits can only happen when low-income countries, particularly those in Africa, build a strong health delivery system.

2.4 THE INFLUENCE OF ECONOMIC FACTORS ON HEALTHCARE SERVICES

Healthcare utilisation and access has been explored by previous researchers (Andersen & Newman, 2005). Ostensibly, individuals in low-income countries tend to have limited access to health services as compared to those in high-income countries (Peters et al., 2008). Cost of service delivery remains an important contributor to the low and sub-optimal uptake of healthcare services, especially in deprived areas (Hangoma, Robberstad, & Aakvik, 2018; Lagarde & Palmer, 2008; Smith et al., 2018). However, there is a paradigm shift of global attention toward universal health coverage with one of the key objectives focusing on protection of individuals from financial risk (WHO, 2019b). This initiative is very crucial given the significant role the economic environment plays on the determinants of the population's health (WHO, 2019c).

Economic inequality is more prevalent in the low-income countries than in high-income countries (Derviş & Qureshi, 2016). In fact, the expenditure on health in low-income countries was estimated to be 5 to 15 per cent of gross domestic product (GDP) (Xu, Saksena, & Holly, 2011). It can therefore be contended that the low expenditure on health in these areas has implications for healthcare services since the amount of health resources available tends to influence health outcomes (Dieleman et al., 2017). Some scholars have suggested the need to improve the efficiency and equity of institutions in low-income countries. Areas highlighted include public sector management, domestic resource mobilisation, and improved financial protection (World Bank, 2005).

There are very key economic factors that notably affect healthcare services. One such factor is the low rate of acquisition of health insurance by individuals and families. According to the World Health Organisation (WHO, 2019d), out-of-pocket payment for health can lead to a catastrophic expenditure by families, which in turn can render them impoverished. Although there is a growing amount of health insurance coverage in low-income countries including African countries, some challenges exist in its efficiency and effectiveness in providing financial protection for the population. For example, a recent impact assessment of Ghana's national health insurance shows that the scheme is threatened financially and operationally by political interference, inadequate monitoring mechanisms, and poor quality care in accredited health facilities among other things (Alhassan, Nketiah-Amponsah, & Arhinful, 2016). There is therefore the need for a reform of the health insurance funding model for Africa to one that takes into account the dynamic needs of the populace.

Another important factor influencing healthcare services is socio-economic status (SES) of clients. Evidence shows that individuals with low SES are more often afflicted by diseases (Flaskerud & DeLilly, 2012) and less likely to be able to afford the cost of care. It is therefore imperative that people are empowered through education, employment, and enhanced income to improve their lives. Furthermore, issues of quality of healthcare services cannot be underestimated in this regard, particularly from the perspective of consumers (Abaerei, Ncayiyana, & Levin, 2017). Thus, the quality of healthcare services hinges on the amount of funding that goes into the service provision. Exploring innovative ways that can enhance resource mobilisation at the facility level would be beneficial. In addition, reduction in wastage in the health system may also yield positive effects. Such innovations can be linked to the influence of technology in healthcare.

2.5 THE INFLUENCE OF TECHNOLOGICAL FACTORS ON HEALTHCARE SERVICES

Technological innovations in healthcare have evolved and are growing at a very rapid pace, influencing almost all processes including patients registration, data gathering and monitoring, laboratory investigations, and self-care services (Laal, 2013). The smartphones and other devices which have emerged should not substitute for the traditional approach to patient monitoring and information management but, instead, could respond to challenges facing healthcare systems (Bardy, 2019). For example, smartphones can be used to increase access to health information. Health records, one of the key segments of health practice, consist of clients' personal information, which is kept as confidential documents used for the purpose of healthcare delivery. Conventionally, health professionals such as physicians, nurses, pharmacists, and laboratory personnel have all had separate formats and files for entering such records. Through the advent of new technology, electronic health records have created greater efficiency in patient care (Riano & Ortega, 2017). The electronic health record is an integrated single platform system which is used for patient data entry including a patient's medical history. It is perceived that consolidated data driven decisions will enable consistency in patient care that could improve patient outcome.

Telemedicine, although not entirely new, is another area considered as one of the fast growing fields in healthcare. In telemedicine, health professionals utilise telecommunication technologies to evaluate, diagnose and treat patients remotely (Bardy, 2019). The application of technology in this sense is perceived as a great advantage for rural settings despite the limited resources. There is evidence that telehealth services reduce hospitalisations (McLean et al., 2013). Mobile health services deal with wireless and cordless devices to enable care professionals and patients to receive instant updates on healthcare processes. The use of smartphones and tablets enables free exchange of information between health providers and their clients at a faster rate. There are mobile tools and applications which professionals use for the purpose of making care decisions, documenting care, and acquiring information for client care. It is perceived that mobile health services are more engaging and that with the use of portable technology, patients have become active actors in their treatments (Ciani et al., 2016). Wireless communications with the use of walkie-talkies and instant messaging are quite new in healthcare deliveries although these forms of communication are not new. Wireless communication systems enhance intra-hospital information sharing among staff, and thus improve security in hospitals (Anand, 1996).

Staffing problems are a major human resource challenge in the healthcare system globally. However, the use of technology such as self-service kiosks has relieved staff burdens for many organisations (Ciani et al., 2016). Self-service kiosks allow patients to carry out registration and payment related tasks without having to wait to talk to service staff. This expedites the hospital registration process and provides comfort for people which enhances service satisfaction. Globally, millions of people have devices at home to monitor their health, which reduce cost and reduce unnecessary visits to the hospital. For example, portable electronic blood pressure machines help individuals to monitor their blood pressure at home. Evidence shows that home monitoring systems reduce readmission rates. With the advent of hospitals being charged penalties for readmissions, remote monitoring tools available to patients at home may be a prudent way for hospitals to avoid such charges. Also, the use of sensors and devices used on the body are additional aids to early detection of abnormalities (Pramanik, Upadhyaya, Pal, & Pal, 2019). These devices are simple machines which could send alerts to health professionals for timely interventions. Undoubtedly, modern trends in health services require adoption of technology for effective and efficient care outcomes. However, there are increased calls to investigate the role of technology in the cost of healthcare delivery (Anand, 1996). For the purpose of sustainability, much is desired from organisational and community leaders in evaluating the spending on new technologies and their efficiencies.

2.6 THE INFLUENCE OF COMPETITIVE FACTORS ON HEALTHCARE SERVICES

In all industries, competition among businesses has long been encouraged as a mechanism to increase value for patients. Competitive factors are features or benefits considered key or essential to the promotion of a product or service to its intended market and should be used in the health sector to attract new clients. The World Health Organisation (WHO) recognises that responsiveness to people's expectations is an essential intermediary goal of a health system and poor responsiveness can negatively affect utilisation of services and the effectiveness of interventions (Moreira, Gherman, & Sousa, 2017).

Traditional competition in healthcare involves one or more elements (e.g. price, quality, convenience, and superior products or services); however, competition can also be based on new technology and innovation (Kurhekar & Ghoshal, 2010). A key role of competition in healthcare is the potential to provide a mechanism for reducing healthcare costs. In the context of these competitive factors, customers would opt for services or healthcare providers/institutions that meet their needs such as cost. Within the African context, there are a lot of customers with low socio-economic status so pricing of healthcare is paramount in attracting customers. The healthcare customer appraises quality of healthcare in several dimensions including attitude of the health personnel (Bloom & Kanjilal, 2012; Murti, Deshpande, & Srivastava, 2013). It is therefore critical that the healthcare provider is committed to maintaining a positive attitude and providing individualised care that will be noticed and appreciated by patients. With modern technology and the internet, customers are more enlightened about their healthcare needs (Haskins, Phakathi, Grant, & Horwood, 2014). Thus, healthcare providers should be abreast of current trends in healthcare services and upgrade their knowledge and skills to meet the standards of the dynamic health system. Indeed, the healthcare facility with knowledgeable and skilful personnel will attract more customers within the competitive market.

Location of healthcare facilities at the convenience of customers plays a role within the competitive discourse. In low- and middle-income countries, access to healthcare facilities can be challenging especially in the less endowed areas. In this regard, building a well-resourced healthcare facility where access is difficult and the clientele within the vicinity of the hospital is poor could lead to major liquidity challenges for the institution. In the long run, such facilities will provide poor services because they cannot pay their skilled staff and maintain the expensive equipment. In a similar vein, healthcare facilities that are close to each other within a well-resourced environment face a lot of competition. Such competition could lead to quality services in the bid to satisfy and attract more customers. It is expected that healthcare facilities regularly assess their competitive advantage and enhance their uniqueness and service advantage. There should be advertisement of the specific service advantage to attract customers to the facility (O'Connor, 2017; Richins, 2015). Customer surveys and effective feedback systems would also reinforce and review services that provide competitive advantage (Al-Abri & Al-Balushi, 2014).

Healthcare competitiveness also hinges on conditions of service of staff. In the African context, conditions of service are generally inadequate (Jaeger, Bechir, Harouna, Moto, & Utzinger, 2018) and salary inequalities exist. For example, healthcare providers including doctors, nurses, and midwives in private practice in Ethiopia, Ghana, Zambia, and Burkina Faso have better conditions of service compared to their counterparts in the public sector (McCoy et al., 2008). It is imperative for employers of health professionals to conduct market surveys and offer competitive salaries and incentives so that they can maintain and attract expert service providers. Poor conditions of service could result in loss of skilled employees to their competitors (Dash & Meredith, 2010). When the staff are paid the right salary, they give of their best and the customers will also be satisfied and continue to seek health services at the facility (Willis-Shattuck et al., 2008). Reducing waiting time, creating effective interpersonal relationships and mutual respect, and adhering to ethical standards would enhance customer satisfaction (Agung, 2018; Bakari Salehe, 2016).

2.7 THE CULTURAL REVOLUTION AND HEALTHCARE

Over the years, healthcare globally has been impacted to a large extent by advancement in many facets of the culture, making ineffective care activities obsolete (Meskó, Drobni, Bényei, Gergely, & Győrffy, 2017; Napier et al., 2014). Now in the twenty-first century, the world is in a time of major transition, especially in the area of technology and innovativeness, and the healthcare system is not an exception. In the past, patients viewed medicine as something beyond their understanding and science was not developed to investigate various health problems. Healthcare customers gave a certain amount of control to doctors and nurses and looked upon the practice of medicine as a kind of magical art that only doctors were competent to perform (Bardhan & Thouin, 2013). Therefore, doctors' decisions were rarely challenged, and patients did not educate themselves on medical matters, in part because medical knowledge was not widely available. However, currently, policy makers aim to empower patients, to transform them into knowledgeable consumers with access to a wide range of healthcare products (Elwyn, Edwards, & Thompson, 2016). Patients are getting more engaged with their medical treatment through information available on the internet, medical chatrooms, and social media. Informed customers will demand quality care and ask questions about their treatment options. The cultural revolution of the information explosion implies that health professionals should be knowledgeable and also educate their clients about their health and treatment options (Cipriano & Hamer, 2013). But although there is a knowledge explosion on the internet and social media, it is not surprising to find customers who do not have adequate knowledge on their disease as they may not be able to read and write (Palumbo, 2017).

The introduction of electronic health (E-Health) services and use of electronic devices to keep health records is another area of cultural revolution in healthcare delivery. The upsurge of E-Health has increased access to healthcare because innovative ways have been used with social media and mobile phones to render healthcare services on the door steps of customers (Li, Talaei-Khoei, Seale, Ray, & MacIntyre, 2013; Ossebaard & Van Gemert-Pijnen, 2016). Overall, electronic data management speeds up services within the health facility. The availability of E-Health services therefore means that contemporary healthcare providers should adjust or redesign their health services to go beyond their hospital premises. However, in low- and middle-income countries, especially in Africa where internet and telephone reception may be a challenge, the use of E-Health is inappropriate to meet the health needs of customers. Moreover, in cases where there is power outage or network failure, the care system is disabled. This calls for back-up power supply and internet connectivity to enhance work. Data management policies should be adhered to and stringent measures should be adopted to protect the privacy of the customer (Tan & Payton, 2010).

Cultural diversity, migration, and cultural infusion have also impacted healthcare to a large extent. Migration of healthcare professionals and customers from one part of the globe to the other calls for health professionals who are culturally sensitive with skills to provide care that meet the needs of their clients (Dell'Osso, 2016). It is expected that health institutions provide training and the enabling environment to accommodate diversity among the staff and customers. Therefore, healthcare institutions that employ professionals from different cultural backgrounds and provide opportunities for diverse people to access services attract more customers (Young & Guo, 2016).

Over the years, health professionals have migrated to different countries and there is the need for multilingual skills to fit within the changing health landscape and provide the expected care to their customers (Meuter, Gallois, Segalowitz, Ryder, & Hocking, 2015).

2.8 THE CHANGING SOCIETAL CONTEXT

The world today is faced with complex and fast processes of change regarding the socio-economic, demographic, and global environment, which requires an all-inclusive conception of determinants of population health (Giles-Corti et al., 2004; McMichael & Beaglehole, 2000). Hitokoto and Tanaka-Matsumi (2014) assert that individuals' psychological health is undermined when a change occurs in socio-demographic conditions. This is because human wellness is relatively the peak of biopsychosocial functioning given preconditions of corresponding behavioural and contextual adaptation. As such, any change will result in modifications to the requirements of the external environment.

Evidence shows that economic growth and the advent of technologies have broadly improved life expectancy in many developed societies (Beaglehole & Bonita, 2004). For example, in economically stable countries there is increased independence and internet usage. However, it is also perceived that such economies are characterised by individualistic lifestyles, associated with an increase in urban populations, one person households, and divorce (McMichael & Beaglehole, 2000). Insufficiencies in social capital adversely affect the panorama of health by predisposing the population to widened rich–poor gaps, inner-urban decay, increased drug trade, and weakened public health systems (Hitokoto & Tanaka-Matsumi, 2014).

Furthermore, the high rate of population growth globally has negatively impacted the global environment in relation to the altered composition of the atmosphere, land degradation, and depletion of terrestrial aquifers and aquatic fisheries (McMichael & Beaglehole, 2000). It happens that man's increased needs for space, resources, and food affect the population of the constantly exploited species of plants and animals, which consequently causes their extinction. At the same time, new invasive species are increasing globally into new non-natural environments as a result of trade and migration. The resultant changes in many regional species have consequential health implications. In equal measure, we can continue to cite similar examples such as man-made degradation of vast lands through erosion, waterlogging, chemicalisation, and salination. Many such losses in our natural ecosystem have necessitated genetic engineering in agro products to increase food production and yet many parts of developing regions such as North Africa are experiencing food insecurity. There are similar threats caused by water body pollutions, with a matching public health crisis. A typical example is the migration of the water hyacinths from Brazil to the East African Lake Victoria, which now serves as a breeding ground for the water snail that transmits the causative organism of schistosomiasis, a genito-urinary, systemic human condition (McMichael & Beaglehole, 2000).

It is obvious that the world is at a crossroads where scientists are challenged with unfamiliar and complex health issues in fast-changing societies (Beaglehole & Bonita, 2004). Societies must advocate for system-oriented influences on health to find, measure, and curb health risk, social behaviours, and environmental factors (McMichael, Butler, & Dixon, 2015).

2.9 THE CONSUMERIST CUSTOMER IN HEALTHCARE

Modernisation has witnessed increased rationalisation of attitudes of actors in the context of the medical field (Clarke & Eales-Reynolds, 2015). The conduct of laypersons has changed with respect to their desires regarding personal health and the way they feel and think about medical care and health professionals (Howgill, 1998). It is obvious that individuals and societies have aligned with the comprehensive sociological concepts of the reflexive self, which is when an individual is empowered to engage in self-betterment as well as being sceptical about expert knowledge. Hence, the consumerist customer in healthcare is perceived as the patient whose conduct is in congruence with a reflexive actor and a rational evaluator who desires to keenly and cleverly assess health services, providers, and health outcomes. No doubt, since the 1960s, the literature has recorded enormous evidence of patient satisfaction assessment of healthcare in many developed countries (Batbaatar, Dorjdagva, Luvsannyam, & Amenta, 2015). Many authors attest that patient assessments of health services have been the fundamental motivation for improvement in healthcare services (Giles-Corti et al., 2004; Howgill, 1998; Lupton, 1997). Thus, a reflection of patients' opinions in the conduct of the health industry influences policies and management procedures in relation to prioritising resource allocation, appropriate services, and training needs.

An integral aspect of medical practice is the doctor–patient relationship. In the past, when medical interventions were mainly disease focussed, doctors were perceived as experts who made all the decisions on behalf of patients. As such, the patient–doctor relationship was more like that of a parent and child, in a model called "paternalistic" or the medical dominance relationship (Sturgeon, 2018). Critics of this model have argued about the restricted position of patients in this concept and have masterminded the agenda for patient autonomy and respect for patient rights to be at the forefront of care. In essence, patients, instead of professionals, are encouraged to be the ultimate decision makers regarding their own bodies and wellbeing. This ideology aligns with the consumerist agenda of healthcare as commodity in which patients, as consumers, have the power to shop around. Thus, a model of privatisation of healthcare with cost implications and a demanding culture of litigation has emerged (Rowe & Moodley, 2013).

The notion of a patient viewed as a customer or consumer in the consumerist ideology comes with additional responsibilities for both patients and service providers (Lupton, 1997; Rowe & Moodley, 2013; Sturgeon, 2018). The patient must be well informed as well as confident to speak out. This happens when patients feel respected and trust that they are at the centre of care. The professionals, on the other hand, must be receptive and open-minded to embrace patients' choice and participation. This implies that there must be an availability of competitive options and patient motivation to select the appropriate and preferred options. Howgill (1998) suggests that if service providers must market their services to appeal to their customers, then they must consider the fundamental marketing principles, which begin with an understanding of the feelings, attitudes, and expectations of their service consumers. However, the introduction of the pro-marketing model of health service provision has also been associated with advantages and disadvantages (Sturgeon, 2018). For example, encouraging competition among healthcare providers may generate both positive and negative outcomes. When patients have the privilege of selecting from competitive value for cost services, healthcare providers commit to quality care. Conversely, in a financially restricted system, patients may compete for limited resources (Schneider & Hall, 2009). Also, not all patients will benefit from participating in the decision-making process of their care (Rowe & Moodley, 2013). For instances, patients in the emergency departments may not have the luxury of time to shop for intervention options, whereas the patient in the general practice settings will (Howgill, 1998). Furthermore, health professionals are required to explain all options available to patients including what they may not recommend based on their technical know-how and experience. However, it can also coincide that some patients may abuse their power of autonomy and the right to refuse expert advice, which can have negative results for both parties.

Ogaji, Giles, Daker-White, and Bower (2015) revealed that patients' view on the quality of care is a growing phenomenon in the sub-Saharan African context. The current limited research evidence on patient's perspective of quality of health services from sub-Saharan Africa suggests that either local research scientists are not interested in the phenomenon or there is poor utilisation of research findings among decision makers. It is also worth noting that, largely within the African context, there are several other competing factors such as poverty, inaccessibility, and a low level of knowledge (Peters et al., 2008). These factors predominantly prevent patients from accessing quality care, as they perceive access as a favour rather than a right. It is therefore recommended that modern medical practice should incorporate diverse models in different contexts (Rowe &

Moodley, 2013). For example, models such as the mutual relationship or the default model may be the most appropriate to a peculiar medical situation. The mutual model also supports the avoidance of passive followers of authority and instead promotes self-determining unrestricted agents. The professional on the other hand recognises the patients' autonomy and adopts a patient-centred, biopsychosocial approach to care. In cases of somatisation, where there is minimal engagement between the physician and patient, the default model is practised (Rowe & Moodley, 2013).

2.10 KEY HEALTHCARE DEVELOPMENTS

Over the decades, diseases and threats to human lives in societies have necessitated pragmatic approaches to health and healthcare, resulting in specific gains and probably some inevitable setbacks in health service delivery. Public health perspectives provide dimensions for discussing key developments in healthcare for contemporary societies. By definition, public health is the art or science of preventing diseases, promoting health, and extending life through the organised efforts of society (Beaglehole & Bonita, 2004). Thus, collectively, the social quests for quality of life and elimination of pains and sufferings have necessitated shared responsibilities for healthcare developments.

To put this discussion into perspective is to first enumerate the major health challenges which face populations in time and geographical spectrum. Over the decades, medical interventions were fundamentally targeted to combat infectious diseases; manage and control the fast-changing pattern of microbial resistance; modify the profile of the major causes of diseases and death as a result of lifestyle, environmental disasters, and pollutions of the natural environment; increase/decrease fertility rates; and regulate the unstable nature of life expectancies and inequalities between the rich and the poor (Giles-Corti et al., 2004). There has also been a need to create measures to combat the rising cost of healthcare, evidence of patient harm, treatment errors and inadequate standards in care (McMichael & Beaglehole, 2000). Although, to a large extent, the above health problems may be generalised to a number of societies worldwide, health interventions have, however, often been tackled as individualised country efforts, resulting in disparities in healthcare developments across nations (Gordon & Shaw, 1999).

From the global health perspective, key healthcare developments can be placed within two contextual divides: the high-income countries and the low- to middle-income countries. This is due to the differences in social and material inequalities, long-term changes in social structures and the natural environment, and the intensity of economic activities within the different divisions. Indeed, major transitions in the health of populations across the social borders have merited the present science-driven inventions and outcomes. Evidence shows that high-income countries, through government machinery, healthcare providers, and funders have recorded major developments in healthcare (Kumar & Bano, 2017; Van Bokkelen, Morsy, & Kobayashi, 2015). These are evident in the changes in social, dietary, sanitation, and material environments. The middle- to lower-income countries have equally recorded key healthcare developments through increased literacy, family spacing, improved nutrition, transfer of knowledge about sanitation, vaccination, and treatment of infectious diseases (Budhathoki et al., 2017).

2.11 CONCLUSIONS

Healthcare in the contemporary world is influenced by a host of factors and this chapter has discussed key players in this arena. It is necessary for healthcare providers, especially those in Africa, and stakeholders to have a contextual, dynamic, and innovative perspective as they assess issues of healthcare provision. The contemporary healthcare consumer is more informed, making it mandatory for healthcare providers to be abreast of current knowledge and skills in their specialty areas. The competition within the healthcare industry has contributed to the complexity and advancement of technology in healthcare. Although Africa has some challenges to match technological advancement, it is imperative to situate healthcare discourse in Africa within the global trend. Issues about competitive cost and provision for cultural diversity within the health system are necessary considerations to promote customer satisfaction particularly in Africa. Cultural diversity within the African context calls for open-mindedness and acknowledgement of individual differences.

REFERENCES

Abaerei, A. A., Ncayiyana, J., & Levin, J. (2017). Health-care utilization and associated factors in Gauteng province, South Africa. *Global Health Action, 10*(1), 1305765. doi:10.1080/16549716.2017.1305765.

Agung, W. A. N. (2018). The impact of interpersonal communication toward customer satisfaction: The case of customer service of Sari Asih Hospital. *MATEC Web of Conferences, 150,* 05087.

Al-Abri, R., & Al-Balushi, A. (2014). Patient satisfaction survey as a tool towards quality improvement. *Oman Medical Journal, 29*(1), 3–7. doi:10.5001/omj.2014.02.

Alhassan, R. K., Nketiah-Amponsah, E., & Arhinful, D. K. (2016). A review of the National Health Insurance Scheme in Ghana: What are the sustainability threats and prospects? *PLoS One, 11*(11), e0165151. doi:10.1371/journal.pone.0165151.

Aluttis, C., Bishaw, T., & Frank, M. W. (2014). The workforce for health in a globalized context: Global shortages and international migration. *Global Health Action, 7,* 23611–23611. doi:10.3402/gha.v7.23611.

Anand, L. C. A. (1996). New medical technology and cost effectiveness. *Medical Journal, Armed Forces India, 52*(3), 181–183. doi:10.1016/S0377-1237(17)30798-0.

Andersen, R., & Newman, J. F. (2005). Societal and individual determinants of medical care utilization in the United States. *The Milbank Quarterly, 83*(4). doi:10.1111/j.1468-0009.2005.00428.x.

Andrews, J. (2011). History of medicine: Health, medicine and disease in the eighteenth century. *British Journal for Eighteenth-Century Studies, 34*(4), 503–515. doi:10.1111/j.1754-0208.2011.00448.x.

Bakari Salehe, D. N. (2016). *Good quality interaction between a registered nurse and the patient.* Degree Programme in Nursing, Seinäjöki University of Applied Sciences.

Bardhan, I. R., & Thouin, M. F. (2013). Health information technology and its impact on the quality and cost of healthcare delivery. *Decision Support Systems, 55*(2), 438–449. doi:10.1016/j.dss.2012.10.003.

Bardy, P. (2019). The advent of digital healthcare. In P. Bardy (Ed.), *The human challenge of telemedicine* (Chapter 1, pp. 3–17). Elsevier.

Batbaatar, E., Dorjdagva, J., Luvsannyam, A., & Amenta, P. (2015). Conceptualisation of patient satisfaction: A systematic narrative literature review. *Perspectives in Public Health, 135*(5). doi:10.1177/1757913915594196.

Beaglehole, R., & Bonita, R. (2004). *Public health at the crossroads: Achievements and prospects* (2nd Ed.). Cambridge, United Kingdom: Cambridge University Press.

Bloom, G., & Kanjilal, B. (2012). *Transforming health markets in Asia and Africa: Improving quality and access for the poor.* Routledge.

Budhathoki, S. S., Pokharel, P. K., Good, S., Limbu, S., Bhattachan, M., & Osborne, R. H. (2017). The potential of health literacy to address the health related UN sustainable development goal 3 (SDG3) in Nepal: A rapid review. *BMC Health Services Research, 17,* 237. doi:10.1186/s12913-017-2183-6.

Bullough, V. L. (1994). Men, women, and nursing history. *Journal of Professional Nursing, 10*(3), 127.

Castillo, M. (2012). The industry of CT scanning. *American Journal of Neuroradiology, 33*(4), 583–585. doi:10.3174/ajnr.A2742.

Ciani, O., Armeni, P., Boscolo, P. R., Cavazza, M., Jommi, C., & Tarricone, R. (2016). De innovatione: The concept of innovation for medical technologies and its implications for healthcare policy-making. *Health Policy and Technology, 5*(1), 47–64. doi:10.1016/j.hlpt.2015.10.005.

Cipriano, P. F., & Hamer, S. (2013). *Nursing, technology, and information systems: Enabling the ordinary: More time to care.* Cerner Clairvia: Kansas City, Missouri.

Clarke, C., & Eales-Reynolds, L.-J. (2015). Human factors paradigm and customer care perceptions. *International Journal of Health Care Quality Assurance, 28*(3), 288–299. doi:10.1108/IJHCQA-05-2014-0067.

D'Antonio, P., Connolly, C., Wall, B. M., Whelan, J. C., & Fairman, J. (2010). Histories of nursing: The power and the possibilities. *Nursing Outlook, 58*(4), 207–213. doi:10.1016/j.outlook.2010.04.005.

Dash, P., & Meredith, D. (2010). When and how provider competition can improve health care delivery. McKinsey & Co. www.mckinsey.com.

Dell'Osso, D. (2016). *Cultural sensitivity in healthcare: The new modern day medicine* (Bachelor of Arts senior thesis). Dominican University of California, Senior Theses and Capstone Projects.

Derviş, K., & Qureshi, Z. (2016). *Income distribution within countries: Rising inequality* (Global Economy and Development at Brookings). Brookings.

Dieleman, J. L., Campbell, M., Chapin, A., Eldrenkamp, E., Fan, V. Y., Haakenstad, A., ... Murray, C. J. L. (2017). Future and potential spending on health 2015–40: Development assistance for health, and government, prepaid private, and out-of-pocket health spending in 184 countries. *The Lancet*, *389*(10083), 2005–2030. doi:10.1016/S0140-6736(17)30873-5.

Elwyn, G., Edwards, A., & Thompson, R. (2016). *Shared decision making in health care: Achieving evidence-based patient choice* (3rd Ed.). New York: Oxford University Press.

Ergin, E., & Akin, B. (2017). Globalization and its reflections for health and nursing. *International Journal of Caring Sciences*, *10*(1), 607.

Flaskerud, J. H., & DeLilly, C. R. (2012). Social determinants of health status. *Issues in Mental Health Nursing*, *33*(7), 494–497. doi:10.3109/01612840.2012.662581.

Giles-Corti, B., Wood, L., Donovan, R., Rosenberg, M., Saunders, J., & Mills, C. (2004). Opportunities and challenges for promoting health in a changing world. *Health Promotion Journal of Australia*, *15*, 17–23. doi:10.1071/HE04017.

Gordon, D., & Shaw, M. (1999). *Inequalities in health: The evidence presented to the independent inquiry into inequalities in health, chaired by Sir Donald Acheson*. Policy Press.

Hangoma, P., Robberstad, B., & Aakvik, A. (2018). Does free public health care increase utilization and reduce spending? Heterogeneity and long-term effects. *World Development*, *101*, 334–350. doi:10.1016/j.worlddev.2017.05.040.

Haskins, L., Phakathi, S., Grant, M., & Horwood, C. (2014). Attitudes of nurses towards patient care at a rural district hospital in the Kwazulunatal Province of South Africa. *Africa Journal of Nursing and Midwifery*, *16*(1), 31–43. doi:10.13140/RG.2.1.3801.7684.

Hitokoto, H., & Tanaka-Matsumi, J. (2014). Living in the tide of change: Explaining Japanese subjective health from the socio-demographic change. *Frontiers in Psychology*, *5*, 1221. doi:10.3389/fpsyg.2014.01221.

Howgill, W. M. (1998). Health care consumerism, the information explosion, and branding: Why 'tis better to be the cowboy than the cow. *Managed Care Quarterly*, *6*(4), 33–43.

Huynen, M. M. T. E., Martens, P., & Hilderink, H. B. M. (2005). The health impacts of globalization: A conceptual framework. *Globalization and Health*, *1*, 14–14. doi:10.1186/1744-8603-1-14.

International Organisation for Migration. (2009). *Migration in Ghana: A country profile*.

Jaeger, F. N., Bechir, M., Harouna, M., Moto, D. D., & Utzinger, J. (2018). Challenges and opportunities for healthcare workers in a rural district of Chad. *BMC Health Services Research*, *18*(1), 7.

Kalipeni, E., Semu, L. L., & Mbilizi, M. A. (2012). The brain drain of health care professionals from sub-Saharan Africa: A geographic perspective. *Progress in Development Studies*, *12*(2–3), 153–171. doi:10.1177/146499341101200305.

Karimi, H., & Masoudi Alavi, N. (2015). Florence Nightingale: The mother of nursing. *Nursing and Midwifery Studies*, *4*(2), e29475-e29475. doi:10.17795/nmsjournal29475.

Kasper, J., & Bajunirwe, F. (2012). Brain drain in sub-Saharan Africa: Contributing factors, potential remedies and the role of academic medical centres. *Archives of Disease in Childhood*, *97*(11), 973–979. doi:10.1136/archdischild-2012-301900.

Kumar, S., & Bano, S. (2017). Comparison and analysis of health care delivery systems: Pakistan versus Bangladesh. *Journal of Hospital & Medical Management*, *3*(1). doi:10.4172/2471-9781.100020.

Kurhekar, M., & Ghoshal, J. (2010). Technological innovations in healthcare industry. *SETLabs Briefings*, *8*, 42.

Laal, M. (2013). Technology in medical science. *Procedia – Social and Behavioral Sciences*, *81*, 384–388. doi:10.1016/j.sbspro.2013.06.447.

Lagarde, M., & Palmer, N. (2008). The impact of user fees on health service utilization in low- and middle-income countries: How strong is the evidence? *Bulletin of the World Health Organization*, *86*(11), 839–848. doi:10.2471/BLT.07.049197.

Lee, K. (2004). Globalisation: What is it and how does it affect health? *Medical Journal of Australia*, *180*(4), 156–158.

Li, J., Talaei-Khoei, A., Seale, H., Ray, P., & MacIntyre, C. R. (2013). Health care provider adoption of eHealth: Systematic literature review. *Interactive Journal of Medical Research*, *2*(1), e7. doi:10.2196/ijmr.2468.

Lupton, D. (1997). Consumerism, reflexivity and the medical encounter. *Social Science & Medicine*, *45*(3), 373–381. doi:10.1016/S0277-9536(96)00353-X.

McCoy, D., Bennett, S., Witter, S., Pond, B., Baker, B., Gow, J., Chand, S., Ensor, T. & McPake, B. (2008). Salaries and incomes of health workers in sub-Saharan Africa. *The Lancet*, *371*(9613), 675–681. doi:10.1016/S0140-6736(08)60306-2.

McLean, S., Sheikh, A., Cresswell, K., Nurmatov, U., Mukherjee, M., Hemmi, A., & Pagliari, C. (2013). The impact of telehealthcare on the quality and safety of care: A systematic overview. *PLoS One*, *8*(8), e71238. doi:10.1371/journal.pone.0071238.

McMichael, A. J., & Beaglehole, R. (2000). The changing global context of public health. *The Lancet, 356* (9228), 495–499. doi:10.1016/S0140-6736(00)02564-2.

McMichael, A. J., Butler, C. D., & Dixon, J. (2015). Climate change, food systems and population health risks in their eco-social context. *Public Health, 129*(10), 1361–1368. doi:10.1016/j.puhe.2014.11.013.

Meskó, B., Drobni, Z., Bényei, É., Gergely, B., & Győrffy, Z. (2017). Digital health is a cultural transformation of traditional healthcare. *mHealth, 3*(9).

Meuter, R. F. I., Gallois, C., Segalowitz, N. S., Ryder, A. G., & Hocking, J. (2015). Overcoming language barriers in healthcare: A protocol for investigating safe and effective communication when patients or clinicians use a second language. *BMC Health Services Research, 15*(1), 371. doi:10.1186/s12913-015-1024-8.

Mittleman, M., & Hanaway, P. (2012). Globalization of healthcare. *Global Advances in Health and Medicine, 1*(2), 5–7. doi:10.7453/gahmj.2012.1.2.001.

Moreira, M. R. A., Gherman, M., & Sousa, P. S. A. (2017). Does innovation influence the performance of healthcare organizations? *Innovation, 19*(3), 335–352. doi:10.1080/14479338.2017.1293489.

Murphy, J. (2007). International perspectives and initiatives. *Health Information and Libraries Journal, 24*(1), 62–68. doi:10.1111/j.1471-1842.2007.00704.x.

Murti, A., Deshpande, A., & Srivastava, N. (2013). Service quality, customer (patient) satisfaction and behavioural intention in health care services: Exploring the Indian perspective. *Journal of Health Management, 15*(1), 29–44. doi:10.1177/0972063413486035.

Napier, A. D., Ancarno, C., Butler, B., Calabrese, J., Chater, A., Chatterjee, H., … Woolf, K. (2014). Culture and health. *The Lancet, 384* (9954), 1607–1639. doi:10.1016/S0140-6736(14)61603-2.

O'Connor, S. J. (2017). Enhancing the depth and breadth of healthcare services in communities: Insights, innovations, and applications. *BMC Health Services Research, 17*(1), 404. doi:10.1186/s12913-017-2338-5.

Ogaji, D. S., Giles, S., Daker-White, G., & Bower, P. (2015). Systematic review of patients' views on the quality of primary health care in sub-Saharan Africa. *SAGE Open Medicine, 3*, 2050312115608338.

Ossebaard, H. C., & Van Gemert-Pijnen, L. (2016). eHealth and quality in health care: Implementation time. *International Journal for Quality in Health Care, 28*(3), 415–419. doi:10.1093/intqhc/mzw032.

Palumbo, R. (2017). Examining the impacts of health literacy on healthcare costs: An evidence synthesis. *Health Services Management Research, 30*(4), 197–212. doi:10.1177/0951484817733366.

Peters, D. H., Garg, A., Bloom, G., Walker, D. G., Brieger, W. R., & Rahman, M. H. (2008). Poverty and access to health care in developing countries. *Annals of the New York Academy of Sciences, 1136*, 161–171. doi:10.1196/annals.1425.011.

Pramanik, P. K. D., Upadhyaya, B. K., Pal, S., & Pal, T. (2019). Internet of things, smart sensors, and pervasive systems: Enabling connected and pervasive healthcare. In N. Dey, A. S. Ashour, C. Bhatt, & S. James Fong (Eds.), *Healthcare data analytics and management* (Chapter 1, pp. 1–58). Academic Press.

Riano, D., & Ortega, W. (2017). Computer technologies to integrate medical treatments to manage multimorbidity. *Journal of Biomedical Informatics, 75*, 1–13. doi:10.1016/j.jbi.2017.09.009.

Richins, S. (2015). *Emerging technologies in healthcare.* New York: Productivity Press.

Risse, G. B. (1999). Health care in hospitals: The past 1000 years. *The Lancet, 354*, SIV25. doi:10.1016/S0140-6736(99)90368-9.

Rowe, K., & Moodley, K. (2013). Patients as consumers of health care in South Africa: The ethical and legal implications. *BMC Medical Ethics, 14*(1), 15. doi:10.1186/1472-6939-14-15.

Sather, R. H. (1992). The social transformation of American medicine: Paul Star. *Philosophical Constructs for the Chiropractic Profession, 2*, 41–47. doi:10.1016/S2214-9163(13)60018-4.

Schneider, C. E., & Hall, M. A. (2009). The patient life: Can consumers direct health care? *American Journal of Law & Medicine, 35*(1), 7–65. doi:10.1177/009885880903500101.

Segouin, C., Hodges, B., & Brechat, P. H. (2005). Globalization in health care: Is international standardization of quality a step toward outsourcing? *International Journal for Quality in Health Care, 17*(4), 277–279. doi:10.1093/intqhc/mzi059.

Smith, K. T., Monti, D., Mir, N., Peters, E., Tipirneni, R., & Politi, M. C. (2018). Access is necessary but not sufficient: Factors influencing delay and avoidance of health care services. *Medical Decision Making Policy and Practice, 3*(1), 2381468318760298. doi:10.1177/2381468318760298.

Stone, J. R. (1984). The social transformation of American medicine. *Chest, 86*(3), 23. doi:10.1016/S0012-3692(16)56060-7.

Sturgeon, D. (2018). The advantages and disadvantages of encouraging consumerist notions of health care at two minor injury units. *British Journal of Nursing, 27*(6), 308–313. doi:10.12968/bjon.2018.27.6.308.

Swain, G. R. (2016). How does economic and social disadvantage affect health? *Focus, 33*(1), 1–6.

Tan, J., & Payton, F. C. (2010). *Adaptive health management information systems: Concepts, cases, and practical applications*. Jones and Bartlett Publishers, LLC.

Van Bokkelen, G., Morsy, M., & Kobayashi, T.-h. (2015). Demographic transition, health care challenges, and the impact of emerging international regulatory trends with relevance to regenerative medicine. *Current Stem Cell Reports, 1*, 102–109. doi:10.1007/s40778-015-0013-5.

Wall, B. M. (2013). The role of Catholic nurses in women's health care policy disputes: A historical study. *Nursing Outlook, 61*(5), 367–374. doi:10.1016/j.outlook.2013.07.005.

Walpole, S. C., Shortall, C., van Schalkwyk, M. C., Merriel, A., Ellis, J., Obolensky, L., … Allen, S. (2016). Time to go global: A consultation on global health competencies for postgraduate doctors. *International Health, 8*(5), 317–323. doi:10.1093/inthealth/ihw019.

Weakland, J. E. (1992). Medieval and early renaissance medicine: Nancy G. Siraisi (Chicago and London: University of Chicago Press, 1990). *History of European Ideas, 14*(2), 302–303. doi:10.1016/0191-6599(92)90273-F.

Willis-Shattuck, M., Bidwell, P., Thomas, S., Wyness, L., Blaauw, D., & Ditlopo, P. (2008). Motivation and retention of health workers in developing countries: A systematic review. *BMC Health Services Research, 8*, 247. doi:10.1186/1472-6963-8-247.

Woodward, D., Drager, N., Beaglehole, R., & Lipson, D. (2001). Globalization and health: A framework for analysis and action. *Bulletin of the World Health Organization, 79*(9), 875–881.

World Bank. (2005). *Financing health in low-income countries*. Retrieved from www.worldbank.org.

World Health Organization. (2019a). Globalisation. Retrieved January 10, 2019, from www.who.int/topics/globalization/en/.

World Health Organization. (2019b). What is health financing for universal coverage? Retrieved January 11, 2019, from www.who.int/health_financing/en/.

World Health Organization. (2019c). The determinant of health. Retrieved January 11, 2019, from www.who.int/hia/evidence/doh/en/.

World Health Organization. (2019d). Financial protection. Retrieved January 12, 2019, from www.who.int/health_financing/topics/financial-protection/en/.

Xu, K., Saksena, P., & Holly, A. (2011). *The determinants of health expenditure : A country-level panel data analysis*.

Young, S., & Guo, K. L. (2016). Cultural diversity training: The necessity of cultural competence for health care providers and in nursing practice. *The Health Care Manager, 35*(2), 94–102. doi:10.1097/hcm.0000000000000100.

3 Strategic Planning and Healthcare Services

Ogechi Adeola and Isaiah Adisa

3.1 INTRODUCTION

All establishments, whether public or private, make plans for marketing services/products to the general public. The complexities of globalisation and the fast pace at which systems are expected to react to societal demands require that institutions do not just plan, but plan strategically. Strategic planning is the source of effective management in any social system (Sadeghifar, Jafari, Tofighi, Ravaghi, & Maleki, 2015). Swayne, Duncan, and Ginter (2006) defined strategic planning as a set of processes which aids in identifying the future desired by an organisation and developing guidelines that will lead to its accomplishment.

Despite the proven efficacies of strategic planning, there is limited evidence of its deployment in healthcare systems of low- and middle-income countries (Sadeghifar et al., 2015). The healthcare industry contributes to a nation's sustainable development goals and is a key component in the social and political sectors of modern economies. Industrialised countries invest substantial amounts of their gross domestic product on healthcare systems, thereby emphasising the importance of that sector to their national development (Najaftorkaman, Ghapanchi, Talaei-Khoei, & Ray, 2015; Organisation for Economic Co-operation and Development, 2011). Unfortunately, steps such as this seem to be missing in African countries.

The healthcare industry operates in a complex environment that is influenced by internal and external factors (Blanco-Topping, 2016) that require healthcare organisations to be more strategic in their service delivery. Due to weak governmental policies, African countries experience great challenges in public healthcare delivery, a prevailing issue in the continent's overall development (Agyepong et al., 2017). Previous attempts to address the healthcare challenges in Africa and particularly in sub-Saharan Africa have yielded little success (World Health Organization, 2012). There is evidence that low- and middle-income countries (LMICs) plan less for healthcare service delivery than high-income countries (El-Jardali, Jamal, Abdallah, & Kassak, 2007; Mills, Brugha, Hanson, & McPake, 2002; Sadeghifar et al., 2015). Although LMICs' limited resources are often the reason for their poor healthcare systems, that fact alone substantiates the need for strategic planning that will place the continent on the path toward sustainable development, fully capable of predicting and managing healthcare challenges.

When strategic planning becomes a priority for health organisations' management activities, their performance will improve. Strategic planning sets priorities, focuses on resources, strengthens operations, ensures employees' roles and responsibilities are aligned with organisational goals, and assesses/adjusts the organisation's platform of operation in response to a changing environment in order to remain relevant. The benefits of strategic planning have been seen in other sectors, like banking and manufacturing (Jimoh, 2003). The banking industry in Nigeria, for example, through strategic planning, reacted to technological changes in the financial market to remain relevant and competitive (Jimoh, 2003). To attract, retain, and satisfy the needs of their customers, banks introduced IT-based products, private banking, telephone banking, smart cards, internet banking, deployment of ATMs, and automated cheque clearing. Most banks were able to easily modify their operational processes because the needed changes had been forecasted earlier, thus mediating the sense of urgency. The African healthcare sector needs to take a cue from the financial sector, now a strong force in the African economy, and formulate strategic plans that anticipate the implementation of prioritised services that would effectively meet the acknowledged challenges.

This chapter focuses on the application of strategic planning to meet Africa's challenges to deliver quality healthcare services and the impact of charting a path that will assure the way forward.

3.2 THE NATURE OF AFRICA'S HEALTHCARE MARKETS

Any conversation about Africa's healthcare markets must begin with the understanding that the healthcare sector in Africa, especially the LMIC countries, is burdened by poor quality service, lack of customer satisfaction, and poor branding and marketing which are all needed in a well-functioning market. From that starting point, the nature of "a market" needs some definition. A market has two essential elements: individuals willing to purchase a commodity or service and individuals willing to provide that commodity or service. A market does not exist if there is not a customer willing to buy or a vendor willing to sell. A healthcare service market, therefore, is formed by a group of consumers, potential buyers, seeking a health-related product or service and a provider of that product or service (Thomas, 2015). The nature of a particular healthcare service market can be conceptualised using four classifications: geographic scope, population characteristics, level of demand, and market potential.

Geographic scope: A market is defined by the geographic scope when the service rendered is available only for individuals who live within a particular location or are able to get there. For example, there are healthcare providers that offer advanced, cutting-edge technology, and skilled practitioners, but these providers operate out of a single location and in certain countries. The market for their services is limited to those who live nearby or are willing to travel to that location (Thomas, 2015). Geography determines accessibility.

Population characteristics: Demographics is often a determiner of healthcare services. Some healthcare providers may serve only children, women, or persons with specialised needs such as cardiology, oncology, or neurology. Hospice or elder care services provide their own specialised market.

Level of demand: Market demand has a direct impact on supply. A growing population around a city or town may increase demand for a general-care clinic. Lengthy wait times to see a specialist may encourage a healthcare provider to expand services to another locale. Recent developments in cancer treatment have generated a demand for previously nonexistent chemotherapy treatments; this is evidence that there is no market when there is no demand. To draw again on the definition of a market as having two essentials, a buyer and a seller, when the public (the buyer) demands a product or service to meet the needs presented by illness or disease, healthcare providers (sellers) have an opportunity to provide their services. A healthcare market is thereby created, becoming a member of the health sector and a contributor to the economy and GNP.

Market potential: A healthcare service market is created when an organisation sees an opportunity to fill a service gap that may be the result of poor or nonexistent providers. Healthcare providers who are proactive in seeking out ways to expand meet the needs of available customers and contribute to the economy

A fifth classification or description of healthcare markets is a new paradigm being discussed in marketing and sales circles: *markets without walls.* Thomas (2015) affirms that "markets without walls" is a concept used to illustrate the victory over the challenges posed by geographical limitations. In a technologically driven world, services of health providers can be received from around the globe. According to Thomas, the advent of telemedicine, for example, allows a specialist in one location to send electronically transmitted test results to a patient's healthcare provider in a different location. Patients and health service providers can share an electronically supported meeting point where services will be rendered, thereby gradually decreasing the reliance on geographically defined markets and increasing the availability for market control by consumer demand, preference, and ability to pay vis-à-vis health challenges unmet by providers or their competitors. Consideration of these factors – geographic scope, population characteristics, level of demand, and market potential, as well as the concept of markets without walls – should be embedded in strategic plans channelled towards building more effective consumer healthcare service markets in Africa.

3.3 STRATEGY DEFINED

To stay relevant, organisations must be flexible in responding to the dynamics of their business environment. Such flexibility can only be achieved through attention to strategy. Businesses and organisations can predict and meet customers' needs and outperform their competitors if they are strategic in their approach to service delivery. Strategy has different meanings to different organisations: The preferred definition is most often determined by the resources at hand and the goals of the organisations (Nickols, 2016). For example, in the military, strategy refers to a general plan of attack or defence; in businesses, strategy is a comprehensive master plan stating how the organisation will achieve its mission and objectives (Nickols, 2016). Strategies can be applied to both long- and short-term business goals, and they can be broken down into elemental parts according to the needs and responsibilities related to a unit's goals. Strategy allows an organisation to bridge the gap between ends and means, now and in the future, predicted circumstances and the dynamics of the business environment. Strategy creates access and direction to the actualisation of a goal, whether that goal is oriented toward increasing profitability, solving problems, or developing new opportunities.

Strategy is tied to a corporate agenda that flows throughout the organisation, creating a path to follow and a foundation for units to build on as they pursue their department goals and objectives. Organisations must be dynamic and evolve with the external business environment so as to remain relevant in their sector. One reason public healthcare systems in Africa are trailing their foreign counterparts is that they have not been strategic in their approach to handling health-related issues before and after their occurrence. It is, therefore, essential that a strategic light is shone on healthcare service delivery in order to support a concentrated effort to predict the occurrence and spread of diseases and put in place measures to quickly and effectively address the populations' healthcare needs.

3.4 THE STRATEGIC PLANNING CONTEXT

Strategic planning is a systematic process of organising, creating, and documenting plans to move from a current situation to desired future outcomes (Perera & Peiró, 2012; Sadeghifar et al., 2015). This systematic process helps in identifying goals and developing guidelines for achieving the goals (Swayne et al., 2006). Mintzberg, Quinn, and Ghoshal (1998) and Sadeghifar et al. (2015) also opined that effective strategic planning begins with acknowledging both the shortcomings and the competencies of an organisation and anticipating changes that can be helpful in achieving a unique and valuable outcome.

A strategic plan guides actions and assigns responsibilities that align with the intended goals. Strategic planning in the health sector requires organisations to assess the realities of their environment and establish mechanisms that will meet customers' needs and health challenges through quality service delivery (Thomas, 2015). In the context of the healthcare sector, a strategic plan should shape employees' behaviour towards patients, attract customers, and render quality service. The strategic plan should include guidelines for mediating substandard service delivery and making adjustments to assure high standards. By establishing the importance of achieving competitive advantage as a primary goal, a strategic plan will seek to place a healthcare organisation foremost in the minds of the public. The strategic plan should direct effective marketing, branding, customer attraction, and service promotion, acting as a set of checks and balances for the organisation's actions. The importance of strategic planning in the organisation and within healthcare service delivery underscores the need for a strategic orientation in health service delivery. When the vision and mission statements align with the strategic plan, healthcare organisations enhance their competitive advantage.

Different perspectives exist on the steps and sequencing of the strategic planning process (Thomas, 2015), but one easy-to-follow process was put forward by Kaye and Allison (2005). The authors recommended a seven-stage strategic planning process that would follow the creation of vision and mission statements: prepare; articulate mission, vision, and values; assess your situation; agree on priorities; write the strategic plan; implement the strategic plan; and evaluate and monitor the strategic plan. Kaye and Allison's seven-stage planning process has been modified in Figure 3.1 to graphically represent the planning process applicable to healthcare services, which should commence from the vision of a healthcare provider to the ultimate goal of customer satisfaction (operational outcomes).

A strategic plan must be flexible, able to respond to the changing dynamics of the healthcare environment. At the stage of monitoring and evaluation, the plan can be adjusted, depending on environmental factors and the outcome of the plan. The process from the vision to the outcome is intended to channel a course of action aimed at achieving the objectives of the organisation. Every organisation in any economic sector – business, finance, manufacturing, or other – and, whether run for profit as a or nonprofit, must have a strategic plan. Healthcare sector organisations are no exception.

3.5 THE STRATEGIC PLANNING PROCESS

Stage 1: Preparation. Those at the helm of an organisation identify the rationale for planning. They are first to ask why the plan is necessary. Is it to increase profits, attract more workers, build a brand, or achieve or sustain competitive advantage? Answers to these formative questions are foundational to the purpose, focus, and goal of a strategic plan. To develop a strategic plan that will channel the organisation towards the attainment of its corporate goals, internal and external factors must be identified. Internal factors include the nature of the healthcare service being provided, as well as the availability of manpower, financial resources, infrastructure, and technology. External factors include government policies, natural disasters, disease outbreaks, the nature of the market, and direct competition. After these internal and external factors have been fully identified and analysed, a strategic plan can be developed that will reflect the vision, mission, and expected outcomes for the organisation.

Stage 2: Articulate Mission, Vision, and Values. After careful planning by organisation leaders, they are expected to articulate the mission, vision, and values in a way that instils in workers the importance of translating the mission, vision, and values into a code of conduct that shapes their service delivery. The vision statement reflects the future goals of the organisation. The mission statement provides direction on what is to be done and how it will be done to achieve the vision statement.

The mission statement should be printed and placed for all to see, serving as a constant reminder to the employees. The vision statement must also be written and shared with employees to achieve a common understanding of the core goals the organisation is striving for. The mission and vision statements will serve to create values that will form the unique image of the organisation – values aimed at customer satisfaction, retention, and quality service delivery. If employees detect inconsistencies between the mission and vision statements, the articulation of values will be incoherent, resulting in disparities in health service delivery.

Stage 3: Assess Your Situation. At this stage of the strategic planning process, the organisation does a review and assessment of the outcomes of its previous plans. The organisation re-examines

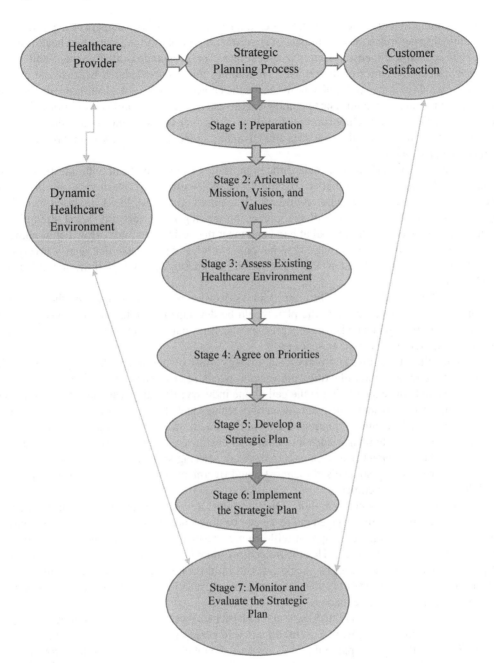

FIGURE 3.1   The Strategic Planning Process in Healthcare. (Source: Authors).

the internal and external factors that could stand in the way of implementing the current strategic plan and prepares a detailed situation assessment. At this stage, the organisation's management has the option to decline, modify, or agree to the implementation of the plans given what they determine to be the likely outcomes predicted by the assessment.

This stage includes assessment of the place of business (location), the kind of health service needed (product), the prices that will need to be charged (returns), and a marketing strategy (promotion) at a cost that will not affect the financial side of the business goal but will attract customers. Application of the PEST analysis – political, economic, social, and technological dynamics – of the country, community, or society of their targeted business audience is also part of the assessment. The political structure defines the impact of government policies and legislation on healthcare services. The economic dimension factors in a location's average incomes, inflation rates, and interest on loans. Social dynamics of the targeted community must be considered because the primary healthcare needs of that population will influence the choice of services the healthcare organisation finds to be in greatest demand. The technological infrastructure in the market will inform decisions related to service delivery. Opportunities for future innovations must be included in the assessment process in order to identify the obstacles and advantages associated with location, product, profitability, and promotion.

The major factor that should decide if the organisation should go ahead with the strategic plan is the SWOT evaluation – strengths, weaknesses, opportunities, and the threats – in the face of the internal and external business environment (i.e., marketing mix, PEST analysis) in which it operates. A SWOT assessment will shape decision-making going forward. What strengths can be leveraged to accomplish the goal at hand and meet the desired outcome? How can weaknesses be mitigated and turned into strengths? What opportunities are available that justify investing in the strategic plan? What threatens the organisation's competitive advantage if the strategic plan is implemented?

Stage 4: Agree on Priorities. The organisation's decision-makers must agree on the fundamentals of the strategic plan and how the plan would be developed, maintained, and sustained. The organisation's management also must agree on the financial commitments and administrative demands required if the plan is to succeed.

A segmenting, targeting, and perception strategy must be applied at this stage. Segmenting means that the organisation identifies the varying needs of customers in specific emerging markets. An example of segmentation is the cell phone industry: Providers can classify customers by benefits and desires, as some customers want high tech gadgets for business activities, others want phones with excellent camera qualities for travelling and tours, and others just want inexpensive phones to communicate with friends and family. A healthcare provider's strategic plan must also segment the health market that it intends to develop, offering services that meet the needs of the community, e.g., highly specialised diagnostic and treatment centres, multi-service hospitals, or walk-in emergency care clinics.

Targeting is a priority-setting activity. Once a healthcare market is identified, a marketing campaign designed to reach the targeted audience can be developed. If the health organisation intends to serve the aged, a targeted campaign will promote services related to maintaining healthy living during the retirement years. Healthcare centres aimed at serving children will focus on the importance of healthy diets, regular check-ups, and child-friendly atmospheres. Targeting supports healthcare organisations' efforts to set service delivery priorities that will give them an advantage in their particular healthcare market.

Perception is built on providing bigger and/or better services than those offered by competitors in their targeted market segment. Careful attention to perception will serve as a big-picture guide in building a marketing campaign that will attract the public's attention with innovations that surpass those of the competition. Segmenting, targeting, and perception building require time and effort, but are the elements of a successful strategic plan.

Stage 5: Develop a Strategic Plan. For a strategic plan to be successful, it must be SMART – specific, measurable, achievable, relevant, and timely or time-bound (Gandolf, 2019). A plan is specific when it has a clearly defined, documented goal. A measurable plan includes a yardstick by which the success or failure to reach the goal can be determined with accuracy. Measurability may also reflect how close the organisation is to meeting a goal so that possibilities for improvement may be communicated to the workers. A successful plan will be relevant when the healthcare service provider assures the community it wishes to serve that they will benefit from its implementation. A strategic plan addresses the importance of being timely; that is, the plan will communicate to stakeholders the time frame established for the goal to be achieved. If the stated time frame is not realistic, failure to meet deadlines will have a negative effect on the attainment of the plan's goals or its implementation.

This fifth stage of the strategic planning process requires that the organisation understands the financial implications of the plan, then documents the steps required to meet all stages of the plan. This document will become the reference source for the creation of goals and objectives for all departments, including finance, recruitment, training, sales, marketing, and production of goods or delivery of services.

Stage 6: Implement the Strategic Plan. It is not enough for a health organisation to have a goal; it must ensure that there is a plan on the ground to achieve the goal. As the French poet, Antonie de Saint said, "A goal without a plan is just a wish" (Gandolf, 2019). Strategic planning mitigates the "wish factor" and helps organisations achieve a goal with all the information they need to manage change and the unforeseen occurrences that are inevitable in the process of implementing a plan. The strategic plan's management team must be able to make adjustments and accommodate unexpected obstacles that may come from any direction without necessarily altering the whole process. One of the characteristics of a good strategic plan is that it is flexible and able to accommodate system change and the dynamics of the market. This sixth stage – implementing the strategic plan – incorporates room for change into its operational plan.

Stage 7: Monitor and Evaluate the Strategic Plan. The last stage of the strategic planning process is to monitor and evaluate the plan after a period of time to assess its validity. Monitoring is important in the process to avoid resource wastage or strategy gap. Monitoring precedes evaluation, and most organisations or health systems miss this step, failing to evaluate the strengths and weaknesses of the plan and its value in achieving its intended goal. Evaluation will reveal how much the plan has achieved, how it has dealt with the challenges it has faced, and how it can be improved in such a way that it will support future growth. This is why it is important that organisations strictly monitor their strategic plans to inculcate updates where needed, upgrading their strategic plans as they predict changes in dynamic environments. Even the best efforts put into strategic plans will have little efficacy or relevance without proper monitoring and evaluation.

3.6 STRATEGIC PLANNING IN HEALTHCARE

Modern healthcare service delivery requires continuous research into the nature and causes of disease and predicting future outbreaks to provide adequate technical measures to tackle them. Achieving this requires that hospitals adopt strategic plans that guide future directions, taking into account the health issues at hand as well as upcoming health challenges. Creating a strategic health plan is an initiative that requires action at national, state, and local administration levels. Healthcare service providers have found that focusing on daily operations is not sufficient to enhance service operations and sustain customer satisfaction, and this has motivated plans in the health sector to inculcate strategic planning into core health service priorities (Blanco-Topping, 2016). According to Jafari, Khalifegari, Danaei, Dolatshahi, and Roohparvar (2010), developing nations must take a cue from the Iranian national accreditation system that hospitals are to have a strategic plan outlining future directions.

Strategic planning in healthcare service delivery is centred on curbing the outbreak of diseases that are inimical to health, and advising government and other policy regulatory bodies on best health practices. This is why refining and developing a quality healthcare service has attracted scientific and strategic discussions (Arah, Klazinga, Delnoij, Ten Asbroek, & Custers, 2003). Evidence abounds (Mills et al., 2002; El-Jardali et al., 2007; Sadeghifar et al., 2015) that having a strategic healthcare service delivery in low- and middle-income countries is more complex, dynamic, and challenging because of the more limited resources available to these countries than to developed nations. As a result of this, low-income countries in Africa and beyond have struggled to manage evolving challenging healthcare issues. However, even with the paucity of resources, proper and effective corporate planning of the healthcare system, taking into cognisance available resources, will result in a change in the status quo. Kaissi, Begun, and Welson (2008) established that health-care organisations with a strategic plan have positive returns in their financial performance as a result of their ability to strategically plan for current and future healthcare needs.

Due to the shift in the nature of modern health challenges, many health organisations are unable to predict and prepare in advance for numerous health issues. Hospitals have to be strategic in their approach to healthcare service delivery if they want to remain viable in the business market. Health organisations must align their services to the needs and demands of the immediate society, which requires a strategic plan that puts in place activities within and outside the organisation that will manage challenges and channel a unique path to goal achievement that will enhance the organisation's competitive advantage through customer satisfaction. Strategic planning would support hospitals' efforts to become more effective and efficient in their service delivery through goal alignment, employee participation, and engagement of all stakeholders in the decision-making process. One example of a strategic plan would be a decision by a primary healthcare provider to expand services to another community, a decision that would depend on that provider's ability to expand its existing strategic goals. The success or failure of such decisions to improve and extend services will depend on a strategic plan that assures collaborative participation between the institution and its stakeholders.

Attention to the healthcare needs of Africa's local markets now and in the future will reduce the loss of manpower and negative impact on the economy. This can be done through strategic planning of healthcare service delivery in Africa.

3.7 STRATEGIC PLANNING AND CHALLENGES OF HEALTHCARE SERVICE DELIVERY IN AFRICA

Among 58.03 million people who died globally in 2005, 10.9 million (18.8 per cent) were from Africa (Kirigia & Barry, 2008). Agyepong et al. (2017) observed that Africa lags behind other continents in health outcomes, the worst occurring in socio-economically fragile countries, rural areas, urban slums, and conflict zones. Without a doubt, Africa as a continent is still struggling to sufficiently meet the health service needs of its inhabitants, and reasons range from ineffective leadership to improper healthcare planning.

Leadership has been an ages-long structural issue in Africa. There is a weak political will to invest rightly in the health sector. Too often, when the government shows commitment to strengthening the health sector, "spoilers" or impediments such as corrupt officials create inefficiencies that render the investments and policies futile. Poor leadership and management of the health sector, inadequate health-related legislation, lack of enforcement, limited community participation, and inefficiencies in resource allocation and use are all to blame for negative outcomes to health service delivery in Africa (Brinkerhoff & Bossert, 2008; Kirigia & Barry, 2008).

A shortage of health workers is another challenge in the African healthcare delivery system. In most public health hospitals in Africa, patients seeking healthcare far outnumber healthcare workers. The lack of health service delivery technologies is another challenge. While most developed countries have moved to technological diagnoses of their patients, most medical centres in Africa still make use of outdated mechanisms and treatments that have, in several instances, led to the death or disability of patients (Agyepong et al., 2017; Kirigia & Barry, 2008).

The service delivery of most African hospitals is still in a deplorable state, with 47 per cent of the population not having access to quality health service and 59 per cent of pregnant women delivering babies without the assistance of skilled health personnel (Kirigia & Barry, 2008; Kirigia & Wambebe, 2006). Without comprehensive health financing policies and strategic plans, the continent's healthcare system remains backwards. Most African health service challenges emanate from a lack of strategic planning by unenlightened health organisations and their leaders. Predicting, understanding, and planning for the healthcare needs of the population and undertaking the exacting process of recruiting and training personnel to meet those needs are the key elements strategic planning would provide to solve many of the problems experienced in Africa's healthcare sector.

3.8 WAY FORWARD

Healthcare organisations in Africa need to go beyond their reactive approach and begin to be proactive in their discharge and management of healthcare services. Healthcare needs of the population will continue to vary by degree and location; healthcare organisations can only meet those challenges if they invest in research and strategies that put in place adequate measures to manage future health situations, whether it is the demands of population expansion or an unforeseeable epidemic. Healthcare organisations have an opportunity to expand their frontiers, opening markets to deliver services in accordance with the new demand. Investment in health research and strategic planning to improve healthcare delivery in Africa go hand in hand. A competitive edge will reward healthcare providers who investigate customers' needs and challenges, then work to create strategic plans that propose manageable action plans. Private health centres that engage in strategic planning that takes into account the parameters of geographic scope, population characteristics, level of demand, and market potential will prepare policies and an operational framework designed to assure satisfaction and attain competitive advantage. For organisations in the health service, strategic planning provides a win–win outcome that should be taken with both hands.

Administration of Africa's healthcare sector by government agencies has often been plagued by poor leadership, poor financial management, inequalities based on ethnicity, and corruption (Agyepong et al., 2017). For a systemic change to have a positive outcome, the government must begin to treat healthcare matters with greater seriousness, providing adequate investment in technology, infrastructure, and human capital. The government must invest in and sponsor health research that will help predict, treat, and eradicate the devastating effects of disease outbreaks across the continent.

The poor administration of the healthcare sector in African countries is made most noticeable by African leaders' failure to patronise their own local healthcare facilities, opting instead for treatment in developed countries. The current President of Nigeria Muhammadu Buhari, former Angolan President Eduardo Dos Santos, Benin President Patrice Talon, and former Zimbabwe Prime Minister Robert Mugabe all have recurrent records of receiving their healthcare services in the United Kingdom, Spain, Paris, and Singapore respectively (Shaban, 2017). To minimise frequent medical tourism and as an accountability measure, policies should be made to encourage public officials to seek treatments in their home country by improving the quality of healthcare. The governments of African nations must be held responsible for poor healthcare service delivery in their countries as the health of their inhabitants is the wealth of their nations. The government and private health organisations have roles to play in ensuring a healthy African continent.

3.9 CONCLUSION

The way forward for African countries' healthcare delivery systems lies in strategic planning to create a healthcare sector that understands the needs of the people. This will require intensive research into market dynamics to assess the internal/external environments, set the right visions and goals, forecast future health challenges, and then implement plans that make needed services available to the public. The healthcare system is supposed to be a haven for the sick, but today, the reverse is the case in Africa. With the adoption of strategic planning, however, Africa can have better healthcare delivery outcomes in the years to come.

REFERENCES

Agyepong, I. A., Sewankambo, N., Binagwaho, A., Coll-Seck, A. M., Corrah, T., Ezeh, A., Fekadu, A., Kilonzo, N., Lamptey, P., Masiye, F., Mayosi, B., Mboup, S., Muyembe, J. J., Pate, M., Sidibe, M., Simons, B., Tlou, S., Gheorghe, A., Legido-Quigley, H., McManus, J., Ng, E., O'Leary, M., Enoch, J., Kassebaum, N., & Piot, P. (2017). The path to longer and healthier lives for all Africans by 2030: The Lancet Commission on the future of health in sub-Saharan Africa. *The Lancet, 390*(10114), 2803–2859.

Arah, O. A., Klazinga, N., Delnoij, D., Ten Asbroek, A., & Custers, T. (2003). Conceptual frameworks for health systems performance: A quest for effectiveness, quality, and improvement. *International Journal for Quality in Health Care, 15*(5), 377–398. doi:10.1093/intqhc/mzg049.

Blanco-Topping, R. (2016). Literature review of quality management and strategic planning in healthcare. *Medcrave Online Journal of Public Health, 5*(1). doi:10.15406/mojph.2016.05.00108.

Brinkerhoff, D. W., & Bossert, T. J. (2008). Health governance: Concepts, experience, and programming options. *Bethesda: Health Systems, 20*, 20.

El-Jardali, F., Jamal, D., Abdallah, A., & Kassak, K. (2007). Human resources for health planning and management in the Eastern Mediterranean region: Facts, gaps and forward thinking for research and policy. *Human Resources for Health, 5*(1), 9.

Gandolf, S. (2019). Are you marketing or just wishing something will happen? Retrieved from www.health-caresuccess.com.

Jafari, G. H., Khalifegari, S., Danaei, K. H., Dolatshahi, P. R. M., & Roohparvar, R. (2010). *Hospital accreditation standards in Iran.* Tehran: Seda publishing company.

Jimoh, A. (2003). Strategic management and the performance of the Nigerian banking industry. *African Review of Money Finance and Banking*, 119–138.

Kaissi, A. A., Begun, J. W., & Welson, T. (2008). Strategic planning processes and hospital financial performance. *Journal of Healthcare Management, 53*(3), 197–208.

Kaye, J., & Allison, M. (2005). *Strategic planning for nonprofit organizations: A practical guide and workbook.* Hoboken: Wiley.

Kirigia, J. M., & Barry, S. P. (2008). Health challenges in Africa and the way forward. *International Archives of Medicine, 1*(27).

Kirigia, J. M., & Wambebe, C. (2006). Status of national health research systems in ten countries of the WHO African Region. *BMC Health Services Research, 6*(1), 135.

Mills, A., Brugha, R., Hanson, K., & McPake, B. (2002). What can be done about the private health sector in low-income countries? *Bulletin of the World Health Organization, 80*, 325–330.

Mintzberg, H., Quinn, J. B., & Ghoshal, S. (1998). *The strategy process.* Revised European edition, Englewood Cliffs, NJ: Prentice Hall.

Najaftorkaman, M., Ghapanchi, A. H., Talaei-Khoei, A., & Ray, P. (2015). A taxonomy of antecedents to user adoption of health information systems: A synthesis of thirty years of research. *Journal of the Association for Information Science and Technology, 66*(3), 576–598.

Nickols, F. (2016). Strategy, strategic management, strategic planning and strategic thinking. *Management Journal, 1*(1), 4–7.

Organisation for Economic Co-operation and Development. (2011). *Health at a glance 2011 – OECD indicators.* Retrieved from www.oecd-ilibrary.org/social-issues-migration-health/health-at-aglance 2011_health_glance-2011-en.

Perera, F. D. P. R., & Peiró, M. (2012). Strategic planning in healthcare organizations. *Revista Española de Cardiología (English Edition), 65*(8), 749–754.

Sadeghifar, J., Jafari, M., Tofighi, S., Ravaghi, H., & Maleki, M. R. (2015). Strategic planning, implementation, and evaluation processes in hospital systems: A survey from Iran. *Global Journal of Health Science, 7*(2), 56.

Shaban, A. R. (2017). Africa's sick presidents and the overseas medical treatment. Retrieved from www.africanews.com/2017/06/21/africa-s-sick-presidents-and-the-overseas-medical-treatment//.

Swayne, L. E., Duncan, W. J., & Ginter, P. M. (2006). *Strategic management of healthcare organizations* (5th ed.). Oxford: Blackwell.

Thomas, R. K. (2015). *Marketing health services.* Chicago, IL: Health Administration Press.

World Health Organization (2012). *National e-Health strategy for improving women & children's health.* Retrieved from www.who.int/goe/publications/ehealth_ex_summary_en.pdf.

4 Marketing in Healthcare Management

Thomas Anning-Dorson, Nii Norkwei Tackie,
Michael Boadi Nyamekye

4.1 INTRODUCTION

Professor Shaker Zahra, in reflecting on the practice of management as postulated by Peter Drucker, explained that marketing centres on demand while innovation creates new value technologies and products to meet emerging needs (Zahra, 2003). We would like to extend this further and assert that marketing combines demand and innovation to meet the aspirations of both the marketer (brand, company, or entity) and the customer who begins and ends the marketing process. Marketing is defined as the identification, anticipation, and satisfaction of customer needs for an organisation or firm's profit (Chartered Institute of Marketing, 2015). In 2018, Google held its annual I/O conference with a particular interest in the development of the artificial intelligence playing a central role among its core applications. An interesting perspective was the use of artificial intelligence in healthcare. The machine was trained to carefully identify cardiovascular risk as well as diabetic retinopathy with the ability to predict within a five-year period the likelihood a patient could have a stroke or a heart attack. This small brief seems to encapsulate the essence of what marketing does in the simplest form, predict through identification and anticipation and then take the requisite measures in order to ensure the customers' needs are met (satisfaction).

The heartbeat of every product or service offered by either private or public organisations is the operationalisation of the marketing orientation in its value delivery (Kotler, 2011; Kotler & Keller, 2016). This customer-centric orientation ensures that the basic aim of profitability and corporate success is met in any business. The total healthcare system is not excluded, with a need for marketing interventions to improve sustainability and profitability (Batalden et al., 2016). This, however, has not been the trend in the healthcare space in most jurisdictions. Research has shown that the healthcare industry has been slow to inculcate marketing principles and techniques in its offerings (Kay, 2007; Saunders & Rod, 2012). Until recently, healthcare was primarily delivered by the government of a country and authorities within the states/cities and municipalities. This could explain why the healthcare industry has traditionally not sought the benefits of improved customer satisfaction and retention which are the end results of successful marketing efforts (Trombetta, 2007). Privatisation and partnerships of the healthcare industry with insurance firms are changing the narrative. In light of this, together with the advancing technological achievements in the healthcare sector, tightened economies, growing access to information on the part of customers, and intense competition, the importance of marketing in the healthcare sector is becoming increasingly clear on a daily basis.

This chapter addresses the importance of marketing in the healthcare industry, carefully bringing to the fore the requisite ingredients to shape marketing thought in relation to healthcare, and the adoption of the marketing orientation in the current and future healthcare environment. The basics of marketing will introduce this chapter with a focus on the marketing orientation – the shift from product-based orientations to the customer centred approach. A case will also be made in order to address the position of healthcare as a service process with a dissection of the product–service nexus. The healthcare system will be assessed as a service and mapped against the 7P's of marketing – the strategic tools for marketing success. The relationship between patient and caregiver as an important element of healthcare marketing will be discussed as well. These topics will be supported finally with a discussion of the future outlook for the healthcare marketing concept and how healthcare institutions can adopt marketing successfully.

4.2 MARKETING BASICS FOR THE NON-MARKETING HEALTH PROFESSIONAL

4.2.1 MARKETING: FROM PRODUCT TO CUSTOMER ORIENTATION

Marketing as a discipline is a pragmatic conduit of economics. Over time it has looked at the demand and supply functions so that firms can adopt a favourable position in order to achieve their desired successes. The philosophies driving it have been affected over time mainly by advances in technology and thus the movement of firms towards a more customer centred approach in achieving their goals effectively (Kotler & Keller, 2016). The marketing concept has evolved from core concepts, most notably the production concept, product concept, and selling concept, before finally becoming the marketing concept. These evolutionary phases are explained below.

The Production Concept: This is the earliest form of marketing practice. It was based on the industrial revolution which championed the socio-economic development of the Western world during the late nineteenth century and early twentieth century. This philosophy was inherently built on the premise that as long as supply exists, there will always be demand for the product. Firms believed that once the product was made available, visible, and cheap, the consumer would buy it. This was especially true at the time, as there was a proliferation of products which were once deemed as luxuries only meant for the most esteemed in society. This translated into a system in which firms were more concerned about ensuring high production efficiency and readily available mass distribution at a reduced cost. This had an impact on product quality, with an apparent disregard for customer specification and customisation. In offering beds to patients, health organisations usually adopt this type of orientation. Patients do not usually consider the type of bed they will lie on in the hospital; they expect it to be readily available and able to deliver on its basic functionality.

The Product Concept: This philosophical approach followed soon after the production orientation. At the height of the industrial age, the era was characterised by intense competition amongst manufacturing firms. This, in turn, pushed supply to exceed demand. In order to compete effectively, firms adopted the belief that once the customer is presented with a "superior" product, they will automatically buy it. When drugs are being prescribed, brands perceived as having superior benefits are often preferred by consumers. Health service personnel play a role in developing this perception and this is a form of the product orientation in the healthcare space. This concept moved firms into hyperdrive in the development of sophisticated products in the belief that it would translate into profitability for the firm. This concept drove innovation in the development of products with less regard for customer needs and wants. Proponents and practitioners of this orientation were yet to see that without the right balance of customer needs and innovation, success would always be a lucky strike.

The Selling Concept: This was the next phase of the evolutionary process, suggesting that unless persuaded, consumers will never buy enough of a firm's products. The strategy was to be aggressively present in the lives of the consumer. Firms were more concerned with selling their products than with meeting the needs of the customer. Dealers in insurance products such as life insurance would usually invade hospitals with banners and flyers in order to continuously shove the importance of insurance in the face of potential clients. For customers faced with health challenges, aggressively letting them relate to their own mortality was meant to open up sales prospects. This type of orientation degenerated into customers cutting ties completely with firms once they were dissatisfied with a product they felt was "forced" on them. Today this strategy is usually used in the sale of unsought goods, most notably insurance products.

The Marketing Concept: Developed in the mid-twentieth century, this is the first concept which developed from the cumulative experience of the earlier approaches. The underlying similarity between those approaches was the complete neglect of the customer's needs. The marketing concept realigns the benefits of all the pre-existing concepts and supports them with the importance of the customer's needs and wants. The concept, therefore, brings the right firms together with the right customer and ensures that they exist in an interlocking mutually beneficial relationship. The creation of customer value plays a central role in the execution of this concept. Firms adopting this concept place emphasis on the customer and the needs of the customer. Research has supported the claim that firms which have adopted this concept have reaped the benefits. The evolution has not ended there; the orientation has seen further evolvement into the holistic marketing orientation, which sees firms revolving all their operations around the customer in order to deliver satisfaction. Customer relationship management and customer delight have been identified as the concepts that have facilitated this transformation and the development of the marketing orientation. In the healthcare industry, this marketing philosophy is not only relevant, but it also positions health organisations so that they can effectively compete. Once patients have the perception that the healthcare service they receive from one healthcare organisation satisfies all their health needs, they are less likely to leave due to the sensitive nature of the industry. A patient who believes his doctors at one hospital are the best will most likely continue to develop that relationship.

4.2.2 Products versus Services: Defining the Concepts

At the core of marketing is the exchange process for value; that value may be derived from a product or service. A service is basically a performance of an activity by one person/entity for another. In the economic sense, services are intangible economic activities offered by one party to another. The performance or delivery of service is often time-based and the performance is meant to produce desired results for which the intended recipient has the responsibility to pay. While the recipient may exchange money, time, and effort for the service delivered, that does not usually result in ownership of any physical element or a good as it does in the case of a physical product. The American Marketing Association (1960) explains service marketing as a function or a set of processes for identifying or creating, communicating, and delivering value to customers and for managing customer relationships in a way that benefits the organisation and stakeholders, of which the customer is the most important. A product is differentiated from a service based on its characteristics of tangibility, heterogeneity (*variability*), inseparability, and perishability (Mudie & Pirrie, 2006). These characteristics are briefly explained below.

Tangibility

Tangibility refers to the ability to "experience" using the five senses to facilitate assessment. Products are therefore of a tangible nature due to their ability to be assessed by the five senses. Services, on the other hand, cannot be experienced without the aid of physical cues and are therefore by nature intangible. One can experience teaching, but without physical cues such as a board, marker, pamphlets, and instruction materials, one cannot assess it.

Heterogeneity (Variability)

Service delivered by service providers tends to be highly variable. This means that the quality of service to be provided highly depends on the one providing the service. Where, when, and to whom the service is being provided also varies, and some medical doctors have bad bedside manners whilst others are quite empathetic towards their clients. Those receiving the service are well aware of the differences between providers and therefore seek to gather information before making a decision. This reduces the risk of receiving a bad service experience. However, it is in the interest of the provider to assure customers by offering quality and service delivery guarantees, although companies that see themselves as market leaders hardly ever take this option.

Inseparability

Physical products are manufactured, inventoried and stored, and later distributed to consumers. Services are normally rendered and used within the same time period and at the same place; that is, it is usually a simultaneous action. The provider of the service usually cannot be separated from the service rendered. This defines the inseparability characteristic of service. For example, visiting the salon, the hairstylist cannot style the hair of a customer without being present. If a service provider renders a service, then the customer must likewise be present. This is why the interaction process between the customer and service provider is a distinct and integral factor of services delivery. The downside of the inseparability element is that it has its limitations with reference to the customer–provider ratio and time. For example, one customer service person can only handle a certain number of customer complaints within a specific time frame. It is, however, possible to get around that. For example, some psychologists have moved from individual-based therapy sessions to holding multiple group sessions of over 50 individuals in large conference halls. A psychiatrist can also spend 30 planned minutes instead of spending 50 free minutes and see more patients.

Perishability

Another characteristic of services is that they cannot be inventoried; therefore, their inability to be stored becomes a huge problem when demand for the service increases. For example, public transport companies must make a point of owning quite a number of cars so that, when it is rush-hour, they can meet demand and also relax when demand decreases. Also, some doctors charge their patients for missed appointments because the service value (availability of the doctor) exists only at the time for which the appointment is set. Managing demand is very important – the right and desired service must be available for production and consumption with the right customers at the right time and at the right place and at the right price in order to maximise profitability from the service delivered.

4.3 THE SERVICE-DOMINANT LOGIC (S-D LOGIC)

The contemporary view of marketing has sought to tone down the strict demarcation between products and services. One perspective (the experience economy perspective) offers that everything is but experience and that whatever customers buy is an experience, irrespective of it being a physical product or service (see Pine & Gilmore, 1999; Anning-Dorson, 2017). The argument for this "experience economy" is that experience is a commodity and that firms use their processes to create different experiences for customers in the form of value. On the other hand, another perspective that emerged in 2004 from Vargo and Lusch was the service-dominant concept (Vargo & Lusch, 2017). The S-D Logic opines that value creation is through exchanges and that this value exchange happens between various actors.

The underlying assumption is that people and entities use their competencies to the benefit of others in return for a service-for-service exchange (Vargo & Lusch, 2017). These proponents heightened the concept of value co-creation which is the basis of all exchanges. The customer is seen as, and actually plays the role of, value creator by partnering with the entity that offers that value. Proponents have now called for the development of the service ecosystems perspective that allows a more holistic, dynamic, and systemic perspective of value creation and an emphasis on institutions and institutional arrangements as coordination mechanisms in such systems (Vargo & Lusch, 2016). The S-D Logic has blurred or even eliminated the differences that existed between physical products and services. The fundamental principle of value co-creation is even more profound in service industries such as healthcare where the participation of the care-receiver is more prominent.

4.4 THE HEALTHCARE SYSTEM AS A DIFFERENT SERVICE

Healthcare is defined as the efforts made to maintain or restore physical, mental, or emotional well-being, mainly by trained and licensed professionals (Kay, 2007). From the above-stated discussion, healthcare falls within the services category. Enthoven and Tollen (2005) identify healthcare as a "service system". Unlike most services where access to information and decision making on the part of the consumer is relatively easy and requires little to no professional knowledge, decisions concerning health-related services are heavily dependent on the medical practitioner delivering the service. Consumers usually have a small window to contemplate on the decisions to be made. This means that consumers of health services find it difficult to assess the healthcare services rendered to them and must appraise the service rendered based on the word of the service provider (Batalden et al., 2016). Increased competition, better access to education, advances in technology, and information access is gradually increasing the capacity of healthcare clients to assess their experiences more.

Another notable difference between healthcare and other services is the level of risk involved. Though different services can in one way or the other have an effect on the wellbeing of an individual, healthcare has a more direct effect on the total wellbeing of an individual. The effects of healthcare services have deeper consequences than those of other services.

Healthcare, unlike other services, is also different in the way it is delivered globally. The way healthcare is managed and delivered in the developed world is totally different from the developing economies' contexts. This means that access to practitioners and other health services is relatively inconsistent and thus marketing issues that affect relationships between healthcare workers and patients may differ significantly. Marketing in healthcare has been shown to have profound effects on behaviour, which have in turn affected the operations of healthcare firms. Kay (2007) cites an example stating that "the growth of direct to consumer (DTC) pharmaceutical advertising in the US has amplified interest in new treatments and stimulated patients to talk to doctors". Promotional campaigns which have been successful have also affected the manner in which drugs are developed and manufactured (Deshpande, Menon, Perri, & Zinkhan, 2004). Moreover, the diffusion of information on disease conditions and treatment regimes, greatly enhanced by internet sites, has enabled consumers to become better informed. Consumers are sharing information on treatments and medications on websites and weblogs, and this has substantially altered many patient–doctor relationships, especially among patients with chronic diseases.

This means that marketing health services must not be done in a reckless or haphazard manner since it can have a detrimental effect on the health of consumers. In a bid to satisfy and offer value, healthcare entities will need marketers who will value the ethics of the medical field and, in turn, balance value with the physical, emotional, and mental wellbeing of consumers in order to deliver services which are relevant but profitable. It also means that practitioners must be informed of the benefits of marketing in order to make it feasible to run the orientation through the entire service ecosystem.

According to Crié and Chebat (2013), marketing in the healthcare industry must be viewed as an integrated system because its objectives are tied to the consumer's wellbeing and are therefore patient centred. It consists of a multi participatory convergence of actors and therefore must be addressed as such. The marketing function must, therefore, respond to actors in a manner that encourages everyone to play their role towards a successful service delivery process.

4.5 THE HEALTHCARE CUSTOMER

In the health and wellness space, customers are often referred to as patients. Customers are individuals with wants, needs, and desires that are satisfied based on their own understanding of what they need and desire (Corbin, Kelley, & Schwartz, 2001). This causes them to search, compare, and eventually make decisions on the product or service they deem capable of satisfying such needs and wants. Customers in the healthcare industry are a bit different in the sense that they are unable to "shop around", most especially in an emergency situation. Customers are most often limited to the expertise of the medical practitioner and the practitioner's preferred method of treating the ailment. Customers in the healthcare space are also prone to having longer term relationships with their practitioners as compared to other services. These relationships are usually intimate and present a chance to develop customer loyalty and delight (Bettencourt, 1997; Enthoven & Tollen, 2005).

Customers in the healthcare industry are usually partakers in the service delivery process and account for the outcomes of the service as a whole. The services marketing literature discourse states that when patients act as participants or temporary "employees" of the organisation, there is value co-creation which yields better value for the customer. Satisfied patients are more vocal about their perceptions of such entities that encourage customer participation (Bettencourt, 1997; Damali, Miller, Fredendall, Moore, & Dye, 2016). This means that healthcare customers are more likely to commend and speak positively about services they have experienced and find satisfactory in nature.

4.6 INTRODUCING MARKETING TO HEALTHCARE

The notion of marketing in healthcare has not been as readily accepted as commercial circles. In fact, Lega (2006) asserts that for some time, marketing has been a prohibited word in the healthcare sector. In countries where there is some form of a National Health System, where health is seen as a right and not a privilege, the notion of marketing has generally been rejected for the healthcare arena. However, in recent years, and in public health sectors around the world, there has been a rising appreciation of how marketing principles can be used to improve the performance of healthcare institutions. The gradual adoption of marketing principles by healthcare organisations can be explained by a number of factors. One such factor is the increasing knowledge of clients of these healthcare providers. Healthcare customers are becoming savvier and are beginning to participate better in the healthcare value delivery process. Additionally, the clients are changing their behaviour and becoming attentive to evaluating both the core service received and the peripheral services. Managers of healthcare institutions are facing pressure to provide better conditions and to respond to the increasingly differentiated market based on age, income, and education. Patient emancipation, as well as regulatory reforms, is enjoining healthcare providers to be increasingly more customer focussed (Crié & Chebat, 2013). Lastly, competition in the various sub-sectors of the health services is increasing, as there are a lot of new entrants as well as increasing demand for better quality health services from patients.

What appears to be missing in healthcare delivery is the issue of "customer focus" since the sector has largely been seen as just meeting the rights of the citizenry. Healthcare marketing has to do with creating and communicating perceivable differences in health service delivery with respect to other competing service providers. Marketing helps in the management of the entire service delivery spectrum to be targeted at meeting the needs of the various stakeholders. Healthcare practitioners and players have to understand the characteristics of the market/their publics, as well as the tools (the marketing mix) and strategies required to achieve their goals. Marketing offers a number of opportunities for better performance of players within the sector. Marketing allows healthcare institutions to understand their markets better through proper segmentation, targeting, and positioning, which has an enormous influence on revenues. Out of that, players are able to devise marketing strategies and plan their marketing programmes to achieve the desired ends. An important aspect of the development of marketing strategies and programmes is to understand the marketing mix. The next section discusses the marketing mix and its relations to healthcare.

4.7 THE 7P'S AND HEALTHCARE MARKETING

In the marketing literature, the traditional marketing mix generally comprises four elements – Product, Price, Place, Promotion – when dealing with physical products, whilst services make use of an additional three – Process, Physical Evidence, and People – which ensure that the services rendered by a service firm are "tangibilised" in order for consumers to experience the service (Goldsmith, 1999; Kotler & Armstrong, 2010; Kotler & Keller, 2016). Even though the 7P's concept has endured and facilitated the adoption of the marketing orientation, it is worth noting that some scholars proposed an alternate 4C's concept, matching the traditional 4P's, which are Customers solution, Cost, Convenience, and Communication. Some scholars have argued that the 7P's concept does not entirely fit into the health service context; however, socio-economic dimensions such as insurance seem to cause this misconception (Grover, 2016; Kahn et al., 1997). In the most basic form, the 7P's clearly facilitate the marketing process in the healthcare industry and the elements are detailed further below.

4.7.1 THE PRODUCT ELEMENT

A product is anything a firm can offer to a market for customers' acquisition, use, consumption, or attention in order to satisfy a need or a want. This means that products must have value to the customer. A product may be a service, physical good, a person, an organisation, an idea, or a place. This element of the marketing mix relates to the development, management, and presentation of the product offered by a firm. In a healthcare space, this will constitute the treatment and the diagnosis of diseases, the educational training of medical students and support staff, and the optimisation of pharmaceutical and emergency services in order to deliver the optimum care to consumers (patients). The healthcare product is anything on offer to improve the health of patrons or actors. The product is the value that customers (e.g. patients) seek to meet their health needs. This is very broad and will vary from one sub-sector in the healthcare industry to another. For example, a spa service will be different from a traditional healer in Tanzania's southern highlands. In the same way, there are variations in the product delivery of a primary healthcare centre in Dodo Kortuma of the Luawa Chiefdom and Kailahun District in Sierra Leone, West Africa, and any of the Netcare Group facilities across South Africa.

4.7.2 THE PRICE ELEMENT

The price is the only element in the marketing mix which generates revenue for the firm, unlike all the other elements which bring costs to the firm. With increasing cost in the delivery of health services, price is an important element in the decision-making process of healthcare patients. Pricing should be delivered on the basis of a well-structured approach which will take into account the cost of operations and financial capability of the target market, in order to deliver the best care at the most affordable cost. Price in healthcare encompasses all efforts, time, pain, and monetary outlays that the healthcare customer would have to expend to access or enjoy the service. The queues and the time spent at public health facilities in Abidjan, Côte D'Ivoire, the social cost a young person would have to endure to access a family planning service in Tamale, Ghana, and the insecure car park at a spa are all part of the cost to the customer.

4.7.3 THE PLACE ELEMENT

The place as an element of the marketing mix explains how value is distributed. Under this element, location plays a central role. The product must always be in the right place and at the right time. The place is where the customer buys, receives, or accesses the service and must be appropriate and convenient for the customer. This element looks at the location of the service delivery together with its general accessibility. Another important aspect of the place is the assessment of what channel is most suitable to deliver the value offered to the client. How customers access a product in terms of convenience and availability is a critical factor in successful healthcare marketing. Additionally, the availability of vital services around the clock is very critical to meeting patient needs.

4.7.4 THE PROMOTION ELEMENT

Promotion is the manner in which a firm communicates its products or services. It includes activities such as advertising, branding, PR, social media outreach, exhibitions, and sales promotions. Promotion must be able to give customers a reason to choose the firm's products and services rather than those of its competitors by delivering an appealing and consistent message. This element will consist of actions undertaken by the healthcare firm in order to make its activities known to the consumer. It generally involves making the consumer aware of the existence of the healthcare facility and of the services it renders as well. From the use of brochures to marketing analytics, healthcare facilities have a large box of tools available to ensure that they can deliver on their promotional intents. Digital marketing has also made it easy for healthcare services to undertake promotional activities. On Facebook and Twitter, or through websites and mobile applications, undertaking promotional activities has never been easier than in this information age (Lammenett, 2019).

4.7.5 THE SERVICES MIX ELEMENTS (PEOPLE, PROCESSES, PHYSICAL EVIDENCE)

The extended marketing mix involves the elements of people, processes, and physical evidence. The people element in the healthcare system involves all individuals who come together in order to make healthcare delivery successful. This includes those who directly affect the delivery of services, such as doctors, nurses, and lab technicians, as well as those who indirectly do so, such as cleaners and other supporting staff. It is important that the people element is addressed because people affect the outcome of how services will be experienced and inform the judgement of clientele. It is therefore important to ensure that the right people are hired, who will drive the operations of the firm towards customer satisfaction (Kemp, Bui, Krishen, Homer, & LaTour, 2017). The information age also presents a challenge as customers can now verify information about the services being rendered. Level of customer knowledge has increased as access to information and verification portals has grown. Healthcare providers must thus be sure to hire highly qualified staff who successfully meet the expectations of the well-informed client base.

The processes element addresses the manner in which the service is rendered to the patient (consumer). Zeithaml, Parasuraman and Berry (1990) explain that it refers to the procedures, mechanisms, and flow of activities through which a service such as a spa, clinic, or a fertility centre is delivered. The process explains the service delivery and operating systems – from the back end to the front end. It usually encapsulates the way a service is delivered to the consumer right from the time of admission all the way through to the time they are discharged from the facility and even to the post-service delivery. This also takes into account the safety of the customer (patient) throughout the delivery of the service. Currently, technology plays a key role in the delivery of this aspect of the element with the integration of health management systems.

Services are intangible and customers continuously refer to the other cues in judging a service offering. Physical evidence in service refers to the "tangibilisation" of a service offering in order to assist the client's evaluation. Physical evidence defines the environment within which the service is delivered as well as the tangibles that facilitate the service delivery process. In the healthcare marketing space, the physical evidence element takes into account issues such as the layout of the healthcare facility, the maintenance of hygiene, cleanliness, the general physical environment, logos, brochures, websites, the physical appearance of personnel, and any other tangibles that are visible to the customer. These offer the customers a sense of what to expect from the healthcare firm and have a great impact on the perceptions of the quality of the services rendered.

4.8 BRANDING AS A TOOL FOR STRATEGIC HEALTHCARE MARKETING

A brand is a symbol, term, name, design, sign, or a combination of any of these factors which is intended to identify and differentiate the goods or services of one entity from that of its competitors (Keller, 2006). With growing competition, ease of access to information, and technology advancements, the role of branding has never been more important, especially in services such as healthcare (Odoom, Anning-Dorson, & Acheampong, 2017). Branding provides customers with the identity of the producers of the product or service. This makes it easier for customers to make decisions in their search process and reduces the risks associated with using an unknown brand. Issues such as quality, pricing, and costs are addressed when strong brands are built. Branding in the sphere of services is considered to be more challenging than in that of physical products. Berry and Seltman (2008) explained service brand to mean a promise of future satisfaction that is conducted through a distinctive performance, consistent messaging, and an appeal to the emotions. Branding is also an important aspect in the marketing of health services even though healthcare services are lagging behind in adopting branding actions (Corbin et al., 2001). Branding can provide healthcare firms with a sense of consistency which is requisite in building customer trust.

In the healthcare industry, branding is a concept being relatively slowly embraced by firms in the space. Branding provides a platform where healthcare institutions can be positioned so as to be perceived as a point of satisfaction for customer needs and wants. It provides the firm with a chance to communicate with customers about the type of health services provided at its facilities. According to Corbin et al. (2001) branding a healthcare firm as a specialised service provider communicates its directed focus to external customers, but, in turn, it also affects how its internal customers (employees) function with the organisation and the community as a whole. Branding, therefore, provides health firms with a chance to stand out from other facilities and develop the trust required to boost their output and profitability, especially in the private sector.

4.9 THE STRATEGIC VALUE OF MARKETING IN HEALTHCARE

In the current dispensation, it has become critical for healthcare companies to market themselves, taking into account the target audience and ensuring the messages and signals sent are to that right audience. Marketing in healthcare is not only for patients to scope for physicians who can treat them, but even for job seeking healthcare workers. The industry is fast evolving and it is important that the industry adapts and keeps consumers well informed. In providing information, it must be timely and significant to ensure credibility. Marketing in healthcare must be done correctly and consumers must be able to trust it. In marketing, the consumer needs to be made aware of why the marketed practice (service) is different from others, and why it is the best in a host of other healthcare providers that may even be, in terms of proximity, closer to the consumer and serve just about the same purpose.

Quality determination in healthcare is subjective and based on the process through which the service is administered, as well as the interaction between the service provider and the customer (Trombetta, 2007). As a result, the five service quality (SERVQUAL) dimensions of "reliability, responsiveness, assurance, empathy, and tangibles" (Parasuraman, Zeithaml, & Berry, 1988) are also applicable in the healthcare service. Within each of these dimensions would be a level of tolerance that a patient possesses in relation to the delivery of healthcare. From the viewpoint of service delivery, it is critical that healthcare providers comprehend these tolerance levels associated with the various dimensions of service quality (Kay, 2007). This has not always been the case in the African context since most of the healthcare institutions were owned by the government; thus, issues such as service quality were not considered in the day to day operations of the organisations. There is increased competition between healthcare providers for the consumer/patient. Additionally, with the significant evolution of healthcare practice into a service sector, patients are now being considered customers. As a result, they are up in arms across the globe expecting better service. Consequently, easy accessibility to healthcare professionals, convenience, and in some cases, luxury are now very significant elements that altogether add to the patient's assessment of the quality of healthcare that they have received. In Ghana, for example, a recent survey to assess the service provided by some private hospitals against developed world standards revealed that at least ten of the hospitals in the country were offering top-notch services amidst growing competition. They are able to differentiate themselves based on the solid brand building activities and the well-defined services mix elements (Glena Healthcare Consultancy, 2018).

It is important for hospitals and related healthcare firms to understand the value of having a respectable brand. As a result of consumers being inundated with information, consumer power has increased. Consequently, in deciding which healthcare provider to patronise, information such as the infection rate, the ranking of the hospital, and the number of specialists on staff all influence consumers' decisions. If hospitals do not cement their position, their competitors will overtake them and create customer attrition. This can be done through word-of-mouth and by leveraging on the fact that consumers now have easy access to data. If a competitor's offering is all patients see, they will be more inclined to believe the competitor than a poorly marketed care provider (Padma, Rajendran, & Sai, 2009; Panchapakesan, Sai, & Rajendran, 2015).

The healthcare space has also changed significantly. With the advent of countries and states positioning themselves for medical tourism, that phenomenon is further shaping the demands and expectations of customers. The rate at which healthcare clients are travelling outside their own country is growing, with countries like Thailand and India benefitting immensely from medical tourism. Marketing in healthcare has also become more intricate and complicated. The traditional use of billboards and print media, or even high-quality television campaigns, is no longer sufficient. There is a need for more interactive customer engagement and not just shoving messages down the throats of consumers. Social media platforms are actively being used to position the brands of healthcare companies. An attractive website is crucial in healthcare marketing, and using video to provide information and even developing seminars for prospects to make a choice as well as learn are all influencing healthcare marketing. The fast-changing technological landscape makes it more imperative for healthcare brands to be at the cutting edge of leveraging technology, not only in the clinical practice, but in marketing efforts as well. Now, the consumer is not only interested in paying for good service, but is also interested in buying into a brand. Some hospitals sponsor free lectures from renowned experts or provide virtual tours of their facility. The use of humour in advertising campaigns is increasing with hospitals letting go of hard-to-digest advertisements and leveraging the appeal of humour (Huhmann & Limbu, 2016).

The debate over the marketing budget of hospitals has been intense. The immense rise of interest of healthcare providers in marketing is at a time when many firms are shutting down facilities, shrinking their budgets, and some are laying off workers. The result is that organisations focussed on consumer protection suggest that hospitals are spending hefty sums of money on marketing rather than focussing on patient care. The rebuttal to the hospitals is that marketing is rather a strategic investment into the sustainable growth of the firms.

4.10 PRIORITISING STRATEGIC MARKETING ADOPTION IN HEALTHCARE

The marketing orientation presumes that institutions or organisations track consumer needs and wants and produce products or services that match them. It is also of the view that consumer behaviour can be both anticipated and managed. This section will look at the factors affecting the healthcare organisation in adopting the marketing orientation.

First, issues concerning healthcare are obviously at the top of the priority list of consumers. This can be attributed to the popular saying that goes "your health is your wealth". Healthcare is associated with happiness, wellbeing, and the quality of life of a person. Increasing the health outcomes would seem to be clearly important for the healthcare organisation but from the viewpoint of the customer this is not the case, because their view tends to be clouded by the complex and complicated nature of healthcare service deliveries and procedures. Healthcare services are generally framed as "credence goods" – for which utility derived from the service rendered is difficult to measure. Consumers rely heavily on trusted experts to provide judgements on the quality of a health service. This makes them vulnerable because they are unable to make judgements for themselves (Aras, 2011). Quality in the eyes of the consumer when it comes to healthcare is seen to be a fundamental issue of concern, unlike some other products or services which compromise this attribute. This is mainly because healthcare deals with the life of a customer, a matter which cannot be taken lightly. Hence, compromising on quality can put the reputation of a healthcare organisation at risk. Even in less serious health situations, customers do not want to accept low service delivery quality. Customers desire the most convenient, rapid, and effective treatment. The above assessment of the customer within the healthcare system is one worthy of note in the adoption of the marketing orientation.

Another factor affecting the adoption of marketing is the shifting of priorities by management. The priorities of management within the healthcare system are continually changing as a result of advancing technology. Tools and equipment that better diagnose the vulnerability of an individual, even as a result of some genetic conditions, are gradually entering the healthcare system, thereby making preventive care and dedicated treatment highly important services to offer. Preventive care is preferable to curative care (Kemp, Jillapalli, & Becerra, 2014). For example, some drugs are given to check and control one's blood pressure from fluctuating which can prevent the threat of hospitalisation due to hypertension. Again, there are some wearables that are able to track one's heart rate and chip implants to monitor patients who are susceptible to heart attacks just to arrest the occurrence in time before it develops. The organisational choices for the evaluation and the assessment of medical uncertainties, processes, and costs are escalating concerns which are largely facilitated by advancing technology. Management priorities should be largely fixated on adopting technology and maximising the complex nature of the health system as well as tracking the needs and requirements for treatment of consumers during the service delivery processes. This has a great effect on the adoption of the marketing orientation.

Ethics and ethical concepts are another important set of elements which affect the adoption of marketing in the healthcare industry. Problems in terms of ethics emanate from the fact that, unlike regular consumer products, medical products such as drugs are consumed based on a particular health situation and as such require tact in their administration and usage. Some medical products are prone to abuse and can in turn damage health as well. The same applies to cut-throat marketing activities, especially in the advertising space, as issues such as over-promising and wrong information can appear. Mistakes in marketing practices may not only lead to customer dissatisfaction, but can also result in death or serious injury. This means that aspects of marketing such as advertising are usually heavily regulated in order to mitigate and monitor these possible negative outcomes in the adoption of marketing.

4.11 MARKETING FROM WITHIN: THE BEGINNING OF SUCCESSFUL HEALTHCARE MARKETING

The last element to consider for marketing in healthcare services is internal marketing. Internal marketing is a philosophy whereby entities treat their employees as customers so that they can, in turn, treat external customers better. The philosophy is focussed on internal customer (employee) satisfaction. The rationale is that marketing oriented entities can influence and motivate employees effectively to be customer conscious, market-oriented, and sales minded if a marketing-like internal approach is adopted and by applying marketing-like activities internally (Grönroos, 1985). Rafiq and Ahmed (2000) capture this succinctly stating:

> Internal marketing is a planned effort using a marketing-like approach to overcome organizational resistance to change and to align, motivate and inter-functionally co-ordinate and integrate employees

towards the effective implementation of corporate and functional strategies in order to deliver customer satisfaction through a process of creating motivated and customer orientated employees. This
means that marketing from within is the beginning of successful marketing. Internal marketing provides the platform for healthcare managers to implement the all-important change in external customer
orientation by creating an atmosphere in which internal customers are motivated and satisfied. As the
fundamental principle of marketing is meeting the value needs of customers (satisfaction), so should
this principle apply to healthcare employees.

The first important principle of internal marketing is hiring/recruiting the right type of employees
and training these employees. The quality of service delivered is largely explained by the quality of
employees delivering the service. Competitive healthcare entities must strive to recruit top-quality
employees and constantly train their staff to meet the challenges of their job and customer expectations. Knowledge is seen as a critical success factor in the increasingly competitive healthcare
landscape. Employees need the requisite knowledge and ability to recognise and solve clients' emotional, physical, and social problems to ensure high-quality service delivery. Investing in employee
training brings about a change in attitudes, increased skills, and job satisfaction which in turn
influence customer satisfaction and loyalty.

Another important principle is employee empowerment. Lack of freedom on the part of healthcare employees stifles innovation and job satisfaction (Anning-Dorson, 2018). Entities must seek
to grow the level of empowerment to engender freedom and respect as well as accountability.
Empowered healthcare employees will continuously seek to provide solutions to clients' problems
– given decision latitude to fix problems without fear of being blamed if something goes wrong. For
effectiveness, empowered staff must be made to understand that it is a matter of life and death in
healthcare, so they must exercise their power responsibly. Another principle is information sharing
which is meant to build trust among employees and functional areas. Employees are able to make
better decisions and judgements (even in their empowered state) when armed with information
which affects such decisions. Pfeffer (1998) argues that information is power; hence, empowered
employees are always armed with information.

Lastly, the issues of better reward, reduced status distinction, and employment security influence
employee satisfaction and external customer satisfaction and loyalty. High basic pay, productivity
gain, sharing, and other forms of reward are important determinants of employee job satisfaction. Competitive and market-oriented healthcare entities seek to incentivise employees above the
industry average and this is one way of getting employees to achieve objectives. Healthcare service
firms must ensure that they reduce the status distinction that makes some workers feel inferior and
less valued, since every single participant (employees) in the value delivery chain in healthcare is
critical. Increasing the worth of employees, especially the lower ranked ones, motivates and creates
a team culture to achieve the organisational objectives. Additionally, employment security gives
healthcare workers the reasonable assurance that they will not be sacked even in tough economic
conditions. Job security works in a reciprocal manner in that employees are committed to entities
that commit to them. This brings about high levels of job satisfaction, low employee turnover, and
trust in management (Bansal, Mendelson, & Sharma, 2001).

4.12 CONCLUSION

In conclusion, the importance of the healthcare sector cannot be overstated regardless of the context – be it in developed or developing countries and markets. Unlike previous thinking, in which
the marketing concept was far apart from the healthcare organisation, changing market conditions
and growing competition have made the adoption of marketing principles and philosophies relevant in today's healthcare environment. In the twenty-first century, different lifestyle trends have
made today's consumers more dynamic and demanding, thereby putting clinicians and managers
in a position to gain loyalty from these consumers and achieve customer value. This has pushed

many healthcare institutions to develop processes that give them competitive advantages in their growing industry. The fact remains that the term "patient" is being increasingly replaced by terms like "consumer" and "customer" which calls for a notable move in the way healthcare organisations structure their marketing strategies. Healthcare managers, most especially in the African setting, must be willing to adopt better marketing and communication strategies to inform customers of the services they offer whilst creating a perception of excellence about the service. Customer feedback systems and mechanisms must also be developed in order to understand customers and deliver on their needs. With growing technology, the convenience of the customer can easily be achieved at a cheaper cost and healthcare managers must make use of such tools. Once managers appreciate that their sustainability is dependent on the satisfaction of customers, marketing will be at the heart of the healthcare system.

REFERENCES

American Marketing Association. (1960). Marketing definitions: A glossary of marketing terms. American Marketing Association.

Anning-Dorson, T. (2017). Innovation development in service firms: A three-model perspective. *International Journal of Services and Operations Management, 28*(1), 64–80.

Anning-Dorson, T. (2018). Innovation and competitive advantage creation: The role of organisational leadership in service firms from emerging markets. *International Marketing Review, 35*(4), 580–600.

Aras, R. (2011). Social marketing in healthcare. *The Australasian Medical Journal, 4*(8), 418.

Bansal, H. S., Mendelson, M. B., & Sharma, B. (2001). The impact of internal marketing activities on external marketing outcomes. *Journal of Quality Management, 6*(1), 61–76.

Batalden, M., Batalden, P., Margolis, P., Seid, M., Armstrong, G., Opipari-Arrigan, L., & Hartung, H. (2016). Coproduction of healthcare service. *BMJ Quality and Safety, 25*, 509–517.

Berry, L. L., & Seltman, K. D. (2008). *Management lessons from Mayo Clinic* (p. 4). McGraw-Hill Professional Publishing.

Bettencourt, L. A. (1997). Customer voluntary performance: Customers as partners in service delivery. *Journal of Retailing, 73*(3), 383–406.

Chartered Institute of Marketing. (2015). CIM 7Ps. *The Chartered Institute of Marketing (CIM)*. Retrieved May 10, 2019, from www.cim.co.uk/media/4772/7ps.pdf.

Corbin, C. L., Kelley, S. W., & Schwartz, R. W. (2001). Concepts in service marketing for healthcare professionals. *The American Journal of Surgery, 181*(1), 1–7.

Crié, D., & Chebat, J. C. (2013). Health marketing: Toward an integrative perspective. *Journal of Business Research, 66*(1), 123–126.

Damali, U., Miller, J. L., Fredendall, L. D., Moore, D., & Dye, C. J. (2016). Co-creating value using customer training and education in a healthcare service design. *Journal of Operations Management, 47*, 80–97.

Deshpande, A., Menon, A., Perri, M., & Zinkhan, G. (2004). Direct-to-consumer advertising and its utility in health care decision making: A consumer perspective. *Journal of Health Communication, 9*(6), 499–513.

Enthoven, A. C., & Tollen, L. A. (2005). Competition in health care: It takes systems to pursue quality and efficiency [Special issue: Project Hope]. *Health Affairs*, 24, Supplement 1.

Glena Healthcare Consultancy. (2018). Top 10 best private hospitals in Ghana. Retrieved May 11, 2019, from www.linkedin.com/pulse/top-10-best-private-hospitals-ghana-dr-joseph-kofi-gyanteh.

Goldsmith, R. E. (1999). The personalised marketplace: Beyond the 4Ps. *Marketing Intelligence & Planning, 17*(4), 178–185.

Grönroos, C. (1985). Internal marketing: Theory and practice. In T. M. Bloch, G. D. Upah, & V. A. Zeithaml, *Services Marketing in a Changing Environment* (pp. 41–47). Proceedings Series. Chicago, IL: American Marketing Association.

Grover, R. (2016). Healthcare marketing: The paradigm shift. *Current Medicine Research and Practice, 6*(3), 138–139.

Huhmann, B. A., & Limbu, Y. B. (2016). Content and compliance of pharmaceutical social media marketing. *Marketing Intelligence & Planning, 34*(7), 977–999.

Kahn, B., Greenleaf, E., Irwin, J., Isen, A., Levin, I., Luce, M., … & Young, M. (1997). Examining medical decision making from a marketing perspective. *Marketing Letters, 8*(3), 361–375.

Kay, M. J. (2007). Healthcare marketing: What is salient?. *International Journal of Pharmaceutical and Healthcare Marketing, 1*(3), 247–263.

Keller, K. L. (2006). Conceptualizing, measuring, and managing customer-based brand equity. *Journal of Marketing*. https://doi.org/10.2307/1252054.

Kemp, E., Bui, M., Krishen, A., Homer, P. M., & LaTour, M. S. (2017). Understanding the power of hope and empathy in healthcare marketing. *Journal of Consumer Marketing*, *34*(2), 85–95.

Kemp, E., Jillapalli, R., & Becerra, E. (2014). Healthcare branding: Developing emotionally based consumer brand relationships. *Journal of Services Marketing*, *28*(2), 126–137.

Kotler, P. (2011). Philip Kotler's contributions to marketing theory and practice [Special issue: Marketing legends]. *Review of Marketing Research*, *8*, 87–120.

Kotler, P., & Armstrong, G. (2010). *Principles of marketing* (3rd ed.). Upper Saddle River, NJ: Pearson.

Kotler, P., & Keller, K. L. (2016). *Marketing management* (15th ed.). Upper Saddle River, NJ: Pearson.

Lammenett, E. (2019). Influencer marketing. In *Practical knowledge online marketing* (pp. 139–170). Wiesbaden: Springer Gabler.

Lega, F. (2006). Developing a marketing function in public healthcare systems: A framework for action. *Health Policy*, *78*(2–3), 340–352. doi:10.1016/j.healthpol.2005.11.013.

Mudie, P., and Pirrie, A. (2006). *Services marketing management* (3rd ed.). Oxford: Elsevier Ltd.

Odoom, R., Anning-Dorson, T., & Acheampong, G. (2017). Antecedents of social media usage and performance benefits in small-and medium-sized enterprises (SMEs). *Journal of Enterprise Information Management*, *30*(3), 383–399.

Padma, P., Rajendran, C., & Sai, L. P. (2009). A conceptual framework of service quality in healthcare: Perspectives of Indian patients and their attendants. *Benchmarking: An International Journal*, *16*(2), 157–191.

Panchapakesan, P., Sai, L. P., & Rajendran, C. (2015). Customer satisfaction in Indian hospitals: Moderators and mediators. *Quality Management Journal*, *22*(1), 10–29.

Parasuraman, A., Zeithaml, V. A., & Berry, L. L. (1988). Servqual: A multiple-item scale for measuring consumer perceptions of service quality. *Journal of Retailing*, *64*(1), 12.

Pfeffer, J.(1998). *The human equation: Building profits by putting people first*. Boston, MA: Harvard Business Press.

Pine, B. J., & Gilmore, J. H. (1999). *The experience economy: Work is theatre & every business a stage*. Harvard Business Press.

Rafiq, M., & Ahmed, P. K. (2000). Advances in the internal marketing concept: Definition, synthesis and extension. *Journal of Services Marketing*, *14*(6), 449–462.

Saunders, S., & Rod, M. (2012). Brand network maps: A multidimensional approach to brand-consumer relationships in the New Zealand pharmacy industry. *International Journal of Pharmaceutical and Healthcare Marketing*, *6*(1), 55–70.

Trombetta, W. L. (2007). Healthcare marketing. *Journal of Hospital Marketing*. doi:10.1300/j043v03n02_02.

Vargo, S. L., & Lusch, R. F. (2016). Institutions and axioms: An extension and update of service-dominant logic. *Journal of the Academy of Marketing Science*, *44*(1), 5–23.

Vargo, S. L., & Lusch, R. F. (2017). Service-dominant logic 2025. *International Journal of Research in Marketing*, *34*(1), 46–67.

Zahra, S. A. (2003). The practice of management: Reflections on Peter F. Drucker's landmark book. *Academy of Management Perspectives*, *17*(3), 16–23.

Zeithaml, V. A., Parasuraman, A., & Berry, L. L. (1990). *Delivering quality service: Balancing customer perceptions and expectations*. Simon and Schuster.

5 Segmentation, Targeting, and Positioning in Healthcare

Ogechi Adeola, David Ehira, Adaeze Nworie

5.1 INTRODUCTION

The concept of marketing as it relates to healthcare has been discussed in the previous chapters. This chapter builds on that background by applying the Segmentation, Targeting, and Positioning (STP) theory to healthcare marketing. Unlike mass marketing, an undifferentiated marketing approach that assumes that consumers will want the same product (e.g., granulated sugar, water, eggs) irrespective of the manner of delivery, pricing system, or promotion, market segmentation recognises the fact that the needs and wants of consumers vary across different categories (Berkowitz, 2017). One significant feature of mass marketing is that there must be homogeneity among the elements (Postrel, 2018). All members of a mass market cluster must share at least one common trait that unites them. STP is a strategic three stage marketing process that organisations utilise to identify their target markets, divide those markets into cohesive segments, and position their products and services, establishing their brand to meet the needs of the identified target segment. When applied to healthcare service delivery, medical providers meet needs, enhance productivity, and reduce costs in an effective and efficient manner (Pleasant, 2014).

Segmentation uses specific criteria to create market categories, dividing a market into groups to support organisations' efforts to target customers based on demographic, psychographic, geographic, or behavioural characteristics (Bruwer & Li, 2017). STP is one of the most frequently used models practised in modern marketing (Santoso, Rahmatullah, Angeline, Raznan, Mubaroq, & Lin, 2018). The model is useful when creating marketing communication plans because it helps marketers prioritise activities and then develop and deliver personalised and relevant messages to engage with different categories of customers. In healthcare services, STP plays a key role. According to Pleasant (2014, p. 71), healthcare providers can no longer look at their industry homogenously as "people that are sick and need care". Unique illnesses require unique attention and treatment techniques, and facilities that cater to those unique illnesses will prove profitable and sustain a competitive advantage in a dynamic marketplace. The "one-stop shop" for taking care of healthcare issues is long gone in the American culture.

5.2 SEGMENTATION, TARGETING, AND POSITIONING IN HEALTHCARE

Application of the STP model is explained in the following three sections: (1) Segmentation in healthcare services; (2) Targeting in healthcare services; and (3) Positioning in healthcare services.

5.2.1 Segmentation in Healthcare Services

Market segmentation groups consumers into homogeneous clusters or market segments, which allows organisations to respond by fashioning one or more elements of the marketing mix

(Berkowitz, 2017; Morton, Anable, & Nelson, 2017). Individuals in a particular market segment exhibit similar behaviours or responses to one or more elements of the marketing communication mix, which includes advertising, direct marketing, personal selling, and other strategies described in the "marketing communication mix" shown in Figure 5.1. Sales promotions, for example, are more effective when the image of a person in an advertisement possesses traits similar to the person viewing the advertisement, who is then more easily persuaded to patronise the product. It has been discovered that advertisements in which targeted communications are employed produce better outcomes than those directed at the general public (Meyers & Morgan, 2013). Advantages associated with market segmentation include:

- Marketing practitioners being able to cut through the complexities that exist in densely populated markets. A segmented market enables a more strategic deployment of the marketing mix – the 4 Ps of marketing (Product, Price, Place, and Promotion) – which in turn enhances the adoption of the product or service.
- Easy identification of homogenous consumers of specific products or services.
- Sales promotions being able to be designed to interest a specific group of customers.
- Economies of scale being enhanced by channelling resources to specific categories of customers.
- Enhanced customer retention: repeat sales of a particular product or service tailored to attract a defined target market.

Market segmentation is tantamount to adjusting supply to suit the will of demand (Berkowitz, 2017). Grouping customers into segments based on homogenous characteristics allows a marketer to identify the shared needs of each segment. Thus, supply can be tailored to meet the customers' needs. For example, Verhoef and van Doorn (2016) segmented consumers according to their actual *purchasing behaviour* of healthcare products, thus simultaneously employing important psychographic and socio-demographic variables common to the distinct segments.

Market segmentation based on the *psychographic method* classifies segments by lifestyle or personality traits or characteristics (Kotler & Armstrong, 2017). Some psychographic descriptors commonly used in healthcare marketing include *consideration of future consequences* (CFC) (Joireman, Needham, & Cummings, 2001), *quality and price consciousness* (van Doorn & Verhoef, 2015), and *health motivation* (Verhoef & Lemon, 2013). c2b solutions (n.d.) classified healthcare consumers into five segments based on psychographic characteristics, including *self-achievers, balance seekers, priority jugglers, direction takers*, and *wilful endurers. Self-achievers* are considered the most proactive when it comes to matters relating to their well-being and appearance, keeping abreast with research, and having regular medical check-ups and screenings. *Balance seekers* are also generally proactive regarding their health and wellness, and seek information from many sources apart from health practitioners in managing their health and well-being. *Priority jugglers* are seen as being too busy handling many responsibilities to take time to properly invest in their own well-being; they are generally reactive regarding health-related issues. *Direction takers* hold their physicians responsible for their healthcare issues because they trust that physicians are most credible when dealing with illness or general healthcare. *Wilful endurers* attribute greater importance to other things in their lives rather than focusing on their future wellness.

The *behavioural method* of market segmentation divides customers based on their knowledge, attitudes, uses of a product, or responses to a product (Kotler & Armstrong, 2017) and has been utilised to segment consumers of healthcare. Behavioural orientations include *egoistic, altruistic*, and *biospheric* (Verhoef & van Doorn, 2016). *Egoistic* consumers fixate on their own individual outcomes regardless of what happens to others, *altruistic* consumers seek the welfare of other people, and *biospheric* customers are mindful of the environmental consequences of their healthcare purchases. Socio-economic features such as gender, age, education, income, and household can also be employed in segmenting users of healthcare (Verbeke, 2005).

Moschis (1992) and Moschis and Friend (2008) applied a *gerontographic technique* to segment healthcare service consumers. Gerontographic segmentation identifies multiple stages and characteristics of the ageing process as well as consumer behaviours (Moschis, 1992; Moschis & Friend, 2008). Since 1987, this technique has proved its superiority as a segmentation model. According to Moschis, Curasi, and Bellenger (2004), the gerontographic technique recognises four segments for those aged 55 years and older: *healthy hermits, ailing outgoers, frail reclusives*, and *healthy indulgers*. *Healthy hermits* are aged persons whose health status is relatively good, but who to some extent are socially withdrawn. *Ailing outgoers* have a relatively poor health status yet choose to be socially active. *Frail reclusives* are aged inactive persons who are often times burdened with health challenges and choose to remain indoors often because their physical security means a lot to them. *Healthy indulgers* include relatively wealthy aged persons whose main focus is on enjoying life as much as possible; this group is said to be more highly related to the so-called baby boomers than any other segment. The gerontographic technique typically analyses the thought patterns and actions that people express in diverse manners (Moschis, 1992) as a basis for segmentation.

Kotler and Clarke (1987) proposed four major core benefit-seeking segments of healthcare services consumers: *quality buyers, value buyers, service buyers*, and *economy buyers*. The *quality buyers* look out for the best product and are less concerned about the cost. For instance, in the hospital industry, a quality buyer might opt for either the best medical centre or the best teaching hospital. *Value buyers* are concerned mostly about how well a rendered healthcare service corresponds with the price paid for that service; they look out for the best value for their money. *Service buyers* seek out the best personal care and nursing attention, assuming that all similar medical care provision is sufficient; a service buyer may prefer a community healthcare centre offering attractive amenities and infrastructure as well as empathetic nurses. *Economy buyers* look for ways to keep costs at a minimum and will look for the least expensive healthcare offerings.

Finn and Lamb (1986) found that health facilities could classify healthcare consumers into four groups: *take care of me, cure me, pamper me*, and *cognitive*. The characteristics of these segments were based on the consumers' expectations related to medical expertise, infrastructure, personalised service, and administrative issues from the hospital (Dey, 2013). The *take care of me* segment is mainly concerned about physical comfort: a comfortable room, suitable bathroom, and good food, for example. Those in the *cure me* segment are mostly concerned about the "me" dimension, valuing privacy and a quiet environment. Those in the *pamper me* group consider personal attention to be highly important as well as personal service delivery; they crave maximum care and attention but are less concerned with the hospital's physical appearance or infrastructure. The *cognitive* consumers are concerned about getting prompt and effective treatment (i.e., what exactly is happening to them) and may not wish to have an extended stay in the hospital. "Cognitives" are the direct opposite of the "take care of me" consumers.

Woodside, Nielsen, Walters, and Muller (1988) categorised healthcare consumers into four groups, the variable being their reasons for hospital preferences: the *old-fashioneds, value conscious, affluents*, and *professional want-it-alls*. The old-fashioneds prefer a hospital with their same religious affiliation or one that is close to their home. The value conscious consumers prefer hospitals that offer lower prices than other hospitals for the same services; getting the greatest value for their money is of utmost concern (Kotler & Clarke, 1987). Affluents seek out a hospital that is popular and known for showing the utmost care and concern for its patients. The professional want-it-all segment has the highest expectations. They want a hospital that is conveniently situated close to their home, has friendly health workers, is well known for emergency care, has the best doctors in the area, and has a good record for treating their condition or illness.

Generally, the segmentation process for healthcare services is influenced by a *concentration approach* or a *multi-segment approach* (Berkowitz, 2017). The *concentration approach* targets only one segment of the healthcare market, applying marketing strategies designed to suit that particular segment. One weakness of this approach is the tendency of the healthcare suppliers to fall into the *majority delusion,* that is, a belief that concentrating on the largest segment of the market will deliver the highest profit (Berkowitz, 2017). When intense competition ensues in such a segment, profitability declines for firms attempting to serve that market. Two variations of the concentration approach are *niche* and *micromarketing.* Niche marketing involves targeting a micro-market segment with a well-defined set of needs. Micromarketing is a one-on-one approach adopted by healthcare providers who customise their marketing strategy to reach individual customers through the internet and social media sales platforms.

Zuckerman and Johnson (2002) identified *disease segmentation,* an approach similar to concentration, which focuses on the services required by people with certain conditions or disorders. By identifying diseases that exceed traditional service lines and require more focused attention, healthcare providers can assess major health status indicators in a community's healthcare area, and gather the data needed to quantify the various diagnoses that are being treated at the community health centre (Zuckerman & Johnson, 2002). For instance, asthma is a major health issue, particularly in children, in some geographical areas. Arthritis, diabetes, heart disease, and vision and hearing loss are prominent health issues within an ageing population. Having identified the major health issues peculiar to a population, a list of required medical services can be compared to existing service lines to identify service gaps. Segmenting a population by diseases can allow hospitals to serve patients better, as well as improve service visibility to targeted healthcare service customers (Zuckerman & Johnson, 2002).

A *multi-segment approach* is one in which the healthcare firm targets several market segments with a diverse marketing mix. Often, companies embark on *product differentiation* by varying one or more of the elements of the marketing mix to suit the needs of different groups. In developing countries, a multi-segment marketing strategy is employed by some popular health maintenance organisations (HMOs) such as Hygeia, Total HealthTrust, and AXA Mansard.

5.2.2 Targeting in Healthcare Services

Targeting involves breaking an existing or potential market into segments and then concentrating efforts on one or a few key segments. A target market is a set of consumers to whom a company directs its marketing efforts. It is a group of consumers or organisations who are most likely to buy a company's products or services. As these buyers are likely to want or need a company's offerings, it is rational for the company to focus its marketing efforts on reaching them. Berkowitz (2017) identified six factors that should be taken into consideration when targeting a particular healthcare market segment: identifiability, accessibility, purchasing propensity, purchasing power, profitability, and desirability.

- *Identifiability:* A good healthcare market segment is easily recognised or profiled in order to ensure an efficient strategic implementation of the marketing mix.
- *Accessibility:* The healthcare market segment can reach the targeted segment geographically and through available distribution channels and promotion efforts.
- *Purchasing propensity:* The members of a targeted segment are predisposed to purchase the healthcare product or service. For example, targeting high-income consumers in a particular geographic sector does not automatically establish a desire to purchase a healthcare product or service and will only amount to a waste of resources.
- *Purchasing power:* Members of a segment have the financial resources to afford the healthcare product or service.
- *Profitability:* The market segment is able to contribute to the organisation's bottom line.
- *Desirability:* Members of the market segment create and maintain a positive brand image. A company may choose to exclude a particular market segment if the characteristics of that segment reflect badly on the company's brand image.

Once targeting decisions have been made, the next step is to determine how to position the health-care service or product to gain visibility, brand recognition, and awareness in the minds of the targeted consumers and other stakeholders.

5.2.3 POSITIONING IN HEALTHCARE SERVICES

The preceding sections described segmentation and targeting – fundamental marketing strategies that set the stage for positioning and the process of establishing an image or identity of a brand or product so that consumers perceive it in a certain way. According to *Business Dictionary* (n.d.), market positioning is "an effort to influence consumer perception of a brand or product relative to the perception of competing brands or products. Its objective is to occupy a clear, unique, and advantageous position in the consumer's mind."

Customers are the centre of focus in any business strategy as they constitute the target market the firm attempts to serve (Cavusgil, Deligonul, Kardes, & Cavusgil, 2018). It is important for a firm to have a good understanding of the customers' purchasing behaviours as well as the factors that influence their purchasing decisions: Why and how do customers buy certain products? Some factors are internal: personal characteristics related to cultural, social, demographic, and psychological influences that shape taste or preferences (Moreno, Santos, Deligonul, Kardes, & Cavusgil, 2017). External factors are market forces created by the economic, technological, and political environment.

In order to establish brand loyalty in the mind of customers, it is imperative to consider how decisions are made. The process for customers' purchasing decision making involves five stages: (1) identify a need or problem to be solved; (2) gather information using both internal and external means; (3) analyse available alternatives; (4) make purchases; and (5) evaluate the purchases, which is known as post-purchase evaluation (Kotler & Armstrong, 2017). Other external conditions derive from the "4 Ps" mentioned earlier: Product, Price, Place, and Promotion.

Companies can strategically position their products and gain competitive advantage through communication strategies that reach targeted consumers: Advertising, sales promotions, personal selling, direct marketing, public relations, and social media are generally included in such strategies (Luxton, Reid, & Mavondo, 2015). The concept of strategic marketing positioning remains contemporary in global marketing literature (Adebiyi & Bello, 2018; Hänninen & Karjaluoto, 2017; Valos, Turner, Scheepers, & Stockdale, 2018). The rationale for the increased attention to this study can be attributed to four important factors. First is the increased recognition by multinational enterprises of the role of strategic marketing positioning in improving brand perception, market performance, and market penetration, as well as creating a favourable reputation for the organisation (Vernuccio & Ceccotti, 2015).

Second, there is now a greater recognition of the role of strategic marketing positioning among directors of marketing who make it an integral part of their marketing plan. An example of this is seen in the incorporation of strategic marketing communication in the overall business strategy of most corporate entities (Adebiyi & Bello, 2018).

Third, the interrelated factors of loss of market share coupled with its attendant marketing challenges – such as unstable social, political, economic, and environmental variables; poor market acceptance; product or service failure (Leeflang, Wittink, Wedel, & Naert, 2013) and other forms of marketing challenges – make strategic marketing positioning highly relevant, especially among market researchers and practitioners. This is further compounded when analysing the pace of penetration in national and global markets.

Fourth, the inability of a wider percentage of business organisations in developing countries to explore new marketing strategies has not gone unnoticed by market researchers and field marketers who continue to study these challenges with the aim of identifying and implementing an integrated marketing communication plan (Turner, 2017).

In this twenty-first century, an era heavily dominated by information technology, marketing positioning has evolved to incorporate digital marketing through the use of mass communication

FIGURE 5.1   Marketing Communication Mix. (Source: Authors).

tools and social media. Strategic marketing positioning is often influenced by the marketing communication mix. As shown in Figure 5.1, the marketing communication mix includes advertising, personal selling, direct marketing, sales promotion, public relations, social media communications, digital marketing, and events and experiences (Luxton, Reid, & Mavondo, 2015).

For the effective positioning of healthcare services in sub-Saharan Africa, digital initiatives such as the mobile health solutions, or "mHealth", have been increasingly adopted as an effective and affordable means of providing healthcare services in constrained rural contexts (Beratarrechea, Moyano, Irazola, & Rubinstein, 2017). Mobile health services in use include audio-visual applications for real-time interaction between patients and health service providers and also more complex platforms like cloud-based solutions for self-diagnosis and treatment support (Crul, 2014). Historical application of mHealth solutions has proven the adoption of this initiative to be a reliable panacea towards ameliorating lack of access to healthcare in the sub-Saharan region (Opoku, Stephani, & Quentin, 2017).

Health promotion interventions through social marketing channels have also been adopted to promote positive health behavioural changes at individual and community levels in sub-Saharan Africa. The behavioural change strategies – health education, social marketing, motivational interviews, and health support – were implemented in the 1990s to promote the awareness of HIV and adherence to various risk reduction and treatment interventions. Work-place programs to facilitate diabetes education and improve physical activity, and school-based programs to reduce sexually transmitted diseases, were implemented using behavioural change strategies (Juma et al., 2018). However, the behavioural change strategies were reported to have little impact on sexual risk behaviours, which led to re-examining the framework to consider socio-economic and cultural factors such as gender identity, stigma, inequality, and poverty (Sepulveda, Carpenter, & Curran, 2007). Despite the introduction of these healthcare intervention programs and the increase in mobile phone adoption across sub-Saharan Africa, the cross-border regional collaborations required to scale and sustain the significant expansion of mHealth programs in this region are severely limited (Lee, Cho, & Kim, 2017).

Marketing positioning involves three basic steps: identify product or service *differentiation* characteristics on which a marketing position could be designed; choose the characteristic that offers the greatest *competitive advantage*; and construct an overall marketing *positioning* strategy (Kotler & Armstrong, 2017). The firm must then communicate all of these throughout the organisation in order to effectively deliver the product or service to the market.

Differentiation in the healthcare market: Differentiation in the healthcare sector is usually associated with competitive pricing (Hagg, Dahinten, & Currie, 2018): lower costs for comparable services. However, market differentiation through traditional marketing variables such as price can be challenging to achieve in the healthcare sector. Healthcare organisations should consider strategically directing their marketing strategies as well as products or services to business organisations that offer healthcare insurance as an employment benefit, an expense that can account for a significant proportion of their cost structure. Liaising with insurance companies or HMOs can also enhance their brand visibility. Market positioning for organisations may require a different strategy from that employed in positioning for individual customers (Berkowitz, 2017).

Competitive advantage: In designing marketing positioning strategies, healthcare marketers should prepare positioning maps that show consumer perceptions of their brands as compared to those of competing products. A positioning or perceptual map provides a graphic display or visual representation to identify and plot a company's brand perceptions in the marketplace and how they compare with competing brands. Only when marketing practitioners understand customers' expectations can they improve service delivery, out-perform their competitors, and build profitable relationships with target customers. A healthcare provider derives competitive advantage when marketing communication is rooted in strategic marketing positioning (Fischer, 2014) that focuses on the provision of superior customer value.

Positioning. Healthcare providers can position their segmentation and targeting strategy by effective use of communication technologies. The internet offers a source of relevant information, increasing visibility, and wider reach and allows providers to establish a competitive position by sharing product and service delivery information with the target audience (Rimal & Adkins, 2003). It is notable that some healthcare consumers will access information about ailments, symptoms, medical diagnoses, and treatment options online instead of or before seeking medical help, and they often exchange medical experiences on online platforms (Keeling, Khan, & Newholm, 2013). This unique positioning will afford healthcare providers the privilege of being regarded as authorities in particular fields of medicine and increase the clientele base.

5.3 INTERNAL MARKETING AND COMPETITOR ANALYSES

Healthcare has been recognised as the bedrock of human well-being (Kyratsis, Atun, Phillips, Tracey, & George, 2017). This is evident in the increasing number of healthcare providers in developing and emerging nations (Hagg et al., 2018). In order to attract customers, healthcare providers often embark on a variety of marketing strategies and sales promotions. One often neglected strategy with great marketing potential is internal marketing (Fortenberry & McGoldrick, 2016). Internal marketing is defined as a range of efforts directed toward all employees of an organisation, educating and enlightening them as to their critical roles in obtaining and retaining the patronage of customers and encouraging proactive efforts to ensure an enhanced customer experience (Fortenberry & McGoldrick, 2016).

Internal marketing is as important as, if not more important than, external marketing efforts and operates under the premise that customers remain with the service provider even after their initial patronage decision, warranting continuous efforts to ensure high satisfaction. The practice and philosophy of internal marketing emerged in the 1970s, ushered in by increasing knowledge and awareness of the impact of employees on the patrons of establishments. Internal marketing places a heavy emphasis on informing and inspiring all employees, regardless of job title, pay grade, or education level. Concerted efforts at internal marketing have the ability to improve healthcare delivery, with the clients being the major beneficiaries (O'Connor, Eze & Heavin, 2017).

As customers increasingly gain access to information online and become more knowledgeable about healthcare, there will be increased competition and therefore increased value in competitor analysis. Healthcare providers should identify competitors providing similar services or serving the same customer segment. An analysis of the elements of competitors' marketing mix (Product, Price, Place, and Promotion) will provide the evidence needed to strengthen a competitive advantage position by improving product offerings through effective targeting that creates value for customers. Value creation communicated to targeted markets allows service providers to gain and hold on to a competitive advantage. Value creation means emphasising the unique and distinct qualities of the service or product in all communication materials. Public image or perception is enhanced when brand promises are fulfilled. When firms capitalise on their core competencies and healthcare specialisations, they reinforce marketing efforts to convey persuasive messages to their customers. Growing competition in the healthcare sector requires strategic customer relationship management (Fischer, 2014).

5.4 RECOMMENDATIONS FOR AFRICA

Healthcare service delivery is critical to the well-being of all nations. This is a particularly urgent priority in the context of developing economies where there is a large disparity between low-income and high-income earners, as well as social, political, economic, and technological challenges compared with advanced countries. Proper segmentation, targeting, and positioning of healthcare delivery will improve market orientation of consumer needs by both public and private healthcare providers. STP will help providers become more responsive to the healthcare sector, developing marketing strategies tailored to meet the unique needs of their target audience. STP will support decisions related to pricing structures, payment schemes, insurance programs, contract terms with companies, and profitability (where applicable). It will also assist in streamlining charging structures and billing processes when the target market is clearly established.

When market segments are identified, targeting becomes easier for healthcare service providers, who are then able to focus their marketing efforts on the appropriate populations. For instance, if the market segment is based on income, i.e., affordability, it becomes clear who should be targeted in any communication materials. When the area of specialisation defines the targeted segment, providers can reach out to desired patients by developing appropriate databases.

Positioning will help establish a healthcare provider's brand and improve competitive advantage, depending on the goal of the organisation. Positioning is manifested in processes, facilities, and other physical evidence in the premises of healthcare providers. Language can be a positioning issue: messages crafted for particular segments, especially rural environments, would use a language or local dialect that customers can relate to and understand. In areas where regulators permit the advertisement of healthcare services, providers of specialised services can emphasise their unique offerings and value to a target audience. For example, x-ray, ultrasound, laboratory, eye surgery, dental services, and paediatrics are a few of the areas of specialisation that can be emphasised.

Quality is also a key differentiator. Hospitals across Africa can improve on the quality of services provided irrespective of the target patients. An emphasis on competent, effective, and safe healthcare attracts patients as well as medical teams, including physicians, who want to be associated with a top-quality healthcare provider. As customers become more knowledgeable and have increased access to information through the internet on healthcare and a plethora of available healthcare services, it is important for healthcare providers to design and implement the right strategy for their target audience. Healthcare providers must apply the right marketing mix in order to be effective, efficient, and competitive.

Applying the marketing mix and appropriately utilising the 4 Ps of Product, Price, Place, and Promotion to STP is a winning strategy for success in healthcare marketing. Products must be distinctively positioned to reach the pre-determined segment who will be the target audience. Pricing of the healthcare service must be in line with the target market's affordability rating and the available insurance scheme(s). Strategic choice of place is important to positioning as the location of a service provider plays a role in the perception of the service. Convenience of location is a key differentiator.

Visibility is essential to promotion as healthcare providers seek to position their brand as the first choice of a target market. Public relations campaigns can play a key role in the positioning strategy of a healthcare provider. Organising a free community presentation on family or personal healthcare or wellness programs can be an avenue to promote the ideals of the service provider. In rural communities, healthcare providers can generate goodwill and visibility and get the necessary buy-in for their programs by including popular opinion leaders and influencers in promotional events. Marketing strategies through social media enhances visibility by utilising demographic information to promote healthy living and its impact on the health and well-being of a targeted audience. For instance, healthcare service providers can deploy sensitisation campaigns on proper diet, weight control, preventable diseases, teenage pregnancy, prostate cancer awareness, breast cancer awareness, menopause management, enhanced lifestyle, and appropriate social behaviours, depending on their target market. Social marketing can also be used to change attitudes towards Africa's prevalent diseases, especially when there are preconceived ideas and locally held beliefs about certain ailments like malaria. This is especially important in countries and communities where traditional herbal treatment takes precedence over modern medicine or where there is apathy or even fear towards healthcare providers. The high rate of infant mortality in Africa can be attributed to some of these practices; therefore, healthcare related social marketing, when implemented, will save lives and improve the health of future generations (Bale, Stoll, & Lucas, 2003).

Although traditional media advertising is popular in Africa, digital media is increasingly playing a key role in the positioning of healthcare services. Websites are being designed to communicate value propositions and promote the healthcare products and services offered. The integration of data and technology can also aid advertising choices when segmentation defines target markets that offer a competitive advantage.

Finally, by applying STP strategies, Africa can fill niches that have been largely neglected, generate revenue, be more competitive, and reduce the high rate of medical tourism to Western countries which contributes to capital outflow. Africa must respond to changes in the global environment and improve in areas of customer service, data utilisation, healthcare funding, education of medical personnel, adequate and advanced infrastructure, best practices, innovation, and proficiency in diagnosis and treatment of diseases.

5.5 CONCLUSION

An effective Segmentation, Targeting, and Positioning strategy has several advantages. STP will lead to proper management of expectations and increased patient satisfaction and proper allocation of limited resources. It can also support the identification of needed healthcare niches and achieve competitive advantage for new service providers or even existing ones. Examples of such niches are affordable cancer treatment centres, clinics for underserved communities, prevention-oriented healthcare services, outpatient care, birthing centres, and nursing home care.

This study recommends STP strategies to build profitable customer relationship management by healthcare providers through an adequate understanding of customers' needs and proper identification of market segments. A healthcare company can gain a competitive advantage by strategically positioning itself to customers as a leading provider of product or service value. A clear understanding of segmentation, targeting, and positioning, together with the appropriate application of the marketing mix, will determine long-term and sustainable success. Overall, emphasis must be placed on the healthcare services provider's mission and vision, clearly identified healthcare market segments, proper targeting and positioning, appropriate product mix, and the deployment of effective marketing strategies.

REFERENCES

Adebiyi, R. A., & Bello, S. (2018). Perception and practice of integrated marketing communication (IMC) among selected marketing communication agencies in Nigeria. *Acta Universitatis Danubius. Communicatio, 12*(1).

Bale, J. R., Stoll, B. J., & Lucas, A. O. (Eds.). (2003). *Improving birth outcomes: Meeting the challenge in the developing world*. Washington, DC: National Academies Press.

Beratarrechea, A., Moyano, D., Irazola, V., & Rubinstein, A. (2017). mHealth interventions to counter noncommunicable diseases in developing countries: Still an uncertain promise. *Cardiology Clinics, 35*(1), 13–30.

Berkowitz, E. N. (2017). *Essentials of health care marketing* (4th ed.) Burlington, MA: Jones & Bartlett Learning.

Bruwer, J., & Li, E. (2017). Domain-specific market segmentation using a latent class mixture modelling approach and wine-related lifestyle (WRL) algorithm. *European Journal of Marketing, 51*(9/10), 1552–1576.

Business Dictionary. (n.d.). What is Market Positioning? Retrieved from www.businessdictionary.com/definition/market-positioning.html.

c2b solutions. (n.d.). Psychographic segmentation: Changing health care consumer behavior by engaging their motivations. Retrieved from www.c2bsolutions.com/psychographic-segmentation, 28 November 2018.

Cavusgil, S. T., Deligonul, S., Kardes, I., & Cavusgil, E. (2018). Middle-class consumers in emerging markets: Conceptualization, propositions, and implications for international marketers. *Journal of International Marketing, 26*(3), 94–108.

Crul, S. (2014). *The mHealth opportunity in Sub-Sahara Africa: The path towards practical application*. The Netherlands: Deloitte.

Dey, D. K. (2013). Market segmentation techniques in the health care industry: A review for applicability in India. *ZENITH International Journal of Multidisciplinary Research, 3*(7), 253–258.

Finn, D. W., & Lamb, C. W., Jr. (1986). Hospital benefit segmentation. *Journal of Health Care Marketing, 6*(4), 26–33.

Fischer, S. (2014). Hospital positioning and integrated hospital marketing communications: State-of-the-art review, conceptual framework, and research agenda. *Journal of Nonprofit & Public Sector Marketing, 26*(1), 1–34.

Fortenberry, J. L., Jr, & McGoldrick, P. J. (2016). Internal marketing: A pathway for health care facilities to improve the patient experience. *International Journal of Healthcare Management, 9*(1), 28–33.

Hagg, E., Dahinten, V. S., & Currie, L. M. (2018). The emerging use of social media for health-related purposes in low and middle-income countries: A scoping review. *International Journal of Medical Informatics, 115*, 92–105.

Hänninen, N., & Karjaluoto, H. (2017). The effect of marketing communication on business relationship loyalty. *Marketing Intelligence & Planning, 35*(4), 458–472.

Joireman, J. A., Needham, T. L., & Cummings, A. (2001). Attachment and empathy. *North American Journal of Psychology, 3*(3), 63–80.

Juma, K., Reid, M., Roy, M., Vorkoper, S., Temu, T. M., Levitt, N. S., Oladepo, O., Zakus, D., & Yonga, G. (2018). From HIV prevention to non-communicable disease health promotion efforts in sub-Saharan Africa: A narrative review. *Aids, 32*, S63–S73.

Keeling, D., Khan, A., & Newholm, T. (2013). Internet forums and negotiation of health care knowledge cultures. *Journal of Services Marketing, 27*(1), 59–75. doi:10.1108/08876041311296383.

Kotler, P., & Armstrong, G. (2017). *Principles of marketing* (17th global ed.). Harlow, UK: Pearson Education Limited.

Kotler, P., & Clarke, R. N. (1987). *Marketing for health care organizations*. Englewood Cliffs, NJ: Prentice-Hall.

Kyratsis, Y., Atun, R., Phillips, N., Tracey, P., & George, G. (2017). Health systems in transition: Professional identity work in the context of shifting institutional logics. *Academy of Management Journal, 60*(2), 610–641.

Lee, S., Cho, Y. M., & Kim, S. Y. (2017). Mapping mHealth (mobile health) and mobile penetrations in sub-Saharan Africa for strategic regional collaboration in mHealth scale-up: An application of exploratory spatial data analysis. *Globalization and Health, 13*(1), 63.

Leeflang, P. S., Wittink, D. R., Wedel, M., & Naert, P. A. (2013). *Building models for marketing decisions* (Vol. 9). Springer Science & Business Media. doi:10.1007/978-1-4615-4050-2.

Luxton, S., Reid, M., & Mavondo, F. (2015). Integrated marketing communication capability and brand performance. *Journal of Advertising, 44*(1), 37–46.

Meyers, J. Y., & Morgan, J. A. (2013). Targeted marketing and African American millennial consumers. *Journal of Research in Interactive Marketing, 7*(1), 6–17.

Moreno, A. M., Santos, L., Deligonul, S., Kardes, I., & Cavusgil, J. A. V. (2017). Proposal for a theoretical model for the analysis of the impact of cultural and personality factors on the demand for tourist services. *ESIC Market. Economic & Business Journal*, *48*(2).

Morton, C., Anable, J., & Nelson, J. D. (2017). Consumer structure in the emerging market for electric vehicles: Identifying market segments using cluster analysis. *International Journal of Sustainable Transportation*, *11*(6), 443–459.

Moschis, G., Curasi, C., & Bellenger, D. (2004). Patronage motives of mature consumers in the selection of food and grocery stores. *Journal of Consumer Marketing*, *21*(2), 123–133.

Moschis, G. P. (1992). Gerontographics: A scientific approach to analyzing and targeting the mature market. *Journal of Services Marketing*, *6*(3), 17–26.

Moschis, G. P., & Friend, S. B. (2008). Segmenting the preferences and usage patterns of the mature consumer health-care market. *International Journal of Pharmaceutical and Health care Marketing*, *2*(1), 7–21.

O'Connor, Y., Eze, E., & Heavin, C. (2017). Trends, findings, and opportunities: An archival review of health information systems research in Nigeria. *Information Systems (JMWAIS)*, *2017*(2), 6.

Opoku, D., Stephani, V., & Quentin, W. (2017). A realist review of mobile phone-based health interventions for non-communicable disease management in sub-Saharan Africa. *BMC Medicine*, *15*(1), 24.

Pleasant, J. T. (2014). *An Overview of Strategic Health Care Marketing*. Georgia: Biblion Publishing LLC, USA.

Postrel, S. (2018). Transaction surplus superiority in canonical market segments: Using the profit map to guide positioning and investment choices across price-rivalry regimes. *Strategic Management Journal*, *39*(6), 1573–1602.

Rimal, R. N., & Adkins, A. D. (2003). Using computers to narrowcast health messages: The role of audience segmentation, targeting, and tailoring in health promotion. In T. L. Thompson, A. M. Dorsey, K. I. Miller, & R. Parrott (Eds.), *Handbook of health communication* (pp. 497–513). Mahwah, NJ: Lawrence Erlbaum Associates Publishers.

Santoso, E. D., Rahmatullah, D., Angeline, L., Raznan, R., Mubaroq, H., & Lin, E. W. H. (2018). Developing tourism business program of Sahid Montana Hotel Malang. *International Journal of Applied Business and International Management*, *2*(3), 1–16.

Sepulveda, J., Carpenter, C., & Curran, J. (2007). *PEPFAR implementation: Progress and promise*. Washington, DC: Institute of Medicine of the National Academy of Sciences, The National Academies Press.

Turner, P. (2017). Implementing integrated marketing communications (IMC) through major event ambassadors. *European Journal of Marketing*, *51*(3), 605–626.

Valos, M. J., Turner, P., Scheepers, H., & Stockdale, R. (2018). Integrating online communities within business-to-business marketing communications: An exploratory study. *Journal of Marketing Communications*, *24*(5), 450–468.

van Doorn, J., & Verhoef, P. C. (2015). Drivers of and barriers to organic purchase behavior. *Journal of Retailing*, *91*(3), 436–450.

Verbeke, W. (2005). Consumer acceptance of functional foods: Socio-demographic, cognitive and attitudinal determinants. *Food Quality and Preference*, *16*(1), 45–57.

Verhoef, P. C., & Lemon, K. N. (2013). Successful customer value management: Key lessons and emerging trends. *European Management Journal*, *31*(1), 1–15.

Verhoef, P. C., & van Doorn, J. (2016). Segmenting consumers according to their purchase of products with organic, fair-trade, and health labels. *Journal of Marketing Behavior*, *2*(1), 19–37.

Vernuccio, M., & Ceccotti, F. (2015). Strategic and organisational challenges in the integrated marketing communication paradigm shift: A holistic vision. *European Management Journal*, *33*(6), 438–449.

Woodside, A. G., Nielsen, R. L., Walters, F., & Muller, G. D. (1988). Preference segmentation of health care services: The old-fashioneds, value conscious, affluents, and professional want-it-alls. *Marketing Health Services*, *8*(2), 14.

Zuckerman, A. M., & Johnson, T. K. (2002). Market segmentation. Sixth in a series examining revenue growth strategies in a difficult health care market. *Health Progress (Saint Louis, Mo.)*, *83*(2), 21.

6 Consumers and Consumer Behaviour

Gideon L. Puplampu, Ama Pokuaa Fenny,
Gwendolyn Mensah

6.1 INTRODUCTION

The consumer and consumer behaviour in healthcare delivery has been a focus of research in contemporary times as a deeper understanding of this concept and its interplay with other factors will enhance service delivery and subsequent consumer satisfaction. A growing literature indicates that consumer patients' behaviour is influenced by several factors in the decision-making process throughout the various phases of healthcare. One major influential factor in that decision-making process is the capacity of consumers to be equipped with information on products, which is essential in determining their behaviours. Adequate information serves as a psychological salve which decreases various kinds of distress across various areas. This review comprehensively organises and integrates the literature on the consumer and consumer behaviour in the management of healthcare, or the inconsistencies between how consumers at present perceive themselves and how they desire to see themselves. The scale of this divergence, however, is dependent on how realistic and believable the contingent market is. This paper gives an overview of eight major features describing the consumer and consumer behaviour concept, which include: (i) introduction to healthcare consumers; (ii) types of healthcare consumers; (iii) features of healthcare consumers; (iv) consumer behaviour and the decision-making process; (v) the pre-encounter phase; (vi) the encounter phase; (vii) post-encounter value outcome evaluation; and (viii) industry buyer behaviour.

A consumer is a person who acquires or buys goods and services for his/her personal use per the definition of the Oxford Dictionary (1997). On the other hand, a healthcare consumer can be said to be a potential or actual patient or client who may benefit from the services of a hospital, community-based health facility, or any other health facility (Mosby's Medical Dictionary, 2009). Consumerism is increasingly becoming popular in the healthcare sector. Easy access to the internet has made it simple and convenient for patients to research online about their symptoms and to find possible treatments before they visit health service providers. This means that patients can actively participate in decision making about their health. Also, health service providers can directly market their services to prospective clients. There are various types of healthcare consumers; hence, it is important for healthcare providers to know each of them, to strive to meet their expectations when they visit the provider's healthcare facilities. This is important because healthcare consumers are concerned about getting the best care when they visit healthcare facilities.

6.2 TYPES OF HEALTHCARE CONSUMERS

There are different types of healthcare consumers; therefore, it is essential to know what each type of consumer expects from their healthcare provider. *Deloitte Center for Health Solutions Review* (Coughlin, Wordham, & Jonash, 2015) on "Rising consumerism: Winning the heart and minds of healthcare consumers" divides healthcare consumers into two main groups, namely, the passive and active categories. Consumers in the passive category are not very particular about their health-care and, as a result, they hardly question their doctors about decisions made in relation to their health. On the other hand, the active category of consumers tend to ask questions about their health and desire to make informed decisions about their health and treatment options. Deloitte further segments them into six (6) types of healthcare consumers, shown in Figure 6.1. These are:

1. The 'casual and cautious' group, which forms 34 per cent of consumers and falls into the passive category. Consumers in this group do not see the need to be very concerned about or involved in their health. In addition, they are cost-conscious and hesitant to spend money, even on their health needs.
2. The 'content and compliant' group, which also falls under the passive group and is about 22 per cent of patients. These are healthcare consumers who are happy with their health-care. They rely very much on their doctors and they trust the doctor's decisions without question.
3. The 'online and on-board' group forms 17 per cent of patients, and can be seen as part of the active group. Consumers in this group are satisfied with their physicians' deci-sions and collaborate with them. They tend to regularly use online resources and health technologies. They assess providers of healthcare and normally compare their treatment options. This group constitutes the greatest percentage of the active category.
4. The 'sick and savvy' group. Consumers in this group have a lot of confidence in their phy-sicians and as a result, they team up with their physicians to make decisions concerning their health. They are financially prepared to handle any cost that comes with the delivery of healthcare. They constitute 14 per cent of all patients and fall under the active category.
5. The 'out and about' group, which forms 9 per cent of patients. They collaborate with their physicians, but still seek information from other health partners and compare them. When they get the needed information, they make independent decisions. They normally seek for customised care.
6. The 'shop and save' group, which is part of the active category and constitutes 4 per cent of all patients. They are the team that believes in quality. They ask questions and look for alternatives, compare, and frequently switch from one health provider to another.

The categories of health consumers as described above from research conducted by *Deloitte Center for Health Solutions Review* shows that healthcare consumers have different perceptions and preferences. Consumers, at the end of the day, want to be healthy through any means possible.

Although consumers of the 'casual and cautious' category do not seem to worry too much about their healthcare, they expect to be healthy no matter the circumstances. On the other hand, even though consumers in the 'content and compliant' category seem to be happy with their healthcare, they would love to see improvements about the care they receive. In contrast, 'online and on-board' consumers who are always online in search for better care are ready to leave if the healthcare rendered to them does not meet their expectations. As a result, for health institutions to keep such consumers, they must be willing to offer the best of care. Furthermore, although the 'sick and savvy' category rely heavily on their physicians and team up with them in order to get the best of care, healthcare providers should not lose sight of the fact that they will always negotiate for the best deals. They will demand the best healthcare available because they want to stay alive in the best of health. The 'out and about' category is made up of consumers who are willing to search for better healthcare alternatives.

Consumers believe in shared decision making. Therefore, as a healthcare provider, if you do not improve on the provision of healthcare, consumers of such services will choose a provider they believe offers better services over yours. Customised service is the way to go if providers want to retain customers in this category. The 'shop and save' consumers are always looking for a better service. They tend to ask questions and frequently change their healthcare providers. In order to maintain this category of consumers, healthcare providers must be competitive.

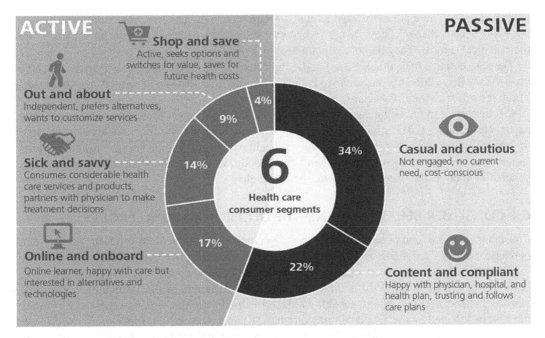

FIGURE 6.1 Categories of Health Consumers. (Source: Deloitte Center for Health Solutions, 2012 consumer survey, segmentation. Graphic: Deloitte University Press, DUPress.com).

Healthcare providers must consider their institutions as business entities the survival of which is based on the quality of care they provide. Regarding the various types of consumers and their different expectations, it is important for healthcare providers to find ways to meet them. Healthcare providers must offer attractive packages in their delivery of care to consumers to improve general healthcare. Providers should be able to attract and retain consumers, which can only be done by offering better healthcare services.

6.3 FEATURES OF HEALTHCARE CONSUMERS

According to the findings of a study conducted by Betts and Korenda (2018) in the US, healthcare users can be featured in four segments – trailblazers, prospectors, homesteaders, and bystanders. Per their findings, trailblazers make up 16 per cent of healthcare users and fall within the highest income earners even though they are the youngest. They are usually tech-savvy, self-directed, and involved in healthy lifestyles. Men make up a larger percentage of this group.

The second segment is made up of the prospectors. They constitute 30 per cent of healthcare users and fall within the second highest income earners bracket as well as being the second youngest group. They trust the recommendations and advice of their friends and family. Also, even though they are willing to use technology to share their health data, this behaviour may be influenced by others that they know who have used the service. There are equal numbers of males and females in this segment.

The third segment is made up of homesteaders who constitute 40 per cent of healthcare users. They are the second oldest group as well as the second lowest income earners. They are more conservative and less likely to use technology to share their healthcare information. They are not very concerned about following a healthy diet or lifestyle; under this segment there are more men than women.

Finally, the last segment is known as the bystanders. They constitute the smallest part of healthcare consumers. They make up 14 per cent and constitute the oldest group as well as the lowest income earners. There are more women in this group than men. They are very traditional and do not easily accept change. They are not tech-savvy and are least likely to use technology to share their medical records. They do not maintain healthy behaviours.

The segmentation of healthcare users above indicates that there is a link between age and income vis-à-vis the disposition of consumers to maintain healthy lifestyles and keep track and share their health records with their physicians.

It is important to know the various types of healthcare consumers present in order to properly engage them. James (2013) stipulates that the engagement of healthcare users could be the solution for enhancing outcomes for users and reducing healthcare costs. This is because healthcare consumers who are more informed about their health conditions and actively participate in decisions concerning their health usually experience better results.

6.4 CONSUMER BEHAVIOUR AND THE DECISION-MAKING PROCESS

Consumer behaviour comprises dynamics that affect their choices. For many products and services, purchase decisions are made based on a meticulous process that may comprise a comprehensive information search, comparison of brands, and evaluation. Behavioural responses to health usage have been analysed in many different settings globally. A variety of patient qualities determine whether patients are willing and capable to make treatment choices. Some of these choices may likewise be affected by social and cultural variables (Kaija & Okwi, 2011; Lindelow, 2005; Sahn & Stifel, 2003). Identifying the factors that influence people to make decisions to seek healthcare can be challenging because of the broad scope of probable factors which span many dimensions such as economic, social, political, and cultural.

Different approaches have been developed to facilitate the understanding of the complexities in healthcare decision making. For instance, Rosenstock's health belief model (Rosenstock, Strecher, & Becker, 1994) describes four central variables by which individuals make decisions to seek treatment and prevent diseases. The model's four main components are conceptualised as susceptibility, severity, effectiveness, and cost. There is also Young's choice-making model that is based on Young's ethnographic assessment of health services usage in Mexico (Young, 1981).

Recently, Andersen's behavioural model of health service utilisation has been adjudged the most inclusive and commonly used service model (Aday & Andersen, 1998; Buor, 2002; Duong, Binns, & Lee, 2004; Jahangir, Irazola, & Rubinstein, 2012; Kamgnia, 2006; Kroeger, 1983; Lopez-Cevallos & Chi, 2010; Nanjin, Bennett, & Luby, 2011; Wolinsky et al., 1989). In 1968, Andersen hypothesised that health service utilisation is a function of (1) predisposition to use services, (2) enabling factors, and (3) need for such services (Andersen, 1968). Predisposing factors include demographic and social factors that affect health service usage such as age, gender, and educational status. On the other hand, enabling factors refer to conditions that enable a person to use a health service. The need for such services denotes perceived and evaluated health status or illness. Andersen's model was later broadened to include the healthcare system (Andersen, 1995). The expanded model assumes that there are various types of health services available and suggests that the use of a specific health service is dependent on a population's characteristics (predisposing, enabling, and need factors) as well as the nature of the health system (policy, resources, and organisation). The use of health services will be based upon the type of services available and the purpose for the use of the healthcare service (Andersen, 1995; Andersen & Newman, 2005). In a nutshell, the revised model suggests that the choice of providers and the frequency of use of health services are determined by both population characteristics and the healthcare system. The outcome of the utilisation of health services, therefore, includes perceived health status, evaluated health status, and consumer satisfaction (see Figure 6.2).

Oladipo (2014) uses the three-stage consumer model in healthcare to analyse the use of healthcare services in both rural and urban communities in Nigeria. The findings of the study indicate that the predisposing, enabling, and need for healthcare services explain the attitudes of individuals

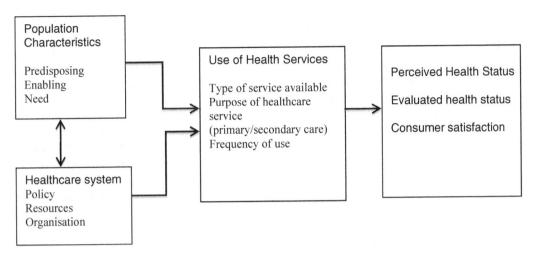

FIGURE 6.2 The Andersen–Newman Expanded Model of Health Service Utilisation. (Source: Andersen & Newman (2005)).

toward the use of healthcare facilities. Based on the findings of the study, Oladipo opines that a three-stage model (predisposing, enabling, and need) is enough to explain the pattern of healthcare usage by urban dwellers. Also, need was the most significant indicator of healthcare usage, while enabling elements were more significant than predisposing elements. He contends that remedies have not been discovered for the challenges of physical inaccessibility and unavailability of healthcare services, especially in rural communities, as well as for financial constraints, which limit the usage of healthcare services. This contrasts with developed countries where healthcare services are easily available and accessible to prospective users. Furthermore, Oladipo states that although health services were not found to significantly affect the use of healthcare, healthcare consumers would like the ability to choose from alternatives if they were available. In addition, while inhabitants of urban communities were more prone to be loyal to their healthcare service providers, rural inhabitants were not. Persons living in rural communities were more preoccupied with the lack of equipment and medical staff at the health facilities available in their communities. Hence, the elements which determine the use of healthcare providers vary for urban and rural inhabitants. Socio-economic and cultural factors of both groups contribute to the difference in healthcare usage.

Furthermore, empirical studies on healthcare utilisation over the years have identified a range of factors influencing the use of health services such as prevalence of the illness, cultural-demographic features (age, sex, race, education, preferences), economic factors (income, cost of services, travel cost, and the value of the consumer's time), ease of geographic access, and supply-side characteristics such as quality of health services (e.g., De Allegri, Sanon & Sauerborn, 2006; Hotchkiss, Mock, & Seiber, 2002; Leonard, Mliga, & Mariam, 2002; Lindelow, 2005; Mariko, 2003; Onah, Ikeako, & Iloabachie, 2009; Pariyo et al., 2009; Sepehri, Moshiri, Simpson, & Sarma, 2008). Wealth or socio-economic position has been found to be an essential component of consumers' healthcare seeking behaviour and usage (Ansah et al., 2009; Blanchet, Fink, & Osei-Akoto, 2012; Mensah, Oppong, Bobi-Barimah, Frempong, & Sabi, 2010). The relative importance of inequalities in this range of factors cannot be determined unless there is an understanding of the connections between resources and health-seeking behaviour.

The health economics approach, on the other hand, considers health as a consumption and investment item. For instance, the Grossman model describes the demand for healthcare as a derived demand (Grossman, 1972). The model assumes that individuals will invest in health until the marginal cost and marginal benefits of its consumption are equal. Over the years, the model has been reviewed and broadened (Grossman, 2000). The notion of utility maximisation and household production of health has its roots in the Grossman model, akin to the model which is utilised in earlier healthcare demand studies (Sahn & Stifel, 2003; Mariko., 2003; Abdulraheem, 2007; Nonvignon et al., 2010). The primary hypothesis is that the rational behaviour of patients who must make health-seeking decisions would be to make their decision based on maximising effectiveness.

The model has been tested empirically to explore issues relating to health and medical care (Case & Deaton, 2005; Cropper, 1981; Erbsland, Ried, & Ulrich, 1995; Muurinen & Le Grand, 1985; Nocera & Zweifel, 1998; Wagstaff, 1986). Yet, it has been criticised for its simplistic way of determining the demand for health (Case & Deaton, 2005; Ehrlich & Chuma, 1990). Others have pointed out that it does not take into consideration the uncertainty of future health status and the uncertainty of future investments in the provision of health services. Many scholars have conducted an extensive review and critique of the Grossman model including Grossman (2000), van Doorslaer (1987), and Zweifel and Breyer (1997). Despite these, the Grossman model underscores the fundamental reasons why individuals choose healthcare and how they respond to changes in healthcare prices.

From the discussion, it can be concluded that consumer behaviour and decision making are affected by several factors. However, in comparison to other goods and services, healthcare is complex and multidimensional; therefore, consumers experience several limitations when making decisions about their care. These include the need, and availability of the care needed; their demography; and the policies as well as the organisation of the health system itself. Usually, the most difficult constraints peculiar to healthcare may be consumers' imperfect medical knowledge and proof of the value of care delivered by providers. Thus, the healthcare provider's key role will be to ensure transparency regarding cost and performance outcomes. In addition, the information provided to healthcare users must be reliable and easily available to provide adequate materials for patients to be able to make informed decisions. The provision of an enabling environment to aid consumers to make the right healthcare decision could yield positive results not only for individuals but for the whole society as consumers would be able to use healthcare services that would be more appropriate for their conditions.

6.5 THE PHASES OF SERVICES CONSUMPTION

Consumer health services are produced and consumed with the full participation of healthcare consumers and the services are not seen as a one-time event, but an interaction that happens in stages or in a process. According to stage theory, the process of consumer services has three stages: pre-encounter, encounter, and post-encounter (Lovelock & Wirtz, 2011; Tsiotsou & Wirtz, 2012). This method is conducive to the healthcare services setting as it aids researchers to create a strong research focus and trend, and administrators to put together goals and to shape consumer behaviour.

6.5.1 PRE-ENCOUNTER PHASE

This phase of the process of service consumption is a complex one as it involves the decision-making process which is time-consuming. According to Tsiotsou and Wirtz (2015), at the pre-encounter phase, a consumer is triggered by a need to begin searching for information and assessing options before they take a buying decision. In healthcare services, there are several triggers to healthcare need: primary prevention of illness, secondary prevention, and tertiary prevention. Consumers can engage in preventive buying of services because of their perceived risk due to age or hazardous health habit such as smoking or exposure to other health risks. In other words, persons who engage in such risk behaviours will seek regular medical services to aid early detection of related health concerns. Preventive healthcare services occur less frequently in low- to middle-income countries due to a lack of the culture of preventive health habits. However, service research has shown the importance of preventive health service culture and its long-term benefits. The secondary and tertiary preventive health services information search process describes conscious consumer decision-making processes when the consumer has a need. Per the concept of planned purchasing behaviour, after consumers identify a need or challenge, they are driven to look for solutions to meet that need or take care of that issue (Figure 6.2).

6.5.2 THE ENCOUNTER PHASE

This stage is characterised by consumer involvement in co-creating experiences and value and co-producing a service while assessing the service experience. Consumer involvement in recent times has received attention from researchers in the branding and services literature (Brodie, Hollebeek, Jurič, & Ilič, 2011). Consumer involvement as described by Goldsmith and Goldsmith (2011) is perceived as the emotional tie which binds consumers to a service provider. Bowden (2009) affirms the view that involvement is a construct especially applicable to services since services commonly include some level of interactivity. Consumer involvement may comprise feelings of confidence, integrity, pride, and passion in a firm/brand (McEwen, 2004). Aside from these affective factors, consumer involvement with service brands is perceived as a behavioural indicator toward a brand or firm that goes further than purchasing and comprises positive word of mouth, endorsements, assisting other consumers, blogging, writing reviews, and even engaging in legal action (van Doorn et al., 2010). Current research has shown that consumer involvement includes cognitive (e.g., preoc-cupation), emotional (e.g., commitment), and behavioural (e.g., energy and communication) factors (Brodie et al., 2011; Patterson, Yu, & de Ruyter 2006). Brodie et al. (2011, p. 260) define customer involvement as "a psychological state that occurs by virtue of interactive, co-creative customer experiences with a focal agent/object in focal service relationships". Therefore, healthcare service encounters could offer the context in which consumers could produce, express, and improve their involvement with a service firm or health institution as a physical environment or servicescape.

Servicescapes – In the service context, consumers experience several elements including the physical service environment. These physical encounters are considered as servicescapes. The servicescape experience assumes a critical role in determining overall service experiences and improving (or undermining) consumer satisfaction, particularly in high-contact people-processing services. Servicescapes identify with the style and appearance of the physical environment in addi-tion to other experiential factors faced by customers at service delivery locations (Bitner, 1992).

As indicated by Lovelock and Wirtz (2011, p. 255), servicescapes serve four purposes: (1) they build consumer experiences and determine consumer behaviour; (2) they communicate the planned image of the firm and bolster its placing and distinction strategy; (3) they constitute part of the value proposition; and (4) they aid the service encounter and improve both service quality and efficiency.

6.5.3 POST-ENCOUNTER VALUE OUTCOME EVALUATION

The final phase of service consumption is the post-encounter stage, which includes consumers' behavioural and attitudinal reactions to the service experience. Consumer satisfaction, as well as perception in relation to service quality, has received much attention in the research agenda at this phase of the service consumption process owing to their connection with business perfor-mance (Brady & Robertson, 2001). Nevertheless, satisfied consumers who have great opinions of service quality do not automatically go back to the same service provider or purchase their services for a second time (cf., Keiningham & Vavra, 2001). Subsequently, there has in recent times been a change in the consumer research trend toward other significant post-purchase results. For instance, perceived service value, consumer fulfilment, consumer responses to service fail-ures (e.g., complaining and switching behaviour), and consumer reactions to service recovery. Customer satisfaction with services has been expounded by a number of conceptual models, for example, the expectancy–disconfirmation paradigm (Oliver, 1980) and the perceived performance model (Churchill & Surprenant, 1982), attribution models (Folkes, 1984), affective models (Mattila

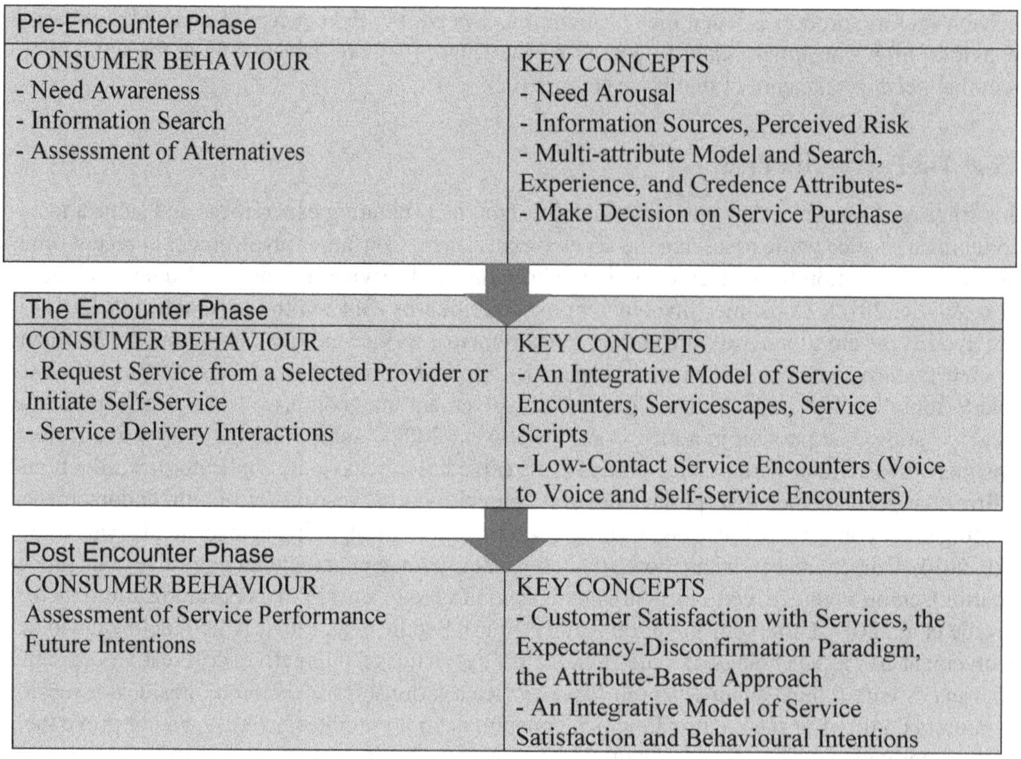

Pre-Encounter Phase	
CONSUMER BEHAVIOUR - Need Awareness - Information Search - Assessment of Alternatives	KEY CONCEPTS - Need Arousal - Information Sources, Perceived Risk - Multi-attribute Model and Search, Experience, and Credence Attributes- - Make Decision on Service Purchase

The Encounter Phase	
CONSUMER BEHAVIOUR - Request Service from a Selected Provider or Initiate Self-Service - Service Delivery Interactions	KEY CONCEPTS - An Integrative Model of Service Encounters, Servicescapes, Service Scripts - Low-Contact Service Encounters (Voice to Voice and Self-Service Encounters)

Post Encounter Phase	
CONSUMER BEHAVIOUR Assessment of Service Performance Future Intentions	KEY CONCEPTS - Customer Satisfaction with Services, the Expectancy-Disconfirmation Paradigm, the Attribute-Based Approach - An Integrative Model of Service Satisfaction and Behavioural Intentions

FIGURE 6.3   The Three-Stage Model of Service Consumption. (Source: Tsiotsou & Wirtz (2015)).

& Wirtz, 2000; Westbrook, 1987; Wirtz & Bateson, 1999), and equity models (Oliver & DeSarbo, 1988). Figure 6.3 summarises the three phases of service experience.

6.6 INDUSTRY BUYER BEHAVIOUR

The healthcare industry all over the world has been recording high growth rates in recent years. Therefore, it is expected that the healthcare industry will continue to make regular purchases to meet the demands of the times and reduce the shortage of healthcare services. In an international study of manufacturing, Deloitte (2003) identified the growing complexity of industries, markets, and supply systems, which makes the search and coordination of information more difficult. As industrial procurement behaviour is largely "a multi-phase, multi-person, multi-departmental, and multi-objective process" (Johnston & Lewin, 1996, p. 1), the growing complexity and dynamics of industrial purchasing places greater requirements on active information searches during the course of the purchasing process (Alejandro, Kowalkowski, Ritter, Marchetti, & Prado, 2011). In view of the current trend illustrated above, it is important to understand how the healthcare industry acts in response to the global changes in buying trends. The healthcare market in Ghana will be used as an example.

Important medical supplies per the regulations and laws of Ghana are bought through public procurement. The purchased medical supplies are stored by the public Central Medical Stores from where they are distributed to the storage facilities of regional medical stores and healthcare facilities in the public and private sectors. The procurement system in the healthcare sector in Ghana has been streamlined by the Ministry of Health in order to ensure that funds are used properly to meet the needs of healthcare consumers. However, the procurement system experiences its fair share of challenges. Bossert, Bowser, Amenyah, and Copeland (2004) note that there are high levels of bureaucracy in Ghana's procurement in the healthcare sector, which hinder procurement decisions.

Furthermore, there are procurement committees at various levels (national, regional, and district) that spearhead procurement of medical logistics and supplies under the Ministry of Health. The procurement committee usually invites tenders for the medical logistics or supplies needed. A supplier is then chosen based on the quality of the products, delivery time, payment terms, cost of products, and durability. However, the procurement process is bedevilled with challenges such as unavailability of funds, delay in reimbursement of National Health Insurance (NHI) claims, and a lack of qualified staff (Adu-Poku, Asamoah, & Abor, 2011). It is worth noting that after decades of haphazard post-colonialism healthcare reforms in Ghana, finally in 2003 by Act 650, the National Health Insurance Fund was established and a social health insurance system started functioning. This system replaced the previous cash and carry system, which was associated with numerous quality-related and access-related problems, as well as with low and inefficient use of healthcare resources However, it soon became clear that the social insurance mechanism was no panacea for these shortcomings because most of them persisted after the National Health Insurance Fund was established (Atanasova et al., 2011). Also, informal cash payments continue to exist even after the implementation of formal co-payments for services covered by the social insurance (Atanasova et al., 2011). Given this double payment burden, it is no surprise that many Ghanaian patients report difficulties in paying for healthcare (Atanasova et al., 2011). At the same time, the private sector has been enlarged in recent years, and as a result, total healthcare expenditure in the country has increased considerably.

According to the findings of a study conducted by Adu-Poku et al. (2011), procurement proceedings are centralised, as procurement is planned by the district health management with very minimal involvement of the managements of various healthcare facilities. Consequently, the medical logistics and goods purchased might not meet the needs of consumers. In addition, purchased medical supplies are stored in cupboards or with nurses, which may result in health workers stealing and mismanaging the supplies. As a result, the monitoring of stocks in store will be affected, which will in turn affect the procurement system. Moreover, findings of the study indicate that the quantities of medical supplies requested by various healthcare facilities are not approved. They are usually given a lesser quantity. Also, about the quality of medical supplies provided, the study found that they were of inferior quality. More than half of the respondents in the study affirmed the inferior quality of the items their facilities were supplied with. The low quality of health supplies provided would adversely affect the health of consumers.

Although, the Ghanaian Ministry of Health has a defined system for the procurement of medical goods and logistics, the centralised approach to planning creates challenges that hinder the success of the system. The findings of Adu-Poku et al. (2011) indicate that there are lapses in the Supplies, Stores, and Drug Management Division of the Ministry of Health, which has the core mandate to ensure that optimum drugs and equipment are available in all healthcare facilities in the nation. Additionally, the division is supposed to ensure that high quality drugs and equipment are purchased for use by the various health facilities. The critical question is what factors influence industrial buyer behaviour.

This review seeks to identify the most critical factors in health-related service buying behaviour that will ensure survival and success in the future. A thematic analysis was done of carefully selected peer-reviewed articles in order to compare results and draw conclusions. It was found that purchasing is influenced by several factors. Understanding these factors will help manage healthcare delivery to a level both the consumer and supplier of healthcare services are satisfied with. Below are the influences that have been identified in the literature that affect industry buyer behaviour including a theoretical framework that describes and predicts buyer behaviour. Influences such as demand, price, economy, and technology all contribute to industrial buying practices. More details of these factors are beyond the scope of this chapter.

Models – Models have also been identified in the literature that indicate why and how industry buying is exhibited. One such model is the Value Analysis Model (VAM). It is a financial analytical tool that can assist buyers to make direct, relative value evaluations and buying decisions in relation to competing goods for a facility. Currently, a lot of managers in charge of materials at medical institutions make expensive buying decisions determined by physicians or cheaper buying decisions determined only by supply price. Sadly, Feldstein and Brooks (2010) report that these approaches do not constantly translate into bottom-line profitability. Per the present economy, it is vital that buying and value evaluation committee members must be able to detect medical products with the best total value (Feldstein & Brooks, 2010). The goal of VAM is to assess and compare the product value in order to save cost.

Therefore, buyers will consider applying a value analysis purchasing approach in the healthcare industry. According to Feldstein and Brooks (2010), value analysis purchasing is choosing medical products that have the primary goal of attaining complete healthcare cost proficiency and optimum clinical outcomes. The authors argue that facilities are not commonly built to collect the cost and outcomes information needed to determine value-based purchasing, and manufacturers have been reluctant to make available such data or have not been able to do so. But this perspective is changing. Buyers now have a source of information to use for their purchasing. This will promote competition and offer value for money.

Source of information – According to Alejandro et al. (2011), there are three main factors influencing industrial buying. They include organisational, personal, and situational elements which influence information searching efforts.

Organisational factors – An industry will search for information about what it wants to purchase based on the level of formalisation of the industry. Formalisation of the institution is a major determinant of data search efforts. Organisations like hospitals have formal structures and are likely to have procurement procedures for purchasing their products. The buyer behaviour will then depend on what guidelines are stipulated in the procedural requirements.

Situational characteristics – Situational factors such as novelty and bargaining power increase the level of information search. An industry will buy a product not only for its functionality, but also for its originality as counterfeit products or replicas are not attractive to buyers. However, there are industries that always buy from the same customer. If a situation defines where to buy, from whom to buy, or how much to buy, it is a critical factor in the industrial buyer behaviour concept. Hence, though such a level of understanding could be difficult to attain because of the complexity of communication networks, knowledge about clients' information search is of key concern to industrial marketing professionals. There are two main sources of data: personal and commercial.

Personal and commercial information – The sources of personal and commercial information are important in industrial buyer behaviour to sale representatives during the buying process. Johnston and Lewin (1996) postulate that buyers will use commercial sources of data to a large degree in the initial phases of the decision-making process, while personal sources of data might come to be very significant as the decision process advances.

In addition, in low complexity buying situations, buyers will use more personal sources of information (Moorman, Deshpande, & Zaltman, 1993). In this situation, purchasers develop confidence in salespersons (sales ads or business presentations) largely at the stage of need recognition and later in the stage of looking for alternative sellers (Moriarty & Spekman, 1984). In the industrial purchasing scenario, both the reliability of the salesperson and the trustworthiness of the selling firm increase the possibility that purchasers anticipate doing continuous and future business with the retailing firm (Doney & Cannon, 1997).

It has also been observed that when high levels of economic risk are involved in the buying process, both personal and commercial information sources are important. Despite confidence in the source of information, purchasers similarly perceive the content as subjective and will not completely trust sales information. This makes industrial buying quite a complex phenomenon as best practices are critical in the decision-making process including good judgement. Additionally, there is a considerable reliance on personal information holders such as consultants outside of the organisation. More current studies likewise indicate the significance of creating trust, building structural mechanisms in new sources of information. In conclusion, industrial purchasers usually utilise various information sources in an intricate decision-making process that enables them to check the value of their information and, thus, reduce their uncertainties in the decision-making process.

6.7 CONCLUSION

This chapter outlined the major features of consumer and consumer behaviour in healthcare, including factors and models that influence and explain consumer behaviour in the decision-making process. The decision to purchase healthcare services or equipment is becoming a complex phenomenon as clients are becoming more knowledgeable and exposed to internet information and new technologies. Clients' characteristics, such as predisposing, enabling, and need factors, influence consumer behaviour and affect the decision-making process in healthcare systems. Consumers desire quality care which they do not often get as a result of unavailability of medical equipment or personnel experts. It is recommended that healthcare providers and policy makers should be more considerate in providing healthcare that meets primary healthcare needs or provides universal healthcare coverage for all the citizenry. The NHI must be improved by expanding coverage to increase funds for health funding and sustainability. Private participation in healthcare must be widened to reach more rural settings to help increase healthcare service choices and to decrease risk of poor healthcare decisions.

REFERENCES

Abdulraheem, I. S. (2007). Health needs assessment and determinants of health-seeking behaviour among elderly Nigerians: A house-hold survey. *Annals of Medicine, 6*(2), 58–63.

Aday, L. A., & Andersen, R. M. (1998). Models of health care utilisation and behaviour. In P. Armitage & T. Colton (Eds.), *Encyclopedia of Biostatistics* (pp. 1841–1845). New York: Wiley.

Adu-Poku, S., Asamoah, D., & Abor, P. A. (2011). Users' perspective of medical logistics supply chain system in Ghana: The case of Adansi South District Health Directorate. *Journal of Medical Marketing, 11*, 176–190.

Alejandro, T. B., Kowalkowski, C., Ritter, J. G. D. S. F., Marchetti, R. Z., & Prado, P. H. (2011). Information search in complex industrial buying: Empirical evidence from Brazil. *Industrial Marketing Management, 40*(1), 17–27.

Andersen, R. (1968). *A behavioral model of families' use of health services.* 25th Series. Chicago: Center for Health Administration Studies.

Andersen, R., & Newman, J. F. (2005). Societal and individual determinants of medical care utilization in the United States. *The Milbank Quarterly, 83*(4), 1–28.

Andersen, R. M. (1995). Revisiting the behavioral model and access to medical care: Does it matter? *Journal of Health and Social Behavior, 36*, 1–10.

Ansah, E. K., Narh-Bana, S., Asiamah, S., Dzordzordzi, V., Biantey, K., Dickson, K., … Whitty, C. J. M. (2009). Effect of removing direct payment for health care on utilisation and health outcomes in Ghanaian children: A randomised controlled trial. *PLoS Medicine, 6*(1). doi:10.1371/journal.pmed.1000007.

Atanasova, E., Pavlova, M., Velickovski, R., Nikoy, B., Moutafova, E., & Groot, W. (2011). What have 10 years of health insurance reforms brought about in Bulgaria? Re-appraising the Health Insurance Act of 1998. *Health Policy, 102*(2–3), 263–269.

Betts, D., & Korenda, L. (2018). Inside the patient journey: Three key touch points for consumer engagement strategies: Findings from the Deloitte 2018 Health Care Consumer Survey. Retrieved May 7, 2019, from www2.deloitte.com/us/en/insights/industry/health-care/patient-engagement-health-care-consumer-survey.html.

Bitner, M. J. (1992). Servicescapes: The impact of physical surroundings on customers and employees. *Journal of Marketing, 56*(2), 57–71.

Blanchet, N. J., Fink, G., & Osei-Akoto, I. (2012). The effect of Ghana's National Health Insurance scheme on health care utilisation. *Ghana Medical Journal, 46*(2), 76–84.

Bossert, T., Bowser, D., Amenyah, J. & Copeland, R. (2004). *Decentralization and the health logistics system in Ghana.* Boston, MA: Harvard School of Public Health, JSI-DELIVER, USAID.

Bowden, J. L. H. (2009). The process of customer engagement: A conceptual framework. *Journal of Marketing Theory and Practice, 17*(1), 63–74.

Brady, M. K., & Robertson, C. J. (2001). Searching for a consensus on the antecedent role of service quality and satisfaction: An exploratory cross-national study. *Journal of Business Research, 51*(1), 53–60.

Brodie, R. J., Hollebeek, L. D., Jurić, B., & Ilić, A. (2011). Customer engagement: Conceptual domain, fundamental propositions, and implications for research. *Journal of Service Research, 14*(3), 252–271.

Buor, D. (2002). Distance as a predominant factor in the utilisation of health services in the Kumasi metropolis, Ghana. *GeoJournal, 56,* 145–157.

Case, A., & Deaton, A. Broken down by work and sex: How our health declines. In D. A. Wise (Ed.), *Analyses in the economics of aging* (pp. 185–212). Chicago: The University of Chicago Press.

Churchill, G. A., Jr, & Surprenant, C. (1982). An investigation into the determinants of customer satisfaction. *Journal of Marketing Research, 19*(4), 491–504.

Coughlin, S., Wordham, J., & Jonash, B. (2015). Rising consumerism: Winning the hearts and minds of health care consumers. *Deloitte Review, 16.*

Cropper, M. L. (1981). Measuring the benefits from reduced morbidity. *American Economic Review, 71,* 235–240.

De Allegri, M., Sanon, M., & Sauerborn, R. (2006). To enrol or not to enrol? A qualitative investigation of demand for health insurance in rural West Africa. *Social Science & Medicine, 62,* 1520–1527.

Deloitte (2003). Chips with everything. Deloitte, London. Retrieved from www.deloitte.com/dtt/cda/doc/content/Chips%20with%20everything.pdf.

Doney, P. M., & Cannon, J. P. (1997). An examination of the nature of trust in buyer-seller relationships. *Journal of Marketing, 61*(2), 35–51.

Duong, D. V., Binns, C. W., & Lee, A. H. (2004). Utilization of delivery services at the primary health care level in rural Vietnam. *Social Science & Medicine, 59,* 2585–2595.

Ehrlich, I., & Chuma, H. (1990). A model of the demand for longevity and the value of life extension. *The Journal of Political Economy, 98*(4), 761–782.

Erbsland, M., Ried, W., & Ulrich, V. (1995). Health, health care, and the environment: Econometric evidence from German micro data. *Health Economics, 4,* 169–182.

Feldstein, J., & Brooks, E. (2010). Optimizing medical device buying. *Mater Mange Health Care, 19,* 20–22.

Folkes, V. S. (1984). Consumer reactions to product failure: An attributional approach. *Journal of Consumer Research, 10*(4), 398–409.

Goldsmith, E. B., & Goldsmith, R. E. (2011). Social influence and sustainability in households. *International Journal of Consumer Studies, 35*(2), 117–121.

Grossman, M. (1972). On the concept of health capital and the demand for health. *Journal of Political Economy, 80*(2), 223–255.

Grossman, M. (2000). The human capital model. In A. J. Culyer & J. P. Newhouse (Eds.), *Handbook of health economics: Volume 1A* (pp. 347–408). Amsterdam: Elsevier.

Hotchkiss, D. R., Mock, N. B., & Seiber, E. E. (2002). The effect of the health care supply environment on children's nutritional status in rural Nepal. *Journal of Biosocial Science, 34*(2), 173–192.

Jahangir, E., Irazola, V., & Rubinstein, A. (2012). Need, enabling, predisposing, and behavioural determinants of access to preventive care in Argentina: Analysis of the national survey of risk factors. *PLoS ONE, 7*(9).

James, J. (2013). Health policy brief: Patient engagement. *Health Affairs.* Retrieved from www.healthaffairs.org/do/10.1377/hpb20130214.898775/full/healthpolicybrief_86.pdf.

Johnston, W. J., & Lewin, J. E. (1996). Organizational buying behavior: Toward an integrative framework. *Journal of Business Research, 35*(1), 1–15.

Kaija, D., & Okwi, P. (2011). *Quality and demand for health care in rural Uganda: Evidence from 2002/03 Household Survey.* AERC Research Paper 214.

Kamgnia, B. (2006). Use of health services in Cameroon. *International Journal of Applied Econometrics and Quantitative Studies, 3*(2), 55–64.

Keiningham, T. L., & Vavra, T. G. (2001). *The customer delight principle: Exceeding customers' expectations for bottom-line success.* New York: McGraw-Hill.

Kroeger, A. (1983). Anthropological and socio-medical healthcare research in developing countries. *Social Science and Medicine, 17*(3), 147–161.

Leonard, K. L., Mliga, G. R., & Mariam, D. H. (2002). By passing health centres in Tanzania: Revealed preferences for quality. *Journal of African Economies, 11*(4): 441–471.

Lindelow, M. (2005). The utilisation of curative healthcare in Mozambique: Does income matter? *Journal of African Economies, 14*(3), 435–482.

Lopez-Cevallos, D. F., & Chi C. (2010). Assessing the context of health care utilisation in Ecuador: A spatial and multilevel analysis. *BMC Health Services Research, 10*, 64.

Lovelock, C., & Wirtz, J. (2011). *Services marketing* (7th ed.). Upper Saddle River, NJ: Prentice Hall.

Mariko, M. (2003). Quality of care and the demand for health services in Bamako, Mali: The specific role of structural, process, and outcome components. *Social Science and Medicine, 56*, 1183–1196.

Mattila, A., & Wirtz, J. (2000). The role of preconsumption affect in postpurchase evaluation of services. *Psychology & Marketing, 17*(7), 587–605.

McEwen, W. (2004, November 11). Why satisfaction isn't satisfying. *Gallup Management Journal Online* (November 11). Retrieved from http://gmj.gallup.com/content/14023/Why-Satisfaction-Isn't-Satifying.aspx [Google Scholar].

Mensah, J., Oppong, J. R., Bobi-Barimah, K., Frempong, G., & Sabi, W. (2010). *An evaluation of the Ghana National Health Insurance scheme in the context of the health MDG's.* (The Human Science Resource Council: Commissioned by the Global Development Network (GDN)). Retrieved May 20, 2018, from www.hsrc.ac.za/Research_Publication-21974.phtml.

Moorman, C., Deshpande, R., & Zaltman, G. (1993). Factors affecting trust in market research relationships. *Journal of Marketing, 57*(1), 81–101.

Moriarty, R. T., Jr, & Spekman, R. E. (1984). An empirical investigation of the information sources used during the industrial buying process. *Journal of Marketing Research, 21*(2), 137–147.

Mosby's Medical Dictionary (2009). 9th ed. Elsevier.

Muurinen, J., & Le Grand, J. (1985). The economic analysis of inequalities in health. *Social Science and Medicine, 20*(10), 1029–1035.

Nanjin, N., Bennett, C. M., & Luby, S. (2011). Inequalities in care-seeking for febrile illness of under-five children in urban Dhaka, Bangladesh. *Journal of Health Population and Nutrition, 29*(5), 523–531.

Nocera, S., & Zweifel, P. (1998). The demand for health: An empirical test of the Grossman model using panel data. In Zweifel P. (Ed.) *Health, the medical profession, and regulation* (pp. 35-49). Boston, MA: Springer.

Nonvignon, J., Aikins, M. K., Chinbuah, M. A., Abbey, M., Gyapong, M., Garshon, B. ... Gyapong, J. O. (2010). Treatment choices for fevers in children under-five years in a rural Ghanaian district. *Malaria Journal, 9*, 188. doi:10.1186/1475-2875-9-188.

Oladipo, J. A. (2014). Utilization of health care services in rural and urban areas: A determinant factor in planning and managing health care delivery systems. *African Health Sciences, 14*(2), 322–333.

Oliver, R. L. (1980). A cognitive model of antecedents and consequences of satisfaction decisions. *Journal of Marketing Research, 17*(4), 460–469.

Oliver, R. L., & DeSarbo, W. S. (1988). Response determinants in satisfaction judgments. *Journal of Consumer Research, 14*(4), 495–507.

Onah, H., Ikeako, L., & Iloabachie, G. (2009). Factors associated with the use of maternity services in Enugu, South-Eastern Nigeria. *Social Science and Medicine, 63*(7), 1870–1878.

Oxford Dictionary (1997). 2nd ed., Additional Series, Vol. 3. Oxford University Press.

Pariyo, G. W., Ekirapa-Kiracho, E., Okui, O., Rahman, M. H., Peterson, S., Bishai, D. M., & Peters, D. H. (2009). Changes in utilization of health services among poor and rural residents in Uganda: Are reforms benefitting the poor? *International Journal for Equity in Health, 8*(39).

Patterson, P., Yu, T., & De Ruyter, K. (2006, December). Understanding customer engagement in services. In *Advancing theory, maintaining relevance, proceedings of ANZMAC 2006 conference, Brisbane* (pp. 4–6).

Rosenstock, I. M., Strecher, V. J., & Becker, M. H. (1994). The health belief model and HIV risk behavior change. In R. J. DiClemente & J. L. Peterson (Eds.), *Preventing AIDS: Theories and methods of behavioral interventions* (pp. 5–24). New York: Plenum Press.

Sahn, D., & Stifel, D. (2003). Exploring alternative measures of welfare in the absence of expenditure data. *Review of Income and Wealth, 49*(4), 463–489.

Sepehri, A., Moshiri, S., Simpson, W., & Sarma, S. (2008). Taking account of context: How important are household characteristics in explaining adult health-seeking behavior? The case of Vietnam. *Health Policy Plan, 23*(6), 397–407.

Tsiotsou, R. H., & Wirtz, J. (2012). *Consumer behavior in a service context: Handbook of Developments in consumer behavior*. UK: Edward Elgar, 147–186.

Tsiotsou, R. H., & Wirtz, J. (2015). The three-stage model of service consumption. In Bryson, J. R., & Daniels, P. W. (Eds.), *The handbook of service business: Management, marketing, innovation and internationalisation* (pp. 105–128). Cheltenham: Edward Elgar.

van Doorn, J., Lemon, K. N., Mittal, V., Nass, S., Pick, D., Pirner, P., & Verhoef, P. C. (2010). Customer engagement behavior: Theoretical foundations and research directions. *Journal of Service Research, 13*(3), 253–266.

van Doorslaer, E. K. A. (1987). Health, knowledge and the demand for medical care: An econometric analysis (Doctoral dissertation, Maastricht University).

Wagstaff, A. (1986). The demand for health: Some new empirical evidence. *Journal of Health Economics, 5,* 195–233.

Westbrook, R. A. (1987). Product/consumption-based affective responses and postpurchase processes. *Journal of Marketing Research, 24*(3), 258–270.

Wirtz, J., & Bateson, J. E. (1999). Consumer satisfaction with services: Integrating the environment perspective in services marketing into the traditional disconfirmation paradigm. *Journal of Business Research, 44*(1), 55–66.

Wolinsky, F. D., Aguirre, B. E., Fann, L., Keith, V. M., Arnold, C. L., & Niederhauer, J. C. (1989). Ethnic difference in the demand for physician and hospital utilization among older adults in major American cities: Conspicuous evidence of considerable inequalities. *The Milbank Quarterly, 67*(3–4), 412–449.

Young, J. C. (1981). *Medical choice in a Mexican village.* New Brunswick: Rutgers University Press.

Zweifel, P., & Breyer, F. (1997). *Health economics.* New York: Oxford University Press.

7 Managing the Healthcare Product

John Muriithi, Abel Kinoti Meru,
Emmanuel Okunga Wandera, Mary Wanjiru Kinoti

7.1 INTRODUCTION

The marketing concept has long been accepted in the pharmaceutical and medical technology devices industries which is hardly surprising as the initial emphasis of marketing theory and practice was focused on physical goods and the four P's of marketing – product, price, place and promotion (Nadowska, 2013). The acceptance of marketing and business management practices in the provision of professional healthcare services was resisted for a long time by medical practitioners who still remain skeptical of the ability of non-physicians to contribute to healthcare (Porter & Teisburg, 2006). Coviello, Brodie, Danaher and Johnston (2002) observed that the initial skepticism towards marketing by professional services was linked to the transactional approach to marketing that was the norm for most of the twentieth century.

Although the concept of relationship marketing has been a long-standing part of business practice, it only gained prominence in marketing theory and practice in the last three decades, driven largely by the growth in services as western economies shifted from being manufacturing based to service based. The growth of relationship marketing has contributed to the increased acceptance and use of marketing by professional services (McColl-Kennedy, Sweeney, Soutar & Amonani, 2008). The significant role played by the private sector in healthcare has also contributed to the growth of healthcare marketing and its effectiveness (Keskinocak & Savva, 2019).

Even though the United States healthcare system is largely market based, there has been a recognition that the system is not working properly. In a normal market, competition usually drives improvements in quality and cost. As the best competitors prosper and grow, the market should expand as prices fall and value improves. This is indeed the norm in industries such as banking and mobile communication, but this does not seem to be the case in healthcare (Porter & Teisburg, 2006).

The private sector plays a key role in the delivery of health services in many developing countries. For instance, in sub-Saharan Africa private healthcare providers account for almost 50 percent of total expenditure, with some countries such as Ghana and Uganda having private sector uptake of over 60 percent (World Bank, 2008). Based on trends in other developing countries in Asia and Latin America, private investment in the African healthcare sector is expected to grow significantly as incomes rise. In Africa, the African Union Model Law, which regulates medical products, has helped standardise the development of health technologies within the region, resulting in accessible and affordable medicine (World Health Organization [WHO], 2017). This chapter delves into the healthcare product and customers and the latest healthcare innovations and design, among other things.

7.2 THE HEALTHCARE PRODUCT

The healthcare product market is divided into two broad categories. The first involves the marketing of pharmaceutical products as well as medical technology devices to doctors and hospitals, while the second involves the marketing of healthcare services by hospitals and healthcare providers to their stakeholders, including patients, medical insurance providers and visiting consultant doctors, among others. The healthcare product is an unsought good or service (Kotler & Keller, 2009). It is described as the service rendered in the health sector (Ahmadi, Pishvaee & Heydari, 2019). One visits a hospital for treatment usually out of necessity and not because one enjoys it. Often it is an emotionally draining experience for both the patient and their family. In this respect, the marketing of healthcare services provides unique challenges as consumers do not look forward to needing medical attention. The role of the healthcare marketer should therefore be not to create demand for treatment procedures, but to encourage patients to choose their clinic or medical facility over other alternatives available.

The dissonance between customer expectations and actual experience is a major problem for hospitals and health insurance providers (Coddington, Fischer & Moore, 2001). Hospitals can advertise a caring environment, yet if no one answers when the patient pushes the nurse call button, that patient will assess the hospital as being negligent and uncaring. Nearly everyone has experienced the long waiting times at doctors' offices and clinics, particularly in Africa, where the doctor–patient ratio is extremely low (Gerein, Green & Pearson, 2006). Supporting this fact, the World Health Organization (WHO, 2010) reported that the ratio of doctors/nurses to patient in Africa was 1:1,000 and Nwaopara (2015) affirm that the ratio has increased to one doctor/nurse per 8,000 patients. The satisfaction level with healthcare insurance acquisition is also very poor in most African markets because the insurance cover is considered poor quality and overpriced, resulting in low penetration levels of insurance on the continent (Mburu, 2017). All these realities have affected the Africa healthcare product and formed a wrong perception of the healthcare service among the masses. The healthcare product market will find it challenging to actualise the goal of preserving, promoting and providing a sound healthcare service delivery if the marketing of health products and services is not improved upon. Importantly, the service rendered in healthcare centers creates a product image in the minds of the masses/customers within a particular society. Through conscious marketing of the healthcare product, which must involve solving the above-mentioned problems and re-orienting the masses about the improved state of healthcare marketing in Africa, the status quo might remain the same. The healthcare product, at present, is not considered attractive and marketable.

The traditional view of healthcare has, for a long time, placed emphasis on disease management rather than overall health. The patient is seen as a passive consumer (McDermott & Pedersen, 2016). However, consumers of healthcare are increasingly informed and assertive, and this has started the shift to a customer relationship building and satisfaction approach to healthcare delivery. In the US, hospitals that have built a customer-oriented marketing culture are outperforming those that see themselves selling visits, tests, and services (Kotler, Shalowitz & Stevens, 2008). Healthcare services, like all services, present the marketer with the challenges of designing offerings that address the challenges of intangibility, inseparability, variability and perishability (Parasuraman, Zeithaml & Berry, 1988).

7.2.1 INTANGIBILITY

Bratucu et al. (2014) note that due to lack of physical evidence, health service attributes cannot be perceived through human senses. To overcome the challenge of intangibility, patients will look for symbols or physical evidence of quality (Bebko, 2000). For instance, nurses' uniforms, the doctor's stethoscopes and well-laid out reception areas have been used for several years as symbols of reassurance, but healthcare services have begun taking a more creative approach to achieve differentiation in a more competitive market place. A neonatal hospital based in Pittsburgh in the US, The Transitional Infant Care Hospital, is so confident of its investment in look, feel and welcoming staff that it invites parents to tour the hospital first before making a decision to transfer their babies there for special care (Gittell & Michelle, 1997).

7.2.2 INSEPARABILITY

Since services are produced and consumed simultaneously, services are inherently inseparable. Traditionally, the interaction between the service provider and consumer is one on one and in a customer's mind, a service is essentially indistinguishable from the person providing it. Bratucu et al. (2014) observed that because of inseparability, patients can get intimate with the service provider. The Hospital Consumer Assessment of Healthcare Providers and Systems (HCAHPS) is a patient satisfaction survey required by CMS (the Centers for Medicare and Medicaid Services) for all hospitals in the United States for adult inpatients (HCAHPS, 2017). In the HCAHPS survey, a consistent finding is that patient satisfaction with a hospital is most powerfully influenced by how well those patients feel their doctors have communicated with them (HCAHPS, 2017). Healthcare marketers should be mindful that patients are often in an emotionally highly strung mindset due to the discomfort of their illness. Continuous training of care givers on the need to engage in a pleasant, professional and respectful manner should be part of the strategy for success in healthcare delivery.

7.2.3 VARIABILITY

Service marketers try to address the challenge of quality variability by standardising their products and processes. Service variability in healthcare can lead to serious medical errors such as filling in the wrong prescription or injecting the wrong medication. In May 2018 there was a nationwide uproar in Kenya when surgeons at the main National Hospital performed a brain operation on the wrong patient (Merab, 2018). Hospitals often try to overcome this challenge through continuous training and developing rigorous quality policies and procedures, as well as measuring and monitoring customer satisfaction (Kotler, Shalowitz & Stevens, 2008). Unfortunately, some service delivery errors are conveniently not reported. To mitigate against this some hospitals have taken the bold step of adopting a less punitive approach to mistakes such as drug errors. The emphasis is on encouraging reporting of service failures so that the organisation can learn from these to improve on quality delivery (Nesreen & Amira, 2016).

7.2.4 PERISHABILITY

Perlman and Levner (2014) observed that medical products are highly perishable and deteriorate fast, necessitating strict adherence to proper storage conditions. Similarly, stock-outs are a threat to human life and the reputation of the health facility, resulting in stock piles, for which at times the cost outweighs the benefit (Sakhaii, 2017). On the patient side, the perishability challenge, in healthcare as in other services, has to do with balancing demand and supply. Since a service cannot be stored, hospitals and clinicians sometimes have challenges coping with high demand peaks. In service sectors where the service providers do not need to be highly skilled, provider organisations can easily hire more workers to manage during peak periods. Doctors, nurses and other medical professionals are almost always in short supply, so extra hands may not always be available at short notice. Some of the other tactics often employed in other sectors, such as setting strict targets on the number of clients served per shift, cannot be easily transferred to healthcare for ethical reasons (Sasser, 1976).

7.3 THE HEALTHCARE CUSTOMER

The main customers that marketers of health services must address, that seemingly fall under healthcare value systems, include patients, consultant doctors and medical insurance providers. According to Kotler, Shalowitz and Stevens (2008), a care receiver or patient extends to close associates, a situation typical in Africa that includes immediate family members, extended family members, guardians, friends and neighbors, as well as institutions catering for disadvantaged persons, such as a home for the elderly. Patients use services provided by clinics and hospitals; doctors are customers because they refer their patients to hospitals and medical investigation facilities; and medical insurance providers are customers because they can influence their clients towards specific hospitals and doctors on their approved list of providers (Celluchi, Wiggins & Farnsworth, 2014).

7.3.1 THE PATIENT AS A CUSTOMER

Caregivers in healthcare still prefer to use the word patient over customer. This is due to their reluctance to view healthcare as a business. The problem with this view is that a patient is considered passive while in the business world a customer is considered active (McDermott & Pedersen, 2016). The change from patient to customer implies that those receiving care want to be more actively involved in their treatment options than was the case in the past (Celluchi, Wiggins & Farnsworth, 2014; Keskinocak & Savva, 2019).

In the past patients had limited knowledge of the treatment options available to them so they depended on referrals from trusted sources such as a family doctor or friends in deciding where to seek medical attention. However, recent trends show that younger consumers of medical services in their thirties are actively searching for health information to prepare for a visit to a doctor or hospital (AlGhamdi & Moussa, 2012). A recent trend in several developing countries with robust private healthcare sectors has been the decision to site hospital clinics in locations convenient to the target population. The Aga Khan University (AKU) Hospital (Pakistan), of which the main hospital is located in Karachi, recently adopted this business model and now has 37 medical centers located in the main cities of Pakistan and a further 170 laboratory testing locations through the country (AKU, 2018). AKU Hospital in Nairobi has adopted a similar expansion strategy, and this has influenced other private hospital brands in Kenya to follow suit.

While patients might consider this development positive due to the attendant convenience, there is a risk that the emergence of large private hospital chains may not lead to lower costs in Africa. The US has had large hospital groups for a long time, yet competition does not seem to have benefited the customer. Africa has a much weaker regulatory environment, and countries like South Africa now have large hospital groups like Netcare, Mediclinic and Life Healthcare. Of the 92,000 hospital beds in South Africa, 37 percent are in private hospitals, yet 53 percent of annual healthcare spending is in the private sector that caters for just 14 percent of the population (Indiana Health Industry Forum, 2017).

7.3.2 THE DOCTOR AS A CUSTOMER

Consultant doctors need to have access to hospitals to treat seriously ill patients or perform procedures that cannot be done in their offices. Doctors will often have admitting privileges at more than one hospital, and hospital executives are well aware that doctors who are not pleased with one hospital will choose to admit their patients in a different hospital. Hospitals, therefore, need to make significant efforts marketing to doctors in order to encourage them to admit an optimum number of patients (Celluchi, Wiggins & Farnsworth, 2014; Ahmadi, Pishvaee & Heydari, 2019). Besides hospitals, pharmaceutical companies also spend significant resources on marketing to doctors. In both cases, it is advisable to adopt a relationship marketing approach. Relationship marketing seeks to develop a mutually beneficial long-term relationship between the marketing organisation and its customer (Berkowitz, 2011). One strategy that is likely to prove useful is to provide opportunities for the doctors to learn of new developments in their respective fields. Doctors need to keep abreast of new knowledge, and, since they are very busy, they will give preferential treatment to organisations that do a great job of assisting them to learn on the go. Conferences, working sessions with visiting renowned physicians and modern comfortable doctors' lounges are among some of the options appreciated by consultant doctors.

7.3.3 THE PAYER AS A CUSTOMER

There are three main types of payers for healthcare services in Africa. These include consumer payers, where the recipient of the services is responsible for settling the bill, the government and private insurance companies. The pricing strategy for healthcare products is heavily influenced by the buyer's decision process depending on who is responsible for making payment (Kotler, Shalowitz & Stevens, 2008; Ahmadi, Pishvaee & Heydari, 2019). Owing to the low penetration of both private and public healthcare insurance in Africa, the consumer is, in most cases, responsible for settling the bill on their own. Since most consumers have low disposable incomes, they are price sensitive and often shop around for affordable healthcare providers. The tendency to shop around is also easily understandable as the individual has limited negotiating power with a doctor and probably less with a hospital. He or she is, therefore, a price taker once the choice of a healthcare provider has been made. In many cases consumers will self-medicate to avoid doctors and hospital charges. The weak regulatory environment in Africa also promotes the habit of self-medication. For example, in Nigeria self-medication is tacitly encouraged because pharmaceutical drugs are freely displayed for sale in unauthorised places such as markets, roadside stalls and other public places not duly licensed to sell them (Ayanwale, Okafor & Odukoya, 2017).

When the government or private insurance company is responsible for settling the bill, then buyer power becomes a key factor (Kotler, Shalowitz & Stevens, 2008). Governments will often set the price they can afford based on the limited financing of healthcare in Africa and hospitals will often have no room for negotiation. Private insurance companies have some leeway in recommending a list of preferred doctors or hospitals, so the providers of healthcare must have good marketing and relationship management strategies in order to remain in the good books of health insurance companies. In the recent past, there has been a demand for predictable pricing by insurance cover providers. Hospitals have responded by adopting fixed aggregate or "package" prices for frequent and relatively routine medical or surgical procedures.

7.4 HEALTH SERVICE INNOVATION AND DESIGN

To better understand the healthcare service roadmap, it is imperative to delve into the three dimensions of healthcare service as enumerated by Kotler, Shalowitz and Stevens (2008), namely: the level of service provided, the nature of medical technology used, and the location of the healthcare service, albeit with minimal delineation. The level of healthcare service may vary from simple to intensive care or from short to prolonged treatment. The medical technology used could be simple to multiple types and, finally, the location of site may be inpatient or outpatient, or a combination of both (Kotler, Shalowitz & Stevens, 2008).

In most developing countries, the majority of the population still lives in rural areas. Most doctors prefer to work in the major cities, so the doctor to patient ratio is even worse in the countryside. In India, for example, 68 percent of the population lives in the rural areas, and over 60 percent of specialist doctor positions in rural and smaller urban center hospitals are vacant (Mathur, Srivastava, Lalchandani & Mehta, 2017). In Africa, the average ratio is 26 doctors per 100,000 persons (Scott & Mars, 2015), but this can be a misleading statistic because some countries such as South Africa, Egypt and Morocco have much higher ratios. In South Africa, 43 percent of patients live in rural areas where the doctor–patient ratio is 13 doctors per 100,000 people, and in some parts of rural Zambia, some provinces operate at a doctor-to-population ratio of 1 : 69,000 (Chanda & Shaw, 2010). The World Health Organization recommends a doctor–patient ratio of 20 : 100,000; in the Organisation for Economic Co-operation and Development (OECD) countries this ratio is 320 to every 100,000 people. Two health service innovations that have been used successfully to improve accessibility to healthcare in Africa are telemedicine and mobile health (m-health).

7.5 MARKETING IN HEALTHCARE: TELEMEDICINE AND MOBILE HEALTH (M-HEALTH)

One of the strategies to deal with this challenge is to promote the use of telemedicine: the remote diagnosis of patients by means of telecommunications technology (World Bank, 2008; Urazimbetoya, 2011). Through a video link, doctors with specialised training assist clinical officers, nurses or junior doctors to diagnose ailments, recommend treatment and perform surgical procedures (World Bank, 2008). Telemedicine has been used to address the shortage and skewed distribution of specialist doctors in developed countries, with documented success. In the United States, more than half the states have passed telemedicine parity laws mandating that commercial insurers reimburse telemedicine visits after studies showed that, among other benefits, its use improved the post-operative management of stroke and heart condition patients while lowering treatment costs (Mehrotra et al., 2016).

The private sector has identified the potential business opportunity of telemedicine in developing countries. In India, the Apollo Hospitals Group has partnered with the Indian government ISRO (Indian Space Research Organisation) to set up over 125 VSAT (very small aperture terminal) enabled peripheral medical centers in the rural areas (Ganapathy & Ravindra, 2009). Nigeria is Africa's largest market for healthcare, and the government has actively encouraged the use of telemedicine to enhance the delivery of healthcare. Recently Shell Nigeria partnered with VSee, a telehealth app and video conferencing Software Company, to enable virtual doctor consultation visits for its employees working in remote offshore drilling sites (Ekanoye et al., 2017).

The high penetration of broadband and smart phones in some African countries such as South Africa and Kenya has contributed to the growth of telemedicine in the recent past. Safaricom, the leading internet and mobile communication company in Kenya, recently partnered with Huawei and the government of Kenya to set up a project that will provide video-based health consultation services to over 200,000 residents in the remote county of Lamu from the main hospital at the Kenyan coast, the Mombasa General Hospital (Safaricom, 2018). Safaricom has a long-term strategy to grow its data and mobile apps businesses by promoting telemedicine and low-cost health insurance products that will ride on its m-pesa (a mobile phone wallet) infrastructure (Safaricom, 2018). Safaricom has been a pioneer in using mobile communication technology to bring financial inclusivity to the bottom of the pyramid (BOP). As of June 2017, m-pesa had 23 million subscribers (Kivuva, 2018) which means that over three out of four adult Kenyans have m-pesa accounts. In 2012, Safaricom partnered with a major Kenyan bank, CBA, to enable vetted m-pesa account holders to access short term micro-credit facilities through its m-shwari mobile app platform.

By 2017, 55 percent of Kenyan adults with registered mobile phones were beneficiaries of microcredit loans through m-shwari and similar mobile phone/commercial bank products in Kenya. Safaricom has also partnered with a Kenyan solar energy company, M-KOPA, to enable over 100,000 Kenyan homes that are not connected to the national electricity grid to acquire a solar energy domestic lighting solution, for which the customers pay monthly over the m-pesa platform (M-KOPA, 2018), enabling them to use their phones to access information. In 2016, Safaricom, in conjunction with a mobile app developer CarePay, and a not-for-profit group, PharmAccess, launched the m-tiba product (m stands for mobile and tiba means "care" in Swahili). This product enables customers who cannot afford traditional private health insurance to access it as they save money monthly to be used for medical treatment when the need arises. To add value to m-tiba, Safaricom and PharmAccess have partnered with donors who contribute to treatment for certain conditions through the m-tiba platform, largely due to the ease of efficient administration and accountability. Within a year, m-tiba had 230,000 users who have been able to access treatment in 311 accredited healthcare centers (Mumo, 2017). Safaricom and its partners are confident that m-tiba will achieve similar success to its other mobile money initiatives and open up healthcare access options to the bottom of the pyramid.

With improved internet connectivity within the region, it is expected that the internet of things (IoT) will make significant inroads in the health sector. Karahoca, Karahoca and Aksöz (2018) note that IoT will greatly shape the healthcare sector due to its ability to map and capture vital health information. For instance, a smart shirt uses GPS down to the exact location to communicate a patient's health complications to the nearest health providers in case of an emergency, and it also tracks the patient's heartbeats and provides an electrocardiogram. This means that lots of patient information will be available at varied internet sites that can be mined to better understand health matters. Morgan (2018) notes that embracing IT to enhance healthcare customer experience through augmented reality (pop up treatment options that appear on-screen as a doctor checks a patient's condition), big data analysis, patient personalisation and use of wearable devices is changing the human face of the sector.

7.6 HEALTHCARE SERVICE BLUEPRINTING

Technological changes in the global environment, with which the organisation must also align in order to remain relevant, require that healthcare providers must have a planning tool or a map that shows how the service is provided, taking into consideration environmental factors. The service blueprint entails aligning the organisation's structure with technology and the need of the markets (Bitner, Ostrom & Morgan, 2008). The healthcare blueprint is a structure of operation that reflects the interaction of the organisation with other stakeholders towards achieving the right customer experience. A healthcare blueprint shows the structure of service delivery, how it would be rendered, and those involved. It allows for comparison between the operational process and the experience gained by customers in their contact with the service organisation.

The service blueprint entails service interactions, identifying gaps in the internal process that might affect an impactful customer's experience. The service blueprint is also used to examine the quality of experience patients have with services rendered by the healthcare service provider. In a technology-driven world, it serves as an asset for marketing healthcare services.

7.7 HEALTHCARE DIGITAL CONTENT MARKETING

Content marketing is the process of creating and sharing original content to generate awareness and interest in a business online without explicitly selling any products or services. The buying decision process for a patient seeking treatment is a high involvement situation. Consequently, healthcare marketers should adopt an educational approach over a promotional one (Berkowitz, 2011). Content marketing's strength lies in building brand recognition and reputation; in a recent study conducted in the United States, hospital reputation was found to be a much bigger determinant of patients' selection of hospitals than recommendations from family or friends (GLC Delivers, 2017).

Since consumers increasingly search for information online before making buying decisions, health service providers who offer invaluable information that educates the public and engenders trust are likely to achieve a competitive advantage over their peers who do not.

The Mayo Clinic is a leading American Hospital brand based in Rochester, Minnesota (Mayo Clinic, 2018). The hospital website has a page on disease symptoms and their possible causes. It also has a page where it shares real patient stories to offer hope and inspiration to potential patients (Mayo Clinic, 2018). The organisation shares the posts widely on social media, too. In addition, Mayo Clinic addresses specific health topics, such as living with cancer and managing chronic conditions. Some of this medical information is available on YouTube video to optimise customer engagement. Some hospitals in Africa have also realised the brand building power of content marketing. The Netcare group of hospitals in South Africa has a web page dedicated to educating visitors on various health conditions (Netcare, 2018) and how best to avoid behavior and/or situations that might aggravate ailments. This information is also available in audio form to make it more engaging and easier to comprehend.

7.8 NEW SERVICE DEVELOPMENT

Rebranding of the healthcare service in Africa will require the development of new services to match the current need of the market and the changing dynamics on which their performance depends. The new service development system must be customer centered and customer driven. To have an effective and efficient new service delivery system, the development process must capture three main frameworks which are: development of the service concept, development of the service system, and the development of the service process (Edvardsson & Olsson, 1996; Lusch & Nambisan, 2015). The main focus of new service development is to ensure there is an efficient customer service delivery process because under this system, the patient is now seen as a customer. Contemporary service delivery systems in the health sector must be aligned with the logic of the customer and create value.

Further Edvardsson and Olsson (1996) and Lusch and Nambisan (2015) stressed that the new service delivery system in the health sector should be geared towards ensuring that a product of the right quality is rendered in the right manner, because the product quality governs the customer's perception and his/her report of the business image in the market. The health sector must see customers as key actors in the long and short run future performance of their health organisation. The service system must be developed in such a way that the service is appropriate to customer's need, which also adds to the organisation's value. Also, the service system should possess the necessary resources needed to have a successful service delivery process. The new service development must coordinate and provide a pathway for a new direction in the organisation's work process. The new service delivery, which is customer oriented, takes the form of a strategic plan which reflects the vision of the organisation. If the organisation's service delivery outcome does not change, it means the new service development system is ineffective and did not capture the service concept, service system and service process put in place

7.9 CONCLUSION

It is evident that marketing over the last couple of decades has made unprecedented inroads in the healthcare sector, which is predominantly service based, driven mainly by the private sector, especially in Africa. The healthcare market consists of marketing of pharmaceutical products, medical technology devices and healthcare services by the providers. Generally, human beings dread going to healthcare centers, so medical goods and services are unsought goods (Kotler & Keller, 2009). This is worsened by the fact that healthcare services are intangible, inseparable, heterogamous and highly perishable, which calls for concerted effort to make them tangible and offer patients a memorable experience.

Today, consumers of healthcare are more active and seek effective and affordable treatment from a wide variety of information communication technologies, compared to yesteryear's customers who were hugely passive. It is imperative to broadly understand that healthcare customer refers to the patient, doctors and clinical officers, as well as the payer (patient, parents, friends, institutions, government and private insurance companies). Recent developments in health technologies in Africa and the rest of world such as telemedicine, m-health and smart technologies have ushered in a new dawn in Africa by closing the physical geographical distance in the provision of healthcare, easing the quest for health for all. Africa's public and private healthcare service providers must ensure that marketing practices are inculcated into their healthcare service delivery systems.

They must begin to see the patients as customers in order to render quality service to them, which will influence their intention to continue with that provider.

REFERENCES

Aga Khan University (AKU) website. www.hospitals.aku.edu/pakistan/medical-and-diagnostics. Retrieved on September 7, 2018.

Ahmadi, A., Pishvaee, M. S., & Heydari, M. (2019). How group purchasing organisations influence healthcare-product supply chains? An analytical approach. *Journal of the Operational Research Society, 70*(2), 280–293.

AlGhamdi, K. M., & Moussa, N. A. (2012). Internet use by the public for health-related information. *International Journal of Medical Informatics, 81*, 363–373.

Ayanwale, M. B., Okafor, I. P., & Odukoya, O. O. (2017). Self-medication among rural residents in Lagos, Nigeria. *Journal of Medicine in the Tropics, 19*(1), 65–71.

Bebko, C. P. (2000). Service intangibility and its impact on consumer expectations of service quality. *Journal of Services Marketing, 14*(1), 9–26, https://doi.org/10.1108/08876040010309185.

Berkowitz, E. N. (2011). *Essentials of health care marketing.* Burlington, MA: Jones and Bartlett Learning.

Bitner, M. J., Ostrom, A. L., & Morgan, F. N. (2008). Service blueprinting: A practical technique for service innovation. *California Management Review, 50*(3), 66–94.

Bratucu, R., Gheorghe, I. R., Purcarea, R. M., Gheorghe, C. M. O., Popa Velea, O. P., & Purcarea, V. L. (2014). Cause and effect: The linkage between the health information seeking behavior and the online environment: A review. *Journal of Medicine and Life.* www.ncbi.nlm.nih.gov/pmc/articles/PMC4233431/. Retrieved on September 8, 2018.

Celluchi, L. W., Wiggins, C, & Farnsworth, T. J. (2014). *Healthcare marketing: A case study approach.* Chicago, IL: Health Administration Press, Foundation of the Amer College.

Chanda, K. L., & Shaw, J. G. (2010). The development of telehealth as a strategy to improve health care services in Zambia. *Health Information and Libraries Journal, 27*(2), 133–139.

Coddington, D. C., Fischer, E. A, & Moore, K. D. (2001). *Strategies for the new health care market place.* San Francisco: Jossey–Bass.

Coviello, N. E., Brodie, R. J., Danaher, P. J, & Johnston, W. J. (2002). How firms relate to their markets: An empirical study of contemporary marketing practices. *Journal of Marketing, 66* (7), 33–46.

Edvardsson, B., & Olsson, J. (1996). Key concepts for new service development. *Service Industries Journal, 16*(2), 140–164.

Ekanoye, F., Ayeni, F., Olukonde, T., Nina, V., Donalds, C., & Mbarika, V. (2017). Telemedicine diffusion in a developing country: A case of Nigeria. *Science Journal of Public Health, 5*(4), 341–346.

Ganapathy, K., & Ravindra, A. (2009). Telemedicine in India: The Apollo story. *Telemedicine Journal and E Health, 15*, 576–585.

Gerein, N., Green, A., & Pearson, S. (2006). The implications of shortages of health professionals for maternal health in sub-Saharan Africa. *Reproductive Health Matters, 14*(27), 40–50.

Gittell, J. H., & Michelle, T. (1997). *Transitional infant care specialty hospital. Harvard Business School Case 898-070.* Harvard: Harvard Business School Press. Revised November, 2000.

GLC Delivers. (2017). Content marketing trends 2018. www.glcdelivers.com/tag/content-marketing-2018/. Retrieved on September 7, 2018.

Hospital Consumer Assessment of Healthcare Providers and Systems (HCAHPS). (2017). Patients' perspectives of care survey. www.cms.gov/Medicare/Quality-Initiatives-Patient-Assessment-Instruments/HospitalQualityInits/HospitalHCAHPS.html. Retrieved on September 6, 2018.

Indiana Health Industry Forum. (2017). Southern-Africa-healthcare-brief-for-GSGP-companies. (2017). www.ihif.org. Retrieved on September 7, 2018.

Karahoca, A., Karahoca, D., & Aksöz, M. (2018). Examining intention to adopt to internet of things in healthcare technology products. *Kybernetes, 47*(4), 742–770, https://doi.org/10.1108/K-02-2017-0045. Retrieved on September 2, 2018.

Keskinocak, P., & Savva, N. (2019). A review of the healthcare-management (modeling) literature published at M&SOM. http://faculty.london.edu/nsavva/healthcare_modeling_May9.pdf.

Kivuva, E. (2018, March 23). www.the-star.co.ke/news/2018/03/23/m-pesa-maintains-top-slot-of-mobile-money-space. Retrieved on September 7, 2018.

Kotler, P., & Keller, L. (2009). Marketing management (13th ed.). Upper Saddle River, NJ: Prentice-Hall.

Kotler, P., Shalowitz, J., & Stevens, R. (2008). *Strategic marketing for healthcare organizations: Building a customer driven health system.* San Francisco, CA: Jossey-Bass.

Lusch, R. F., & Nambisan, S. (2015). Service innovation: A service-dominant logic perspective. *MIS Quarterly*, *39*(1).

Mathur, P., Srivastava, S., Lalchandani, A, & Mehta, J. L. (2017). Evolving role of telemedicine in health care delivery in India. *Primary Healthcare*, *7*(1), www.omicsonline.org/…/evolving-role-of-telemedicine-in-health-care-delivery. Retrieved on September 6, 2018.

Mayo Clinic. (2018). Website. www.mayoclinic.org/. Retrieved on September 7, 2018.

Mburu, J. M. (2017). Penetration and uptake of insurance in Kenya (Unpublished MBA thesis, USIU Africa).

McColl-Kennedy, J., Sweeney, J., Soutar, G., & Amonani, C. (2008). Professional service firms are relationship marketers. *Australasian Marketing Journal*, *16*(1), 30–47.

McDermott, A. M., & Pedersen, A. R. (2016). Conceptions of patients and their roles in healthcare: Insights from everyday practice and service improvement. *Journal of Health Organization and Management*, *30*(2), 194–206, https://doi.org/10.1108/JHOM-10-2015-0164.

Mehrotra, A., Jena, A. B., Busch, A. B., Souza, J., Uscher-Pines, L,, & Landon, B. E. (2016). Utilization of telemedicine among rural Medicare beneficiaries. *JAMA*, *315*(18), 2015–2016.

Merab, E. (2018, March 1). Horror at KNH as doctors open skull of wrong patient. *The Daily Nation online edition*. www.nation.co.ke/news/KNH-doctors-perform-surgery-on-wrong-patient/1056-4325292. Retrieved on September 6, 2018.

M-KOPA. (2018). M-KOPA makes high quality solar affordable for everyone. www.solar.m-kopa.com/about/our-impact. Retrieved on September 7, 2018.

Morgan, B. (2018). The top 5 trends in customer experience in healthcare. www.forbes.com/sites/blakemorgan/2018/01/09/the-top-5-trends-in-customer-experience-for-healthcare/#522c8d5623e6. Retrieved on September 8, 2018.

Mumo, M. (2017, April 3). Safaricom's m-tiba uptake on the rise. *The Daily Nation online edition*. www.nation.co.ke/business/Safaricom-healthcare-app-MTiba-nets-230-000/996-3876690-nuvjfwz/index.html.

Nadowska, A. (2013). Services marketing in the health care industry: Elekta in Sweden (Unpublished MBA thesis, University of Gavle). www.diva-portal.org/smash/get/diva2:661128/fulltext01.pdf. Retrieved on September 7, 2018.

Nesreen, M., & Amira, I. (2016). The importance of medication errors reporting in improving the quality of clinical care services. *Global Journal of Health Sciences*, *8*(8), 243–251.

Netcare. (2018). Website. www.netcare.co.za/Careers/Education-and-training. Retrieved on September 7, 2018.

Nwaopara, A. U. (2015). Doctor to patient ratio and infrastructure gap in a psychiatric hospital in oil rich Eket, Nigeria. *International Journal of Basic, Applied and Innovative Research*, *4*(3), 72–85.

Parasuraman, A., Zeithaml, V. A., & Berry, L. (1988). Servqual: A multiple-item scale for measuring consumer perceptions of service quality. *Journal of Retailing*, *64*(1), 12–40.

Perlman, Y., & Levner, I. (2014). Perishable inventory management in healthcare. *Journal of Service Science and Management*, 2014, 7, 11–17. Published online February 2014 (www.scirp.org/journal/jssm). http://dx.doi.org/10.4236/jssm.2014.71002.

Porter, M. E., & Teisburg, E. O. (2006). *Redefining health care: Creating value-based competition on results*. Harvard: Harvard Business School Press.

Safaricom. (2018). Sustainability report. www.safaricom.co.ke/sustainabilityreport. Retrieved on September 7, 2018.

Sakhaii, M. (2017). Inventory policy for a hospital supply chain with perishable inventory (Unpublished MSC science thesis, Russ College of Engineering and Technology of Ohio University). https://etd.ohiolink.edu/!etd.send_file?accession=ohiou1480597038799773&disposition=inline. Retrieved on September 8, 2018.

Sasser, W. E. (1976). Matching supply and demand in service industries. *Harvard Business Review*. www.hbr.org/1976/11/match-supply-and-demand-in-service-industries. Retrieved September 6, 2018.

Scott, R., & Mars, M. (2015). Telehealth in the developing world: Current status and future prospects. *Dove Press Journal* (3), 25–37.

Urazimbetoya, S. (2011). A case study: On patient empowerment and integration of telemedicine to national healthcare services. https://pure.au.dk/ws/files/53744533/A_case_study_on_patient_empowernment_and_…pdf.

World Bank. (2008). *The business of health in Africa: partnering with the private sector to improve people's lives (English)*. International Finance Corporation. Washington, DC: World Bank. worldbank.org/curated/en/878891468002994639/The-business-of-health-in-Africa-partnering-with-the-private-sector-to-improve-peoples-lives. Retrieved on September 7, 2018.

World Health Organization. (2010). *World health statistics 2010*. World Health Organization.

World Health Organization. (2017). *Towards access 2030: WHO essential medicines and health products strategic framework 2016–2030*. Geneva: World Health Organization.

8 Utilisation and Pricing of Healthcare Services

George Acheampong and Solomon Yaw Agyeman-Boaten

8.1 INTRODUCTION

The utilisation and pricing of healthcare services have been discussed extensively in the literature of developed countries such as North America, Australia, England, the Netherlands, and Germany, among others. One reason ascribed to the numerous studies in these areas is the availability of data on utilisation and cost of healthcare, whereas there is limited or no such available data in developing countries. Insight into healthcare utilisation trends is required to inform policy as well as to develop interventions (Wammes et al., 2017). Studies in this aspect of the health sector are essential and need to be explored further, especially in developing countries such as countries in Africa.

Mushi (2014) defined access to healthcare services as "the number or proportion of people reporting for medical attention in health-care facilities". The problem with access to care is shown by low-income individuals or people using fewer services in certain areas of the country. Mushi (2014) noted in a study conducted in Tanzania that people who are not poor report higher morbidity rates than those who are poor, so they utilise more healthcare services than the poor. A number of households are unable to access medical care due to the fees being charged in the public healthcare facilities. In a similar manner, utilisation of healthcare was also referred to as "the number or proportion of the consulting patients that are given medical services including medical consultation" (2014).

Healthcare services are sometimes categorised into a wide range of services, to include outpatients, inpatients, medical aid and advice, primary healthcare, maternity care, hospitals and specialists, mental care, care from general practitioners, allied healthcare (comprising dietary advice, occupational therapy, speech therapy, physiotherapy), complementary medicine (which consists of acupuncture, natural medicine, homeopathy, and osteopathy), and transportation. Services are also provided for specific diseases such as ischaemic heart disease and circulatory disorders, treated in 53 per cent of the top 1 per cent of high-cost beneficiaries in Netherlands (Wammes et al., 2017). In Malaysia, endocrine disorder and cardiovascular disorders, followed by central nervous system and musculoskeletal disorders, are the most common diseases identified (Ud din Babar, Ibrahim, & Bukhari, 2005).

According to Canavan, West, and Card (2016), outpatients' appointments, day-case admissions, primary healthcare utilisation, inpatient rates, and colonoscopy rates over time have all demonstrated a similar trend of utilisation increase before referral. Except for colonoscopy, rates of utilisation in all healthcare domains increase with decreased deprivation (Canavan et al., 2016). In Tanzania, attendance and utilisation of health facilities has improved due to cost sharing between government and patients. This has doubled access and quality of healthcare in all the categories of patients as of 2005. This worked through improved availability of drugs, minor rehabilitations including expansion of physical facilities, the government paying utility bills and paying for security guards for the health facilities, and through quality control and resource management improvements (Mushi, 2014).

8.2 DEFINING HEALTH SERVICE DEMAND

Demand analysis for healthcare services is used to explain variations in the use of healthcare services. Generally, demand is the amount of product or service that a household is willing and able to purchase at different prices, at a given period. Likewise, healthcare services demand is the units of healthcare services that a household is willing and able to purchase at different prices, at a given period. Thus, the ability and willingness to use a healthcare service is backed by purchasing power. Ability and willingness to buy will depend on the price of the good or service in the marketplace, notwithstanding whether the market is in equilibrium. Moreover, just desiring to purchase a product or service does not constitute demand. Consequently, Feldstein (1966) distinguished between need for care and demand. He explained that "need is the amount of care believed necessary by medical authorities while demand is the actual use of medical care services". Factors that account for discrepancies between demand and the need for care include the unawareness of the value of medical care of an individual who may demand more care than medically required. Furthermore, he could be unaware that "specialized facilities and services could be available to him or he could be without the financial resources for the medical care he needs". Concluding, Feldstein posits that the need for a community health facility may be very great, but it will remain empty if it does not reflect these factors in its usage.

Another aspect of the topic espoused extensively by Feldstein (1966) is the distinction between public and private demand for healthcare services. Some healthcare services involve elements that are not counted in the community's total demand for healthcare. These are traditionally provided by the government via public health programmes. The purchase of these kinds of services provides benefits to persons other than the purchaser, so a less than optimum level of such service will be provided if left in the hands of the individual to provide. The demand for healthcare services of this nature is what is termed as public demand for healthcare. Examples include deriving knowledge from a medical research. Aside the "public good" provided by government, it also provides what is usually classified as private goods and services in medical care. The provision of such assistance is through government subsidies or direct provision of services which affects empirical estimates of personal demand for healthcare.

Baer (1963) defined medical care as "the service consisting of the control and/or management of diseases (or other unwanted physical or mental conditions) be they actual or potential". These services include drugs, hospital and physician care, and nursing homes. The various components in the definition are "used together when treating an illness and must therefore be considered both complementary and interchangeable" (Feldstein, 1966). Empirically the components measuring demand "have generally been expressed as units of service such as hospital admissions, patient days, length of stay and physician visits" (Fieldston, Ragavan, & Jayaraman, 2012).

Friedman and Kuznets (1945) suggest that the dollar amount a person spends is the appropriate dependent variable for medical care in demand studies, since the physician will provide a set of components of treatment for a given expenditure. Feldstein (1966), on the other hand, argued that

> an empirical measure such as medical care expenditures may bias the effects of the factors believed to influence demand (prices and income), if it is not first adjusted for price changes and for changes in the product itself, e.g., quality changes.

He added that

> although measurement is difficult, a clear advantage may be gained by discussing the price of medical care in terms of treatment price, allowing for quality changes that have occurred, rather than by merely observing the changes in prices for the components of medical care.

Feldstein (1966) further explained that "the demand for medical care is the demand for a treatment, and variations in demand are variations in either number of treatments or in their quality". Sahn,

Younger, and Genicot (2003) added that "the quality of medical care has large effects on health demand" and this quality stems from "the quality and availability of doctors/nurses, drugs and the clinic environment".

According to a systematic search for papers by Polley and Pilkington (2017),

> any reported reduction in demand for health services applies only to the cohort of patients referred to social prescribing.... In some cases, patients who failed to engage fully with social prescribing had much higher rates of health service use both before and after referral.
>
> (Dayson & Bashir, 2014)

Usually, demand is initiated by the patient. The physician provides what Feldstein (1966) calls "inputs" such as their own service or the hospital service to provide a treatment of a given quality. He considers these demands for "inputs" as derived, since initial demand for a treatment determines which inputs are needed. Treating illness of patients is based on the physician's awareness of the patient's financial resource, how much the patient can afford to pay, as well as the physician's medical knowledge, and other constraints. These to a high extent influence the kind of inputs to be prescribed.

According to Feldstein (1966) the demand for healthcare rests on two elements of choice: "the amount of medical care purchased and in the way which the components of care are combined to produce a given treatment". Likewise, the degree of choice, whether on the part of the patient or his physician, hinges on knowledge and availability of substitutes. The knowledge of a medical condition and the availability of substitutes influence the decision made by both patients and physicians. He further explained that, unlike other markets, the patient does not usually make this choice directly in healthcare, but it is the physician that combines components of care into treatment based on their knowledge acquired. For that reason, "the physician has an element of choice available to him that produces observed variations in usage". For physicians to provide a relatively low cost of medical care to both the patient and themselves, they must consider components of care such as their availability and the financial and physical cost to the patient and themselves. For instance, health insurance cover would influence the relative price to a patient. In conclusion, "arriving at the demand for any one of the components of care, both the patient and physician influences must therefore be considered" (Fieldston et al., 2012).

8.3 FACTORS INFLUENCING HEALTH SERVICE DEMAND

Feldstein (1966) designed a framework of the demand for medical care. This model comprises three phases: factors that affects a patient's demand for treatments, factors that affects a physician's use of the components of care, and derived demands for the components of care. Simkhada, Teijlingen, Porter, and Simkhada (2008) categorised "Socio-demographic factors, availability, accessibility, affordability, characteristics of health services, women's position in the household and society, and women's knowledge, attitudes, beliefs and culture" as the factors that affect the use of antenatal care (ANC) services in developing countries.

Incidence of illness, cultural-demographic characteristics, and economic factors are considered to be the factors that affect a patient's demand for medical care. Since healthcare services cannot generally be obtained for free, families are limited by their scarce financial resources among alternative desires. Specifically, the amount spent would thus partially depend on the amount of income and wealth available and also on the price of medical care relative to the prices of other goods and services. Incidence of illness and cultural-demographic characteristics are said to shape a family's "desire" for medical care, and depend primarily upon the family's perception of a health deficiency and belief in the efficacy of medical treatment (Simkhada et al., 2008).

Feldstein (1966) postulates that incidence of illness by itself generates need. It is the interrelationship of illness with other factors that generates demand. Although illness is considered as a random event for individuals, it has a fair degree of predictability based on certain characteristics of the population such as age and sex. Therefore, "having greater predictability for population groups has been the basis for planning medical care services through the use of mortality rates, bed per population ratios, and physician per population ratios as indications of need".

Physiological condition, perception of illness, and attitudes toward seeking medical care are deemed cultural-demographic factors that impact on a patient's demand for medical care. Measuring these factors requires specific population characteristics such as age, sex, marital status, family size, education, and residence (rural or urban) as a proxy indicator since they in themselves can rarely be measured. Someone who is well informed of the risks of ill health and is desirous of treatment will in all likelihood incur quite large expenditure for preventive services, but may incur lower expenditure for treatment of morbid physiological conditions because they have been averted. Cultural-demographic factors do not suddenly change (Feldstein, 1966).

There is extant literature on the relationship between utilisation of healthcare components and various characteristics. Feldstein (1966) observed the following relationships. The "relationship between age and use of medical care services is not a simple linear one". Thus, it is "predictable that age and sex would affect demand for care in that they affect morbidity". Moreover, "marital status is also considered to affect the consumption of certain components of medical care". Ashford and Pearson (1970) confirmed this assertion, stating that "marital status has been shown to influence the demand for medical care, with widows characteristically requesting care more frequently than married women". Family size is also observed to have a significant impact on healthcare demand. Apart from the above, Banks, Beresford, Morrell, Waller, and Watkins (1975) add to the findings of Feldstein (1966), stating that education and area of residence have consistently been demonstrated to influence the demand for healthcare. Banks et al. (1975) deduced from earlier studies that "lower demands for medical care occur among those who proceeded beyond the age of fifteen in their education". For social class Banks et al. (1975) found complex and conflicting results.

The study by Jacob (1969) revealed that "a high neuroticism score, using the Maudsley Personality Inventory, occurs in those patients who make frequent demands for medical care due to a variety of episodes of illness". It also revealed that introverted patients had higher demands of healthcare than the extroverted. Similar to Jacob's findings, Banks et al. (1975) established that "a high anxiety level in women was found to be associated with both consultation behaviour and symptom perception.... Whatever the level of symptom perception, women with more anxiety were more likely to consult their General practitioner". Scheffler and Miller (1989) equally estimated demand for mental health services by blacks, Hispanics, and whites, as well as males and females, using a three-part regression model, by examining the probability of mental health use and the level of outpatient and inpatient use. Their result showed that "all user subpopulations sharing this plan have the same coverage, so differences in demand and utilization are related to ethnic and racial background, age, salary, outpatient visit co-payment and market area characteristics, including the supply of psychiatrists". With regard to the mental health component of healthcare, Scheffler and Miller (1989) found from the sociological and health service research literature that "women utilize ambulatory mental health services to a greater extent than men". They further stated that "numerous studies drawing upon different populations and treatment settings have demonstrated an inverted 'u' relationship of age with both probability of use and level of use" (1989).

The third component of the factors that affect patient's demand for medical care according to Feldstein (1966) consists of the economic factors. In addition to price and income affecting a person's decision whether or not to seek healthcare, they affect the extent of care as well insofar as treatment is undertaken. A lower price of service corresponds with consumption increase. Both the direction and the extent of price change are considered. A study conducted in Africa (rural Tanzania) by Sahn et al. (2003) confirms that "price increases or user fees will result in small percentage of people opting for self-treatment". Such instances serve as an inducement to a high degree of substitution between public and private care. They assert that these findings on health demand are not different from previous research conducted in some African countries such as Ghana (Waddington & Enyimayew, 1990), Kenya (Mwabu, Mwanzia, & Laimbila, 1995), Swaziland (Yoder, 1989) and Zambia (Kahenya & Lake, 1994).

Consequently, an introduction of the economic term "elasticity" which indicates "the responsiveness of changes in consumption to a change in one of the factors affecting consumption" becomes relevant. Unlike the estimates of elasticity in economics, there is an assumption in the field of health that "changes in prices have little effect on the use of medical care services" (Feldstein 1966). Sahn et al. (2003) indicates that "own price elasticities of demand for all health care options are high, although less so for public clinics and dispensaries than other choices".

Once more in the health sector, the out-of-pocket price to patients is utilised. Therefore, "the effect of health insurance, 'free' care, and the tax deductibility aspects would first have to be eliminated, for these factors [to] actually reduce the price the patient pays for services" (Phelps, 2016, p. 57). Theoretically, health insurance is used as a proxy for the price variable. According to Feldstein (1966), insurance has two effects: the "Income Effect", which "reduces the over-all price of medical care to the patient with insurance, hence increasing his consumption of medical care services"; and the "Price or Substitution Effect", which "causes components of care that are covered to be substituted for those that are not". Both are difficult to measure empirically.

Generally, studies have shown that "families with higher incomes have higher expenditures signifying higher consumption for medical care, but the percentage of income spent on medical care decreases with higher levels of income". Additionally, "illness may result in higher medical care spending and, at the same time, reduce family income by causing the debility of a wage earner" (Feldstein, 1966).

The model of demand formulated by Feldstein (1966) includes factors that affect the physician's ability to use the set of components that would result in lowest cost to the patient. Some of these limitations may come as a result of "institutional arrangement, extent of his knowledge of different methods of treatment, some hospitals having sanctions that preventing the physician from prolonging a patient's stay unnecessarily when other forms of care are available" (1966). Meanwhile, physicians act in the interest of both the patient and themselves when combining the components of care. Thus, any change caused by the above factors results in lower cost to the patient, the physician, or both.

A summary of this is to note that patient characteristics, such as cultural and economic factors, in addition to their relative cost, influence the amount and type of healthcare a physician will prescribe.

8.4 PREDICTING THE DEMAND FOR HEALTHCARE SERVICES

Predicting the future demand for healthcare services is essential for strategic planning and management of the health sector. Feldstein (1966) explained that the unexpected nature of illness in individuals and the fluctuating or random element in demand on a day-to-day basis with respect to individual hospitals have prompted a number of studies that deal with predicting demand. A basic assumption underlying the use of these studies in predictions of hospitalisation is that admission is based on incidence of illness and that length of stay in the hospital, except for scheduling problems, is also based on medical necessity. Feldstein (1966) added that a

> random component should also be used for determining the number of beds to be built, for if facilities are built according to the mean expected level of use, the cost is a penalty of not being able to satisfy demand in excess of that mean level.

Both the demand and supply factors must be known to predict actual use and a study of demand is a study of only one part of the complete model.

Lynch, Edington, and Johnson (1996) argue that health risk appraisals (HRAs) help predict which individuals are most likely to develop serious and expensive illnesses in the long-term future.

On the other hand, cost–risk assessments identify individuals at greatest risk of using healthcare services in the near future. To investigate variations in utilisation of medical care is to decide upon the best approach to adopt. A model, based on hypotheses about the expected relationships, could be constructed to gather data and analyse relationships.

A number of studies have used various models to examine the utilisation of medical care and predictions of hospitalisation. Feldstein (1966) posits that "persons with knowledge of operations research have reasoned that if they could ascertain the underlying probability distribution of 'need' that best fits the utilization data, they will have developed an explanatory model as well as an accurate predictive device". Al Nuaimi (2014) developed "different data mining techniques in order to build four models to assist decision makers in predicting the demand for healthcare services in Abu Dhabi Emirate". These models are to predict the district's current needs for hospitals; predict the district's future needs for hospitals (i.e. potentially oversupplied, undersupplied); predict the district's current need for clinics; and predict the district's future needs for clinics. The experimental results showed that "there is real demand for healthcare services in some districts" (2014). Similarly, the Health and Social Care Modelling Group in the United Kingdom (2013) developed a web-based system with different forecasting methodologies which include "exponential smoothing, Holt-Winters exponential smoothing, linear regression analysis, single layer artificial neural networks, and grey systems prediction". Li (2012) too "designed a grey dynamic prediction model according to grey system theory and subsequently forecasted the demand of the Heilongjiang professional health technicians from the years 2011 to 2020". Two models of health demand used in estimating the probability of using any service and modelling the number of visits among users were adopted by Skordis-Worrall, Hanson, and Mills (2011) to estimate the demand for health services in four poor districts in Cape Town, South Africa. Predicting the demand for physician workforce, Tsai, Eliasziw, and Chen (2012) used a multiple stepwise-linear regression to derive the physician density prediction model. The study identified population, physician, healthcare system, and economics as the four theoretical factors that are required in estimating the number of physicians a country needs. They concluded that "a large Physician Density discrepancy in a country indicates the needs to examine physicians' workloads and their wellbeing, the effectiveness or efficiency of medical care, the promotion of population health and the team resource management" (2012).

According to Frees & Lee (2011), in modelling medical services utilisation, "two-part models (TPMs) have been a widely used tool to model frequency and cost of medical services". They therefore

> extend the TPM by using more detailed information about the frequency of use and to improve the prediction of annual expenditures at an individual or group level.... Given a set of individual-level characteristics such as demographics, economic attributes, and health history at the beginning of a year

to model observable variables, frequency and expenditure – specifically, point predictions (annual expenditure model and alternative models) and simulations of predictive distribution (2011). The authors further recommended the "use estimates of coefficients, smearing factors, and individual random effects based on 2003 data to predict expenditures for individuals from the 2004 MEPS survey" and found that "explanatory variables such as demography, education, regional, health status, and economic factors significantly explained the variation in counts of inpatient admissions and outpatient visits; however, most of the variables were not significant in explaining expenditures per visit" (2011).

Van Genugten, Heijnen, and Jager (2003) examined the potential impact (in terms of hospitalisations and deaths) of pandemic influenza in the Netherlands and analysed the effects of several possible interventions. They concluded that

> a combined strategy of pneumococcal vaccination of risk groups for influenza together with the therapeutic use of neuraminidase inhibitors for all patients with influenza like illness (within 48 hours after onset of symptoms) is the best strategy in preventing hospitalizations and deaths.

In conclusion, "forecasting utilization of medical care services depends essentially upon finding relationships between the variables to be forecasted and the other factors which determine the variables' magnitude" (Feldstein, 1966).

8.5 PRICING

Pricing investigates what price is to be paid by purchasers for the health service and how the prices to be paid can be calculated. Waters and Hussey (2004) posit that "pricing health services is a key component of the broader activity of resource allocation and purchasing in health care systems". They outline and discuss the various methods used in different types of provider payment systems of healthcare. The study states that

> these methods are required for assigning indirect cost to the services that patients directly consume and are paid for by the purchasers. There is the need for an effective mechanism to link prices that purchasers pay for service to the actual cost of these services.

In determining the prices of healthcare services that purchasers pay, Waters and Hussey (2004) enumerated

> the availability of information on costs, volumes and outcomes; methods of provider payment; methods for calculating providers' costs, and characteristics of purchasers and providers (including the regulatory environment, provider autonomy, the degree of competition and negotiating power)

as the main factors that influence pricing decision.

8.6 DEMOGRAPHIC CONCLUSIONS ON UTILISATION AND PRICING OF HEALTHCARE SERVICES

Utilisation of healthcare service cannot be separated from its cost even if a health insurance system has been put in place. Previous scholars analysed the linkage between the two in relation to demographic characteristics such as age, sex, education level, and income levels of the users. For instance, Canavan et al. (2016) calculated the "stratified overall annual mean costs and gamma distribution parameters according to sex, age at referral, duration of IBS, socioeconomic status, smoking status and comorbidity status". This section elaborates on some of these issues discussed in the literature.

Allocating cost to "cost centres" or health services could be direct or indirect. Direct cost includes drugs and suppliers whilst indirect encapsulates support activities such as housekeeping and laundry and administrators' salaries. Allocations can also be activity-based costing, usually applied in the United States, and traditional costing. "The main factors influencing how prices are set are the unit and method of payment, the measurement of costs, and the characteristics of purchasers and providers" (Waters & Hussey, 2004).

In England, Canavan et al. (2016) found that "the presence of comorbid conditions increased patients' healthcare utilisation in all domains, with the exception of colonoscopy, by approximately 20%". In Germany, "95% of the respondents had at least one contact with an outpatient physician in a survey to elicit reference values of medical and non-medical health care utilisation and costs" (Grupp, König, & Konnopka, 2016). Heinrich et al. (2008) also found that pharmaceuticals and outpatients' physician services were used by 98 per cent of patients from a bottom-up costing study executed by using a cross-sectional primary care sample aged above 75 in Germany. "Women, older patients, smokers and patients with greater comorbidity utilised more healthcare resources, which generated higher costs" (Canavan et al., 2016). A model by Diehr, Yanez, Ash, Hornbrook, and Lin (1999) showed that "the relationship of age to utilization is linear and that regression lines which are parallel for men and women assume a linear relationship with different slopes for men and women". Another model showed "a quadratic relationship that is different for men and women". He further found (1999) that

> the curves that show the actual relationship of cost to age are nonlinear and differ by sex. Very young children have high utilization. Males and females have similar utilization until puberty, at which time women increase their utilization because of childbearing. Men's utilization is low until about age 40.

Grupp et al. (2016) added that women have higher outpatient visits relative to men, although the figures for men increase with age. In terms of specialist visits, the mean values tend to be higher for women between 30 and 59 years of age due to menopause and childbearing. Heinrich et al. (2008) stated that "despite significant differences in service utilization between women and men, mean total direct cost does not differ significantly". At the national level, Peters et al. (2008) found that "people in poor countries tend to have less access to health services than those in better-off countries, and within countries, the poor have less access to health services". Low- and middle-income countries "account for 90% of the global burden of disease but for only 12% of global spending on health" (Gottret & Schieber, 2006).

Diehr et al. (1999) pointed out that "an important area of research is prediction of total health care costs for a group of people for a year, so that providers can be paid appropriate rates for caring for those people". According to the study of Heinrich et al. (2008) "the main cost components accounting for 78% of total direct costs were inpatient care, pharmaceuticals, and outpatient physician services". Heinrich et al. (2008) further found that the total mean direct costs do not differ significantly between sexes. The yearly mean total direct costs per respondent summed to €3,730. Inpatient care accounted for 34 per cent of the total yearly direct cost representing the main category of healthcare. Pharmaceuticals were used by most respondents surveyed (98 per cent). A study conducted by Canavan et al. (2016) indicated that prescriptions accounted for over half of the total cost each year. Grupp et al. (2016, p. 162) discussing the pricing of healthcare service also found that

> direct costs partially reflected the age and gender related pattern in utilisation rates and duration of utilisation. On average, women have substantially higher costs of outpatient physician and therapist visits as well as informal care, whereas costs of mobile nursing services, domestic helps, rehabilitation and hospital treatments showed only marginal differences between men and women. Costs of outpatient physicians and therapists rise steadily in men, but highest in women from the age 30 to 69.

Similar to the pattern of utilisation, cost of domestic help, informal care, and mobile nursing services strongly increase at the age of 80 in both sexes. The differences between women and men younger than 30 years had been small in relation to the aggregated direct cost according to gender. The costs in women's care almost doubles in the age group 30 to 39 whereas costs in men remain the same. The aggregated direct costs remain steady in women but rise in men, between the ages of 40 and 69. At the age of 80, aggregated direct cost strongly rises in both sexes. The rise in utilisation of mobile nursing service, domestic help, and informal care caused the strong cost increase in later life. The share of outpatient physician and therapist cost on aggregated direct costs reduced from 31 per cent in the youngest age group to 11 per cent in the oldest age group. Langton et al. (2015) confirmed this assertion by stating that "the last year of life is one of the most resource and cost intensive periods in cancer care". Moreover, the results of Heinrich et al. (2008) additionally showed that a movement from lower to middle education and a point rise in chronic disease score (CDS) are allied with a rise in mean direct cost. Interestingly, overall, 1.3 per cent of the difference of total direct cost may be clarified by age, sex, education, and family status, with no independent variable being significant. Two per cent of the total direct cost resulted from transportation cost. Finally, Grupp et al. (2016) discovered "a non-linear relationship between the number of sick days and indirect costs". Since wage rates rise with age, indirect costs are higher in the age group 50 to 59. Although women often had sick leave, there are lower indirect costs in women in the age group 60 to 65.

8.7 PRICING STRATEGIES IN HEALTHCARE

8.7.1 PROVIDER PAYMENT METHODS

As stated earlier, "the principal constraint on the development of provider payment systems in low- and middle-income countries is the limited availability of information on costs, volumes, and patient characteristics" (Maceira, 1998). Previous studies determined prices by calculating the unit cost of the health service paid for, that is, all services related to diagnosis (per case), each healthcare service provided (fee-for-service – FFS), all services provided to all patients over a period of time (global or line-item budgets), or all services for a patient over a period of time (capitation) (Maceira, 1998). Waters and Hussey (2004) divided payments into retrospective and prospective. Retrospective payments such as per case are computed and paid for after the service has been delivered, whilst prospective payments, such as line-item and global budgets and capitation, are made before delivery of the service. The retrospective payment price must reflect the actual cost whereas with the prospective payments, the price should reflect the anticipated cost of the services to be provided. In setting the price, another aspect of the provider payment system is whether it is fixed or variable. The aggregated amount of payment service is proportionate to the volume of activity in the variable payment system whilst there is a limit on total payments for the fixed system (Jegers, Kesteloot, De Graeve, & Gilles, 2002).

In middle-income and low-income countries, the most common reimbursement methods for hospitals are line-item and global budgets. They, however, do not provide any incentive to ensure quality. They are prospective and have fixed aggregate payments for some period of time. Kutzin (1995) and Preker and Feachem (1996) are cited in Waters and Hussey (2004) stating that "their level of payment is grounded on previous payment levels adjusted by inflation factors". Whilst the global budgets permit the reallocation of resources across service categories, the line-item budgets do otherwise. Public hospitals in Chile are conventionally paid via the global budgets.

The capitation payments are prospective but have fixed aggregate payments per patient for a specified period of time. Langenbrunner and Wiley (2002) added that "although capitation payments offer a strong control on the price and volume of service, they also encourage under-provision or poor-quality care if payment levels are too low".

> The price of services under a capitated payment system is therefore the rate paid to the provider per insured individual consistent with the time period. If prices impeccably equalled expected cost, any remaining surplus or deficit in revenue for the provider could be because of random events and treatment patterns. If prices are under anticipated costs, providers can be expected to make up for the deficit by reducing expected costs by way of choosing decrease risk patients.
>
> (Waters & Hussey, 2004)

Whilst the use of inpatient services has decreased, the use of ambulances has been extended in the capitation of Thailand.

Payment per case can be "prospective or retrospective and has variable payments made per hospital discharge, usually weighted by diagnosis" (Jegers et al., 2002). It encourages accelerated hospital admissions but limits costs by type of service. Public sector purchasers in Organization for Economic Cooperation and Development (OECD) countries are increasingly using diagnostic-based per case payment techniques, considerably so in Japan, France, and Australia (Imai, Jacobzone, & Lenain, 2000; Imai 2002).

Unlike the other payment systems, fee-for-service payments set variable payments for each service provided. While such payments are forthright, failure to cap hospital payments could lead to increased hospital cost and insolvency of insurance funds (Langenbrunner & Wiley, 2002). "Many low- and middle-income nations are moving beyond line-item budgets for provider reimbursement and exploring fee-for-service (FFS) approaches for outpatient care and per diem (per day) for inpatient care". Experiences from those nations and from OECD nations demonstrate that fee-for-service normally ends in upsurge in health prices because the purchaser, instead of the providers, bears the financial risk (Waters & Hussey, 2004).

Waters and Hussey (2004) further explain that

> the features of those basic payment systems may be blended; mixing incentives for both providers and patients. For instance, The Federal Unified Health System (SUS) in Brazil also introduced a mixed case-based, fee-for-service approach to reimburse each public and private provider.

Korea and Taiwan have largely used fee-for-service purchasing in the context of growing public medical health insurance programmes. "Mixed payment techniques and price negotiations can assist to limit the undesired consequences such as under-band overutilization that emerge from unsuitable price levels" (Waters & Hussey, 2004).

8.7.2 Methods for Calculating Healthcare Costs

In order to limit incentives for under- or overutilisation, the price that clients pay for healthcare services should be associated with the actual unit costs of services. Establishing the genuine unit cost of health service is a complex proposal. The unit costs provide the national average cost of every type of care episode, at the same time as a healthcare resource group (HRG) offers the particular cost generated by that patient for that occasion (Canavan et al., 2016).

Waters and Hussey (2004) write that the methodology

> used to trace cost in health care has been categorized into top-down and bottom-up. Top-down costing comprises disaggregating total expenditure to units of service consisting of patient's visits or patient's hospital days. This is accomplished via allocating costs to 'cost centres' (units of service activity which includes hospital wards), figuring out the number of units of service per cost, and subsequently allocating cost to units of services. Bottom-up costing on the other hand entails aggregating the costs of every input used to offer a service.

Patient-level utilisation data for bottom-up costing are used to calculate both the number and kind of service offered to every patient per cost centre (Wiley, 1993). In setting prices proportional to cost, unit costing studies are very important; however, in instances in which correct unit costs are not available, other options exist for fixing prices as they should be. There are limited studies on costing of healthcare services, which are used in turn to set prices paid by purchasers in middle- and low-income nations found in Africa and Asia. This can be ascribed to the high cost of data acquisition and the limited data available for such purpose.

8.8 CONCLUSION

The utilisation and pricing of healthcare services remain crucial in the healthcare systems all over the globe. Developed economies have seen a substantial improvement leading to the equilibrium of healthcare demand and supply. The availability of health sector data in these economies has also helped the investigation of challenges and the provision of amicable solutions for elements such as utilisation and pricing. These studies have also aided the prediction of healthcare demand. Although a tremendous improvement in healthcare demand and supply has been realised over the years in developing countries, a lot more needs to be done to improve upon all aspects of healthcare in these countries. In view of these points, more empirical studies on healthcare service utilisation and pricing should be encouraged in Africa as well as other developing countries to elucidate the healthcare needs and right price to pay. This can be achieved if the governments of these countries, health service providers, and international organisations like the World Health Organization, along with stakeholders in the field, can devote time and resources for such a worthy cause. Much investigation will help to disclose the dynamics of healthcare in such areas, in terms of demographics and economics among other things, which will lead to solutions for various challenges. Although health insurance schemes in many countries, especially those in sub-Saharan Africa, have their own challenges, proper health insurance systems devoid of corruption should be rolled out by health service providers to deal with the numerous difficulties associated with healthcare pricing and utilisation in developing countries. Finally, in addition to finding solutions to better healthcare services, preventive healthcare services should be prioritised by health service providers. These measures, among others, are expected to alleviate the difficulties experienced in the healthcare utilisation and pricing systems.

ACKNOWLEDGEMENT

The authors are grateful for the support received from the Skills Development Fund MSc. International Business Degree Support Fund held at the Department of Marketing and Entrepreneurship, University of Ghana.

REFERENCES

Al Nuaimi, N. (2014, November). Data mining approaches for predicting demand for healthcare services in Abu Dhabi. In *2014 10th International Conference on Innovations in Information Technology (IIT)* (pp. 42–47). IEEE.

Ashford, J. R., & Pearson, N. G. (1970). Who uses the health services and why? *Journal of the Royal Statistical Society: Series A (General)*, *133*(3), 295–346.

Baer, D. V. T. (1963). *The economics of medical care*. Unpublished paper, March 20, 1963, p. 18.

Banks, M. H., Beresford, S. A. A., Morrell, D. C., Waller, J. J., & Watkins, C. J. (1975). Factors influencing demand for primary medical care in women aged 20–44 years: A preliminary report. *International Journal of Epidemiology*, *4*(3), 189–195.

Canavan, C., West, J., & Card, T. (2016). Calculating total health service utilisation and costs from routinely collected electronic health records using the example of patients with irritable bowel syndrome before and after their first gastroenterology appointment. *Pharmacoeconomics*, *34*(2), 181–194.

Dayson, C., & Bashir, N. (2014). *The social and economic impact of the Rotherham Social Prescribing Pilot: Main evaluation report*. Centre for Regional Economic and Social Research (CRESR), Sheffield Hallam University.

Diehr, P., Yanez, D., Ash, A., Hornbrook, M., & Lin, D. Y. (1999). Methods for analyzing health care utilization and costs. *Annual Review of Public Health*, *20*(1), 125–144.

Feldstein, P. J. (1966). Research on the demand for health services. *The Milbank Memorial Fund Quarterly*, *44*(3), 128–165.

Fieldston, E., Ragavan, M., Jayaraman, B., Metlay, J., & Pati, S. (2012). Traditional measures of hospital utilization may not accurately reflect dynamic patient demand: Findings from a children's hospital. *Hospital Pediatrics*, *2*(1), 10–18.

Frees, E. W., & Lee, G. (2011). Rating endorsements using generalized linear models. *Variance*, *10*(1), 51–74.

Friedman, M. and Kuznets, S. (1945). Income from independent professional practice. New York, NT: National Bureau of Economic Research, 1945, pp. 157–158.

Gottret, P., & Schieber, G. (2006). *Health financing revisited: A practitioner's guide*. Washington, DC: The World Bank.

Grupp, H., König, H. H., & Konnopka, A. (2016). Health care utilisation and costs in the general population in Germany. *Health Policy, 120*(2), 159–169.

Health and Social Care Modelling Group (HSCMG). (2013). Forecasting patient demand for NHS continuing healthcare. Retrieved on 30 May 2014, from www.healthcareanalytics.co.uk/wp-content/uploads/LPPDemand-Planning-Tool-Branded-v2.pdf.

Heinrich, S., Luppa, M., Matschinger, H., Angermeyer, M. C., Riedel-Heller, S. G., & König, H. H. (2008). Service utilization and health-care costs in the advanced elderly. *Value in Health*, *11*(4), 611–620.

Imai, Y. (2002). *Health reform in Japan*. Organization for Economic Cooperation and Development (OECD), Economics Department Working Papers No. 321.

Imai, Y, Jacobzone, S., & Lenain, P. (2000). *The changing health system in France*. Organization for Economic Cooperation and Development (OECD), Economics Department Working Papers No. 269.

Jacob, A. (1969). The personality of patients in the "artificial" practice. *Journal of the Royal College of General Practitioners, 17*, 299.

Jegers, M., Kesteloot, K., De Graeve, D., & Gilles, W. (2002). A typology for provider payment systems in health care. *Health Policy, 60*(3), 255–273.

Kahenya, G., & Lake, S. (1994). *User fees and their impact on utilization of key health services*. Lusaka: UNICEF.

Kutzin, J. (1995). Experience with organizational and financing reform of the health sector (No. WHO/SHS/CC/94.3. Unpublished). Geneva: World Health Organization.

Langenbrunner, J. C., & Wiley, M. M. (2002). Hospital payment mechanisms: Theory and practice in transition countries. In M. McKee & J. Healy (Eds.), *Hospitals in a Changing Europe* (Chapter 8). Buckingham, UK: Open University Press.

Langton, J. M., Srasuebkul, P., Reeve, R., Parkinson, B., Gu, Y., Buckley, N. A., ... & Pearson, S. A. (2015). Resource use, costs and quality of end-of-life care: Observations in a cohort of elderly Australian cancer decedents. *Implementation Science, 10*(1), 25.

Li, F. (2012). Demand prediction of Heilongjiang professional health technicians: Based on gray dynamic model. In *2012 International Conference on Management Science & Engineering (19th)*, Dallas, TX, 20–22 Sept. 2012.

Lynch, W. D., Edington, D. W., & Johnson, A. (1996). Predicting the demand for healthcare. In *Healthcare Forum Journal, 39* (1), 20–25.

Maceira, D. (1998). *Provider payment mechanisms in health care: Incentives, outcomes, and organizational impact in developing countries*. Major Applied Research 2, Working Paper 2. Bethesda, MD: Partnerships for Health Reform Project, Abt Associates Inc.

Mushi, D. P. (2014). Impact of cost sharing on utilization of primary health care services: Providers versus household perspectives. *Malawi Medical Journal, 26*(3), 83–89.

Mwabu, G., Mwanzia, J., & Laimbila, W. (1995). User charges in government health facilities in Kenya. *Health Policy and Planning, 10*, 164–170.

Peters, D. H., Garg, A., Bloom, G., Walker, D. G., Brieger, W. R., & Hafizur Rahman, M. (2008). Poverty and access to health care in developing countries. *Annals of the New York Academy of Sciences, 1136*(1), 161–171.

Phelps, C. E. (2016). *Health economics*. Routledge.

Polley, M. J., & Pilkington, K. (2017). *A review of the evidence assessing impact of social prescribing on healthcare demand and cost implications*. University of Westminster.

Preker, A. and Feachem, R. G. A. (1996). *Market mechanisms and the health sector in Central and Eastern Europe*. World Bank Technical Paper 293. Washington, DC: World Bank.

Sahn, D. E., Younger, S. D., & Genicot, G. (2003). The demand for health care services in rural Tanzania. *Oxford Bulletin of Economics and Statistics, 65*(2), 241–260.

Scheffler, R. M., & Miller, A. B. (1989). Demand analysis of mental health service use among ethnic subpopulations. *Inquiry, 26*(2), 202–215.

Simkhada, B., Teijlingen, E. R. V., Porter, M., & Simkhada, P. (2008). Factors affecting the utilization of antenatal care in developing countries: Systematic review of the literature. *Journal of Advanced Nursing, 61*(3), 244–260.

Skordis-Worrall, J., Hanson, K., & Mills, A. (2011). Estimating the demand for health services in four poor districts of Cape Town, South Africa. *International Health, 3*(1), 44–49.

Tsai, T. C., Eliasziw, M., & Chen, D. F. (2012). Predicting the demand of physician workforce: An international model based on crowd behaviors. *BMC Health Services Research, 12*(1), 79.

Ud din Babar, Z., Ibrahim, M. I. M., & Bukhari, N. I. (2005). Medicine utilisation and pricing in Malaysia: The findings of a household survey. *Journal of Generic Medicines, 3*(1), 47–61.

Van Genugten, M. L., Heijnen, M. L. A., & Jager, J. C. (2003). Pandemic influenza and healthcare demand in the Netherlands: Scenario analysis. *Emerging Infectious Diseases, 9*(5), 531.

Waddington, C., & Enyimayew, K. A. (1990). A price to pay, Part 2: The impact of user charges in the Volta region of Ghana. *The International Journal of Health Planning and Management, 5*(4), 287–312.

Wammes, J. J. G., Tanke, M., Jonkers, W., Westert, G. P., Van der Wees, P., & Jeurissen, P. P. (2017). Characteristics and healthcare utilisation patterns of high-cost beneficiaries in the Netherlands: A cross-sectional claims database study. *BMJ Open, 7*(11), e017775.

Waters, H. R., & Hussey, P. (2004). Pricing health services for purchasers: A review of methods and experiences. *Health Policy, 70*(2), 175–184.

Wiley, M. (1993). Costing hospital case-mix: The European experience. In M. Casas & M. Wiley (Eds.), *Diagnosis related groups in Europe* (pp. 138–154). Berlin: Springer-Verlag.

Yoder, R. (1989). Are people willing and able to pay for health services? *Social Science and Medicine, 29*, 35–42.

9 Distribution in Healthcare Markets

Mahmoud Abdulai Mahmoud

9.1 INTRODUCTION

Distribution in healthcare markets is made up of several players. All these players in the healthcare provision have their unique roles to play to ensure success of the system. Effective and efficient healthcare distribution markets will at least ensure productivity in the sector. The primary motive of healthcare distribution markets is to provide convenience to healthcare consumers. A healthcare distribution system which meets the needs of patients will ensure optimal performance of both material and human resources. For instance, ineffective healthcare distribution markets, policy makers and healthcare workers are often blamed for the suboptimal performance of the healthcare markets. Anecdotal evidence indicates that due to poor distribution of healthcare markets, many lives are lost that could have been saved if healthcare resources were properly distributed.

Inadequate healthcare coverage also serves as a catalyst to review the distribution of healthcare markets. It is possible healthcare resources could be skewed towards certain regions more than others. This might occur to the detriment of some segment of the population who do not receive healthcare resources at all. Therefore, a review of the distribution of healthcare markets is relevant and timely. Distribution in healthcare markets may be formally presented as a set of interdependent organisations participating in the process of making a healthcare product or service available for use or consumption. These are the set of pathways a healthcare product or service follows after production culminating in purchase and consumption or by final end user (Kotler & Keller, 2016).

In distributing healthcare products and services, some intermediaries take title to the goods or services. These categories of healthcare distributors are referred to as merchants. Mostly, they are predominant in the retail sector. However, they are also present in the wholesale distribution sector as well. Others, such as producers, manufactures, representatives or sales agents, do not take title to the goods and services. They negotiate on behalf of the manufacturers; they are called facilitators. Distribution channels of all types play an important role in healthcare markets and affect all other management decisions. Managers of healthcare facilities should judge them in the context of the entire process by which healthcare products and services are made, distributed, sold and serviced.

The main objective of this paper is to review literature on distribution in healthcare markets. The remainder of the paper is structured as follows. A literature review is carried out considering subdivisions such as centralisation and decentralisation in healthcare markets, market segmentation in healthcare markets and supply chain management. The structure of the healthcare delivery system in Ghana, and its health insurance, is considered. Finally, some conclusions are drawn for academics and practitioners alike. The next section focuses on the literature review.

9.2 LITERATURE REVIEW

9.2.1 CENTRALISATION VERSUS DECENTRALISATION

In healthcare distribution, the issue of centralisation and decentralisation is an ongoing debate among researchers and policymakers all over the world. As some countries are shifting from centralisation to decentralisation, others are doing the reverse. For instance, while Italy and Spain have undertaken immense changes to decentralise the organisation of their healthcare systems (Mosca, 2006), countries such as Norway and the other Scandinavian states are adopting centralisation in their healthcare structures (Byrkjeflot & Neby, 2008). However, decentralisation is more commonly practised and has gained extensive attention in conceptual and empirical research (Peckham, Exworthy, Greener & Powell, 2005; Magnussen, Hagen & Kaarboe, 2007; Bossert & Mitchell, 2011). Irrespective of the possible setbacks of decentralisation, proponents indicate its numerous advantages, emphasising the potential improvements to resource allocation, welfare, and access to healthcare due to local knowledge and the effective and flexible use of resources to address local needs (Peckham et al., 2005; Bossert & Mitchell, 2011).

The definitions of centralisation and decentralisation in extant literature have covered a wide range of disciplines including politics, public administration, health services research, economics, management, sociology and organisational studies. The understanding of the concepts should go beyond organisational and geographical lenses solely. It is suggested that the delivery of healthcare should not be undertaken without recognition of the individual as well as the organisational contexts, particularly as there is increasing focus on professional autonomy and regulation and patient involvement, self-determination and choice (Peckham et al., 2005).

Centralisation of healthcare services refers to the accumulation and concentration of resources, including specialised services in a few specific institutions (Yoong et al., 2013). Champions of centralisation argue that patients admitted to hospitals with sufficient staff are more likely to receive prompt treatment and will be provided better quality of care through cooperation and coordination among healthcare providers (Robinson & Casalino, 1996; Casalino, Devers, Lake, Reed & Stoddard, 2003). Although it is argued that centralisation yields economies of scale by sharing facilities, jointly purchasing supplies and coordinating administrative services, decentralisation is highly preferred. There is an empirically tested relationship that exists between decentralisation and organisational performance.

In the distribution of healthcare services, decentralisation is primarily the preferred choice, even in the phase of recent rhetoric on professional autonomy, as it helps improve the access to and quality of care by enabling timely and convenient healthcare services to patients. The competition resulting from decentralisation may also incentivise the improvement of quality of care by healthcare providers. In sum, the primary objective of decentralising healthcare services is to enhance performance and/or improve health outcomes with emphasis on what is being decentralised and for what purpose.

9.2.2 MARKET SEGMENTATION – A KEY INGREDIENT IN HEALTHCARE DISTRIBUTION

Market segmentation is key in delivering marketing solutions – "divide to conquer!" Market segmentation is a managerial tool used to group customers into well-defined homogeneous groups. In traditional marketing, segmentation strategies can increase efficiency and profitability of marketing activities through the product/service offering, advertising, pricing and distribution (Alt & Iversen, 2017). According to Swenson, Bastian and Nembhard (2016), effective health marketing strategies imported from traditional marketing applications and techniques, serve as a means to improving health promotions for patients. They further iterate that effective delivery of healthcare is enhanced through customer-based market segmentation by providing the focus and precision required to personalise healthcare. This is done through the identification of the latent relationships between attributes found in individual electronic medical records, customer surveys and/or demographic data. These relationships help define patient clusters or segments which hospitals, health systems, insurers and affiliated healthcare agencies can use to refine health marketing efforts.

By segmenting and targeting health promotions to specific market segments, efficiency is enhanced, health promotion costs reduced, and patient-centred care as well as personalised healthcare goals improved (Ginter, Duncan & Swayne, 2018; Alt & Iversen, 2017; Sahoo & Ghosh, 2016). Similar to traditional marketing, the primary bases upon which the healthcare market can be segmented include the geographic, demographic, psychological, psychographic or behavioural. Peculiar to healthcare marketing, the market may also be segmented based on type of illness, medical conditions, preferences and demand for certain specialised services. Health market segmentation is essential for effective and efficient distribution of healthcare and resources. Policymakers rely extensively on market segmentation to allocate health personnel, medications, equipment and devices, and funds to the various parts of the nations. Private practitioners, pharmaceutical retailers and insurance firms also utilise market segmentation to maximise efficiency and profitability. Essentially, it is right to conclude that market segmentation is a key ingredient in healthcare distribution.

9.2.3 Healthcare Supply Chain Management

The healthcare supply chain is an essential topic in the discussion of healthcare distribution. As competition in the healthcare industry intensifies (Hillestad & Berkowitz, 2018; Ho & Lee, 2017), firms are applying ways of cutting down costs and overheads wherever possible. One of the ways of being cost efficient in the healthcare industry is through effective supply chain management, considering that the supply chain is a significant driver of cost in the industry, accounting for about one-third of the operational costs for hospitals (Roark, 2005). Various stakeholders in the industry, particularly hospitals and regulators, are fervently interested in new sources of competitive advantage and cost reduction strategies through the supply chain. The government is also concerned about how the supply chain in the healthcare industry could improve operational efficiency, accessibility and quality of service. Compared to other industries, supply chain management is more intricate in healthcare because of the complexity of the nature and roles of players involved. Essentially, an effective management of the supply chain in the healthcare industry is necessary for meeting both service and cost objectives.

A model developed by Mustaffa and Potter (2009) comprises five levels in the supply chain, starting with the primary manufacturers and going through to the hospitals and other healthcare providers who deliver end-user services to patients. The primary manufacturers create the active ingredients and generic compositions of the medications. They are mass producers. The next level in the supply chain is the secondary producers. These producers convert the active ingredients manufactured by the primary manufacturers into useable medications such as tablets, capsules, infusions, among others. This is the birth of many brands of healthcare products. Altricher and Caillet (2004) estimate that there can be as many as 200 secondary producers arising from a single primary manufacturer at this level of the supply chain. Shah (2004) also observes that the secondary producers are not necessarily situated in the same geographical location as the primary manufacturers. In fact, due to increasing globalisation within the industry, secondary producers are geographically dispersed in order to supply local and regional markets. At the next stage of the healthcare supply chain model, a number of channels are involved to distribute the finished products to the market. The prominent intermediate member of this group is the wholesaler (Mustaffa & Potter, 2009), accounting for about 80 per cent of volume flows in the UK. It is also noted that the retailers and hospitals who require very high demand may order direct shipments from manufacturers without the use of wholesalers. Similarly, some hospitals form consolidations to leverage their bargaining power to enjoy economies of scale (Roark, 2005). For instance, Group Purchasing Organisations are common in the UK and other Western countries, while in most developing

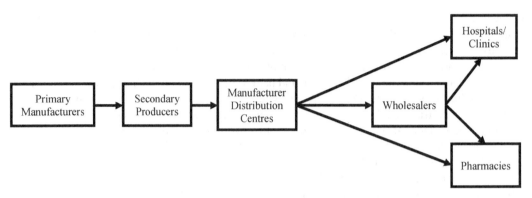

FIGURE 9.1   Healthcare Supply Chain Model. (Source: Adapted from Mustaffa & Potter (2009)).

countries the hospitals purchase large volumes through the government medical stores. This model is diagrammatically represented in Figure 9.1.

Another healthcare supply chain model was developed by Mathew, John and Kumar (2013). In this model, Mathew et al. stress the flow of products and information as well as the involvement of different stakeholders as requirements for achieving efficiency in the delivery of products, cost reduction and quality service delivery. They stipulate that there are three main groups in the healthcare supply chain, namely: Producers, Purchasers, and Providers. Ryan (2005) agrees that the interconnected relationships among these groups are further augmented by the involvement of government institutions, regulatory agencies and insurance companies. This network of relationships is presented in Figure 9.2. The distribution in the healthcare sector starts with manufacturers and ends with final consumers at the healthcare providers, with several intermediaries operating independently. However, some service providers may purchase directly from the manufacturers to enjoy cost savings and economies of scale. Schneller and Smeltzer (2006) observes that this inconsistency and fragmentation complicate the supply chain, making it expensive and inefficient. It is also noted by Mathew et al. (2013) that the level of independence and autonomy of the groups of

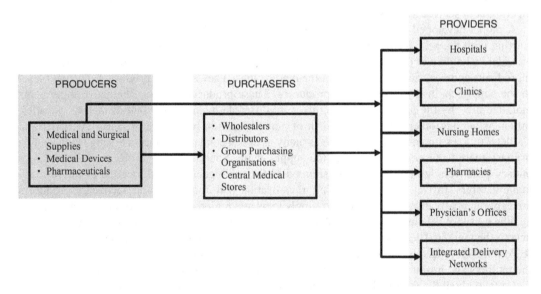

FIGURE 9.2   Healthcare Supply Chain Management. (Source: Adapted from Mathew, John & Kumar (2013)).

the supply chain leads to misaligned and conflicting goals inhibiting the cohesive operation of the supply chain as a single system. This further creates a barrier for adoption and application of the supply chain management practices.

A trend analysis of the distribution of healthcare products in sub-Saharan Africa reveals that in 1990, the public sector was responsible for 33.2 per cent (Bennett, Quick & Velásquez, 1997). However, it is noted that there were stark variations in the estimates for various countries. For example, Senegal had as low as 16 per cent of their healthcare distribution controlled by the public sector, while the Zimbabwean public sector controlled 50 per cent of its healthcare distribution (Foster, 1991). In the era of increased globalisation and intense competition in the healthcare industry, the estimates for distribution by the government have changed. McCabe (2009) identify that as much as 70–90 per cent of the healthcare distribution in Malawi is controlled by the government, whereas in Mali and Ghana, the public sector controls only 15 per cent and 10 per cent respectively. It is, however, noted that the estimates in terms of value may not reflect the true picture, as to a large extent the majority of companies in the private sector distribute the more expensive branded and innovator medicines, thereby inflating the private share of distribution.

In the public sector of the sub-Saharan African countries, the procurement and distribution of healthcare supplies are done through a central or parastatal entity. These entities are called "pharmacie d'approvisionnment" (or similar) in the French-speaking countries or central medical stores (CMS) in the anglophone countries (Dowling, 2011). In other countries, the health ministries execute this responsibility through their pharmacy departments. The central medical stores have different levels of autonomy in the various countries. For example, in Ghana and Malawi, the central medical stores are wholly owned and run by the government through the Ministry of Health (MoH), while the Centrale d'Achats des Médicaments Essentiels Génériques et des Consommables Médicaux in Burkina Faso enjoy a relatively larger degree of operational and financial independence.

The central medical stores play varying roles and responsibilities. Primary among these is to acquire, store and distribute medicines from a central store location to the regional or district level. In some other countries (e.g. Ghana, Malawi), there are regional medical stores (RMS), which store and distribute supplies to the health providers. There are ten regional medical stores in Ghana, eight in Senegal and three in Malawi. In a USAID report by Dowling (2011), it is observed that some regional medical stores can independently procure supplies. In the distribution of supplies, there is generally an order process, occurring consistently on a monthly or quarterly basis.

In Ghana, the distribution and management of healthcare supplies are operated in three levels. These comprise the Central Medical Store, regional medical stores, and service delivery points. As noted earlier, the Central Medical Store performs the role of procurement, receipt, storage and distribution of supplies through the Ministry of Health. The lower levels apply the "pull" and "demand" system to get supplies from the Central Medical Store.

The Central Medical Store acquires medicines and healthcare supplies from manufacturers, local private suppliers and through international competitive bidding. Central procurement for the Central Medical Store is done annually, and semi-annually for some items, by the Procurement Unit of the Ministry of Health. Deliveries to the Central Medical Store come in large quantities at a time. The standard procedure is for the regional medical stores and teaching hospitals to procure their supplies through the Central Medical Store and other local private suppliers. Staff of the regional medical stores usually travel to the Central Medical Store in Accra to pick up their deliveries. Quantification is done on all levels mainly based on consumption data versus stock on hand, while cash shortages limit procurement volumes leading to purchasing of smaller increments more frequently. The service delivery points in turn procure from the regional medical stores in their respective regions. Service delivery points do not have procurement capacity and use mainly shopping to buy the drugs that are not available at the nearest regional medical stores. Even though the Ministry of Health has a policy requiring all public health facilities to procure supplies from the public sector system, unless there are shortages, it is observed that significant purchases are

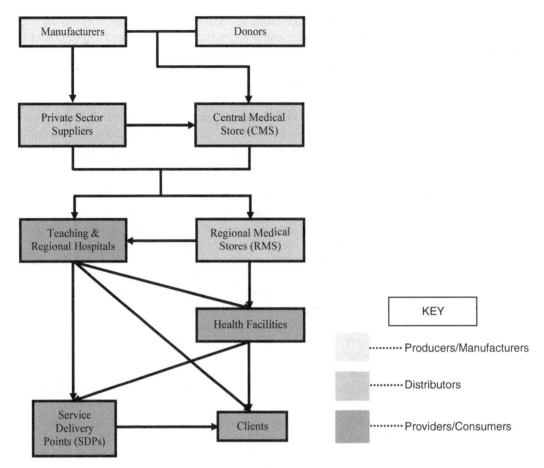

FIGURE 9.3   The Distribution Structure of Health Supplies in the Public Sector of Ghana.

made from the private sector at all levels. At the regional medical stores and service delivery points level, a high percentage of purchases (in several cases over 80 per cent) are made directly from the private sector rather than from the Central Medical Store or regional medical stores. This has been necessitated by the poor transportation system for distribution, especially for essential drugs. In addition, when drugs ordered have not been delivered, in many cases, it serves as justification to purchase from the private sector. Figure 9.3 presents the structure of the distribution system for Ghana's healthcare.

The current state of the supply chain management in the healthcare industry is a complex one, riddled with several complex issues resulting in inefficiencies and poor service delivery. Several of these issues are present in the distribution of products from the manufacturers to the providers and retailers. Common observed problems include the following:

- *Product Life Cycle* – It takes a very long time for patented active ingredients to be developed into useable products. Papageorgiou, Rotstein & Shah (2001) observe that once an active ingredient is created by a primary manufacturer, the requirements for licensing and clinical trials can take 8–10 years before the ingredients can be used to manufacture marketable/branded products. This lengthens the time it takes to churn out new products to the market. It slows the flow of products in the supply chain. Moreover, until a patent expires, the supply of a patented product is usually restricted and prices high. This also exacerbates the complications in the supply chain management in the healthcare industry. It must, however, be noted that new technology is shortening the life cycles of products (McKone-Sweet, Hamilton & Willis, 2005), further creating new pressures on the distribution channels (Mustaffa & Potter, 2009).

- *Lack of Supply Chain Education* – There is generally inadequate education about the supply chain, especially among the service providers (hospitals, pharmacies, etc.). Supply chain awareness and campaigns are limited among groups in the healthcare supply chain. According to Mathew et al. (2013), this lack of supply chain education renders managers of health institutions and service providers incapable of controlling the supply of medications.
- *Forecasting* – One of the pertinent issues crippling healthcare supply chain management is the non-existence of accurate consumer data, and lack of synchronisation among stakeholders in the supply chain management. The consequence of this lack of data is the difficulty in making accurate prediction for demand and supply. This creates an unbalanced distribution of products resulting in intermittent excess and shortages. This also affects the accessibility and delivery of quality healthcare.
- *Profit Margins* – Prices of pharmaceutical products are generally high, especially at the pharmacies and retail centres. This is also because the number of intermediaries in the distribution chain is greater. However, in spite of the high value per unit prices for pharmaceutical products, Lauer (2004) observes that in the wholesaler sector of the value chain operating margins are small. One significant reason for this is the pricing control and purchasing power held by hospitals, retailers and manufacturers. Group purchasing organisations are able to demand lower prices for the hospitals and retailers from the wholesalers. The wholesalers are usually on the "losing" end, with very low profit margins due to cut-throat competition. The lack of any pricing system and consistency in price regulations across the distribution chain are issues that need to be addressed.
- *Inadequate Collaboration, Regulation and Control* – This is a major challenge in developing countries, for there exists an ever-expanding private health sector but the government lacks the resources for effective control and regulation. There is also very little collaboration among the industry players. This increases redundancy and duplication, and supports an uneven urban/rural distribution of basic resources and services.
- *Financing* – Another common problem in the supply chain in developing countries is financing and flow of funds in the public sector supply chain. The system is designed to ensure cash flow from all levels. However, leakages, forecasting problems with partial oversupplies of drugs that cannot be sold, losses due to storage conditions, unforeseen financing costs, delayed payments from insurance schemes, etc., have depleted the funds at various levels, accumulating debt over time. To address the increasing indebtedness, some facilities raise sales prices over the officially permitted levels in order to stay afloat. Since the involved public entities cannot sue each other for the owing, the arrears accumulate.

9.3 STRUCTURE OF THE HEALTH DELIVERY SYSTEM IN GHANA

In Ghana, and most countries alike, the government plays a central role in the distribution and regulation of healthcare products and services. The role of government is to ensure there is a balance of both social and economic interests in the presence of intense competition among players. The highest governmental unit in charge of health is the Ministry of Health (MoH). The MoH is responsible for policy design. Implementation and management of the health service delivery is carried out by the Ghana Health Service, established in 2003. The MoH practises decentralisation in the delivery of health services in Ghana. The Ghana Health Service has under its umbrella the headquarters, Regional Health Management Teams (RHMTs), and District Health Management Teams (DNMTs).

The health service facilities in Ghana are divided into primary, secondary and tertiary health institutions. The primary institutions comprise all public sector providers (hospitals, health centres, and clinics) and individuals, including private, public or traditional. In the primary healthcare system at the district level, there is a subdivision of 4–6 sub-districts, with each district responsible for a geographical area of 20,000–30,000 people. The clinics and health centres, together with the communities, provide clinical, public health and maternity services through a recipe of clinic-based, regular outreach and public campaigns.

The secondary health institutions are the polyclinics, district hospitals and regional hospitals. The district hospitals are the first referral point in the healthcare system. They also provide outpatient and inpatient clinical services, maternity services and backup services for the health centres in their respective districts. The regional hospitals serve as the second referral point. They provide technical services for specialised clinical and diagnostic care in medicine, general surgery, paediatrics, obstetrics and gynaecology, among other expert services.

At the apex are the teaching hospitals. They are the tertiary institutions and serve as the final referral point in the health system in the country. In addition to the provision of health services, they also provide undergraduate and postgraduate training and research for health professionals.

9.3.1 PHARMACIES

Availability and accessibility of market data in the Ghanaian pharmaceutical market is weak. Unlike in larger markets that have market research companies with established data collection systems at critical points of sale, the data that are available in the literature are based on aggregate estimates from various market participants. In 2008, the total market was estimated at US$300 million at the retail price level. This estimate was predicted to reach US$1 billion by the end of 2018 at a growth rate of 6–8 per cent from 2008. The growth in the market is spurred by the development of the National Health Insurance Scheme established in 2003.

The health products manufactured and/or imported into the country are regulated and restricted by the Food and Drugs Authority and Ghana Standards Authority. The Ghana Pharmacy Council is a statutory regulatory body established by an Act of Parliament, The Pharmacy Act, 1994 (Act 489). The Pharmacy Council monitors and ensures timely processing of registration and renewal of applications, as well as re-certification of pharmacists and other pharmaceutical care providers. The pharmaceutical firms also have an association (Pharmaceutical Manufacturers Association of Ghana) comprising 32 members, with 11 of them as active manufacturers, of which seven can be considered major producers in the national context (Entrance Pharmaceuticals, Ayrton Drugs, Danadams Ltd, Ernest Chemists Ltd, LaGray Chemical Company, Kinapharma, and Phyto Riker).

As of July 2016, the pharmaceutical industry in Ghana employed some 2,050 registered pharmacists in the country, with about 400 of them working in the public sector. The local pharmaceutical sector is ranked as the tenth most attractive market in Africa and comes in at twenty-first place out of 31 countries analysed in the Middle East and Africa. However, the local manufacturers make up only 30 per cent with 70 per cent of the health products imported, mainly from Europe, India and China (Ghanaweb.com, 2018). Some of the most common multinationals competing for market share in the Ghana consumer healthcare market include, but are not limited to, GE Healthcare, Johnson & Johnson, Roche, Philips Healthcare, Omron, GlaxoSmithKline (GSK), Bayer Healthcare Pharmaceuticals, Norvatis. There are about 150 licensed or registered national or regional wholesalers of pharmaceutical products. Further, about 60 companies act as importers of pharmaceutical products and they sell these products to local distributors based on their own networks. The total number of businesses involved in active drug import and distribution is between 200 and 300.

The key composition of the pharmaceutical market is as follows:

- *Local Manufacturers* – Producers of finished pharmaceutical goods from raw materials (especially on a large industrial scale) within Ghana.

- *Importers of Pharmaceutical Products* – Importers for customs purposes – the party who makes (or on whose behalf an agent or broker makes) the import declaration, and who is liable for the payment of duties (if any) on the imported pharmaceutical goods. Normally, this party is named either as the consignee on shipping documents or as the buyer on the exporter's invoice.
- *Wholesalers* – Firms that buy large quantities of goods from various producers or vendors, warehouse them and resell to retailers.
- *Licensed Chemical Sellers* – Facilities registered by the Pharmacy Council to trade in Class B medicines in accordance with the Pharmacy Act 64.

9.3.2 INSURANCE COMPANIES

The biggest health insurer in Ghana is the National Health Insurance Scheme (NHIS), a social intervention programme introduced in 2003 by the government to provide financial access to quality healthcare for residents in Ghana. The NHIS is largely funded by: the National Health Insurance Levy (NHIL), which is a 2.5 per cent levy on goods and services collected under the Value Added Tax (VAT); 2.5 percentage points of Social Security and National Insurance Trust (SSNIT) contributions per month; the return on National Health Insurance Fund (NHIF) investments; and premiums paid by informal sector subscribers. NHIS subscribers fall into two broad groups, the informal and exempt groups. It is only the informal group that pays a premium. Members of the exempt group do not pay any premium. They include: formal sector employees and the self-employed who contribute to the Social Security and National Insurance Trust (SSNIT contributors); children (persons under 18 years of age); persons in need of ante-natal, delivery and post-natal healthcare services (pregnant women); persons classified by the Minister for Social Welfare as indigents; categories of differently abled persons determined by the Minister responsible for Social Welfare; persons with mental disorder; pensioners of the Social Security and National Insurance Trust (SSNIT pensioners); and persons above 70 years of age (the elderly).

Several categories of healthcare facilities have been credentialed by the National Health Insurance Authority (NHIA) to provide services to subscribers. These are:

- Community-based Health Planning and Services (CHPS)
- Maternity homes
- Health centres
- Clinics
- Polyclinics
- Primary hospitals (district hospitals, Christian Health Association of Ghana primary hospitals, quasi-government primary hospitals and private primary hospitals)
- Secondary hospitals
- Tertiary hospitals
- Pharmacies
- Licensed chemical shops
- Diagnostic centres

The health insurance industry is also supported by private companies providing health insurance products. As a free market, private companies are allowed to also compete with the National Health Insurance Authority (NHIA). However, the NHIA is mandated by National Health Insurance Act, 2012 (Act 852) to regulate Private Health Insurance Schemes (PHIS) in Ghana. In performing its regulatory functions, the NHIA registers, licenses and supervises the operations of PHIS in Ghana. There are two types of private health insurance schemes:

- Private Mutual Health Insurance Scheme (PMHIS)
- Private Commercial Health Insurance Scheme (PCHIS)

As at the first quarter of 2019, there were 14 licensed private commercial health insurance companies in Ghana.

The health insurance market is a catalyst for development and growth in the pharmaceutical market. An effective and efficient delivery of the insurance services ensures affordability, accessibility and availability of pharmaceutical products across all parts of the country. This facilitates growth in the distribution and supply of healthcare supplies.

9.4 CONCLUSIONS

Distribution in healthcare markets relies heavily on various channels rendering their service. The majority of firms operating in the healthcare sector depend on the service of their intermediaries to reach their target markets. A review of this nature is paramount to highlight what arrangements exist in the healthcare markets for key stakeholders. It is also important since there are several ways by which players in the healthcare sector can reach their target market. It calls for critical decision making with respect to the composition of the channel of distribution. Management in the healthcare sector has an important role in making decisions with regards to the products or service to be delivered. These decisions are important since they have an impact on healthcare distribution performance. Healthcare distribution decisions need to be given the attention they deserve. If properly constituted, the distribution system frees researchers and manufactures to focus on their jobs. It also provides ready markets for manufacturers and producers and, equally, delivers convenience to consumers of healthcare products and services. Manufacturers have alternative means of reaching their target market. They can either sell directly to consumers or through intermediaries in the healthcare distribution markets. This will reduce the risk associated with distribution without alternative modes.

9.4.1 MANAGERIAL IMPLICATIONS

In terms of managerial implications, distribution in healthcare markets is made up of professionals with varying backgrounds. It is imperative to motivate and train channel members to perform their various roles. For instance, inadequate training and low motivation may result in healthcare workers committing errors such as the administration of the wrong dosage of medicine to a patient by any member of the distribution channel such as a physician, pharmacy or a nurse. This can impact negatively and have serious consequences on healthcare distribution markets. This calls for due diligence in the healthcare distribution system in executing their duties.

Distribution in the healthcare markets is not static; it keeps on experiencing changes due to several reasons. These include new entrants into the markets, government policies and regulations on the healthcare sector based on global best practices, change in organisational structures and so on. Related to the dynamic nature of the distribution of healthcare markets is technology introduction in the distribution of healthcare products and services. This has facilitated the distribution of healthcare services and products.

In addition, distribution in the healthcare markets has experienced some level of channel integration. What this means is that it is feasible for one to visit a health facility and be able to access a number of services within the same facility without being referred to a different facility. However, there is more work to be done in this channel integration efforts. Instances of patients being asked to move from one facility to another just to undertake an X-ray or MRI scan are common knowledge. Largely, channel integration is low in the healthcare distribution sector. For instance, pharmaceutical firms focus on the production and distribution of medicines whereas hospitals and clinics concentrate on their main duties.

Moreover, distribution in healthcare markets is not free from conflicts and competition. Conflicts are unavoidable in every distribution relationship including healthcare markets. The most important issue is to how to handle this conflict. Competition is another feature of distribution in the healthcare markets. There are direct and indirect competitors in every level of distribution of healthcare products and services. The public and private healthcare institutions are competing for patients' attention. Usually, those who can afford it would patronise the private healthcare institution since they charge high prices. It is important to note that ethical and legal considerations should guide every aspect of the distribution of healthcare products and services. But to the contrary, healthcare markets are normally confronted with legal and ethical challenges that must be addressed, particularly in the testing and distributing of newly developed medicines.

9.4.2 RECOMMENDATIONS FOR AFRICA

Particularly for developing economies and African markets, the following recommendations will aid in the efficient and effective distribution of health services to ensure adequacy, availability and accessibility of quality healthcare.

- Governments of developing nations should encourage private investment in healthcare facilities as existing health infrastructures are highly inadequate, leading to excessive pressure on and inaccessibility of health services and products, especially in rural areas. This can be done by relieving the private investor of tax burdens for a period, and relaxing investment regulations to attract foreign direct investments into the health sector.
- The above must also be complemented with the necessary regulations to ensure fair and equitable distribution of health products and services. This is because without such regulations and control the private health sector would be largely driven by profitability, thereby siting health centres and products only in selected profitable locations at the neglect of poorer communities. This is a necessity as access to quality healthcare is a universal right for all, considering also that majority of people who need critical healthcare may reside in poorer and rural areas of the country.
- Also, tax policies and incentives should be favourable to local manufacturers of healthcare products to boost the affordability and accessibility of essential medicines and health products. Similarly, the government should foster development in private manufacturers and distributors of healthcare products to ensure the continual provision of quality healthcare at affordable prices.
- Lastly, it is important to control the menace of corruption in the administration and distribution of health products and services. All too often, the distribution and management of healthcare services and products in some developing countries is marred with corruption, where essential medications are diverted to certain areas instead of where they are intended for. Failure to address these corrupt practices will result in poor distribution of quality healthcare.

REFERENCES

Alt, J., & Iversen, T. (2017). Inequality, labor market segmentation, and preferences for redistribution. *American Journal of Political Science, 61*(1), 21–36.

Altricher, F., & Caillet, T. (2004). SCM in a pharmaceutical company. In H. Stadtler & C. Kilger (Eds), *Supply chain management and advanced planning: Concepts, models, software and case studies* (pp. 355–370). New York, NY: Springer-Verlag.

Bennett, S., Quick, J. D., & Velásquez, G. (1997). *Public-private roles in the pharmaceutical sector: Implications for equitable access and rational drug use*. Health Economics and Drugs Series No. 5. Geneva: World Health Organization.

Bossert, T. J., & Mitchell, A. D. (2011). Health sector decentralization and local decision-making: Decision space, institutional capacities and accountability in Pakistan. *Social Science & Medicine, 72*(1), 39–48.

Byrkjeflot, H., & Neby, S. (2008). The end of the decentralised model of healthcare governance? Comparing developments in the Scandinavian hospital sectors. *Journal of Health Organization and Management, 22*(4), 331–349.

Casalino, L. P., Devers, K. J., Lake, T. K., Reed, M., & Stoddard, J. J. (2003). Benefits of and barriers to large medical group practice in the United States. *Archives of Internal Medicine, 163*(16), 1958–1964.

Dowling, P. (2011). *Healthcare supply chains in developing countries: Situational analysis*. Arlington, VA: USAID| DELIVER PROJECT.

Foster, S. D. (1991). Pricing, distribution, and use of antimalarial drugs. *Bulletin of the World Health Organization, 69*(3), 349–363.

Ghanaweb.com. (2018). Drugs industry hits US$1bn in value, 70% imported. Retrieved June 10, 2019, from www. ghanaweb.com/GhanaHomePage/business/Drugs-industry-hits-US-1bn-in-value-70-imported-665950.

Ginter, P. M., Duncan, W. J., & Swayne, L. E. (2018). *The strategic management of health care organizations*. John Wiley & Sons.

Hillestad, S. G., & Berkowitz, E. N. (2018). *Health care market strategy*. Jones & Bartlett Learning.

Ho, K., & Lee, R. S. (2017). Insurer competition in health care markets. *Econometrica, 85*(2), 379–417.

Kotler, P. and Keller, K. L. (2016), *Marketing management* (15th ed.). Upper Saddle River, NJ: Pearson Prentice Hall.

Lauer, T. W. (2004). The risk of e-voting. *Electronic Journal of E-government, 2*(3), 177–186.

Magnussen, J., Hagen, T. P., & Kaarboe, O. M. (2007). Centralized or decentralized? A case study of Norwegian hospital reform. *Social Science & Medicine, 64*(10), 2129–2137.

Mathew, J., John, J., & Kumar, S. (2013, May). New trends in healthcare supply chain. In *International Annual Conference, Production and Operations Management Society, Denver, Colorado*.

McCabe, A. (2009). Private sector pharmaceutical supply and distribution chains: Ghana, Malawi and Mali. Retrieved from http://apps.who.int/medicinedocs/documents/s17508en/s17508en.pdf.

McKone-Sweet, K. E., Hamilton, P., & Willis, S. B. (2005). The ailing healthcare supply chain: A prescription for change. *Journal of Supply Chain Management, 41*(1), 4–17.

Mosca, I. (2006). Is decentralization the real solution? A three country study. *Health Policy, 77*(1): 113–120.

Mustaffa, N. H., & Potter, A. (2009). Healthcare supply chain management in Malaysia: A case study. *Supply Chain Management: An International Journal, 14*(3), 234–243.

Papageorgiou, L. G., Rotstein, G. E., & Shah, N. (2001). Strategic supply chain optimization for the pharmaceutical industries. *Industrial & Engineering Chemistry Research, 40*(1), 275–286.

Peckham, S., Exworthy, M., Greener, I., & Powell, M. (2005). Decentralizing health services: More accountability or just more central control? *Public Money & Management, 25*(4), 221–228. doi:10.1080/09540 962.2005.10600097.

Roark, D. C. (2005). Managing the healthcare supply chain. *Nursing Management, 36*(2), 36–40.

Robinson, J. C., & Casalino, L. P. (1996). Vertical integration and organizational networks in health care. *Health Affairs, 15*(1), 7–22.

Ryan, K. Jennifer. (2005). *Systems engineering: Opportunities for health care – Building a better delivery system: A new engineering/health care partnership*. National Academy Press

Sahoo, D., & Ghosh, T. (2016). Healthscape role towards customer satisfaction in private healthcare. *International Journal of Health Care Quality Assurance, 29*(6), 600–613.

Schneller, E. S., & Smeltzer, L. R. (2006). *Strategic management of the health care supply chain*. Jossey-Bass.

Shah, N. (2004). Pharmaceutical supply chains: Key issues and strategies for optimisation. *Computers & Chemical Engineering, 28*(6–7), 929–941.

Swenson, E. R., Bastian, N. D., & Nembhard, H. B. (2016). Data analytics in health promotion: Health market segmentation and classification of total joint replacement surgery patients. *Expert Systems with Applications, 60*, 118–129.

Yoong, J., Park, E. R., Greer, J. A., Jackson, V. A., Gallagher, E. R., Pirl, W. F., … & Temel, J. S. (2013). Early palliative care in advanced lung cancer: A qualitative study. *JAMA Internal Medicine, 173*(4), 283–290.

10 Integrated Marketing Communications in the Healthcare Sector

Insights from sub-Saharan Africa

Golda Anambane and Robert Ebo Hinson

10.1 INTRODUCTION

Healthcare is one of the basic needs or wants of humanity as indicated in Article 25 of the United Nations' Universal Declaration of Human Rights (United Nations, 2013). The presence of healthcare facilities improves not only access to medications and quality care, but also economic opportunities in nations since people will be able to be active in the workforce because they have sound health (Eggoh, Houeninvo, & Sossou, 2015; Mahmud & Parkhurst, 2007; Stenberg et al., 2017). Consequently, the healthcare sector is among the most rapidly growing segments in the world economy (World Health Organization, 2002). A report by Deloitte (2017) estimates the growth rates of the health sector across different regions of the world by the year 2020: Asia and Australasia, 5 per cent; North America, 4.3 per cent; Middle East and Africa, 4.2 per cent; Western Europe, 4 per cent; and Latin America, 2.4 per cent. These growth rates presuppose that that competition within the industry will increase, albeit the industry in most countries is already competitive. Chapman (2014) maintains that the increasing competition in the healthcare industry across nations can be attributed to liberalization policies that allow private individuals to own and operate private hospitals (commercialization of the health sector). The healthcare delivery sector in Ghana, for instance, has witnessed commercialization and is one of the most competitive sectors, as private and public service providers are competing for same customers (Atinga, Abekah-Nkrumah, & Domfeh, 2011). The dramatic changes in the healthcare industry, leading to keener competition in the health sector, are compelling healthcare organizations to seek new strategies for survival and growth (Zarei, Daneshkohan, Pouragha, Marzban, & Arab, 2015); one of these strategies is effective integrated marketing communications (IMC).

The concept of IMC reflects a process that assimilates and aligns strategic and tactical marketing communication decisions (Luxton, Reid, & Mavondo, 2015). It is a relevant theory that goes beyond the simple integration, coordination, and unification of communication instruments to cover the strategic positioning, relationship building, and managerial, organizational, and human resource issues (Andrews & Shimp, 2017; Finne & Grönroos, 2009; Kliatchko, 2008). The recognition for discussions on IMC in research can be attributed to the concept's potential to offer competitive advantage, influence business performance, and ensure consistent and effective communication, as well as enhance brand equity (Luxton et al., 2015; Madhavaram, Badrinarayanan, & McDonald, 2005). Even though Bruhn and Schnebelen (2017) highlight that research on IMC reached its peak several years ago and has declined in recent times, Kitchen and Burgmann (2010) assert that academic research on the subject of IMC has been inadequate. It is therefore not surprising that academic discourse that explores IMC in the context of healthcare is scant. Although optimizing marketing mixes (of which marketing communications is one) has been of interest in marketing literature, Haughton et al. (2015) note that little published research on that subject has been devoted to the healthcare industry. Additionally, the few extant pieces of research that focus on integrated marketing communications have largely been conducted in the Western world, raising the need for research to be conducted on the phenomenon within the African context and therefore sub-Saharan Africa (SSA).

The healthcare sector is unique amongst business sectors in the nature of the services rendered (Osei-Frimpong, 2016). As a service, healthcare is delicate and there is no room for service failure as it could lead to death and other eventualities which cannot be reversed or recovered. As such, consumers will often want to patronize healthcare delivery firms that they are sure of, hence the relevance of marketing communications in the sector. The practice of marketing communications is being propagated in the healthcare industry to reach outward to prospective customers in hopes of gaining patronage (Fortenberry & McGoldrick, 2016). In most jurisdictions, the healthcare sector consists of pharmaceutical firms, medical insurance companies, and companies that provide or facilitate the provision of healthcare to patients. This chapter concentrates on organizations that provide healthcare: hospitals. These entities are of interest to the chapter because of the concerns about direct-to-consumer (DTC) marketing communications programs within the healthcare sector of several nations. Liang and Mackey (2011) reveal that in the Western world, DTC marketing communications programs are known to be legal in the USA and New Zealand only. However, in Ghana and other African nations, marketing communications in the healthcare sector are allowed to be undertaken by some hospitals, especially the private ones, albeit with some restrictions and limitations. This chapter therefore explores how hospitals in sub-Saharan Africa make use of IMC in view of the communication mix proposed by Armstrong, Adam, Denize, and Kotler (2008): advertising, public relations, sales promotion, personal selling, and direct marketing. The chapter proceeds to discuss the use of IMC in the health sector under various relevant headings.

10.2 THE COMMUNICATION PROCESS MODEL IN HEALTHCARE SERVICE DELIVERY

The complications of human communication present an extremely difficult challenge to the study of marketing communications (Barnlund, 2017), especially in the service sector. Communication has been defined as the transfer of information, ideas, emotions, or attitudes from an individual or a group to another, mainly using symbols (Theodorson & Theodorson, 1969). Ineffective communication in healthcare leads to negatives such as misdiagnosis, delayed treatment, errors in medication, and the like (Foronda, MacWilliams, & McArthur, 2016). Over the years, scholars have developed models to explain the concept of communication or how communication occurs. The basic communication models have indicated that communication begins with the sender (organization) conceiving an idea it wants to send to a target audience. The idea conceived by the sender or organization is encoded using words, symbols, colours, and other elements to create a message. The created message is then transmitted to the receiver (customer) via a means (medium). The mode of transmission could be radio, television, newspaper, billboard, internet, among others. The receiver, upon getting the message sent by the sender through a transmission mode, then decodes it to give meaning to the message. After the message is understood by the receiver, feedback is expected by the sender. In the context of marketing communications, feedback could be the purchase of a product or the performance of a particular action. The communication process can, however, be distorted by noise. "Noise" represents anything that has the potential of interrupting the successful receipt and understanding of the message sent. In marketing communications, noise could be other messages by competing firms. The basic communication model is presented in Figure 10.1.

However, there has not been much done with respect to the design of a communication model that fits the healthcare sector since the sector has been identified as being a unique service sector (Chandra, Finkelstein, Sacarny, & Syverson, 2016). Hence, scholars have largely relied on the general communication model in studies relating to health. Gheorghe (2012) indicates that the

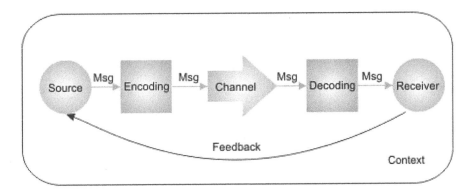

FIGURE 10.1   The Basic Communication Model.

communication process in the healthcare context emanates from the source through to the receiver who then gives feedback, which echoes the basic communication model. According to Gheorghe (2012), the source of the message (hospital) encodes the message whilst the receiver (consumer/patient) decodes the message. The author acknowledges that some marketing communications within the healthcare sector are unplanned; hence, the marketing communications of a healthcare facility could be planned and unplanned. Planned messages result from planned marketing communication campaigns and are usually sent through controlled channels such as printed advertising. On the other hand, the unplanned messages result from the experiences consumers have with health organizations, after which they engage in positive or negative word of mouth. Unplanned messages play the role of indirect feedback and cannot be controlled by the healthcare institutions. The integrated model of the communication process in the healthcare sector as proposed by Gheorghe (2012) is depicted in Figure 10.2.

After an organization understands the communication process, the next step is to integrate the communication marketing mix components in an IMC strategy (Purcarea, Gheorghe, & Gheorghe, 2015). An understanding of the communication process within the healthcare sector will enable hospitals to deliver marketing messages to the right audience using the appropriate communication tools.

10.3 CHALLENGES TO EFFECTIVE COMMUNICATION IN THE HEALTHCARE SECTOR IN AFRICA

Marketing communications are imperative in the healthcare sector. They inform consumers about where to patronize desired services, persuade them to buy, as well as remind them about the existence of the health service. As such, several health facilities in SSA are beginning to realize their relevance. However, there are times when communication does not achieve its intended purpose. In the SSA context, some factors act as barriers to effective communication. These include government regulations/code of ethics, culture, and poor health literacy.

To begin with, the healthcare sector is characterized by government regulations and a code of ethics for health practitioners that have largely limited advertising in the healthcare sector. Countries such as Ghana, Nigeria, and Uganda have these rules and regulations making it difficult, if not impossible, for hospitals to advertise their services intensively. Also, the language barrier is the bane of effective marketing communications in the healthcare sector of most SSA countries. The increasing diversity in countries across SSA makes healthcare providers come into contact with consumers with different languages. However, marketing communications by healthcare facilities are generally often written using national languages like English and French, which leaves people who do not understand these languages in the dark. Additionally, culture and

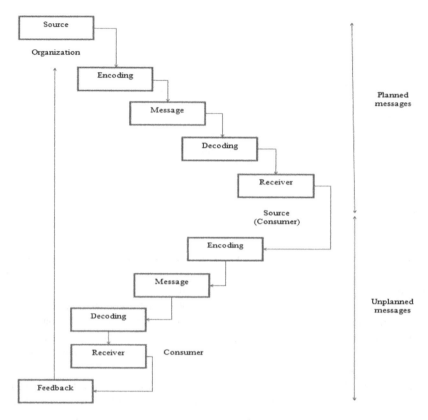

FIGURE 10.2 The Integrated Model of the Communication Process in the Healthcare Sector. (Source: Adapted from Gheorghe (2012)).

superstition are critical issues affecting effective healthcare sector communications. The majority of persons in SSA perceive that healthcare facilities are to be patronized when one is unwell. As a result, hospitals or healthcare have been successfully linked to misfortunes. This perception makes it difficult for them to effectively advertise, engage in personal selling, and the like. Such acts make consumers feel they are being wished evil. This can be likened to the criticism coffin manufacturers in recent times have received in Ghana especially, regarding the morality of their business. Lastly, the healthcare sector is unique and technical. Thus, consumers need to understand some terminology to understand the marketing communications. People with poor literacy skills especially have difficulty understanding most healthcare information. There is a vast disparity in how people receive and understand health information (Batterham, Hawkins, Collins, Buchbinder, & Osborne, 2016). Low health literacy is not only applicable to consumers who have low levels of education but even affects consumers who are literate. A recognition and understanding of the barriers to effective communication in the healthcare sector is instrumental to effective marketing communications.

10.4 INTRODUCING THE INTEGRATED COMMUNICATIONS MIX

Communications are essential for marketing professionals and organizations. This is because in the absence of effective marketing communications the consumer is unaware of the products and services they need to satisfy a need or a want (Kalla, 2016). Marketing communications represent the interaction between a firm and its customers which occurs in the pre-selling, selling, consuming, and post-consuming stages of a business transaction (Kotler, 2003). Kotler and Keller (2008) define marketing communications as "the means by which firms attempt to inform, persuade and remind their customers (directly and indirectly) of products and brands they sell". The marketing communication mix, otherwise known as promotional mix, refers to the combination of tools used to convincingly communicate customer value to customers and build relationships with customers (De Pelsmacker, Geuens, & van den Bergh, 2003; Ozturk, Nusair, Okumus, & Hua, 2016). According to Wirtz and Lovelock (2016), the marketing communication mix is a combination of elements like personal selling, advertising, public relations, sales promotions, and direct marketing (as presented in Figure 10.3) that companies use to reach their target markets during marketing programs. Todorova (2015) observes that successful marketing communications are dependent on the mixture of advertising, sales promotion, direct marketing, and public relations that allows firms to communicate effectively with a target audience.

The service sector has gained much attention in recent times. This could be attributed to the sector's significant contributions to economies (Wirtz, Tuzovic, & Ehret, 2015). The marketing communications mix for services is not different from the traditional marketing communications espoused by scholars: advertising, sales promotion, direct marketing, personal selling, and public relations. Hinson and Abor (2005) maintain that the communication mix for services covers every communications tool available to the organization which is relevant to marketing. The various elements of the marketing communications mix play different roles in overall marketing programs for stimulation of interest (Keller, 2001). For instance, whereas advertising seeks to create awareness, sales promotion seeks to stimulate sales. Additionally, marketing communications go beyond advertising, sales promotion, and so on, to cover a firm's packaging, product's styling, price, and the salesperson's mannerism and appearance (Rundh, 2016; Underwood, Klein, & Burke, 2001). All these communicate an idea to the consumer. In the healthcare sector, all these variables or activities together either strengthen or weaken a customer's perception of the healthcare provider. Hence, the marketing communications mix elements must be integrated to deliver a consistent message to achieve strategic positioning in the healthcare sector.

Events in the contemporary marketplace have led to changes in the practice of marketing communications (Šerić, Gil-Saura, & Ruiz-Molina, 2014). Kitchen, Brignell, and Jones (2004) highlight that a single marketing communication tool hardly achieves marketing communications purposes considering the changing media preferences of consumers. The challenges presented by new media, changing media patterns, advancement in information communication technology, and divided consumer attention call for the integration of marketing communication tools (Batra & Keller, 2016). IMC is a more efficient and sophisticated approach to marketing communications

FIGURE 10.3   The Marketing Communication Mix Elements. (Source: Adapted from Kotler & Keller (2008)).

as it responds rapidly to such changing market needs or conditions as are being witnessed in the healthcare sector of most economies (Kim, Han, & Schultz, 2004).

10.5 ADVERTISING

The word "advertising" emanates from the French word "réclame", which means to "evoke" as Todorova (2015) observes. According to Kotler and Keller (2012, p. 56), advertising represents any paid form of non-personal communication (presentation and promotion of ideas, goods, or services) by an acknowledged sponsor. Seldon, Jewell, & O'Brien (2000) describes advertising as any non-personal form of communication regarding a firm, product, or idea, that is paid for by an exact sponsor. Advertising portrays a one-way communication from a firm to its target audience. It uses a variety of media such as the print media (newspapers), electronic media (radio), outdoor displays (billboards), transportation, direct mail, advertising specialties or novelties (T-Shirts), catalogues, and directories and films. In the healthcare sector, advertising occurs when a hospital sends a communication to its target audience via radio, televisions, newspapers, among others. Advertising promotes a health facility's image, reputation, or ideas and has the capacity to influence the sale of services and stimulate demand for specialist care. Although advertising fulfils multiple functions, its key functions are to inform, persuade, remind, and create the perception of extra usefulness to consumers (Todorova, 2015).

In 1994, Andaleeb predicted that the act of advertising will become a progressively more important and common marketing tool in the healthcare industry, considering changes in the regulatory environment against advertising in several jurisdictions. For instance, the code of ethics of the American Medical Association (AMA) embedded a ban on advertising (Leibenluft & Pollard, 1981). However, after the Supreme Court made it unconstitutional for lawyers to be prohibited from advertising, in a case known as "Bates and O'Steen v. The State of Arizona", the AMA then reviewed its guidelines and made advertising more acceptable in the healthcare sector (Saad Andaleeb, 1994). However, in most SSA countries such as Ghana, Nigeria, and Uganda, the act of advertising is still problematic in the healthcare sector due to government regulations and policies as well as guidelines issued by regulatory bodies. Consequently, some patients in most SSA countries are still clueless about where to get certain medical services due to regulations and policies which do not allow medical practitioners and facilities to intensively advertise their competences (Makinde, Brown, & Olaleye, 2014).

In the Ghanaian context, for instance, there are regulations regarding advertising by healthcare organizations in Ghana as indicated in Section 114 of the Public Health Act 2012 (Act 851). The Act states that

> the advertisement of a drug, a herbal medical product, cosmetic, medical device or household chemical substance to the general public as a treatment, preventive or cure for a disease, or an abnormal physical state, is prohibited unless it has been approved by the Ghana Medical Association.

Also, hospitals under the Ghana Health Service, per the code of ethics of the service, are not permitted to engage in mass advertising or advertising through the mass media. In the light of these restrictions, adverting is not alien in the sector. Within the healthcare sector in Ghana, advertising is minimally used due to the restrictions stated in the preceding paragraph. Owing to legal restrictions within the sector, hospitals are not visibly seen in the advertising space or heavily engaged in advertising. Since hospitals under the Ghana Health Service are prohibited from advertising to the mass market, only a few specialist private hospitals are seen in the advertising space. Whereas some of these of these specialist hospitals advertise through mass media such as television (which gives them the opportunity to showcase the equipment they have), others indirectly advertise on radio or television stations where they have health professionals host health related programs. During most of these health related programs, members of the public are allowed to phone in to ask health related questions. This gives these hospitals the platform to inform, persuade and remind consumers about the offers they present. For instance, Nyaho Medical Centre (a health facility located in the Capital of Ghana – Accra), indirectly advertises to the public by hosting a health programme on preventive health on Citi FM (one of Ghana's vibrant and prestigious radio stations) every Thursday at 3:20 p.m. (Nyaho Clinic, n.d.). Aside advertising in the media, hospitals in Ghana make good use of signage as an advertising tool. Most often, these hospital signs are found around the business premises. It creates awareness of not only the existence of the hospitals but services on offer as well as times of operation. The use of displays such as billboards as advertising tools is largely absent in hospital advertising.

In Uganda, healthcare advertising is not so different from the Ghanaian situation but the situation is more extreme. Healthcare practitioners and facilities in Uganda are prohibited from engaging in advertising or campaigning for patients in any form in line with the code of ethics of The Uganda Medical and Dental Practitioners Council (Section 12). At the extreme, health practitioners in Uganda are prohibited from publicizing names and registered professional category on letterheads, business cards, and other means for informational purposes.

10.6 PUBLIC RELATIONS

The purpose of public relations is to develop, maintain, protect, and improve an organization's or an individual's image presented to the public or target audience (Juska, 2018). Tomic, Lasic, and Tomic (2010, p. 25) indicate that public relations in healthcare is the "communication process of health institutions (hospitals, primary healthcare centres, etc.) with its internal and external public, in order to achieve mutual respect, understanding and achieving mutual interests." Public relations can be grouped into media relations, government relations, community relations, and employee relations. Percy (2008) maintains that public relations can contribute to a firm achieving its overall brand communication goals via activities such as media relations, sponsorships, corporate communication, events, and publicity. Public relations has been traditionally described as a one-way communication. Hence, Grunig and Grunig (1991) opine that marketing communications via other communication tools will not achieve the same results as public relations in the healthcare sector. However, in contemporary times, the theory is that public relations is a two-way communication (Grunig & Grunig, 1989; Kent & Taylor, 2002). Additionally, competitive pressures within the health sector have led several healthcare organizations to practise public relations (Grunig & Grunig, 1991). Berkowitz (2008) documents that the practice and discipline of public relations has evolved in the healthcare sector over the years. Historically, public relations within healthcare organizations occurred as a one-way communication that was often reactive in nature: managing crises as they occurred in the organization. However, recent theoretical development within the discipline suggests that public relations goes beyond managing crisis to relationship building and ongoing dialogue with key publics (Kim, 2016; Wilcox, 2006). This shift can be attributed to the evolution on the internet, particularly blogging and podcasting. Blogging and podcasting as public relations tools have, however, been underutilized in the healthcare sector though they have significant potential for marketing communications. Newsom, Turk, and Kruckeberg (2000, p. 399) state that "it is virtually impossible to practice effective public relations today without using the internet". This is explained by the fact that consumers of healthcare services are increasingly seeking for more information about healthcare facilities from the web.

Further, public relations has always been a key tool of hospitals' marketing communications over the years. Before marketing became a major functional area of healthcare management, hospitals only relied on public relations as a tool for delivering messages to audiences and gaining a position in the market. The relevance of public relations in the healthcare sector still remains in contemporary times even in the face of the ever more cluttered message-overloaded healthcare marketplace (Berkowitz, 2008). Kehinde and Igbozuruike (2016) find a positive relationship between good public relations practices and healthcare management performance of hospitals in Nigeria.

Nonetheless, public relations is not new in the Ghanaian healthcare sector. It has been a function by which hospitals get their stories out to the public. Most hospitals in Ghana have public relations officers and have so far used them for a one-way flow of information to stakeholders: government agencies, the community at large, foundations, or the community in which the healthcare organization operates. The common public relations Ghanaian hospitals engage in is more of a reactive activity, in which the hospitals engage in public relations to control crisis rather than build relationships. For example, the year 2018 witnessed negative reportage about the inability of most hospitals in Ghana to provide bedding facilities to patients, which even led to the death of a 70-year-old man. To mitigate the effects of these negative reports on the image of Korle-Bu Teaching Hospital, a story was released by the hospital informing the Ghanaian public that the teaching hospital will temporarily desist from admitting patients who are transferred from other health facilities. They added that the move is part of actions taken to decongest the facility after overcapacity of patients has made it difficult for doctors to work at the surgical and medical emergency unit (Zurek, 2018). Also, in November 2018, a man alleged via Facebook that upon going through laboratory tests at a private lab, the blood he received from the Okonfo Anokye Teaching Hospital (KATH) was HIV and syphilis contaminated. KATH released a public relations item to debunk such claims and informed the public that a five member committee had been set up to investigate the issue.

Furthermore, the Nigerian healthcare sector has witnessed the use of public relations over the years. Public relations has mainly been used by hospitals to tackle issues like fistula and polio. However, the public relations on fistula has mainly been used by specialist hospitals mostly set up by expatriates who are keen on alleviating the problem with little effort by local health facilities. In the year 2003, efforts to eradicate polio in Nigeria through vaccinations faced resistance, especially in Northern Nigeria. This occurred because of the strong perception that the program was rather aimed at reducing population through birth control. Eventually, the leadership of Nigeria's Kano, Kaduna, and Zamfara states vehemently opposed the administering of the polio vaccine to the children. To address this issue, public relations activities were carried out by health institutions and organizations, and other stakeholders, to enlighten the public through radio, television, and door to door campaigns. The role of the Aminu Kano teaching hospital in achieving the acceptance of polio vaccinations cannot be overlooked.

It is observed that although literature has stated that the practice of public relations has moved from being a one-way communication to a relational communication, it is still practised in several healthcare sectors in SSA as a one-way communication where hospitals use it for crisis management. Such practices are likely to cause public distrust in health facilities. The argument is that consumers will perceive the public relations item as self-seeking and not for the good of the public.

10.7 SALES PROMOTION

Sales promotion is a marketing communications tool that motivates potential buyers to buy a product or more of it (Kotler & Keller, 2012). In sales promotions, the offers that act as motivators are financial incentives or extra rewards, available only within a limited period of time. Sales promotions often last for a clear stipulated period: a few hours, days, or weeks. Popular sales promotions strategies used include coupons, free samples, cash back, sweepstakes, contests, free gifts, low interest rates, bonus rewards, new experiences, and owner loyalty programs. The most relevant part of a sales promotion is its measurability. The impact of the sales promotion is often realized through consumers' response to a promotional offer. This can be ascertained by examining the number of sweepstakes entries, coupons redeemed, points obtained, among others (Juska, 2018). In the services industries, one marketing strategy that enhances customer loyalty is sales promotions (Yeboah-Asiamah, Quaye & Nimako, 2016). This presupposes that sales promotions can be applied in the healthcare sector to enhance patient/consumer loyalty.

The practice of sales promotion in the healthcare sector has not been fairly explored in academic discourse and even in practice. Over the years, hospitals in SSA have relied on sales promotion to a limited extent as a stimulant of sales. This could be because of the nature of the services rendered by these hospitals. Within the SSA context, a visit to the hospital is not a desirable activity as the widely held perception is that people patronize hospitals when ill. Therefore, one cannot buy the services of a hospital more often just because there are ongoing sales promotions. However, considering the increasing commercialization of the health sector in modern times and the increasing health concerns and propagation of advice for regular hospital check-ups, sales promotions can be relied on for increasing sales. Some hospitals, especially the private hospitals, are innovatively using sales promotions. For instance, ProVita Specialist Hospital (a fertility specialist hospital located at Tema, Ghana) offers a free hospital consultation to consumers (ProVita Specialist Hospital, n.d.). Aside the ability of this free consultation to induce customer repurchases for the firm, it has the tendency of triggering positive word of mouth from consumers, which contributes to the marketing communications efforts of the hospital.

10.8 DIRECT MARKETING AND DIGITAL COMMUNICATIONS

The digital age has modified consumers' expectations of branded communications (Chaffey & Ellis-Chadwick, 2019; Killian & McManus, 2015). The concept of direct and digital marketing is rooted in direct mail activities and is beneficial to both organizations and consumers (Armstrong, Adam, & Denize, 2014). Direct and digital marketing makes it possible for organizations to break the barriers of distance to reach target audiences across regions. These marketing communication tools are also interactive and immediate (Armstrong et al., 2014). According to Groucutt, Leadley, and Forsyth (2004), one advantage of direct marketing is the ability to target the right people. Direct marketing is successful when the organization or marketer is able to reach the right target audience, at the right time, and with the right message. A variety of channels are used in direct marketing and these include direct mail, telemarketing, e-mail marketing, social media marketing, website marketing, and mobile marketing (Amirkhanpour, Vrontis, & Thrassou, 2014).

Dodson, Dotson, and Cussimanio (1990) emphasize that direct marketing offers a new marketing arena for most hospitals. To reiterate, Sanchez (2000) indicates that hospital website marketing (an aspect of direct marketing) witnessed explosive growth towards the end of the 1990s. Several hospitals have acknowledged the relevance of direct/digital marketing. Health facilities and practitioners in SSA have extended face-to-face selling towards direct marketing via phone, mail, and computer. The utilization of the internet for marketing communications in the healthcare sector is growing steadily. Irrespective of this, the use of asynchronous communication tools for healthcare regions remains undeveloped (Newhouse, Lupiáñez-Villanueva, Codagnone, & Atherton, 2015), causing delays in responses. Health facilities in the SSA region are beginning to adopt directing marketing to mitigate the effects of the inability to advertise effectively in the sector. Hospitals in countries such as Ghana, Kenya, Nigeria, Uganda, Togo, among others, have internet presence through their websites.

In the Ghanaian context, the majority of hospitals are actively using direct marketing. The most dominant of these direct marketing is website marketing. A search on the internet reveals that most hospitals in Ghana have websites via which they communicate with their target audience as well as receive feedback from customers. Search engine optimization is also used by most of these hospitals to make them more visible on the internet. Emphasizing the importance of direct marketing in the healthcare sector, the Trust Hospital in Ghana expressly states:

When we started, Information and Communications Technology (ICT) was not an added value to any healthcare facility in Ghana. However, as we progressed, the age of ICT has caught up with us and it has become necessary to evolve with the times. In today's ICT world, the website of an organisation does not only communicate or give information to clients but also afford clients the opportunity to interact with us and give feedback as far as our services is concerned.

(The Trust Hospital, n.d.)

The dominance of website marketing in the healthcare sector in SSA is not enough in terms of digital marketing, considering the high illiteracy rates and poverty in the sub-sector. A person's level of education determines his/her ability to use a hospital's website when seeking information. A focus on website marketing translates to a focus on the middle class and literate. It can therefore be deduced that higher rates of illiteracy and poverty are the bane of effective digital marketing in the healthcare sector in SSA. However, hospitals can still use digital marketing to reach the under-privileged (uneducated). Hospitals and network companies can work together to provide certain healthcare information in the local dialects of the people. With this, through telemarketing, the illiterate can also benefit from the marketing communications of hospitals.

10.9 PERSONAL SELLING

Belch and Belch (2004) define personal selling as a way of personal communication by which a vendor tries to identify potential customers for a product. It encompasses direct contact between buyer and seller, either face to face or by telephone. Personal selling allows the seller to evaluate the reaction of potential buyers and adapt the marketing message in line with specific needs. An advantage of personal selling is that it implies a two-way interaction between the salesperson and the potential customer.

In the healthcare sector, where the sale of non-standardized, highly technical, intangible services occurs, personal selling is effective (Bowers, Powers, & Spencer, 1994; Purohit, 2018). Bowers and Powers (1991) indicate that the promotion of healthcare has advanced from stressing advertising to personal selling. In line with practices in other service industries, healthcare providers are also relying on non-advertising tools such as personal selling as Rothschild (1979) indicates. The need for a move from advertising to personal selling within the healthcare sector has been reinforced by a lack of marketing quality control (Booms & Bitner, 1981). The used of personal selling has been documented in the Western world (see Bowers & Powers, 1991). Thomas (2008) opines that the practice of personal selling by hospitals is relatively recent. The author adds that in recent times, "healthcare providers have become active in personal sales, with hospital representatives calling on referring physicians, employers, and other organizations to promote the hospital's emergency room, sports medicine program, or a particular service line" (Thomas, 2008, p. 106). However, there has not been much personal selling by hospitals witnessed in the SSA context. In a cultural context in which the perception is that hospitals become necessary after a person has taken ill, a majority of consumers might find it awkward should they be contacted for hospital services to be marketed. Those who are superstitious might perceive that they are being wished evil.

10.10 IMPLICATIONS FOR POLICY

In the light of the commercialization of the healthcare sector in most SSA countries, it has become imperative for the sector to have flexible policies that allow operators to effectively use each tool of the marketing communications mix. Currently, the application of integrated marketing communications in the sector is problematic due to policies and regulations that have limited the use of some marketing communications tools. Hence, it has become imperative for the removal of outdated healthcare sector policies that do not promote effective marketing communications. The continued existence of such policies only limits the growth of the healthcare sector in SSA. Therefore, the code of ethics of medical associations in several countries in SSA need revision to be in line with changing market trends and needs.

10.11 CONCLUSION

Marketing communications has become imperative in the healthcare sector in SSA, in view of the commercialization of the sector. The healthcare sector in several SSA countries comprises both government and private owned healthcare providers who are competing. As a result, the need for marketing communications and its integration has risen. Kitchen et al. (2004) highlight that a single marketing communication tool hardly achieves marketing communications purposes considering the changing media preferences of consumers and therefore highlights the need for a move towards integrated marketing communications. Generally, hospitals in SSA have largely used most of the marketing communication tools: advertising, public relations, sales promotion, direct or digital marketing, and personal selling. The marketing communication tools most widely used by hospitals in SSA are public relations, digital/direct marketing, and advertising. Sales promotions and personal selling are minimally used. Therefore, although IMC is adopted by most hospitals in SSA to send consistent marketing communications to the public, not all the communication mix elements are intensively explored. The limitations in the use of the identified marketing communication tools are rooted in the perception of the African populace as to what the role and purpose of hospitals is. It is recommended that hospitals find innovative ways of using sales promotions and personal selling. For example, aside offering free consultation as a form of sales promotion, a specialist gynaecological hospital can institute sales promotion by offering a free Pap smear to every tenth woman to take such a test in a month.

Even though public relations has over the years been the most widely used marketing communication tool by hospitals, it has mainly been used as a reactive tool rather than relative (to build relationships). The chapter therefore suggests that hospitals should begin using public relations to build valuable relationships with the public and other stakeholders rather than maintaining their current usage for crisis management only. Again, the chapter argues that high illiteracy rates and poverty have been the bane of effective website marketing as a communication tool. Many people in SSA are faced with poverty and illiteracy. This does not allow them to experience the benefits of digital or website marketing.

This chapter calls for a revision of outdated healthcare sector policies that do not promote the effective use of some marketing communication tools such as advertising. In recent times, several governments of SSA countries have been targeting stimulating economic growth and development through tourism. One sector of tourism that is gaining ground is medical tourism. Medical tourism refers to the act of travelling to a different country to seek medical, surgical, and dental care (see Fetscherin & Stephano, 2016). The inability of health facilities in SSA to efficiently advertise limits them in becoming medical tourism centres. For instance, health facilities such as the Maritime Hospital, Ghana, which is an ultra-modern hospital facility offering specialized services and even providing a helipad to receive patients flown in for treatment, can be positioned to become a medical tourist centre if marketed properly through communications. Therefore, the tourism potential of several effective hospitals in SSA is in limbo because their potential is not communicated due to regulations.

REFERENCES

Amirkhanpour, M., Vrontis, D., & Thrassou, A. (2014). Mobile marketing: A contemporary strategic perspective. *International Journal of Technology Marketing*, *9*(3), 252–269.

Andrews, J. C., & Shimp, T. A. (2017). *Advertising, promotion, and other aspects of integrated marketing communications*. Nelson Education.

Armstrong, G., Adam, S., Denize, S., & Kotler, P. (2014). *Principles of marketing*. Australia: Pearson.

Atinga, A. R., Abekah-Nkrumah, G., & Ameyaw Domfeh, K. (2011). Managing healthcare quality in Ghana: A necessity of patient satisfaction. *International Journal of Health Care Quality Assurance*, *24*(7), 548–563. doi:10.1108/09526861111160580.

Barnlund, D. C. (2017). A transactional model of communication. In *Communication theory* (pp. 47–57). Routledge.

Batra, R., & Keller, K. L. (2016). Integrating marketing communications: New findings, new lessons, and new ideas. *Journal of Marketing, 80*(6), 122–145. doi:10.1509/jm.15.0419.

Batterham, R. W., Hawkins, M., Collins, P. A., Buchbinder, R., & Osborne, R. H. (2016). Health literacy: Applying current concepts to improve health services and reduce health inequalities. *Public Health, 132*, 3–12. doi:10.1016/j.puhe.2016.01.001.

Belch, G. E., & Belch, M. A. (2004). *Advertising and promotion: An integrated marketing communications perspective* (6th ed.). New York, NY: McGraw-Hill.

Berkowitz, E. N. (2008). The evolution of public relations and the use of the internet: The implications for health care organizations. *Health Marketing Quarterly, 24*(3–4), 117–130. doi:10.1080/07359680802125154.

Booms, B., & Bitner, M. J. (1981). Marketing strategies and organizational structures for service firms. In J. Donnelly & W. R. George (Eds.), *Marketing of services* (pp. 171–177). American Marketing Association.

Bowers, M. R., & Powers, T. L. (1991). Personal selling in health care organizations: A status report. *Marketing Health Services, 11*(3), 19.

Bowers, M. R., Powers, T. L., & Spencer, P. D. (1994). Characteristics of the salesforce in the US health-care service industry: A comparative study of selling professional services. *Journal of Services Marketing, 8*(4), 36–49. doi:10.1108/08876049410070718.

Bruhn, M., & Schnebelen, S. (2017). Integrated marketing communication: From an instrumental to a customer-centric perspective. *European Journal of Marketing, 51*(3), 464–489. doi:10.1108/EJM-08-2015-0591.

Chaffey, D., & Ellis-Chadwick, F. (2019). *Digital marketing.* UK: Pearson.

Chandra, A., Finkelstein, A., Sacarny, A., & Syverson, C. (2016). Health care exceptionalism? Performance and allocation in the US health care sector. *American Economic Review, 106*(8), 2110–2144. doi:10.1257/aer.20151080.

Chapman, A. (2014). The impact of reliance on private sector health services on the right to health. *Health and Human Rights, 16*(1), 122–33.

Deloitte. (2017). 2017 global healthcare sector outlook. Retrieved from www2.deloitte.com/content/dam/Deloitte/global/Documents/Life-Sciences-Health-Care/gx-lshc-2017-health-care-outlook-infographic.pdf.

De Pelsmacker, P., Geuens, M., & van den Bergh, J. (2003). *Marketing communication.* Grada Publishing as.

Dodson, D. C., Dotson, M. J., & Cussimanio, L. (1990). Direct hospital marketing: An idea whose time has come. *Journal of Health and Human Resources Administration, 12*(3), 336–344.

Eggoh, J., Houeninvo, H., & Sossou, G. A. (2015). Education, health and economic growth in African countries. *Journal of Economic Development, 40*(1), 93. Retrieved from http://jed.or.kr/full-text/40-1/4.pdf.

Fetscherin, M., & Stephano, R. M. (2016). The medical tourism index: Scale development and validation. *Tourism Management, 52*, 539–556. doi:10.1016/j.tourman.2015.08.010.

Finne, Å., & Grönroos, C. (2009). Rethinking marketing communication: From integrated marketing communication to relationship communication. *Journal of Marketing Communications, 15*(2–3), 179–195.

Foronda, C., MacWilliams, B., & McArthur, E. (2016). Interprofessional communication in healthcare: An integrative review. *Nurse Education in Practice, 19*, 36–40. doi:10.1016/j.nepr.2016.04.005.

Fortenberry, J. L., Jr, & McGoldrick, P. J. (2016). Internal marketing: A pathway for healthcare facilities to improve the patient experience. *International Journal of Healthcare Management, 9*(1), 28–33. doi:10.1179/2047971915Y.0000000014.

Gheorghe, I. R. (2012). *Marketing communications in health care services. An electronic word of mouth approach* (Doctoral thesis. Academy of Economic Studies, Bucharest, Romania).

Groucutt, J., Leadley, P., & Forsyth, P. (2004). *Marketing: Essential principles, new realities.* Kogan Page Publishers.

Grunig, J. E., & Grunig, L. A. (1991). Conceptual differences in public relations and marketing: The case of health-care organizations. *Public Relations Review, 17*(3), 257–278. doi:10.1016/0363-8111(91)90022-D.

Grunig, J. E., & Grunig, L. A. (1989). Toward a theory of the public relations behavior of organizations: Review of a program of research. In J. E. Grunig & L. A. Grunig (Eds.), *Public relations research annual* (pp. 37–74). Routledge

Haughton, D., Hua, G., Jin, D., Lin, J., Wei, Q., & Zhang, C. (2015). Optimization of the promotion mix in the healthcare industry. *International Journal of Pharmaceutical and Healthcare Marketing, 9*(4), 289–305. doi:10.1108/IJPHM-03-2013-0008.

Hinson, R., & Abor, J. (2005). Internationalizing SME nontraditional exporters and their Internet use idiosyncrasies. *Perspectives on Global Development and Technology, 4*(2), 229–244. doi:10.1163/1569150054738998.

Juska, J. M. (2018). *Integrated marketing communication.* Taylor & Francis.

Kalla, N. (2016). Marketing communication mix of government of Rajasthan for various healthcare and family welfare schemes: A case study of western rural Rajasthan. *International Journal of Social Sciences and Management, 3*(2), 135–140. doi:10.3126/ijssm.v3i2.14810.

Kehinde, O. J., & Igbozuruike, R. C. (2016). Public relations as a tool for effective healthcare management. *Innovative Journal of Business and Management, 5*(4), 81–88.

Keller, L. K. (2001). Mastering the marketing communications mix: Micro and macro perspectives on integrated marketing communication programs. *Journal of Marketing Management, 17*(7–8), 819–847. doi:10.1362/026725701323366836.

Kent, M. L., & Taylor, M. (2002). Toward a dialogic theory of public relations. *Public Relations Review, 28*(1), 21–37. doi:10.1016/S0363-8111(02)00108-X.

Killian, G., & McManus, K. (2015). A marketing communications approach for the digital era: Managerial guidelines for social media integration. *Business Horizons, 58*(5), 539–549. doi:10.1016/j.bushor.2015.05.006.

Kim, C. M. (2016). *Social media campaigns: Strategies for public relations and marketing.* Routledge.

Kim, I., Han, D., & Schultz, D. E. (2004). Understanding the diffusion of integrated marketing communications. *Journal of Advertising Research, 44*(1), 31–45. doi:10.1017/S0021849904040024.

Kitchen, P. J., & Burgmann, I. (2010). Integrated marketing communication. In *Wiley international encyclopedia of marketing.* doi:10.1002/9781444316568.wiem04001.

Kitchen, P. J., Brignell, J., Li, T., & Jones, G. S. (2004). The emergence of IMC: A theoretical perspective. *Journal of Advertising Research, 44*(1), 19–30. doi:10.1017/S0021849904040048.

Kliatchko, J. (2008). Revisiting the IMC construct: A revised definition and four pillars. *International Journal of Advertising, 27*(1), 133–160. doi:10.1080/02650487.2008.11073043.

Kotler, P. (2003). *Marketing management.* Prentice Hall International Editions.

Kotler, P., & Keller, K. L (2008). *Marketing management.* Mate.

Kotler, P., & Keller, K. L. (2012). *Marketing management: Global edition.* Harlow: Pearson.

Leibenluft, R. F., & Pollard, M. R. (1981). Antitrust scrutiny of the health professions: Developing framework for assessing private restraints. *Vanderbilt Law Review, 34*, 927.

Liang, B. A., & Mackey, T. (2011). Direct-to-consumer advertising with interactive internet media: Global regulation and public health issues. *Jama, 305*(8), 824–825. doi:10.1001/jama.2011.203.

Luxton, S., Reid, M., & Mavondo, F. (2015). Integrated marketing communication capability and brand performance. *Journal of Advertising, 44*(1), 37–46. doi:10.1080/00913367.2014.934938.

Madhavaram, S., Badrinarayanan, V., & McDonald, R. E. (2005). Integrated marketing communication (IMC) and brand identity as critical components of brand equity strategy: A conceptual framework and research propositions. *Journal of Advertising, 34*(4), 69–80. doi:10.1080/00913367.2014.934938.

Mahmud, A., & Parkhurst, M. (2007). *The role of the health care sector in expanding economic opportunity.* Corporate Social Responsibility Initiative Reports (21). John F. Kennedy School of Government, Harvard University.

Makinde, O. A., Brown, B., & Olaleye, O. (2014). The impact of medical tourism and the code of medical ethics on advertisement in Nigeria. *The Pan African Medical Journal, 19.* doi:10.11604/pamj.2014.19.103.5217.

Newhouse, N., Lupiáñez-Villanueva, F., Codagnone, C., & Atherton, H. (2015). Patient use of email for health care communication purposes across 14 European countries: An analysis of users according to demographic and health-related factors. *Journal of Medical Internet Research, 17*(3). doi:10.2196/jmir.3700.

Newsom, T., Turk, J., & Kruckeberg, D. (2000). *This is PR: The realities of public relations* (7th ed.). Belmont, CA: Wadsworth.

Nyaho Clinic (n.d.). Nyaho Clinic website. www.nyahomedical.com/.

Osei-Frimpong, K. (2016). Examining the effects of patient characteristics and prior value needs on the patient-doctor encounter process in healthcare service delivery. *International Journal of Pharmaceutical and Healthcare Marketing, 10*(2), 192–213. doi:10.1108/IJPHM-01-2016-0005.

Ozturk, A. B., Nusair, K., Okumus, F., & Hua, N. (2016). The role of utilitarian and hedonic values on users' continued usage intention in a mobile hotel booking environment. *International Journal of Hospitality Management, 57*, 106–115. doi:10.1016/j.ijhm.2016.06.007.

Percy, L. (2008). *Strategic integrated marketing communications.* Routledge.

ProVita Specialist Hospital (n.d.). ProVita website. www.provitaspecialisthospital.com/.

Public Health Act. (2012). Retrieved from http://extwprlegs1.fao.org/docs/pdf/gha136559.pdf.

Purcarea, V. L., Gheorghe, I. R., & Gheorghe, C. M. (2015). Uncovering the online marketing mix: Communication for health care services. *Procedia Economics and Finance, 26*, 1020–1025. doi:10.1016/S2212-5671(15)00925-9.

Purohit, B. (2018). Salesperson performance: Role of perceived overqualification and organization type. *Marketing Intelligence & Planning, 36*(1), 79–92. doi:10.1108/MIP-06-2017-0108.

Rothschild, M. L. (1979). Marketing communications in nonbusiness situations or why it's so hard to sell brotherhood like soap. *The Journal of Marketing, 43*(2), 11–20. doi:10.1177%2F002224297904300202.

Rundh, B. (2016). The role of packaging within marketing and value creation. *British Food Journal, 118*(10), 2491–2511. doi:10.1108/BFJ-10-2015-0390.

Saad Andaleeb, S. (1994). Hospital advertising: the influence of perceptual and demographic factors on consumer dispositions. *Journal of Services Marketing, 8*(1), 48–59. doi:10.1108/08876049410053302.

Sanchez, P. M. (2000). The potential of hospital website marketing. *Health Marketing Quarterly, 18*(1–2), 45–57. doi:10.1300/J026v18n01_04.

Seldon, B. J., Jewell, R. T., & O'Brien, D. M. (2000). Media substitution and economies of scale in advertising. *International Journal of Industrial Organization, 18*(8), 1153–1180. doi:10.1016/S0167-7187(99)00010-7.

Šerić, M., Gil-Saura, I., & Ruiz-Molina, M. E. (2014). How can integrated marketing communications and advanced technology influence the creation of customer-based brand equity? Evidence from the hospitality industry. *International Journal of Hospitality Management, 39*, 144–156. doi:10.1016/j.ijhm.2014.02.008.

Stenberg, K., Hanssen, O., Edejer, T. T. T., Bertram, M., Brindley, C., Meshreky, A., ... & Soucat, A. (2017). Financing transformative health systems towards achievement of the health Sustainable Development Goals: A model for projected resource needs in 67 low-income and middle-income countries. *The Lancet Global Health, 5*(9), e875–e887. doi:10.1016/S2214-109X(17)30263-2.

Theodorson, S. A, & Theodorson, A. G. (1969). *A modern dictionary of sociology.* New York, NY: Cassell.

The Trust Hospital (n.d.). Retrieved from https://thetrusthospital.com/gms-message/.

Thomas, R. K. (2008). *Health services marketing: A practitioner's guide.* Springer Science & Business Media.

Todorova, G. (2015). Marketing communication mix. *Trakia Journal of Sciences, 13*(1), 368–374. doi:10.15547/tjs.2015.s.01.063.

Tomic, Z., Lasic, D., & Tomic, T. (2010). Public relations in health care. *Materia Socio-Medica, 22*(1), 25.

Underwood, R. L., Klein, N. M., & Burke, R. R. (2001). Packaging communication: Attentional effects of product imagery. *Journal of Product & Brand Management, 10*(7), 403–422. doi:10.1108/10610420110410531.

United Nations. (2013). United Nations Universal Declaration of Human Rights. Retrieved from www.un.org/en/universal-declaration-human-rights/.

Wilcox, D. L. (2006). The landscape of today's global public relations. *Anàlisi: Quaderns de comunicació i cultura,* (34), 67–85.

Wirtz, J., & Lovelock, C. (2016). *Services marketing.* World Scientific Publishing Company.

Wirtz, J., Tuzovic, S., & Ehret, M. (2015). Global business services: Increasing specialization and integration of the world economy as drivers of economic growth. *Journal of Service Management, 26*(4), 565–587. doi:10.1108/JOSM-01-2015-0024.

World Health Organization. (2002). *Health and the international economy.* Retrieved from http://apps.who.int/iris/bitstream/handle/10665/42520/9241590122.pdf;jsessionid=D6F48349C86DE6F25CD134B3CF71373E?sequence=1.

Yeboah-Asiamah, E., Quaye, D. M., & Nimako, S. G. (2016). The effects of lucky draw sales promotion on brand loyalty in mobile telecommunication industry. *African Journal of Economic and Management Studies, 7*(1), 109–123. doi:10.1108/AJEMS-09-2013-0076.

Zarei, E., Daneshkohan, A., Pouragha, B., Marzban, S., & Arab, M. (2015). An empirical study of the impact of service quality on patient satisfaction in private hospitals, Iran. *Global Journal of Health Science, 7*(1), 1. doi:10.5539/gjhs.v7n1p1.

Zurek, K. (2018). No-bed syndrome: Korle Bu informs hospitals not to refer patients. Retrieved from www.graphic.com.gh/news/health/no-bed-syndrome-korle-bu-informing-hospitals-not-to-refer-patients.html.

11 Branding the Healthcare Experience

Oluwayemisi Olomo and Olutayo Otubanjo

11.1 INTRODUCTION

Meeting the needs of the healthcare consumer in the twenty-first century goes beyond providing functional products and services for those needs. Unlike previous decades, in which information was one-sided and the consumer passive, the advent of the internet and related technologies has led to more sophisticated consumers who are knowledgeable about their health and have an increased awareness about suitable product and service choices to meet those health needs. As consumers seek products and services that promote health and well-being, they are confronted with an array of choices – all of which seek to fulfil the same need. With several competing choices, it becomes necessary for health marketers to differentiate themselves in the mind of the consumer, not just in terms of products and services, but also in terms of coordinating these products and services into brand experiences for the healthcare consumer. This is made possible either by positioning healthy living and lifestyles as brands in the mind of the consumer or positioning the healthcare organization itself as a brand in the mind of the consumer (Evans & Haider, 2008; Evans, Blitstein, Vallone, Post & Nielsen, 2014). This is the essence of health branding and the premise upon which this chapter is written.

For healthcare marketers seeking to brand the healthcare experience, this chapter seeks to enlighten such readers on how to achieve such an objective. Therefore, in the first section of this chapter, the fundamentals of brand building are discussed in brief – namely, the concepts of brand identity, brand image and brand equity; the three stage process of brand development; developing brand consistency; brand architecture and healthcare services; the benefits of building a strong healthcare brand; and the relevance of health branding to sub-Saharan Africa.

It is pertinent to mention that before meaningful brand experiences can be created for the consumer, it is necessary for the healthcare marketer to be acquainted with the various world-views or epistemologies that drive the healthcare branding landscape. Several worldviews shape the way health brands are perceived and in the second section of this chapter, existing models of healthcare branding are examined with a view to acquainting health marketers with the various schools of thought or perspectives that govern the field of health branding. Chrysochou (2010), for instance, adopts a pragmatic viewpoint in order to investigate the role of marketing mix elements and public discourse in creating a healthy brand image. On the other hand, Kemp, Jillapalli and Becerra (2014) examine one of the constructs of health brands – consumer brand relationships from a positivist perspective – while Evans, Blitstein and Hersey (2008) investigate the relationship between branded message exposure, brand equity and health behaviour change from a positivist lens.

In the third section of the chapter, an additional perspective, the social constructionist view of health branding, is introduced. Unlike the positivist view, in which causal explanations and the quantitative measurements of facts are sought, the social constructionist view holds that individuals search for understanding of the world in which they live and work; therefore, individuals develop subjective meanings of their experiences (Easterby-Smith, Thorpe & Jackson, 2015). In the fourth and fifth sections of the chapter, a social constructionism model of health branding is presented while the benefits of looking at healthcare branding from a social constructionist viewpoint are discussed in the sixth and concluding section of the chapter.

11.2 THE FUNDAMENTALS OF BRAND BUILDING

As healthcare consumers make more informed choices via the internet and other consumer referrals, health marketers can no longer rely on the traditional business model of management – controlled organizational communication to reach the consumer. Today's healthcare marketers need to take into consideration the fact that marketing is now a two-way affair, involving simultaneous dialogue between the company and the consumer (Lovejoy & Saxton, 2012). Not only are consumers speaking with the company in order to make informed choices, consumers are also speaking with each other and influencing each other in order to make informed decisions on the healthcare products and services they wish to purchase.

It is pertinent to note that just as commercial brands have either functional or symbolic attributes that distinguish them from others, healthcare brands can have similar attributes, and the application of branding techniques to healthcare is no different from the way products and services in the commercial sector are branded. In the sections that follow, the fundamentals of brand building and the relevance of health branding to sub-Saharan Africa are discussed.

11.2.1 BRAND IDENTITY, BRAND IMAGE AND BRAND EQUITY

While there is no universally agreed definition of brand identity, the term is often used interchangeably with the term brand reputation (Black & Veloutsou, 2017). Therefore brand identity can at best be described as the core character of the brand and the definition of the brand (Barnett, Jermier & Lafferty, 2006; Black & Veloutsou, 2017)

Kapferer (2012) posits that brand identity should be represented by a hexagonal prism known as the brand identity prism, which comprises six facets, namely: physical, personality, culture, relationships, customer reflections and customer self-images. These six dimensions, according to Kapferer (2012), define the identity of the brand and the boundaries within which it is free to change or to develop.

While brand identity emanates from the company, brand image refers to consumer perceptions and entails a set of beliefs that consumers have about the brand (Nandan, 2005). Brand equity, on the other hand, is said to be driven by brand image. Farquhar (1989) defines brand equity as the added value with which a brand endows a product and posits that this added value can be viewed from the perspective of the firm, the trade or the consumer. Brand equity can also be regarded as the differential preference and response to marketing effort that a product obtains because of its brand identity (Datta, Ailawadi & Van Heerde, 2017).

11.2.2 THE THREE STAGE PROCESS OF BRAND DEVELOPMENT

The three stage process of brand development can be described as the steps marketers need to take in order to develop a brand. A strategic mindset is adopted for developing the brand, and the three stages which are intertwined include (i) developing a brand identity; (ii) brand image; and (iii) brand equity. Developing a brand therefore begins with having an identity. Kapferer (2012) posits that having an identity means "being your true self, driven by a personal goal that is both different from others and resistant to change". Closely related to the concept of brand identity is the concept of brand image. Brand identity and brand image are related but distinct concepts, and can be regarded as essential ingredients or the building blocks of strong brands

(Nandan, 2005). In the context of healthcare, brand equity becomes a great source of competitive advantage because of the credence nature of healthcare services (Bharadwaj, Varadarajan & Fahy, 1993).

11.2.3 DEVELOPING BRAND CONSISTENCY

Considered one of the key antecedents of brand authenticity, brand consistency refers to the standardization and preservation over time and place of a defined brand image and associated meanings through names, symbols and positioning themes (Bengtsson, Bardhi & Venkatraman, 2010; Beverland, Wilner & Micheli, 2015). Brand consistency is considered a core principle of successful brand development and stems from consistent corporate communications (Olins, 1995; Knox and Bickerton, 2003). Brand consistency is thought to be dependent on the understanding of the brand throughout the organization (Hemsley-Brown & Goonawardana, 2007) and has been argued to have both strategic and consumer benefits which include enhancing brand equity, serving as a heuristic for consumer decision making and achieving harmony in cognitive structures. Lee, O'Cass and Sok (2017) suggest that firms may enhance their capacity to build strong brands when they are supported and governed by a formalized structure. With a formalized structure, brand oriented firms are able to prescribe specific rules and procedures that guide how brand-directed tasks are completed, which in the long run reduces behavioural variance, enforces uniformity and ultimately creates the consistency fundamental to effective brand management (Aaker & Joachimsthaler, 2000; Lee et al., 2017).

11.2.4 BRAND ARCHITECTURE AND HEALTHCARE SERVICES

Brand architecture refers to an organization's approach to the design and management of its brand portfolio (Devlin, 2003; Devlin & McKechnie, 2008; Strebinger, 2014). Laforet and Saunders (1994, 2007) reveal three general patterns of brand architecture, namely: corporate dominant, product dominant and mixed structures. While corporate dominant brand architectures are based on visibility for the organization and the corporation as a global driver of brand value, within product dominant structures individual brands are developed for every product, while the mixed pattern of brand architecture incorporates both the corporate brand and the product brand (Uggla, 2006). Aaker and Joachimsthaler (2000) extend work on brand architecture strategies by highlighting four main strategies, namely: branded house, sub-brand, endorsed brand and house of brands.

Devlin (2003) notes that brand architecture decisions in particular are concerned with the number of brands to utilize, the role of specific brands and the relationship between such brands. The author notes that, in the context of services, it has been posited that services organizations tend to adopt a corporate brand approach to the management of their brand architecture, having the propensity to rely largely on one overarching brand.

11.2.5 BENEFITS OF BUILDING A STRONG HEALTHCARE BRAND

The benefits of building a strong healthcare brand are numerous. For example, having a strong brand gives the healthcare organization or service provider a unique identity and image such that it can be easily and positively identified and distinguished from the competition (Nandan, 2005). Branding also reduces the high perceived risk associated with healthcare services as healthcare services are regarded as high in credence attributes, to the extent that even after consumption of service their performance cannot be judged (Shekhar Kumar, Dash & Purwar, 2013). In addition, building a strong brand increases its visibility to the point where it can be used as a distinguishing and strategic competitive factor in the marketplace.

11.2.6 Relevance to Sub-Saharan Africa

The need for branding the healthcare experience in sub-Saharan Africa becomes urgent in the light of emerging healthcare trends, some of which have begun to change the healthcare landscape of the continent. Some of these trends include: the shift in focus of African health systems from curative to preventive care; the transfer of healthcare decision making to the local level; the ascendancy of telemedicine and mobile-phone technology as the dominant means of delivering healthcare advice and treatments; the actualization of a universal health coverage which gives all Africans access to a basic package of benefits; and a reduction in international donor support as a result of continued global instability, leaving governments to fill the gaps. Coupled with these trends is the increasing public–private mix of healthcare delivery across the continent as well as the rise of a growing middle class population that can afford better treatment (Economist Intelligence Unit, 2012; Hattingh, Russo, Sun-Basorun & Van Wamelen, 2012)

With a strong demand for quality, international-standard healthcare coming from these various groups – the emerging middle classes, overseas investors, governments and health insurers (Economist Intelligence Unit, 2012) – the need to build strong health brands that can deliver on their brand promises should be seen as a strategic objective in order to ensure the continued relevance and sustainability of firms operating within the healthcare space.

In this regard, healthcare organizations can seek to position themselves along the line of emerging market trends. For example, some healthcare brands can choose to build their brands by leveraging technology. MOBIcure, for instance, is a social enterprise company that uses mobile technology to provide healthcare solutions to pressing health problems in Nigeria and the African Continent, particularly in the area of maternal and child health (MOBIcure, 2019). MOBIcure's products include the myPaddi and the OMOMI app. While the myPaddi app provides young people with access to accurate, unbiased and youth-friendly sexual and reproductive health information, and ensures they remain totally anonymous, the OMOMI app provides pregnant women and mothers with access to life saving maternal and child health information. Both apps provide access to health professionals in a real time chat.

11.3 WHAT IS THE MEANING OF HEALTH BRANDING?

Despite the array of studies seeking to elucidate what the health branding phenomenon is about, one topical issue that remains unclear is the question of its meaning. Over the last decade, the meaning of health branding has been constructed theoretically as an image (e.g. Chrysochou, 2010), a social process (e.g. Anker, Sandøe, Kamin & Kappel, 2011) or as a strategy (Gordon, Hastings, McDermott & Evans, 2008; Basu & Wang, 2009). Chrysochou (2010), for instance, defines health branding as 'the practice in which marketing strategies are adopted to communicate the value of health'. The author similarly posits that a health brand is developed when a corporate organization intentionally attempts to communicate implicitly or explicitly a value universe that links a product or the corporate organization itself to the value of health and consumers are also able to associate the product/company with this value. Adopting a critical realist approach, Chrysochou (2010) seeks to explore health branding from a managerial perspective. Using case research as a research method, the author examines the practice of health brands and health branding, specifically, the role of elements of the marketing mix in conveying a healthy brand image. In addition, the author explores the way the marketing mix and public discourse interact to shape certain aspects of the health brand.

Five companies based in the Danish food industry are selected using the purposive sampling strategy – maximum variation sampling – and qualitative data is collected in two stages using discourse analysis and key informant interviews. The five cases used in the study include a low-fat, a functional, a fitness, an organic and a fake health brand. Based on the findings from the five cases used in the study, Chrysochou (2010) develops a conceptual model containing propositions on the role various marketing mix elements play in the formation of a healthy brand image. The author posits that a healthy brand image is built through the adoption of health stimuli emanating from the marketing mix elements of a brand. Furthermore, the degree to which the marketing mix elements convey a healthy brand image depends on factors external to the health brand, such as regulation and internal contextual factors including corporate branding strategy, brand type, product type, communication strategy types, brand management stage and the manager's capability. Chrysochou (2010) also notes that the marketing mix elements and their effect are moderated by public discourse on the brand.

Anker et al. (2011) present a conceptual analysis of potential ethical problems in commercial food health branding. In the study, the authors argue that while other researchers have attempted to provide definitions of health brands (Evans & Hastings, 2008; Evans et al. 2007) and isolate the key components of health brands (Evans et al. 2008), there is no prior research into the ethics of health branding. Drawing on Evans et al. (2008)'s conceptual definition of health brands, Anker et al. (2011) define the health brand as "a set of features that identifies and distinguishes a health product (or service) from its competitors by promising functional and symbolic consumer–brand benefits which are to emerge in a process of consumer–brand interaction".

The study subsequently focuses on three health brand elements, namely functional claims, process claims and health symbols, and examines the potential ethical issues related to the application of the three health brand elements. The authors propose a distinction between epistemic and emotional ethical problems, noting that functional and process claims assign descriptive content to a health brand, while health symbols impart symbolic meaning and assign emotional and persuasive content. While the study does not carry out any empirical investigations, the authors posit that the conceptual analysis of health branding advances the academic literature in applied marketing ethics and provides an important point of reference for marketing practitioners who want to conduct ethically responsible health branding.

Kemp et al. (2014) examine how emotionally based relationships are developed in a healthcare context. Previous studies have conceptualized consumer brand relationships (e.g. Fournier, 1994, 1998) and explored the various forms brand relationships take, namely *cognitive, habitual* or *emotional*. In the present study, the authors investigate the phenomena of developing emotional or affect-based relationships for healthcare organizations using a mixed methods approach. Based on evidence from marketing literature and findings from the interviews conducted in the study, the authors posit that several factors contribute to the development of affective commitment between consumers and a brand. The most important factor identified is trust, which, in turn, is suggested to be driven by several distinct factors such as the consumer's attitude toward the brand, perceived quality of the brand, prestige of the brand and the display of customer-oriented behaviour. Based on the findings from their study, Kemp et al. (2014) posit that trust, referent influence and corporate social responsibility are key variables in establishing affective commitment in consumer brand relationships in a healthcare context, noting that once affective commitment is established, consumers may come to identify with the healthcare brand, form a self–brand connection and ultimately serve as advocates for the brand via word-of-mouth promotion. While Kemp et al. (2014) examine the development of emotionally based consumer–brand relationships from a positivist perspective, Evans et al. (2008) also adopt a positivist approach in their study on public health brands. The authors explore the relationships among three variables – namely: brand message exposure, brand equity and health behaviour change – and posit that public health brand equity operates as a mediator between branded message exposure and health behaviour change.

From the foregoing, it can be seen that there is no generic definition of health branding and the models developed thus far by health branding researchers have largely positivist orientations. Positivist research has a deterministic philosophy in which causes most likely determine effects or outcomes (Creswell & Creswell, 2017) and the key assumptions of the positivist view include: the hypothetical nature of knowledge (as it is assumed that absolute truth can never be found); the testing of theories in which claims are made and then refined or abandoned in favour of other claims that have stronger justifications; empirical observation and measurement; the development of true, relevant statements that can explain a situation of interest or describe causal relationships as well as objectivity as an integral part of competent enquiry (Phillips & Burbules, 2000).

Therefore, although these models advance the existing knowledge on health branding, due to their positivist orientations, they are unable to accommodate some of the issues of concern to the social constructionist lens of health branding. For instance, while the models demonstrate the mandatory presence of interaction among the elements (see Anker et al., 2011) they fail to recognize the notion of *ongoing*, which is responsible for initiating a continuous interaction between brands and consumers. The idea of the ongoing is, however, an essential requirement for the development or maintenance of desired corporate images or reputation (Otubanjo, 2008). Furthermore the models do not take into consideration the important roles of the pillars of social order, direction and stability in the health branding formation process. Otubanjo, Melewar and Cornelius (2008) note that the above mentioned pillars provide the basis and structural foundation upon which social interactions between brands and consumers occur.

In addition, the positivist models lack the ability to understand that meanings can be generated through frequent and ongoing repetition of corporate activities. Taking into account the weaknesses identified in the positivist models, the authors propose an alternative approach that seeks to clearly explain the health branding process – the social constructionist approach. The social constructionist view is discussed in detail in the next section.

11.4 THE HEALTH BRANDING EXPERIENCE FROM A SOCIAL CONSTRUCTIONIST LENS

The previous section brought to the fore the focal topic being investigated in this chapter, which is health branding. The previous section proposed that a suitable approach capable of investigating the health branding phenomenon is the social constructionist philosophy. This section strengthens this proposition by providing ontologically grounded reasons why the study of health branding can be approached from a social constructionist perspective. Social constructivism is a contrasting epistemology to positivism and is concerned with the empathic understanding of human acts rather than with the forces that act on them (Bell, Bryman & Harley, 2018). Social constructivism focuses on the ways people make sense of the world via the medium of language; reality is therefore construed by people rather than by objective and external factors (Easterby-Smith et al., 2015). Its intellectual heritage includes Max Weber's *Verstehen*, the hermeneutic-phenomenological tradition and symbolic interactionism (Bell, Bryman & Harley, 2018).

Social constructionism is regarded as a paradigm popularized by sociologists Berger and Luckmann (1966), who argue in their book *The social construction of reality* that 'reality is socially constructed and that the sociology of knowledge must analyze the process by which this occurs'. Burr (2015) notes that Berger and Luckmann's account of social life argues that human beings together create and then sustain a social phenomenon through social practices. In addition, Berger and Luckmann demonstrate that the world can be socially constructed by the social practices of people and at the same time be experienced by people as if the nature of their world is pre-determined and fixed (Burr, 2015).

Social construction consequently seeks to examine the ways social phenomena and trends are produced, shaped, entrenched and made into custom by groups and individuals (Hacking & Hacking, 1999). With respect to the social construction of reality, Berger and Luckmann (1966) refer to an enduring process, created and recreated by people given their interpretations and knowledge of such changing processes.

Otubanjo (2008) notes that social constructionism is based on two epistemological assumptions, the first being that people attempt to understand society as an external, objective reality and the second that people experience and approach society as an internal subjective reality

Looking at people's understanding of society as an external, objective reality, the author notes that societies impose specific norms, values and ways of life repetitively to which both old and new members must conform, failing which designated actors may be forced to invoke sanctions to ensure compliance. These forceful dictates and impositions based on societal beliefs, norms and behaviours appear to individuals as *objective reality*.

Internal subjective reality, on the other hand, occurs when individuals attempt to break away from objective reality by making sense of their own worlds and identifying with people of their own class, thoughts and beliefs (Otubanjo, 2008). Specifically, internal subjective reality emerges when individuals consistently challenge or query the dictates of institutionalized objective reality by interpreting and making meanings of all activities within society and acting on these interpretations. At this point, individuals acquire a subjective, coherent, plausible identity which in the long run influences society, and society in turn experiences these individual actions as objective reality (Otubanjo, 2008). Consequently, there is a cyclical and ongoing relationship between objective and subjective reality which according to Berger and Luckmann's (1966) epistemology indicates that the pursuit of specific actions based on an individual's experience triggers the development of a subjective version of reality, which in turn is presented as objective reality to other individuals. Elucidating further, Burr (2015) observes that Berger and Luckmann (1966) see the relationship between individuals and society as operating in dual directions, with human beings continually constructing the social world which then becomes a reality to which they must respond.

Berger and Luckmann identify three aspects of this circular process, namely: externalization, objectivation and internalization. Basic to this cycle, the authors note, is "human beings' ability to create symbols, things that carry meanings in the here and now", adding that language is a system of symbols that allow human beings to represent events (Burr, 2015). Drawing on Berger and Luckmann's thesis, Otubanjo et al. (2008) posit that the cyclical and ongoing relationship between external objective reality and internal subjective reality is being shaped by seven important ontological assumptions namely: *social order, direction, stability, habitualization, social interaction, institutionalization, control* and *historicity.* Each of these ontological assumptions is examined in detail below:

Ontological assumption 1 (*social order, direction* and *stability*): This position assumes that human activity is built on the pillars of social order, direction and stability, with social order referring to those facets of society which are stable over time (Hechter & Horne, 2003), while direction is the course towards a well-defined goal. Social stability refers to the state in which social institutions operate steadily, peacefully and cohesively (Rowe, 2002) and Hechter and Horne (2009) argue that social order holds to the extent that the actions of multiple individuals within a system generate collectively beneficial outcomes. The problem, however, is that it is difficult to estimate the extent to which social order affects human conduct (Otubanjo et al., 2008).

Ontological assumption 2 (*social interaction*): This position assumes that men together produce the human environment based on ongoing psychological formations or mental representations (meanings) of actors' interactions. However, this position fails to provide details of how mental representations come about. A number of authors have attempted to fill this gap by providing detailed cognitive processes of how human interactions trigger mental associations (Otubanjo et al., 2008).

Ontological assumption 3 (*habitualization*): This position assumes that the frequent repetition of human activities, along with the total psychological formations or mental representations that come with these repetitions, become cast into a behavioural pattern and subsequently habitualized. A drawback of this position, however, is that it fails to establish exactly at what point human actions become habitualized (Otubanjo et al., 2008).

Ontological assumption 4 (*institutionalization*): This position assumes that institutionalization develops on the basis of a variety of reciprocal typifications of habitualized actions alongside psychological formations or mental representations (i.e. meanings and interpretations) that emerge in the course of the reciprocal typification of these actions. This position is, however, considered weak due to the fact that it approaches institutionalization as a phenomenon that develops from repetitive actions alone (Otubanjo et al., 2008).

Ontological assumptions 5 and 6 (*history and control*): Otubanjo et al. (2008) note that insti-tutionalization develops over time through history and this is controlled in an ongoing manner by codes of conduct. Burr (2015), however, notes that even though human beings construct the social world, they cannot construct it in any way they choose, because at birth they enter a world already constructed by their predecessors and this world assumes the status of an objective reality for them and later generations.

Ontological assumption 7 (*communication*): According to Berger and Luckmann (1966), the ongoing transmission or communication of stable or changed actions produces reality. The authors note that the shaping of the world is an ongoing activity that is fully transparent to those who initially carried out specific actions. In addition, the originators of such actions understand the meanings of these actions fully, and consequently the ability to change or abolish these practices, which hitherto might have been stable over a long period of time, lies within their willpower and authority. As a result, these actors are capable of changing, stabilizing and communicating these actions continuously to new generations.

11.5 HEALTH BRANDING FROM A SOCIAL CONSTRUCTIONIST PERSPECTIVE

The previous section addressed the meaning of social construction based on Berger and Luckman's (1966) epistemology and ontological assumptions. This section attempts to extend the notion of social construction to the concept of health branding. From an epistemological point of view, tra-ditional health branding research is based on an objectivist, functionalist and rationalistic under-standing of the interaction between individuals, organization and society. Consequently, it is taken for granted that there is an objective reality "out there" which it is possible to grasp by following certain scientific methodological rules which in turn produce accurate, testable and predictable knowledge (Zhao, Falkheimer & Heide, 2017). In addition, stakeholders are viewed as a homogene-ous group, sometimes divided into "target groups" from the senders' perspective but rarely seen as interpretative actors in different contexts and situations (Zhao et al., 2017).

As a result, the traditional approach to health branding research is organization-centred and characterized by managerialism (see Chrysochou, 2010; Anker et al., 2011). The alternative approach, the social constructionist view, was developed as a reaction to the traditional approach which concentrates on managers' interest and assumes that managers are in the best position to solve all organizational problems. Rather than question the existence of a reality "out there", what the alternative approach seeks to do is to emphasize human relations to it – in other words, what it means to different people (Zhao et al., 2017).

11.6 THE DEVELOPMENT OF A SOCIAL CONSTRUCTIONIST BASED MODEL OF HEALTH BRANDING

Drawing on Berger and Luckmann's (1966) work on social constructionism and Otubanjo et al.'s (2008), social constructionist model of corporate identity, which equally draws from Berger and Luckmann's thesis, a social constructionist model of health branding is presented. This chapter follows Otubanjo et al.'s (2008) views on social constructionism and develops a model based on the identified central concepts of social constructionism. The model is represented in Figure 11.1.

The starting point for the social constructionist model for health branding is the premise that all activities between corporate actors (in this case, all employees) and all stakeholders take place within the context of the pillars of social order, direction and social stability. These pillars form the structural foundation upon which ongoing interactions between firms and stakeholders occur. As Otubanjo et al. (2008) note, no human activities, whether business or social, can be successfully accomplished without the underlying forces of social order, direction and social stability.

Once the pillars of social order, direction and social stability are firmly established, it is pos-sible for firms to pursue various corporate personality activities related to health in an ongoing

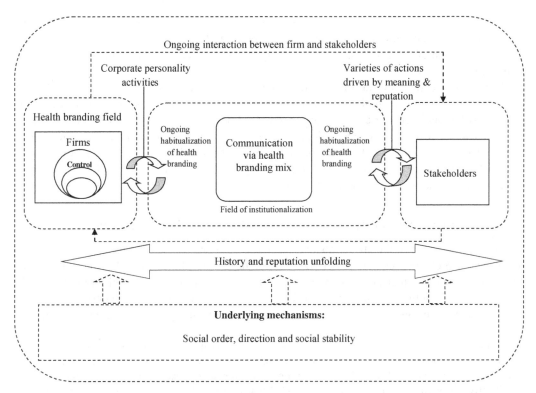

FIGURE 11.1 A Social Constructionist Model of Health Branding. (Source: Developed by authors but inspired by Otubanjo et al. (2008)).

manner. These activities are pursued with a view to developing the firm's corporate identity on the basis of health. The repeated or ongoing pursuits of these activities generate meanings. This is because frequent repetition of actions casts human actions into habits; therefore, meanings are generated from the repetition of these activities over time. In the process of generating these meanings, firms are endowed with a history and reputation based on the repetition of these actions (Otubanjo et al., 2008).

The sovereignty to repeat these corporate personality activities provides firms the autonomy to inject corporate control into the meanings generated from these activities, particularly if the meanings are negative. In more precise terms, the control of these activities (corporate identity) through corporate policy making and implementation allows firms to re-examine and re-define what exactly the firm is and what it is not as well as other issues that pertain to corporate identity. In addition, the use of corporate control allows the firm to spell out exactly what it does and what it does not do, what the firm stands for and what it does not, etc. (Otubanjo et al., 2008).

The frequent ongoing repetition and implementation of these policy measures generates desired meanings, stimulates good corporate reputation and builds up corporate history. With the passage of time, these intangible assets come to exemplify and epitomize the firm's personality. The conceptualization of the meaning, reputation and history of a firm's corporate identity based on ongoing habitualization and control of activities in turn sets the stage for ongoing communications through the health branding mix – either one or a combination of visual signs, behaviour or corporate advertising (Otubanjo et al., 2008).

Following the consistent, repetitive and ongoing construction of corporate identity through the health branding mix, corporate personality messages are received and interpreted by stakeholders in an ongoing and repetitive manner. Consequently, the meanings generated from the interpretation of the messages are acted upon by stakeholders through various actions (e.g. the boycott or contin-ued patronage of health products or brands, investments and divestments etc.). The frequent and ongoing repetition of these actions is subsequently cast into a pattern and habitualized over time (Otubanjo et al., 2008).

The repetitive actions by stakeholders in response to the meanings generated from the formal and informal communication of corporate activities (which constitute the corporate identity) trig-ger the institutionalization of a variety of relationships. The institutionalization of these relation-ships in turn is reflective of the reciprocity and types of relationships emerging from the meanings of the repetitive or habitualized interactions between the firm and stakeholders over time. Lastly, the varieties of reciprocal actions derived from the ongoing relationships between firms and stake-holders (institutionalization) accumulate into history and reputation (Otubanjo et al., 2008).

11.6.1 A Social Constructionist View on the Meaning of Health Branding

The conceptualization of the above model (see Figure 11.1) provides an insight into the workings and mechanism of the social constructionism based health branding model. The development of this model raises an important issue with respect to how the meaning of health branding should be perceived. Given the new insights emerging from this new model, a social construction based perspective on the meaning of health branding is suggested. Consequently, it is conceived that:

> Health branding is a phenomenon that emerges from ongoing interactions between health-oriented firms and stakeholders. It is a signification of several corporate personality actions, which like many human activities, is founded on the pillars of order, direction and social stability. Health branding is reflective of how corporate personality is controlled and constructed repeatedly or (habitually) through the health branding mix, and the varieties of ways that stakeholders reciprocate and respond to these constructed personalities.

The essence of this new definition is that it emphasizes the possibility of generating meanings from both stakeholder interpretations of health branding and the ongoing construction of health brand-ing. Meanings are embedded in the repetitive expression of health branding over time.

11.7 CONCLUSION

In the first section of this chapter, the fundamentals of brand building were discussed, namely: the concepts of brand identity, brand image and brand equity; the three stage process of brand devel-opment; developing brand consistency; brand architecture and healthcare services; the benefits of building a strong healthcare brand; and the relevance of health branding to sub-Saharan Africa.

In the second section, the meaning of health branding was explored from various epistemologi-cal mindsets, which were identified to be largely positivist in orientation. In the third section, an alternative approach – the social constructionist approach – was examined alongside its epistemol-ogy and ontological assumptions drawn from Berger and Luckmann's work. In the fourth and fifth sections, the health branding experience was viewed from a social constructionist perspective and a social constructionist model of health branding presented. In the sixth and final section of this chapter, the benefits of looking at health branding from a social constructionist perspective are presented, along with recommendations on the practice of health branding for practitioners.

Reflecting on the intellectual context in which Berger and Luckmann's (1966) *Social construc-tion of reality* emerged, Gergen (2018) suggests that while the Berger and Luckmann thesis provides a major catalyst to the emerging dialogues, subsequent developments in critical, literary and rhe-torical theory as well as the history of science have added important dimensions to understanding.

Gergen (2018) notes that while the earlier emphasis on social phenomenology was largely clouded by a concern with the linguistic construction of reality, discussions of social structure and individual experience were largely replaced by a focus on the social or dialogic construction of reality. These dialogues, in Gergen's (2018) view, are having a profound effect on the social sciences such that they liberate the professions from the debilitating grip of logical empiricism by adding a concern with the social and political effects of inquiry and invite a pluralist inclusiveness in forms and functions of enquiry, as well as encouraging innovation in both theory and research methods. The social constructionist worldview is typically seen as an approach to qualitative research (Creswell, 2009) and most qualitative research rejects a positivist epistemology, adopting instead interpretative, constructionist or critical methodological approaches (Green & Thorogood, 2018).

Social constructionism also emphasizes purposeful creation of knowledge (Thomas, Menon, Boruff, Rodriguez & Ahmed, 2014), and two key concepts to a social constructionist perspective are the incorporation of the environment or social context into knowledge building and the attention of groups on joint creation of knowledge (Thomas et al., 2014). In the context of health, Pirnejad, Niazkhani, van der Sijs, Berg and Bal (2008) note that healthcare is provided in a social environment, which provides the context for interactions between people. In addition, knowledge building in healthcare comes from various disciplines trained in separate spheres and paradigms, which require a bridge (Dayton & Henriksen, 2007; Manojlovich, Squires, Davies & Graham, 2015). Social constructionism provides such a bridge across distinct knowledge bases because it is premised on the fact that knowledge is socially constructed, meaning that people create knowledge through their interactions, which are mostly accomplished through communication (Berger & Luckmann, 1966; Manojlovich et al. 2015). This is particularly important in the context of health brands, as consumers are seen as co-creators of brand experiences and brand benefits (Anker et al., 2011). Therefore studying the health branding phenomenon through a social constructionist lens provides details into how co-creation of knowledge occurs between various parties in the health brand promise (i.e. brands and consumers).

In terms of managerial implications, the social constructionist approach becomes important in the context of healthcare branding because healthcare practitioners, managers and policy makers have increasingly turned to the qualitative methods of social enquiry used within the social sciences to enhance their understanding of health, health behaviour and health services, as well as improve the management and provision of health services (Green & Thorogood, 2018). Qualitative methods of enquiry such as ethnographic studies, in-depth interviews and customer focus groups, for example, yield rich consumer insights that healthcare marketers and organizations can use to improve on their products and services or brand partner relationships with customers. This becomes particularly important in an era when consumers have become co-creators of brand experiences. With the increasing digital savviness of customers, a lot of consumer insights can also be unravelled through the use of diverse digital marketing tools to conduct online market research.

Therefore in terms of brand building, the process of branding should not be limited to just the "brick and mortar context" alone; with the advent of the social media and other forms of new media, healthcare marketers and healthcare administrators can begin to increase their organizations' visibility through the use of various social media platforms, which can complement the traditional forms of branding used in offline environments.

REFERENCES

Aaker, D. A., & Joachimsthaler, E. (2000). The brand relationship spectrum: The key to the brand architecture challenge. *California Management Review*, *42*(4), 8–23.

Anker, T. B., Sandøe, P., Kamin, T., & Kappel, K. (2011). Health branding ethics. *Journal of Business Ethics*, *104*(1), 33.

Barnett, M. L., Jermier, J. M., & Lafferty, B. A. (2006). Corporate reputation: The definitional landscape. *Corporate Reputation Review*, *9*(1), 26–38.

Basu, A., & Wang, J. (2009). The role of branding in public health campaigns. *Journal of Communication Management*, *13*(1), 77–91.

Bell, E., Bryman, A., & Harley, B. (2018). *Business research methods*. Oxford University Press.

Bengtsson, A., Bardhi, F., & Venkatraman, M. (2010). How global brands travel with consumers: An examination of the relationship between brand consistency and meaning across national boundaries. *International Marketing Review, 27*(5), 519–540.

Berger, P. L., & Luckmann, T. (1966). *The social construction of reality*. New York: Doubleday.

Beverland, M. B., Wilner, S. J., & Micheli, P. (2015). Reconciling the tension between consistency and relevance: Design thinking as a mechanism for brand ambidexterity. *Journal of the Academy of Marketing Science, 43*(5), 589–609.

Bharadwaj, S. G., Varadarajan, P. R., & Fahy, J. (1993). Sustainable competitive advantage in service industries: A conceptual model and research propositions. *Journal of Marketing, 57*(4), 83-99.

Black, I., & Veloutsou, C. (2017). Working consumers: Co-creation of brand identity, consumer identity and brand community identity. *Journal of Business Research, 70*, 416–429.

Burr, V. (2015). *Social constructionism*. Routledge.

Chrysochou, P. (2010). Food health branding: The role of marketing mix elements and public discourse in conveying a healthy brand image. *Journal of Marketing Communications, 16*(1–2), 69–85.

Creswell, J.W. (2009). *Research design: Qualitative, quantitative, and mixed methods approaches*. Thousand Oaks, CA: Sage.

Creswell, J. W., & Creswell, J. D. (2017). *Research design: Qualitative, quantitative, and mixed methods approaches*. Sage Publications.

Datta, H., Ailawadi, K. L., & Van Heerde, H. J. (2017). How well does consumer-based brand equity align with sales-based brand equity and marketing-mix response? *Journal of Marketing, 81*(3), 1–20.

Dayton, E., & Henriksen, K. (2007). Communication failure: Basic components, contributing factors, and the call for structure. *The Joint Commission Journal on Quality and Patient Safety, 33*(1), 34–47.

Devlin, J. (2003). Brand architecture in services: The example of retail financial services. *Journal of Marketing Management, 19*(9–10), 1043–1065.

Devlin, J. F., & McKechnie, S. (2008). Consumer perceptions of brand architecture in financial services. *European Journal of Marketing, 42*(5/6), 654–666.

Easterby-Smith, M., Thorpe, R., & Jackson, P. R. (2015). *Management and Business Research*. Sage.

Economist Intelligence Unit (2012). Economist intelligence report. Retrieved June 15, 2019, from www.eiu.com/public/topical_report.aspx?campaignid=Industries2012.

Evans, W. D., & Haider, M. (2008). Public health brands in the developing world. In W. D. Evans & G. Hastings (Eds.), *Public health branding: Applying marketing for social change* (pp. 215–232). Oxford University Press.

Evans, W. D., & Hastings, G. (Eds.). (2008). *Public health branding: Applying marketing for social change*. Oxford University Press.

Evans, W. D., Blitstein, J., & Hersey, J. C. (2008). Evaluation of public health brands: Design, measurement, and analysis. In W. D. Evans & G. Hastings (Eds.), *Public health branding: Applying marketing for social change* (pp. 43–72). Oxford University Press.

Evans, W. D., Blitstein, J., Vallone, D., Post, S., & Nielsen, W. (2014). Systematic review of health branding: Growth of a promising practice. *Translational Behavioral Medicine, 5*(1), 24–36.

Evans, W. D., Renaud, J., Blitstein, J., Hersey, J., Ray, S., Schieber, B., & Willett, J. (2007). Prevention effects of an anti-tobacco brand on adolescent smoking initiation. *Social Marketing Quarterly, 13*(2), 2–20.

Farquhar, P. H. (1989). Managing brand equity. *Marketing research, 1*(3).

Fournier, S. (1994). *A consumer-brand relationship framework for Strategic Brand Management* (Unpublished doctoral dissertation, University of Florida).

Fournier, S. (1998). Consumers and their brands: Developing relationship theory in consumer research. *Journal of Consumer Research, 24*(4), 343–373.

Gergen, K. J. (2018). The social construction of reality: Traces and transformation. In M. Pfadenhauer & H. Knoblauch (Eds.), *Social constructivism as paradigm?* (pp. 259–272). Routledge.

Gordon, R., Hastings, G., McDermott, L., & Evans, W. D. (2008). Building brands with competitive analysis. In W. D. Evans & G. Hastings (Eds.), *Public health branding: Applying marketing for social change* (pp. 73–90). Oxford University Press.

Green, J., & Thorogood, N. (2018). *Qualitative methods for health research*. Sage.

Hacking, I., & Hacking, J. (1999). *The social construction of what*. Harvard University Press.

Hattingh, D., Russo, B., Sun-Basorun, A., & Van Wamelen, A. (2012). *The rise of the African consumer*. McKinseys Africa Consumer Insights Center.

Hechter, M., & Horne, C. (2003). *Theories of social order: A reader*. Stanford University Press.

Hechter, M., & Horne, C. (2009). *Theories of social order*. Palo Alto.

Hemsley-Brown, J., & Goonawardana, S. (2007). Brand harmonization in the international higher education market. *Journal of Business Research, 60*(9), 942–948.

Kapferer, J. N. (2012). *The new strategic brand management: Advanced insights and strategic thinking.* London, Kogan Page publishers.

Kemp, E., Jillapalli, R., & Becerra, E. (2014). Healthcare branding: Developing emotionally based consumer brand relationships. *Journal of Services Marketing, 28*(2), 126–137.

Knox, S., & Bickerton, D. (2003). The six conventions of corporate branding. *European Journal of Marketing, 37*(7/8), 998–1016.

Laforet, S., & Saunders, J. (1994). Managing brand portfolios: How the leaders do it. *Journal of Advertising Research, 34*(5), 64–77.

Laforet, S., & Saunders, J. (2007). How brand portfolios have changed: A study of grocery suppliers brands from 1994 to 2004. *Journal of Marketing Management, 23*(1–2), 39–58.

Lee, W. J., O'Cass, A., & Sok, P. (2017). Unpacking brand management superiority: Examining the interplay of brand management capability, brand orientation and formalisation. *European Journal of Marketing, 51*(1), 177–199.

Lovejoy, K., & Saxton, G. D. (2012). Information, community, and action: How nonprofit organizations use social media. *Journal of Computer-Mediated Communication, 17*(3), 337–353.

Manojlovich, M., Squires, J. E., Davies, B., & Graham, I. D. (2015). Hiding in plain sight: Communication theory in implementation science. *Implementation Science, 10*(1), 58.

MOBIcure (2019). Retrieved from https://mobicure.biz/.

Nandan, S. (2005). An exploration of the brand identity–brand image linkage: A communications perspective. *Journal of Brand Management, 12*(4), 264–278.

Olins, W. (1995). *The new guide to identity.* Hampshire: Gower.

Olutayo Otubanjo, B., Melewar, T. C., & Cornelius, N. (2008). *Practitioner conceptualisations of corporate identity, 1945–2008: Review and analysis.* Electronic copy available at: http://ssrn.com, abstract 1299764.

Otubanjo, B. O. (2008). *Industry construction of the meaning of corporate identity in Nigeria's banking services sector: An interpretive analysis of corporate advertisements, 1970–2005* (Doctoral Dissertation, Brunel University, London).

Phillips, D. C., & Burbules, N. C. (2000). *Postpositivism and educational research.* Rowman & Littlefield.

Pirnejad, H., Niazkhani, Z., van der Sijs, H., Berg, M., & Bal, R. (2008). Impact of a computerized physician order entry system on nurse–physician collaboration in the medication process. *International Journal of Medical Informatics, 77*(11), 735–744.

Rowe, W. T. (2002). Social stability and social change. In W. J. Peterson (Ed.), *The Cambridge history of China: Vol. 9, Part 1: The Ch'ing empire to 1800* (pp. 473–562). Cambridge University Press.

Shekhar Kumar, R., Dash, S., & Chandra Purwar, P. (2013). The nature and antecedents of brand equity and its dimensions. *Marketing Intelligence & Planning, 31*(2), 141–159.

Strebinger, A. (2014). Rethinking brand architecture: A study on industry, company- and product-level drivers of branding strategy. *European Journal of Marketing, 48*(9/10), 1782–1804.

Thomas, A., Menon, A., Boruff, J., Rodriguez, A. M., & Ahmed, S. (2014). Applications of social constructivist learning theories in knowledge translation for healthcare professionals: A scoping review. *Implementation Science, 9*(1), 54.

Uggla, H. (2006). The corporate brand association base: A conceptual model for the creation of inclusive brand architecture. *European Journal of Marketing, 40*(7/8), 785–802.

Zhao, H., Falkheimer, J., & Heide, M. (2017). Revisiting a social constructionist approach to crisis communication: Investigating contemporary crises in China. *International Journal of Strategic Communication, 11*(5), 364–378.

12 Branding for Small and Medium Sized Healthcare Institutions

Raphael Odoom and Douglas Opoku Agyeman

12.1 INTRODUCTION

I must say that I have a special connection – even an emotional tie to my clinic. Every time I drive by the small clinic with my three-year-old in the car, she says "that's where I was born." This is heart-warming. Besides, they have great milkshakes there.

(Lauren, cited in Kemp, Jillapalli & Becerra, 2014, p. 1)

In today's world, branding is regarded as an important function in every performance driven organisation (Dhawan & Prior, 2017). Over the years, branding has been upheld as an effective response to increased market concentration and competition. It offers the potential outcomes of centralised control and format standardisation, and an additional value- or cost-driven procedure which can be utilised to differentiate the company's offering and fortify market positioning (Schmidt & Pioch, 2005). Often, when discussing branding and brands, individuals have a propensity for envisioning enormous global brands with huge thoughts and much greater spending plans. Likewise, books and articles in general utilise global brands or huge local companies as examples. However, a solid brand is just as critical to a small business as it is to a big enterprise (Mitchell, Hutchinson & Quinn, 2013).

Global competition has made it compulsory for small and medium sized enterprises (SMEs) to leave their shell of moderate business strategies and transform themselves according to the need of changing market tastes and preferences. As a result, the branding process is particularly important for SMEs that desire to become players outside their domicile. While branding has for decades been customarily associated with or practised by consumer-packaged goods organisations, it is also a key device that can create a solid impact within service-oriented industries, specifically the healthcare industry.

In recent years, the healthcare industry in both developed and developing parts of the world, especially sub-Saharan Africa (SSA), has changed. Intense market transparency, high mortality rates, increased competition and number of private healthcare providers within the region have warranted the need for healthcare SMEs, particularly in SSA, to consider robust branding practices to promote to and satisfy their clients (Khosravizadeh, Vatankhah & Maleki, 2017). Like other industries, healthcare has become consumer driven (Kumar, Jacob & Thota, 2014). Google gets a massive amount of searches every day. It is quite interesting to realise that 5 per cent of all these Google searches are health related. This implies that each day a great number of people see content or information relating to healthcare service organisations and/or their brands. Customers see organisations and their competitors. Patients, suppliers and any other persons who purchase healthcare or devices have developed a superpower of information. Further, healthcare has become one of the most important, yet personalised, services a consumer will experience. In effect, for a high-trust industry like healthcare, the rewards of branding can be extremely compelling, irrespective of their size and nature. It can possibly draw in more patients and funding. Its identity can, likewise, coordinate the conduct of workers and help pull in the best talent which is crucial to the organisation's prosperity.

Although branding is essential to healthcare institutions, it appears that big healthcare organisations rather understand the power of brands. Perhaps, this is due to the close and very individualised nature of healthcare decision making. Big healthcare institutions appreciate that their brands assume a key role in capturing market share from other healthcare organisations, particularly smaller healthcare institutions (Snyder, 2013). That is the reason why they spend a lot of money yearly on advertising directly to prospective patients, re-positioning their brand as more secure, better, faster and of higher quality. Hence, we ponder, do small healthcare institutions need to brand themselves in a sector or industry that one could envision as being somewhat unusual for branding? Can branding provide small healthcare institutions with a tool to communicate their value to the public as potential consumers of their services?

To this question, Lauren gives an answer in the quote above. She has a special connection – even an emotional tie – to her small clinic. Moreover, as a response to the strategic brand moves by big hospitals, as well as the turbulent changes in the industry, small healthcare institutions need to pull out all the stops on branding in order to achieve success. More and more SMEs in healthcare are now developing their own brands, expanding the scope of their operations to include not only services but also marketing, and reorienting themselves from the regional (host) market to focus on the global market as a whole. Thus, for small healthcare institutions, strong brands are now viewed as essential to the sustainability of the business in both domestic and international markets. Besides, earlier studies have shown that small healthcare institutions which operate a strategy of a unique marketplace specialism are inherently more successful. Even though healthcare organisations are branding their services, however, most healthcare SMEs, especially in SSA, seem to be content with their web module of promotion, with very few making any effort towards full-fledged branding motives. The question is, how can SMEs in small healthcare businesses institute the requisite branding strategies to achieve success? This paper develops this line of argument by addressing whether there is the need for SMEs in healthcare services to brand themselves.

The chapter is structured in four sections. The following section provides the general introduction to branding with specific reference to small healthcare institutions. The second part looks at the various definitions of branding and its significance, especially to healthcare SMEs in SSA. The third section of the chapter discusses the branding strategies of healthcare institutions. The fourth section presents the implications and the concluding thoughts on the chapter.

12.2 DEFINITIONS OF BRANDING AND ITS SIGNIFICANCE

In seeking to understand the concept of SME healthcare branding, the first question that needs to be answered is, "what is branding?" In the brand management field, varied definitions of branding have been put forward by scholars and practitioners, dependent upon the paradigmatic approach adopted. These paradigms can be broadly categorised into the product, the projective, adaptive, relational, and the emotional paradigms. With regard to the product paradigm, the brand is characterised by product elements such as logos, trademarks, features and other identifiers. Berry (2000) proposes that branding services is not quite the same as branding goods as a result of the characteristics (intangible qualities) that make services different from goods. In effect, a successful brand in this perspective can be a name, symbol, design or some combination of these, that identifies the product or service of a vendor or group of vendors and distinguishes them from those of competitors. Conversely, the projective paradigm takes the view that product traits do not signify sustainable brand attributes (Simoes & Dibb, 2001), but rather buyers define branding as a holistic firm-wide identity system. From a seemingly different perspective, the adaptive paradigm characterises the brand from the buyers' point of view (Wood, 2000), whereby they translate brand messages to form a collection of brand associations for brand meaning. Taking this into consideration, the relational paradigm characterises the brand as the bond between client and firm, which acts as the fundamental source of brand differentiation (Fournier, 1998). Nonetheless, in contrast, the emotional paradigm gives prominence to the intimacy of brand–customer bonds (Cova & Cova, 2002), which can form brand communities. However, branding is not just about the logo, variation or recognition either. The fundamental point of branding is to increase value to the client (as that enhances the value of the organisation in the long run) irrespective of whether it is a service, good, company, art, person, event, etc. (Gad, 2001).

In the healthcare context, the best definition of branding has nothing to do with name, logo, image or colour scheme. There are undoubtedly some auxiliary advantages from perfecting your design elements. However, they do not make up the core of what a brand means to healthcare institutions. Rather, their brand characterises precisely how their service offerings are perfectly aligned with the needs of their patients. At the end of the day, branding to healthcare organisations is winning an individual's (i.e. patient's) trust by giving the best treatment. Healthcare branding has to do with endowing healthcare institutions (whether hospitals or clinics) and services with the power of the brand equity. The brand equity affirms the value of the healthcare organisation in the sight of the patients. And this can be achieved if the healthcare has a favourable brand image in the eyes of the patients. Thus, a health institution's brand image is the sum of beliefs, thoughts and impressions that a patient holds towards a healthcare organisation (Kotler, Shalowitz & Stevens, 2008). A brand image of a healthcare organisation is not absolute; it is relative to brand images of competing healthcare institutions. Consumers (patients) develop a brand image of healthcare organisation from their own medical experiences. DeVries and McKeever (2008) also add that with regard to health services organisations, branding is the major component linking business objectives, worker conduct, advertising correspondence and the capacity to convey uncommon encounters; that is, dealing with the patients with added value.

But why do healthcare institutions need to develop a brand? Brands themselves are valuable intangible resources that should be managed with consideration as they offer advantages to clients, employees and employers. The key importance of branding is that consumers perceive differences between brands in a product or service category. One notable reason is that a brand name and trademark can give legitimate assurance to a product or a service, keeping the organisation's rivals from replicating it. Branding, likewise, encourages market segmentation; a brand can assist an organisation with cultivating customer loyalty, consequently looking after stable sales volume and guaranteeing long term profitability. Onkvisit and Shaw (1989) observed the favourable circumstances of having a brand from the perspective of a service firm. They found that brands assume a vital role in service organisations since they cultivate trust from customers for intangible performance factors (Berry, 2000), creating the possibility for clients to readily visualise and understand them. They lessen clients' perceived monetary or social dangers in purchasing services, which are an obstruction to assessing services effectively before purchase. Similarly, service brands can help consumers by guaranteeing them a uniform level of service quality (Krishnan & Hartline, 2001). Arguably, this presupposes that branding of services is even more critical than branding of goods since the customer has no tangible attributes when evaluating the brand.

12.3 WHY BRANDING MATTERS FOR SMALL HEALTHCARE INSTITUTIONS

Until the early 1970s, hospitals, clinics, nursing homes, hospices, birth centres, managed care organisations, rehabilitation centres and other healthcare institutions did not consider branding. Healthcare experts and organisations cautioned against the amalgamation of the words "healthcare" and "branding" in the same phrase. Many misinterpreted branding as advertising, and advertising for healthcare services was viewed as unfitting. Along these lines, healthcare service providers had long opposed the integration of formal branding activities into their operations.

Fast forward to today, the healthcare industry is globally undergoing a rapid change; growing lifestyle, expanding populace, related medical issues, cheaper cost of treatment, improved health insurance penetration, increasing disposable income and government initiatives. In SSA, for instance, as new hospitals emerge, and more healthcare options become available to consumers (for example, minute clinics in drug stores, after-hour urgent care clinics), more competition will be real within the industry. Previously, individuals had the same physician for years, perhaps their entire life, and doctors were trusted without criticism. However, patients now have resources to learn more about their health and their options for care. They are more sophisticated. They have higher desires. They will decide whether to remain in their community or go to a specialist or to an urgent care centre or a clinic. Considering the changes in the industry, effective healthcare systems will perceive these changes as catalysts for developing new strategies that satisfy their societies' healthcare needs. Further, most healthcare institutions, especially in SSA, have failed due to lack of government support and insufficient resources in their healthcare management (Khosravizadeh et al., 2017). As a result, branding is now considered as a conceivable strategy to support the growth and success of healthcare organisations, especially in SSA.

This has created a need for developing a brand for healthcare institutions, as branding is a valuable intangible asset and differentiator for any organisation (Wu, 2011). In general, organisations in the healthcare sector need to be trusted and the service provided has to be satisfactory and professional. They need to provide added value for the patient. Therefore, effective healthcare institutions need to look beyond the tradition; they need to start a different way of thinking about the organisation as a whole and increase the role of branding. Thus, effective branding strategy will require healthcare institutions, regardless of the size, to develop a strong brand identity. Healthcare organisations should have in mind that they possess profitable tangible and intangible resources that should keep up with care as they offer advantages to patients, employees and employers. The brand is not only for the clients; great branding can take a healthcare organisation to the next level (Green Communications, 2006). In the healthcare industry, branding of clinics or hospitals for the most part depends on converting each patient into a brand representative for that health organisation. Consequently, it is essential for a healthcare organisation to always brand its service, if the business wants to be identified, differentiated and perceived as more than just one more institution providing similar services to others. Hence, it is evident that, regardless of what size the healthcare organisation is, the most successful ones are simply those that have positioned themselves as leaders in the industry by developing a strong brand. How good a brand is is not related to the size of an organisation.

Consequently, the line of argument for this chapter is justified that small healthcare institutions need to brand themselves as well. Arguably, small healthcare organisations need to engage in effective brand management in order to survive the wild changes in the industry. A recent report by Blue Cross Blue Shield in the US also confirmed that prospective patients seeking for quality healthcare will drive directly past their local, smaller clinic to persevere through the maze of admissions, testing and treatment at a much bigger hospital; this is despite the fact that prospective patients can receive equal – even possibly better – care at their small facility or clinic. These patients were thought to accept this extra travel because of 1) the established brand and perceived value of the larger hospital, and 2) anxiety/fear that they will receive sub-standard treatment options at a local, smaller facility. Accordingly, in this competitive healthcare environment, small healthcare institutions need to focus their marketing efforts on effective and strategic brand management.

In addition to these points, Green Communications (2006) argues that every healthcare organisation, whether a low-cost care or a specialist, stands for a certain image or brand value in the minds of clients or prospective clients. Customers already have an idea in their minds of what that organisation (brand) or the business means to them. Therefore, branding a small healthcare organisation means that it conveys its message more successfully to the customers so that they associate the organisation more positively with their needs and requirements. Hence, it is essential that every staff member, from the CEO or owner manager to the volunteer at the reception desk, communicates the mission of the organisation effectively. The result is a brand-guided organisation. Good branding can take even a small healthcare organisation to the next level.

Accordingly, it is strongly argued that small organisations in healthcare services can also create effective brands. To be more precise, small healthcare institutions need to develop effective brands in the midst of industry changes, especially as they compete for care and quality outcomes. Considering the paucity of research material on SME healthcare branding in the SSA context, sub-Saharan Africa is a region in dire need of development and perhaps with the greatest need of research attention. In view of the many benefits that can accrue for SSA countries that successfully implement branding initiatives, a study that focuses on such an under researched part of the African region is relevant and the need for it cannot be overemphasised.

12.4 BENEFITS OF BRANDING TO SMALL HEALTHCARE INSTITUTIONS

As a result of recent increase in competition, and the reframing of the consumer experience, the healthcare delivery system is getting considerably more complicated, and big healthcare organisations appear to be distinct as far as their healthcare services offered are concerned. This has made it a prerequisite for small healthcare organisations to develop a brand. What benefits can small healthcare institutions accrue from engaging in effective brand management?

First, it is important to note that effective branding for small healthcare organisations will allow them to create a filter through which all decisions will be observed. Branding services provided by small healthcare institutions will set a key position over rivals in the market and among consumers. Thus, a favourable brand image is regarded as a critical element of an organisation holding on to its market position. This is so because the brand can be considered as a valuable intangible resource, which is difficult to copy and which is beneficial to attaining sustained performance. In SSA, for instance, small healthcare institutions need to understand that advertising alone is not sufficient to defeat the challenge, but creating a brand for the organisation is a crucial part of setting up a strong spot in the competitive market. Van Niekerk, former Global Head of Marketing for Investec notes that most SME healthcare institutions in sub-Saharan Africa do not know the most important aspects of branding, hence the need to improve the branding know-how required to spur the growth of healthcare SMEs (Global Entrepreneurship Monitor, 2017).

As a result, many popular small healthcare institutions such as the Mayo Clinic and Cleveland Clinic (both in the US), Manipal Heart Foundation (Bangalore), etc., have increased efforts to reinforce their brands (Thomaselli, 2010). As small healthcare organisations engage in branding, it is possible for them to create a direct and simple message of "why" their brand should matter to the consumer (patient). The majority of clients do not have the time or inclination to figure this out on behalf of the organisation. The brand must create a story that answers the question, "why you?"

Moreover, by building up a solid brand image, reappearance of the patients at the healthcare centre will increase. This is because branding creates a favourable image which provokes patient loyalty, and furthermore upgrades patient satisfaction through the improvement of service quality and reduces patients' perceived risks in buying services (Kim et al., 2008). The presence of enough patients to treat is essential too, since a healthcare service ends up pointless without them. Concentrating on developing impressions of a quality trusted healthcare provider which understands patient needs can entice new patients and retain existing ones (Wu, 2011). Patient experience is equally critical to enhancing satisfaction and expanding positive word-of-mouth referrals. Further, patients or customers connect with healthcare institutions through the mode of the healthcare brand, and the brand creates a solid connection between the institution and the customer. It is almost impossible for customers or prospective patients to emotionally cement a positive connection in their minds if the business does not have a reliable way of deploying its brand at all points of contact.

Moreover, choosing a brand for a small healthcare organisation can be vital to advance the services offered by that organisation in the market, as well as enhance the money related status of the organisation. Misbranding of a small healthcare organisation may influence its money related outlook (for example market share loss and financial loss). Establishing a brand can also motivate the employees of a small healthcare organisation. Any organisation can hire workers, but only a strong brand can contract motivated employees who are impelled to move the vision and mission of the organisation forward. At a point where your brand feels pride, your workers do as well. Having a solid brand is critical for employee morale and efficiency.

Small healthcare organisations should also consider that a successful brand will increase the value of the business, which can attract prospective customers, investors or franchisees. This is because a developed brand indicates that the business understands its purpose and goal. It shows that you are not just another organisation competing in a noisy space. Investors will be eager to work with organisations which are organised (Green Communications, 2006). Technology adaptation, clinical steps forward, national accreditations and quality rankings are instances of healthcare branding strategies. We can see that as the healthcare services industry is moving towards corporatisation, branding prompts this corporatisation culture. We will now consider how to apply Gelb's brand trust model to explore how small healthcare institutions can build successful brands.

12.5 BRAND BUILDING STRATEGIES FOR SMALL HEALTHCARE INSTITUTIONS

Now, this chapter points out clearly why a healthcare brand is important and why it is risky not to have one. The next big question is: how can a small healthcare organisation develop an effective brand strategy? A brand strategy can be difficult to define but will comprise: what the brand stands for; what promises the brand makes to clients; what identity the brand sends through its marketing. Nevertheless, it is different when we observe this in the healthcare industry. The healthcare sector revolves around trust and recognition. The healthcare branding strategies should lay emphasis on trust, staff–patient relationships and professionalism, doing what the business claims it does and keeping it clear and simple. However, it is worth keeping in mind that patients do not just want to trust a healthcare institution, they prefer experiences and added value for themselves (DeVries & McKeever, 2008). To be more precise, when it comes to healthcare institutions, branding strategies should be tied to business goals, employee behaviour, marketing communication and the ability to deliver excellent experiences – that is, to taking care of the patients with added value (DeVries & McKeever, 2008). For the purposes of this discussion, and considering the nature of the industry, we consider Gelb's brand trust model to explore how small healthcare institutions can build their brands (see Figure 12.1). We summarise these branding strategies into four themes, namely: customer value, consistent brand experience, competitive difference and familiarity. Within an organisation, these tasks are usually undertaken by the entire staff in that organisation.

Gelb's brand trust model is based upon the empirical observation that familiarity is a crucial element of successful brand building, while the choice element and differentiation establish brands. Nevertheless, it is also the customer's experience and trust (as calculated by probability of

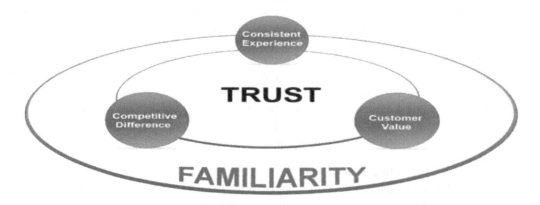

FIGURE 12.1 Gelb's Brand Trust Model. (Source: Gelb Consulting (2011)).

recommendation) that create brand equity. The model scrutinises the central elements to developing a sustainable competitive advantage (that is, a solid healthcare brand). The elements inside the circle consist of customer value (the benefit of high importance), competitive difference (reputation based on brand personality) and consistent experience (continuous customer satisfaction). The three (3) aspects combined create the trust that the consumers or patients have for the healthcare business (DeVries & McKeever, 2008)

12.5.1 CONSISTENT EXPERIENCE (CONTINUOUS CUSTOMER SATISFACTION)

Consistent brand experience is how well the brand delivers on its promise; it drives customer satisfaction and loyalty. That is, experience has been characterised as displaying a relatively high level of familiarity with a specific brand, which is acquired through some sort of exposure to the brand. For example, a consumer who has experienced the process of information search, decision making and/or service patronage would be viewed as experienced. As consumers' brand experiences deepen, it is proposed that their capacities to classify brands by attributes are improved (Weinberg, 2001). However, the level of brand experience can vary to some degree, which is because improved brand experience is not only associated with familiarity. This also impacts critically on understanding, appreciating, upgrading and developing the brand.

Consequently, regarding the healthcare sector, a crucial part of the healthcare branding strategy is to ensure that the experience offered by the brand is consistent and organised across every point of contact. This is because brand consistency converts into reliability in the mind of the consumer. Hence, a patient–healthcare relationship, based on brand experience, may positively affect the level of brand trust. In healthcare branding, experience is one of the key issues, no matter the size of the practice or organisation, because the greatest impact in healthcare comes through interactions between the staff and the patient, their family members and others.

In the attempt of small healthcare institutions to achieve this, daily positive and helpful brand experience should be encouraged by recognising and encouraging positive behaviour. Small healthcare organisations should understand that healthcare branding is an emotional connection between the practice and the people it serves. Hence, the staff and employees are the main conduit for making that people-to-people connection. Therefore, for a healthcare brand (specifically, small healthcare) to endure, the brand must be easily understood, internalised and acted on by the staff (Grensing-Pophal, 2011). The staff in a small healthcare organisation play a key role in delivering the brand experience, because they are the ones interacting with patients, their families and potential customers. If the employees do not understand the brand completely they might send mixed messages to customers that conflict with what the brand stands for. On the other hand, when employees understand the brand and that they are part of the process, they know they will be dealt with more respectfully and they are more likely to come along with the vision and even turn into brand ambassadors (Grensing-Pophal, 2011).

Moreover, the experiences patients have with the healthcare service can be linked to its physical environment (healthcare facility or office). The healthcare facility has a message. When a new patient crosses the threshold for the first time, they get an immediate message about the physical environment. What if a doctor's office looks messy and papers are lying around? Will the brand message be delivered to the patient when they walk to the office and expect reliable and efficient service? The facility has a message and the worst case scenario is that it might have a negative impact on the brand. It might be good to consider the impact of the location, building appearance and office interiors to the brand image (Hirsch & Gandolf, 2011). On the other hand, small healthcare institutions can start to bring their desired brand experience in line with reality by also improving the organisation's online experience with a user-friendly website, patient portals and online scheduling. Thus, to achieve consistent brand experience, the brand personality should extend from the smiles on your employees' faces to the user-friendliness of your website's interface.

This presupposes that branding begins from an inside-out outlook, as the brand has to be clearly understood, believed and delivered by the owners and the employees as much as by the current and potential customers (Grensing-Pophal, 2011). In effect, to achieve consistent brand experience, it is crucial for small healthcare institutions, especially in sub-Saharan Africa, to train the staff in the branding message; they need to understand the goals, and why and how they are reached, as well as their role. Second, branding should also be brought to the hiring process and to the organisational culture as it is important to hire and retain the right people who inspire a positive environment.

12.5.2 Competitive Difference (Reputation Based on Brand Personality)

Competitive difference defines how brands are distinguished; it drives the reputation of the firm. That is, reputation is based on the personality of the brand. To truly differentiate the healthcare organisation from others, the healthcare business needs to think long and hard about how it can distinguish itself in the industry. This can be achieved by rightly positioning the healthcare brand and creating a solid brand identity. Brand positioning is suggested to be the conceptual place the healthcare business wants to own in the potential consumer's mind that sets the brand apart: that is, the benefits the firm wants the customers to think of when they think about the brand.

This suggests that establishing a healthcare brand that is trustworthy and reliable amid the competition will go a long way to ingratiate the healthcare organisation with its customer base. By considering the overlap of the firm's services and attributes, the competitor's offerings and market needs, the firm can distil its brand position. Greenawalt (2001) mentions that several variables are involved in positioning a brand in the health sector. These variables include: vision, brand's meaning and parameters of relevance. Vision is the brand's roots. It defines why the healthcare organisation exists and where it is headed. The vision must be sustainable so as to ensure visibility, greater market share, financial performance and overall growth. Meaning defines what the organisation's brand represents in the industry, while parameters of relevance refer to the limit to which the healthcare brand can be extended. The development of an effective brand combines these variables.

Consequently, in achieving a solid brand positioning, small healthcare organisations must study the competitive landscape in which the brand operates so that the firm can hope to identify opportunities for differentiation. Ginter, Duncan, and Swayne (2018) also explain that the traditional brand positioning for achieving competitive difference in healthcare involves one or more elements (for example, price, quality of service, convenience, operational efficiency, expense control and superior services). Nevertheless, positioning can also be based on new technology, innovation and geographical focus. For example, the healthcare institution may be the sole provider for a certain demographic in a specific region. This powerful claim, matched with aligned services, will communicate a beneficial difference to the patients the business wants to reach. For instance, the Mayo Clinic in the US is uniquely positioned to advance medicine and bring discovery to practice more efficiently and effectively. Mayo Clinic's Center for the Science of Health Care Delivery works to innovate and validate effective, affordable and accessible healthcare delivery models to benefit healthcare for people everywhere.

Considering the above example, there is a variety of sources of differential advantage. These include technological capability, name or image, clinical expertise, distribution network, geographic focus, narrow product line, targeted segment and operational efficiency. Each of these sources of differential advantage has inherent strengths and weaknesses. Therefore, the choice of strategy for small healthcare institutions should rely on the consideration of benefits to the client, perception by the client, uniqueness and sustainability.

Under these circumstances, small organisations in healthcare business need to identify their brand uniqueness in order to arrive at the right positioning and also generate options for core messaging. And this should be aligned with research (both qualitative and quantitative). Only by collecting qualitative and quantitative data can the business progress to identifying its brand strategy. Additionally, Ginter et al. (2013) suggest that achieving a competitive difference is the actions of that healthcare institution (specifically the small healthcare institution) to obtain the best resources (including human resources, infrastructure) that will provide a differential advantage over other similar entities and help the entity maintain leadership in the market for that segment of the population served.

On the other hand, small healthcare firms can achieve competitive difference by creating a solid brand identity for the healthcare. A brand identity strategy is how the healthcare organisation seeks to identify itself. It is the promise the healthcare makes to people along with the mission, personality and competitive advantages. It is a means for healthcare businesses to find a position in the market and consumer's mind. A well-built brand identity will effectively communicate a healthcare organisation's personality and its value to potential customers, and will help in building brand recognition, association and loyalty. Aaker (2011) proposed that brand identity encompasses: healthcare's internal perceptions, expected quality or a promise defined within the healthcare business, and the functional and emotional relationship with patient. Subsequently, Aaker (2011) added that a healthcare brand identity should consist of core identity and extended identity. Core identity is the essence of the brand and that aspect of the identity that remains intact even over time. Extended identity in turn reflects those aspects of a brand's identity that may change over time and between different markets, such as logo/wordmark, colour scheme, text used on ads, website, documents and designs.

For example, the brand identity for Vista Community Clinic (VCC) is centred on a rejuvenated signature – that is, a fresh visual representation of the organisation's welcoming approaches to community health and hope (see www.vistacommunityclinic.org). Their colour green symbolises growth and vitality, while blue conjures trust and confidence. The VCC wordmark is illustrated so as to evoke caring and open arms. And the handwritten tagline symbolises the personal and human touch that every patient can expect to encounter at VCC facilities. However, small healthcare firms should understand that to be successful with brand identity, it must be tightly aligned with the brand position. In other words, to achieve a successful competitive difference, the firm's brand position and brand identity should be aligned together.

12.5.3 Customer Value (The Benefit of High Importance)

To build an effective brand strategy, the healthcare business needs to ask the following questions. What are the benefits expected from the healthcare brand? What are the key strengths and weaknesses? How willing are customers to pay a premium for the health services provided? How often do customers prefer the healthcare brand? This is called customer value. Value has various connotations. To some, value means price, to others it means benefit. It also means the worth of something. That is why we often hear the phrase "value for money" (meaning they are price sensitive); and others who prefer "money for value" (meaning they are willing to pay for what they consider as benefits, as from a brand or a better service, or more convenience etc.). In healthcare branding, customer value is the perception of how much the healthcare provided is worth to the consumer (patient) versus the possible alternatives. Researchers have found that the value benefits of healthcare brands increase as the values, beliefs and emotions of consumers are incorporated into brand messages.

In seeking to achieve this task, the healthcare organisation has to understand the customer value concept: what patients or customers perceive as value, how a customer's value needs change over time and how to get customer feedback. The organisation must realise that patients patronise services that create the most value over competing options. Therefore, for small healthcare institutions to create real value, the business must identify what a customer perceives as value. The firm must understand how the customer views other healthcare institutions. What is important to the customers in their buying decisions? Is price more important or are benefits? Are you good at delivering what the customer believes is important? Are you able to deliver more than your competition on these factors?

Creating customer value for patients enhances patients' satisfaction and the patient experience. The reverse is also true; a good customer experience will create value for a customer. Creating customer value (better benefits versus price) increases loyalty and market share, reduces errors and increases efficiency. Higher market share for the healthcare organisation and better efficiency leads to higher profits. Some examples of how healthcare institutions can create customer value include:

1. Giving a price that makes patients believe they are getting more than they pay for in the benefits they get versus competitive offers.
2. Reducing the price or keeping the same price and giving something extra over competition (this could be better attention or some added value to the service or treatment).
3. Making it convenient for the customer to access the healthcare, and to buy and pay for it.
4. Smiling at and being attentive to a patient, which creates value for him or her.
5. Making it easy for the patients to contact the organisation and instilling an assurance that an answer will be given when and how promised.

In effect, for healthcare organisations, customer value is the ability of the healthcare institution to solve the problem of patients with added value. That is customer value.

12.5.4 FAMILIARITY

Familiarity is defined as the awareness and knowledge that targeted customers have of your brand. It is based on experience with your brand. Thus, forming brand familiarity might depend on consumers' perceptions based on brand experience. To build successful brand value for the healthcare firm, customers or patients must not only recognise the firm, but also be able to place it into a category of service. This is called brand familiarity, which goes beyond just name recall and involves a reasonable relationship with specific healthcare services. Once familiarity is attained, clients assess how well the firm competes, normally on the basis of rational components. These would incorporate excellent healthcare service, convenience of location and even out-of-pocket expenses.

Familiarity also shows that the organisation has been heard of (awareness) and somebody (friend, family, recommendation in a magazine or on the internet) has used it (experience). Brand familiarity with healthcare services is derived from the frequency of brand-related experiences the consumer has had. This suggests that for a small healthcare institution to achieve brand familiarity, the organisation must be capable of providing excellent and consistent brand experience for its patients. Baker, Hutchinson, Moore, and Nedungadi (1986) also add that brand familiarity is a unidimensional construct that is directly related to the amount of time spent processing information about the healthcare, regardless of the type or content of the processing involved. It means that in developing strong brands, the healthcare institution must make sure its brand stays at the forefront of the mind.

Nevertheless, it is critical for small healthcare institutions to understand that familiarity is also linked with preferability. If someone has mentioned the firm, they must have liked the service (reputation, perceived quality, overall satisfaction). As Accountability Information Management (AIM) says "a customer can be familiar with the brand, but not prefer, or you can be familiar and prefer, but a customer cannot prefer what he or she is not familiar with". This presumes that to develop a solid brand strategy, small healthcare institutions should focus on brand familiarity and preference elements.

12.6 CONCLUSIONS AND IMPLICATIONS

Branding existed before, during and after the era of slavery. Today branding remains very significant to all organisations around the world. Small firms are branding, medium firms are branding, while large firms are also branding. All organisations are branding themselves. Analysis of issues in this chapter has revealed that small healthcare organisations should brand because competition has become intense and technology has espoused patients or customers to varied brands. Therefore, branding healthcare institutions will enhance business identification and differentiation and enhance brand trust more than just any other institution providing similar services as others will. In effect, branding creates a solid brand image, leading to re-purchase intentions on the part of patients. In view of this, the chapter recommends that small healthcare institutions, particularly in sub-Saharan Africa, should offer branding a commanding place in their resource allocation. Healthcare institutions should be charged with sufficient resources to create brand content that is appealing, creative and innovative for customers. All operational staff from security personnel to the manager should be oriented to deliver quality healthcare, since they represent the number one source of brand for the organisation.

Arguably, building a strong brand is a very difficult task for small healthcare institutions around the world. This phenomenon is evident in SSA, where small healthcare outfits are noted for avoidable marketing and branding errors, thus resulting in high mortality. This difficulty originates from the inability of small healthcare institutions to deliver their promise and also communicate their brand value. Analysis of Gelb's brand trust model has revealed that there are four building strategies for small healthcare organisations. Hence, we conclude that consistent experience, competitive differences and customer value create high level familiarity, thus influencing brand trust among patients.

How well the brand conveys and delivers on its promise drives high brand familiarity leading to brand trust and a strong brand. To achieve consistent brand experience for strong brands, this chapter recommends that small healthcare institutions, especially in sub-Saharan Africa must train their staff in the branding message; staff must understand the goals and why and how they are reached, as well as their role in the branding message. Small healthcare institutions in SSA should hire and retain the right people with the right attitude to the organizational branding culture and who can inspire a positive environment.

We also contend that distinguishing and differentiating a brand result in high brand familiarity and trust, leading to strong brands. This implies that in establishing trustworthy and reliable healthcare brands amid competitive intensity, it is important to differentiate the brand and connect with its customer base. Hence, this chapter recommends that, to achieve solid brand positioning, small healthcare organisations must study the competitive environment of their brand to identify opportunities for differentiation. Small healthcare institutions in SSA must identify their brand novelty and the uniqueness of their brands in order to position them and also generate options for communicating the core value of the brand.

This chapter further maintains that brand value also creates brand familiarity, leading to brand trust and hence a strong brand. Therefore, it is recommended that for small healthcare institutions to create real value, there is the need to understand what patients or customers perceive as value, how the value needs of the customer change over time, and how to get customer feedback to create value. The organisation must understand that patients patronise a healthcare service that creates a value greater than what competitors are offering. This chapter has established that there is a relationship between brand building strategies and customer value, leading to brand familiarity and trust, and hence strong brands.

REFERENCES

Aaker, D. A. (2011). *Brand relevance*. San Francisco, CA: Wiley.

Baker, W., Hutchinson, J., Moore, D., & Nedungadi, P. (1986). Brand familiarity and advertising: Effects on the evoked set and brand preference. *North American Advances in Consumer Research, 13*, 637–642.

Barbis, D. (2012). *Brand model creation for a small healthcare service* (MBA thesis, Helsinki: HaagaHelia university of applied sciences).

Berry, L. L. (2000). Cultivating service brand equity. *Journal of the Academy of Marketing Science, 28*(1), 128–137.

Brennan, I., & Babin, L. A. (2004). Brand placement recognition: The influence of presentation mode and brand familiarity. *Journal of Promotion Management, 10*(1–2), 185–202.

Cova, B., & Cova, V. (2002). Tribal marketing. *European Journal of Marketing, 36*, 595–620.

Devers, K. J., Brewster, L. R., & Casalino, L. P. (2003). Changes in hospital competitive strategy: A new medical arms race? *Health Services Research, 38*(1, Pt. 2), 447–469.

DeVries, K., & McKeever, J. (2008). Constructing a better brand: High-performance brands begin with a solid foundation. *Marketing Health Services, 28*(4), 15.

Dhawan, P., & Prior, D. (2017). Internal branding and leader-member exchange: Role of cultural capital in employee's service delivery behaviour in healthcare sector: An abstract. In *Academy of Marketing Science World Marketing Congress* (pp. 259–259). Cham, Switzerland: Springer.

Dominiak, M. C. (2004). The concept of branding: Is it relevant to nursing? *Nursing Science Quarterly, 17*(4), 295–300.

Du Plooy, T., & De Jager, J. (2007). Measuring tangibility and assurance as determinants of service quality for public health care in South Africa. *Professional Accountant, 7*(1), 96–111.

Farid, I. M. F. (2008). Development of a model for healthcare service quality: An application to the private healthcare sector in Egypt. Maastricht School of Management, New Delhi. Retrieved January 1, 2015, from www.msm.nl/resources/uploads/2013/10/Appendix-12a-Fikry.pdf [Google Scholar].

Fournier, S. M. (1998). Consumers and their brands: Developing relationship theory in consumer research. *Journal of Consumer Research, 24*(4), 343–373.

Gad, T. (2001). *4-D branding: Cracking the corporate code of the network economy.* Pearson Education.

Gelb Consulting. (2011). Brand trust model. Retrieved February 19, 2019, from www.gelbconsulting.com/brand-research.

Ginter, P. M., Duncan, W. J., & Swayne, L. E. (2018). *The strategic management of health care organizations.* John Wiley & Sons.

Global Entrepreneurship Monitor. (2017). *GEM 2016/2017 global report.* Retrieved July 6, 2019, from www.gemconsortium.org/report/gem-2016-2017-global-report.

GREEN Communications. (2006). Guide to creating a brand). Retrieved October 19, 2011, from www.green-blog.co.uk/files/quide-to-creating-a-brand.pdf.

Greenawalt, B. J. (2001). Can branding curb burnout? *Nursing Management, 32*(9), 26–31.

Grensing-Pophal, L. (2011). Practice branding starts from inside. *Medical Economics, 88*(14), 36.

Hirsch, L., Gandolf, S. (2011). How to build your brand through staff, office and location. Retrieved February 19, 2019, from www.healthcaresuccess.com/articles/brand-building.html.

Kemp, E., Jillapalli, R., & Becerra, E. (2014). Healthcare branding: Developing emotionally based consumer brand relationships. *Journal of Services Marketing, 28*(2), 126–137.

Kent, T. (2003). 2D23D: Management and design perspectives of retail branding. *International Journal of Retail & Distribution Management, 31*(3), 131–142.

Khosravizadeh, O., Vatankhah, S., & Maleki, M. (2017). A systematic review of medical service branding: Essential approach to hospital sector. *Annals of Tropical Medicine and Public Health, 10*(5), 1137.

Kim, K. H., Kim, K. S., Kim, D. Y., Kim, J. H., & Kang, S. H. (2008). Brand equity in hospital marketing. *Journal of Business Research, 1*(61), 75–82.

Kotler, P., Shalowitz, J., & Stevens, R. (2008). *Strategic marketing for health care organizations.* Jossey-Bass.

Krishnan, B. C., & Hartline, M. D. (2001). Brand equity: Is it more important in services? *Journal of Services Marketing, 15*(5), 328–342.

Kumar, N. P., Jacob, A., & Thota, S. (2014). Impact of healthcare marketing and branding on hospital services. *International Journal of Research Foundation of Hospital & Healthcare Administration, 2*(1), 19–24.

Mitchell, R., Hutchinson, K., & Quinn, B. (2013). Brand management in small and medium-sized (SME) retailers: A future research agenda. *Journal of Marketing Management, 29*(11–12), 1367–1393.

Onkvisit, S., & Shaw, J. J. (1989). Service marketing: Image, branding, and competition. *Business Horizons, 32*(1), 13–19.

Pinkerton, S. (2002). Marketing and branding (Retention and recruitment). *Nursing Economics, 20*(1), 42–44.

Schmidt, R. Ä., & Pioch, E. A. (2005). Community pharmacies under pressure: Can branding help? *International Journal of Retail & Distribution Management, 33*(7), 494–504.

Simoes, C., & Dibb, S. (2001). Rethinking the brand concept: New brand orientation. *Corporate Communications: An International Journal, 6*(4), 217–224.

Snyder, M. 2013. Regaining market share for small city and rural hospitals. Retrieved February 20, 2019, from https://themekgroup.com/regaining-market-share-for-small-city-and-rural-hospitals/.

Speak, K. D. (1996). The challenge of health care branding. *Marketing Health Services, 16*(4), 40.

Thomaselli, R. (2010, June 28). Health-care reform stokes spending by top hospitals, clinics. *Advertising Age.*

Weinberg, B. D. (2001). Research in exploring the online consumer experience. *North American Advances in Consumer Research*, *28*, 227–232.

Wood, L. (2000). Brands and brand equity: Definition and management. *Management Decision*, *38*(9), 662–669.

Wu, C. C. (2011). The impact of hospital brand image on service quality, patient satisfaction and loyalty. *African Journal of Business Management*, *5*(12), 4873–4882.

13 Managing Healthcare Employees

Andrews Agya Yalley

13.1 INTRODUCTION

The healthcare workforce referred to in services as "people" can best be described as large and diverse and representing a conglomeration of employees and professionals from different backgrounds and professional associations (Ali and Aameed, 2016). They represent the highly skilled professionals and experts and the semi-skilled employees and trainees occupying both the frontline and the backstage in the delivery of healthcare services. They include the nurses, doctors, ward assistants, physician assistants, obstetricians, psychiatrists, paediatricians, surgeons, therapists and laboratory technicians, amongst others. These employees are indispensable and the lifeline of a healthcare organisation's internal, external and interactive marketing, and they represent the visible and invisible hands in the delivery of superior and holistic healthcare to patients.

From the patient's perspective, the inseparability, and the delicate, sensitive and emotional nature, of healthcare delivery puts healthcare employees, particularly frontline employees, in a privileged position as: the patient's first port of call; patients' emotional and physical support; creators and enhancers of patient experience; patients' friends; and relationship builders. Patient outcome and perception of healthcare quality are, therefore, largely influenced by healthcare employees (Osei-Frimpong and Owusu-Frimpong, 2017). From the employers' perspective, healthcare employees are a source of competitive advantage; a core part of the organisation's products and brand; a source of patient information; drivers of patient service quality, productivity and loyalty; and part-time marketers (Kotler and Keller, 2012; Yalley and Sekhon, 2014; Bowen, 2016; Sharma et al., 2017; Yalley and Agyapong, 2018). Healthcare employees are, therefore, an efficient and effective channel for understanding and anticipating patient needs; delivering high-quality care; building relationships and loyalty with patients; enhancing brand value; and, ultimately, influencing healthcare outcomes.

Despite the importance of healthcare employees, there are a number of concerns for healthcare employees and employers in Africa. First, employment is below the global benchmark as compared to its counterparts in developed countries, and by 2030 it is estimated that Africa will have a deficit of 5,843,806 healthcare workers (World Health Organization [WHO], 2016; Liu et al., 2017). This has negative implications for healthcare professionals and institutions in Africa as well as for the quality of patient care. Second, the physical and emotional nature of healthcare jobs results in employee injuries, tiredness, stress-related illness, dissatisfaction, absenteeism and turnover, which consequentially impact on patient outcomes and fatalities as well as on organisational performance and reputation (Gates et al., 2011; McHugh et al., 2011; Koinis et al., 2015). Third, the multiplicity of employees' roles as boundary spanners, in their bid to satisfy management and patients, results in role conflicts and difficulties in meeting management and patient expectations, thus affecting healthcare outcomes. Addressing these concerns requires leveraging healthcare employees' privileged position in the service marketing triangle and getting the best out of them.

Kwame and Ruth met for the first time at a health conference after completing nursing training college four years ago. After the conference, the two college friends sat down to share their life-after-college stories. Kwame was posted to a large government hospital as a nurse and four years through a career, he is dissatisfied with his employer and attributed this to the government posting system. He also explained that he was not paid for almost two years after starting his work at the government hospital, which had demotivated his interest in nursing. He further expressed the ambiguity in his workplace attributing it to the unclear job description and inaccessible policies and procedures. He described the stressful nature of his job dealing with a large number of patients daily with limited resources and support from management and inadequate opportunities for professional development. He highlighted the growing number of patient complaints, dissatisfaction and mortality rate at his hospital and he is contemplating migrating abroad for a nursing job or starting his own trading business.

Ruth's story, on the other hand, is a happy one. Having completing nursing training, Ruth preferred working for a private hospital. It took a year to get a job at her favourite hospital after a thorough recruitment and selection process. She described her interview and assessment process as intensive and challenging and since being employed, she has all the support from her employers and she is being mentored by her supervisor in taking a leadership role at the hospital. She is paid regularly and she has recently been promoted and awarded the best employee of the year. Ruth attributes this to the excellent care she provides to patients, which has been necessary as a result of the hospital's clear policies and procedures and the training, motivation and support from management. Her future plan is staying with the hospital for the next fifteen years in order to take on leadership positions and finally to open her own hospital.

FIGURE 13.1   Healthcare Professional Life after College Chit-Chat.

Successful and customer-driven healthcare organisations are, therefore, the ones that get the best out of their employees through the application of human resource management practices. The stories shared by the two nurses in Figure 13.1 demonstrate the importance of managing healthcare employees.

13.2 HUMAN RESOURCE MANAGEMENT PRACTICES IN HEALTHCARE SERVICES

The importance of healthcare employees justifies the significance of managing the human resource of healthcare organisations. By human resource, we are referring to the people employed by healthcare organisations in delivering efficient and effective patient care; and their management is critical in getting the best out of them. This is termed human resource management (HRM) and is defined as "a strategic approach to managing employment relations which emphasizes that leveraging people's capabilities and commitment is critical to achieving a sustainable competitive advantage or superior public services" (Bratton and Gold, 2017: 5). The importance of HRM includes employee motivation, satisfaction and turnover; improved performance and service quality; and improved patient care and satisfaction. Successful implementation of HRM practices can also bridge the service quality gaps and contribute to the employee cycle of success. The role of HRM in healthcare entails resourcing and retaining efficient and effective employees and managing their performance towards the attainment of organisational goals and objectives. Other roles include providing guidance on the legal and ethical issues of patient care; health and safety of employees and patients; careers and labour union issues; and job analysis and design (Ali and Aameed, 2016).

13.2.1 HRM Issues and Challenges in Healthcare

A World Health Organization report almost two decades ago identified that one of the biggest challenges of the healthcare sector in Africa is its poor human resources management (WHO, 2000). This challenge still remains and has contributed to the low morale and high absenteeism and dissatisfaction amongst healthcare employees; to strikes and increasing staff shortages and workloads; to poor patient care and dissatisfaction; and to poor performance. The key HRM issues and challenges in the African healthcare sector are as follows:[1]

13.2.1.1 Centralised Recruitment and Selection

The recruitment and selection of healthcare professionals in most African countries are carried out using the centralised recruitment and selection approach via the posting system. "Posting system" refers to the making of decisions regarding where health employees work, and their geographic mobility within the health system. It entails a two-stage process: first, form filling and submission; and, second, a regional-level interview (Kwamie et al., 2017). The popularity of the centralised recruitment and selection method in most African countries can be attributed to its ability to ensure cost efficiency and the consistency and expertise associated with its processes, as well as its ability to balance the maldistribution of healthcare workforce in cities, rural and deprived areas (Njovu, 2013).

Despite its advantages, it also comes with several disadvantages. First, the processes and systems are inflexible to the diverse needs of the different healthcare institutions as well as to the uniqueness of health issues in the different parts of the country, particularly in the rural and urban areas. Second, as highlighted by Ali and Aameed (2016), the assessment of prospective healthcare employees at the time of recruitment and selection is inadequate in most developing countries. This can be attributed to the centralised recruitment approach which side-lines the in-depth interview and other relevant selection methods for evaluating a prospective employee's ability to cope with the physical, emotional and psychological demands of the healthcare job.

Third, the low involvement of prospective healthcare employees and management of healthcare institutions in the recruitment and selection process creates "personal fit" problems and possible conflicts between employees and their managers. This is attributed to the limited management participation in the recruitment and selection process or the posting process, thereby depriving management of the opportunity to assess and evaluate the values, expectations and personalities of prospective employees against those of their respective institutions. Similarly, prospective employees are deprived of the opportunity to select and work for the healthcare institution that fits their personal values, lifestyle and personalities. Finally, based on a reflection on the Ghanaian centralised posting system, Kwamie et al. (2017) identified that it breeds corruption at a higher level; operates on the logic of "who you know"; leads to absenteeism, low morale and inefficiency amongst healthcare employees; affects the balance between institutional needs and healthcare employee needs; and ultimately impacts negatively on the health system's accountability and patient outcomes.

13.2.1.2 Staff Shortages

Employment in the African healthcare sector is below the global benchmark as compared to its counterparts in developed countries. According to a WHO report, almost all African countries fall below the global benchmark of 2.5 health workers per 1,000 population (WHO, 2016). In addition, it is estimated that about 70 per cent of the healthcare workforce are lost to developed nations, and approximately 70,000 and 65,000 African-born nurses and doctors, respectively, are working in developed countries (Clemens and Pettersson, 2008; Aluttis et al., 2014). Further, it is estimated that by 2030, Africa will have a deficit of 5,843,806 healthcare workers as compared to its counterpart in Europe with a surplus of 11,016,996 healthcare workers (Liu et al., 2017). This disparity is attributed to some extent to the brain-drain of healthcare professionals to Western countries; poor investment and training of healthcare professionals; changes in career; and morbidity and premature mortality of healthcare employees (Kinfu et al., 2009; Andalón and Fields, 2011; Soucat et al., 2013). As a result, healthcare professionals in Africa are overworked and undergo physical and emotional exhaustion and this has a negative effect on the quality of healthcare outcomes.

13.2.1.3 Unclear and Inaccessible Policies and Procedures

Several scholars have reported poor, unclear and inaccessible policies and procedures facing healthcare institutions in Africa (e.g. Keers et al., 2013; Shayo et al., 2014; English et al., 2017) and these findings have been supported by a recent interview with healthcare professionals in Ghana. From the interview, most healthcare institutions have unclear and inadequate policies and procedures and most documents on policy and procedure are inaccessible to employees. Subsequently, newly recruited employees rely on advice and guidance from existing employees regardless of its correctness, thereby impacting negatively on employee socialisation, learning, development and performance and, ultimately, patient outcomes.

13.2.1.4 Inadequate Training and Development

The training provided for nurses and doctors by training colleges and universities is inadequate and does not prepare them for the challenges pertaining to developing countries' healthcare, particularly for the rural healthcare setting (Ali and Aameed, 2016). Healthcare professionals and employees are provided with limited training on interpersonal communication, doctor–patient and doctor–staff interactions, and counselling, which results in a failure to equip them with the necessary skills, knowledge, competency and expertise as compared to their counterparts in developed nations (Ali and Aameed, 2016). Also, from the interview, whilst on the job, healthcare institutions have failed to provide employees with adequate induction, orientation and reorientation courses as well as opportunities for further training and development. This is consistent with the findings of Kamati et al., on the challenges of nurses in Namibia (Kamati et al., 2014).

13.2.1.5 Inadequate Performance Appraisal

Performance appraisals for healthcare professionals are conducted in an informal and ad hoc fashion, sometimes during times of crisis, and are consummated by either unconstructive feedback or no feedback at all (Awases et al., 2013). From the interviews conducted, performance appraisals in healthcare tend to be routine, biased and standardised using generic indicators, and they fail to make any constructive review for performance improvement. This has a negative consequence on employees' motivation, morale, performance and service delivery, and subsequently on patient outcomes.

13.2.1.6 Poor Reward Systems and Management

Healthcare workers in Africa are poorly rewarded both intrinsically and extrinsically (Awases et al., 2013; Lutwama et al., 2013), and rewards are not based on performance but on grade, years in service and seniority (Kamati et al., 2014; Ali and Aameed, 2016). An example is Ghana's Single Spine Pay Policy implemented in 2010. In addition, from the interview, newly employed nurses in

Ghana, for instance, get their first salary a year or two after starting work. This has implications for employee motivation and morale, performance and patient outcomes.

13.2.1.7 Long Working Hours and Poor Working Conditions

Healthcare work in Africa is characterised as entailing long working hours, limited break or rest periods and long night shifts, and this is attributed to shortages of healthcare professionals. This also has negative implications for employees' performance and quality of patient care and patient safety (Wu et al., 2013). Another challenge is the poor working conditions and inadequate equipment and resources that characterise most healthcare institutions in developing countries (Kamati et al., 2014). These include inadequate resources (gloves, needles, ambulances, health equipment) and inadequate staff rooms, changing rooms and cafeterias. This has an impact on employee performance, self-efficacy and patient outcome (Kamati et al., 2014; Sekhon et al., 2016).

13.3 MANAGING EMPLOYEES IN HEALTHCARE ORGANISATIONS

Successful healthcare organisations are the ones that have built a competitive advantage and differentiated themselves by recruiting, selecting and retaining the best employees. The Mayo Clinic, Johns Hopkins Hospital, Gambro Healthcare, As-Salam International Hospital and Netcare Group are examples of healthcare organisations that have achieved this successfully. This was not attained by accident but through the strategic and careful recruitment, selection and management of employees. To address the aforementioned challenges facing African healthcare institutions, the following human resources management strategies are recommended:

13.3.1 STRATEGIC RECRUITMENT AND SELECTION

The deployment of healthcare employees has implications for the accessibility and quality of healthcare outcome;, therefore, a better alternative to the centralised recruitment and selection of healthcare professionals is paramount. What is required is a strategic approach to the recruitment and selection of employees through an in-depth and appropriate recruitment and selection process and the alignment of people towards the strategic direction of the organisation (O'Meara and Petzall, 2013). Several scholars and practitioners have recommended the decentralised approach to the recruitment and selection of healthcare professionals through in-depth interviews and further selection processes (Barnett et al., 1997; Hasenan, 2010; Adu-Gyamerah and Ali, 2018). This section will first discuss the recruitment and selection process, followed by a discussion on its application in the decentralised context.

13.3.1.1 Recruitment and Selection

The recruitment and selection of employees provide the vehicle for achieving competitive advantage and differentiation. Recruitment refers to the process of finding and engaging the people requirement of the organisation (Armstrong, 2014). The recruitment process for healthcare employees starts with a clear specification of the qualifications, knowledge, abilities, competence and skills requirement for the job through the job/person specification. This becomes the organisational value proposition to prospective employees and enables healthcare organisations to attract the best candidates that fit the requirement of the organisation, as opposed to the way in which the centralised recruitment of healthcare employees works.

Following the job/person specification, strategies should be in place to ensure that the proposed value is communicated to prospective employees using appropriate mediums, including online recruiting sites, social media, advertising, recruitment agencies, outsourced recruitment processes and direct approaches to educational establishments, as well as the corporate website, to attract the most talented and best employees nationally and globally. A direct approach through educational establishments provides the best medium for the recruitment of healthcare professionals including doctors and nurses in Africa.

Selection, although part of the recruitment process, is concerned with decisions on the appointments of candidates to jobs (Armstrong, 2014). The selection process entails both interviews and testing methods, including psychological, psychometric, intelligence, personality, ability, emotional intelligence and aptitude tests, to demonstrate a candidate's levels of abilities, intelligence, personality and aptitudes in coping with the physical, emotional and psychological demands of healthcare jobs.

Therefore, whilst recruitment is about how people are attracted to an organisation, selection, on the other hand, is about how the organisation selects people for employment in an organisation. However, it should be noted that the recruitment and selection process of healthcare employees is not complete until references and criminal checks are done, as well as follow-ups. References provide confirmation of a candidate's performance and character whilst criminal checks provide assurance to patients and relatives of the safety of vulnerable patients in the care of healthcare professionals. And follow-ups ensure employees are well inducted and have settled in the job.

13.3.1.2 Decentralised Approach to Recruitment and Selection

Decentralised recruitment and selection refer to moving the decision-making, authority, power and management in the recruitment and selection of employees to lower level management. This in the healthcare sector entails the delegation of recruitment and selection processes for healthcare employees to managers of individual healthcare institutions. For example, the Ghana Health Service (GHS) recently abolished its centralised posting approach and adopted the decentralised approach, whereby health professionals after graduation can search and apply for jobs and attend interviews (Adu-Gyamerah and Ali, 2018).

The advantages associated with this approach are as follows. First, it gives managers the flexibility to recruit and select employees in accordance with their specific institutional needs and priorities, thereby providing management with the opportunity to recruit and select the right candidate for their respective healthcare institutions and overcoming the "personal fit" problem associated with the centralised approach. Second, it increases the transparency, accountability and local responsiveness of individual healthcare institutions (Barnett et al., 1997; Hasenan, 2010). Third, management involvement in the recruitment and selection process leads to high morale and empowerment amongst management and a sense of responsibility toward employees' success. Finally, it empowers prospective employees in applying and working for their preferred healthcare institution that fits their personal values, lifestyle and personalities. This, together with management involvement in the recruitment and selection process, has the potential of overcoming the "personal fit" problem and building good working relationships between employees and their managers.

Taken altogether, the decentralised recruitment and selection of healthcare professionals through in-depth interviews and selection process has positive implications for healthcare management, employees and patient outcomes. However, as cautioned, this approach is associated with corruption and the tendency of encouraging favouritism and nepotism (Prud'homme, 1994; Tessema et al., 2009). Also, the decentralised recruitment and selection approach can be costly and can lead to oversights in its processes, as most healthcare managers lack the requisite management skills in the recruitment and selection of employees.

13.3.2 Development of Policies and Procedures

Healthcare services entail a set of processes consisting of a series of activities aimed at addressing patient healthcare problems. Undertaking such processes and activities requires clear guidelines in directing employees' actions and behaviour. Such guidelines should translate patients' and other stakeholders' expectations into policies and procedures. A policy refers to a statement that guides the decision-making process of employees in the processes and activities undertaken by organisations regularly (Hollnagel et al., 2014). Procedures, on the other hand, refers to the desired and intentional actions and steps to be taken by specified persons to achieve a certain objective in a defined set of circumstances

(Irving, 2014). The importance of policies and procedures includes promoting workplace safety; regulatory compliance; delivery of safe and high-quality patient care; reduction in practice variability that may result in substandard care and patient harm; and serving as a resource for employees (Irving, 2014). In South Africa, as a result of the delicate issue of the importance of religion to patients, policies and procedures have been extended to include patient spiritual care (De la Porte, 2016).

Policy and procedures may be developed for occupational health and safety, manual handling, sexual harassment, drug dispensing and hand washing, and such policies and procedures should be made clear and accessible to all employees. This entails developing policies and procedures that are understandable by employees and easy to comply with; providing copies to new employees; furnishing staffrooms with copies; and making them available through the organisational intranet.

13.3.3 SOCIALISATION

Socialisation provides the platform for successful integration of employees within the healthcare environment. This relates to the process through which an individual employee secures appropriate job skills and supportive social interactions with co-workers and adapts to the organisational culture (Taormina, 2004). Its emphasis on the induction and orientation given to healthcare employees upon starting a new job and its importance has been associated with employee self-efficacy and performance (Luthans et al., 2010; Bauer and Erdogan, 2012). In a study in the South African healthcare sector, it was observed that socialisation through induction has positive effects on newly qualified professional nurses in terms of their confidence, competence and attrition rate (Makua, 2015).

13.3.4 TRAINING AND DEVELOPMENT

Training and development of healthcare employees is a strategic essential for competitive advantage, differentiation, innovation and creativity. By training and developing healthcare employees, the skills and knowledge endowment is enhanced, which is reflected in employee innovativeness, capacity to accept new technologies and techniques, satisfaction, loyalty and performance, as well as in patient care, health outcomes and organisational performance and competitiveness (McNamara, 2008; Falola et al., 2014). Provision of professional development opportunities in the South African healthcare sector has been identified as influencing healthcare professionals' confidence, competence and independence (Makua, 2015). In addition, the World Health Organization has highlighted the importance of the training and development of professional nurses in Africa, drawing examples from Haiti and Rwanda (Kurth et al., 2016)

The training and development of healthcare employees starts with a clear definition of the training and development needs of each employee and the setting of training and development objectives through performance review. This should be followed by developing a training and development plan detailing how each need will be provided and the resources required. This should be done in direct consultation with employees. Following that, the training and development plan should be implemented by providing a full range of training and development opportunities and ensuring each employee is given equal opportunity. Finally, the process should be consummated by evaluating the outcome of the training and development programs in comparison with the training and development objectives set. The process of employee training and development are presented in Figure 13.2.

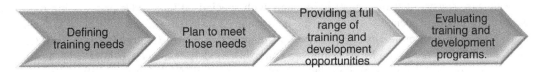

FIGURE 13.2 Employee Training and Development Process.

13.3.5 Reward Management and System

Attracting and retaining high-quality healthcare professionals and employees is contingent on the reward management and systems in place. Reward management systems deals with the strategies, policies and processes required in ensuring that the contribution of people to an organisation is recognised (Armstrong, 2014). For an effective reward management system, the following has been recommended:

- Rewards should be linked to employees' and organisational goals and should reflect the expected performance culture of the organisation.
- Rewards should be fair, equitable and consistent amongst employees.
- Rewards should be used as a tool for attracting, motivating and retaining the right people.
- Rewards should be influenced by market rates, competence and performance.
- Rewards should be holistic (total reward management). This should include extrinsic reward (pay and wages) and intrinsic reward (praise, learning and development opportunities and recognition).

(Manus and Graham, 2003; Armstrong, 2014)

13.4 EMPLOYEE EMPOWERMENT AND TEAMWORK IN HEALTHCARE

The strategic role of healthcare employees in the delivery of superior healthcare to patients has resulted in employee empowerment and team working becoming critical in healthcare management.

13.4.1 Employee Empowerment in Healthcare

Employee empowerment has its origin with its sister terms "employee participation" and "employee involvement" and refers to the transfer of power to employees from management. It involves "giving individuals and teams more responsibility for decision-making and ensuring that they have the training, support and guidance to exercise that responsibility properly" (Armstrong, 2014: 146). In addressing the complexity of patient needs and the challenge for managers in controlling employee behaviour and performance in healthcare, employee empowerment provides the tool for this. Its importance includes increased employee responsibility, motivation, commitment, satisfaction and self-efficacy; trust in colleagues, superiors and the organisation; reduced work-related stress; effective and efficient healthcare delivery; improved individual and organisational performance; and patient satisfaction and loyalty. Table 13.1 presents the strategies for empowering employees in healthcare.

13.4.2 Teamwork in Healthcare

The African adage "the strength of the broom lies not in the power of a single frond but in the resilience of its united fronds" hold true in the delivery of holistic, seamless, multidisciplinary and interconnected healthcare. Healthcare delivery involves a team of healthcare professionals from different backgrounds working together in providing patient-centred and superior healthcare. These teams may be large or small, connected or disconnected, temporary or permanent, but all contribute to the seamless and holistic delivery of patient care (Weller et al., 2014). Teams in healthcare consist of two or more individuals with specialised knowledge and specific roles, performing interdependent tasks and sharing a common goal such as safe care for patients (Salas et al., 2008). The Interprofessional Education for Collaborative Patient-Centred Practice (IECPCP) and TeamSTEPPS are examples of healthcare teamwork models developed in improving healthcare professionals' team working knowledge, attitudes and skills (Baker et al., 2010). A National Health Service report emphasises the importance of teamwork by stating: "The best and most

TABLE 13.1
Strategies for Empowering Healthcare Employees

Strategy	Explanation
Clearly Define Roles and Responsibilities	• Clearly define roles, job specification and assignment of responsibilities, authority and power, linking each to its accompanying accountability.
Support Employee Independence	• Create the necessary conditions and environment through the development of policies and procedures and the provision of employee socialisation, training and development opportunities to build employee self-efficacy, confidence and leadership skills. • Re-design and enrich jobs by emphasising employees having greater control over assigned tasks.
Cultural Change	• Shift organisational and management culture to a culture of trust, open communication and information and power sharing.
Appreciate Empowerment Efforts	• Develop and implement reward policies and performance management systems that motivate, reward and promote employee empowerment in the organisation and its departments.

cost-effective outcomes for patients and clients are achieved when professionals work together, learn together, engage in clinical audit of outcomes together, and generate innovation to ensure progress in practice and service" (Borrill et al., 2001: 13).

Team working thus becomes an asset for healthcare organisations and employees as well as a necessity for patient care, and its importance includes reduction in employee workload and burnout; fostering of cohesion amongst employees; reduction of medical errors; improvements to patient care and satisfaction; and, above all, positive outcomes for patient, employees and employers (Carter and West, 1999). However, as cautioned, its malfunction can result in compromised patient care, patient harm, staff distress and inefficiency (Alvarez and Coiera, 2006; St.Pierre et al., 2008). The challenges of teamwork in healthcare have been highlighted by the Audit Commission report, drawing attention to a major gap between rhetoric and reality:

> Separate lines of control, different payment systems leading to suspicion over motives, diverse objectives, professional barriers and perceived inequalities in status, all play a part in limiting the potential of multi-professional, multi-agency teamwork … for those working under such circumstances efficient teamwork remains elusive.
>
> (Audit Commission, 1992)

The key challenges of healthcare teams according to Weller et al. (2014) can be classified under **educational** (poor knowledge and skills related to team working communication); **psychological** (the professional silos, conducts, ethics and hierarchies associated with the different healthcare professionals); and **organisational** (geographically dispersed teams leading to communication failures and poor information sharing). In overcoming these challenges, Figure 13.3 presents the training approaches recommended by Thomas (2011) for healthcare professionals. Strategies for developing high-performance healthcare teams are also presented in Table 13.2.

13.4.3 CONFLICT MANAGEMENT IN HEALTHCARE TEAMS

The importance and indispensable role of healthcare teams in the delivery of holistic, seamless, multidisciplinary and interconnected patient care also comes with the stark reality that conflicts

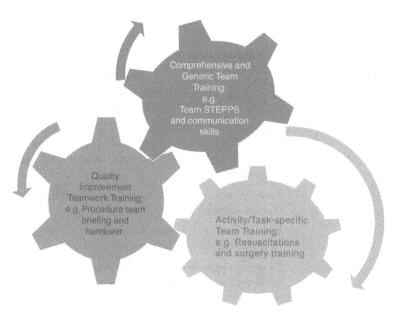

FIGURE 13.3   Training Approaches for Healthcare Professionals.

TABLE 13.2

Strategies for Developing High-Performance Healthcare Teams

Strategy	Explanation
Develop and Grow Teams and Members	• Allow teams and their members to develop and grow naturally. This implies allowing members of the multi-disciplinary team to go through the forming, storming, norming, performing and adjourning stages of Tuckman's model of team development.
Clearly Define Teams and Members' Roles and Responsibilities	• A clear definition of each team and its member objectives, roles and responsibilities and accountability, as well as the establishment of a code of conduct amongst teams and members, are key ingredients in developing healthcare teams.
Empower and Motivate Teams and Members	• Create the necessary conditions and environment for empowering teams and their members, and reward teams and members intrinsically and extrinsically.
Mutual Trust and Respect	• The survival of teams and its members depends on mutual trust and respect amongst teams and members.
Communication Flow	• Ensure patient care information flows vertically and horizontally amongst multidisciplinary healthcare teams in ensuring the effective delivery of healthcare. • In ensuring information sharing and coordination of patient care, confidentiality and "need to know" must be emphasised • The use of face-to-face communication, supplemented with technologically mediated communication channels including Facebook, WhatsApp and Trello, is a powerful tool in engaging with multidisciplinary teams and their members.
Manage Conflict	• Positive conflict should be encouraged and negative conflict should be managed carefully. • Create an environment that fosters communication flow, clarity of expectations, intra- and inter-professional collaboration; and mutual trust and respect. • Forcing, accommodating, collaborating, avoiding and compromising, accompanied by strong leadership, are effective strategies for managing teams and their members' conflict.

are inescapable for the following reasons. First, the individuals within teams come with different personalities, cultures, demographics, interest, working styles and values. Second, these individuals also come from different professional silos with their accompanying conduct, ethics and hierarchies. This is likely to lead to a conflict in their endeavour of working together for the achievement of specific healthcare goals. Conflict may occur nurse–nurse, nurse–doctor, doctor–doctor and between the different multidisciplinary teams.

Conflicts can be positive or negative for healthcare teams. Positive conflicts may be healthy and productive and may result in the development of strong, innovative, efficient and effective employees and teams, thereby affecting healthcare outcomes. Negative conflicts, on the other hand, can be harmful and counterproductive and may result in employee dissatisfaction, turnover, work-related stress and inefficiency, and may create a culture of fear, suspicion and blame in the workplace, which ultimately may impact negatively on patient care. As a result, positive conflicts should be encouraged and managed to reap their benefits whilst negative conflict should be discouraged and managed strategically to avoid its spill-over effect.

All conflict has an underlying meaning and cause and should be understood, mitigated and managed successfully. Healthcare managers and team leaders should create an environment that fosters communication flow, clarity of expectations, intra- and inter-professional collaboration and mutual trust and respect. Emphasis should also be placed on developing communication and team working skills and the emotional intelligence of employees. A team working ethos, ethics and policies and procedures should be developed to ensure consistency and understanding amongst teams and their members towards the holistic delivery of patient care. Table 13.3 provides an explanation of the different types of conflicts amongst healthcare teams and their corresponding mitigation strategies.

13.5 PERFORMANCE MANAGEMENT

Institutions in the healthcare sector in Africa, particularly state-owned institutions, are the poorest performing institutions across the world and this is reflected in the irregularities in facilities' openings; staff absenteeism, unprofessionalism and hostility; misdiagnosis; unavailable medicines; increasing patient complaints; poor patient satisfaction; long waiting times; and other patient horror stories (O'Donnell, 2007). These performance issues are attributed to funding problems; limited resources; the widening patient/healthcare professional ratio; increasing pressure on existing healthcare facilities and other key resources; inadequate training; poor communication; blurred policies and procedures; unpaid and lower salaries amongst employees; and a climate of low motivation, emotional and physical exhaustion, job dissatisfaction and strikes. These challenges have contributed to the low-performance culture in healthcare institutions in Africa.

Developing a high-performance culture amongst healthcare employees in Africa is, therefore, critical and requires providing the necessary environment for achieving performance objectives. Performance management (PM) provides the mechanism for developing a high-performance culture and achieving performance objectives and it is defined as "a continuous process of identifying, measuring and developing the performance of individuals and teams and aligning performance with the strategic goals of the organisation" (Aguinis, 2005: 2). PM, therefore, is an ongoing process between healthcare employees and their managers/supervisor and entails planning, acting, monitoring and reviewing employee performance. Its objectives include: communicating organisational strategic expectations to employees; developing employees; building relationships between managers and employees; and employee evaluation, accountability and motivation (Shields, 2007: 24).

13.5.1 Principles of Employee Performance Management in Healthcare

Employee PM in the healthcare sector traditionally can best be described as a form filling, paper-intensive exercise, a standardised, rigid, pay-focussed process. In addition, management lacks the necessary management and communication skills to undertake PM. Thus, the traditional approach

TABLE 13.3

Conflict Types and Mitigating Strategies in Healthcare

Conflict Type	Explanation	Mitigation Strategy
Values Conflict	Occurs when there is an incompatibility of standards of behaviour and practices amongst healthcare teams and their members.	• Create a corporate culture and organisation-wide shared values on standard of care.
Interpersonal Conflict	Occurs when team members have incompatible personal needs, goals and work styles.	• Create a cross-cultural sensitisation training program. • Create employee socialisation programs.
Power Conflict	Occurs when a team or a member of a team exerts or maximises influence in decision making. An example is doctors' exertion of power over nurses.	• Develop a clear and well-specified job description. • Establish an inter-professional understanding of each team role and responsibility. • Establish lines of communication and reporting systems. • Create a participatory management culture that values the importance and contribution of each team and employee.
Economic Conflict	Occurs when teams compete over limited organisational resources. This includes competition over medical equipment, budget, allowances and technology.	• Create avenues for negotiations and bargaining for the different teams on the allocation of resources. • Coordinate resource allocation among teams using: • Pareto optimality. • Resource scheduling. • Adopt a priority-based allocation of resources approach. • Adopt a performance-based allocation of resources approach.

Organisational Conflict	Occurs when there is a clash between management and employees or teams on managerial decisions that affect employees or teams adversely.	• Create a participatory management culture centred on:
		  − Bottom-up decision making.
		  − Vertical communication.

Inter-professional Conflict	Occurs when the conduct, ethics and hierarchies associated with the different healthcare professionals working together towards the achievement of specific healthcare goals contradict.	• Establish an inter-professional understanding of each team role and responsibility. • Create a corporate culture and organisation-wide shared values on standards of care.
Interdependence Conflict	Occurs when teams depend on each other for a successful healthcare outcome. For example, nurse–doctor dependency for the safe recovery of patients.	• Create a culture of mutual respect and trust. • Create awareness of each team's roles and responsibilities. • Establish multi-team lines of communication and reporting systems.

to PM neglects essential aspects of PM, which are communication, consultation, mutual under-standing and the provision of necessary resources and training in developing a high-performance culture and achieving performance objectives. And as a result, PM is reluctantly embraced by employees with suspicion and uncertainty. Further, most PM evaluation indicators in the healthcare sector are efficiency focussed and over-reliant on objectives and lagging metrics; they are therefore misleading and inadequate in capturing the reality of today's healthcare sector and hinder oppor-tunities for employee performance improvement.

To develop a high-performance culture in the healthcare sector:

- The PM process should be simple, clear, flexible and unbiased.
- PM should be about managing and developing employees rather than being used as carrot and stick in the evaluation of employee performance and rather than focussing on systems or paperwork.
- PM communication should focus on a two-way communication process providing oppor-tunities for both employees and their managers in understanding the process and the benefits.
- PM indicators should be aligned with organisational performance culture and objectives.
- PM indicators in the healthcare sector should be clearly defined and should focus on effi-ciency, effectiveness and outcome measures as well as objective and subjective measures.
- PM indicators for employees should include: work–life balance; participation in well-ness programs; participation in teamwork/activities; overtime hours; absenteeism rate; patient complaints and complements about the employee; service quality rating; creativ-ity; patient-to-staff ratio; number of errors by employees; revenue per employee; return on investment in human capital; training and developmental activities; job function; patient waiting time; bed turnover; average length of stay; infection rate; and readmission rate.
- Evaluation of employee performance should be holistic, entailing a 360-degree feedback from the employee, patients, colleagues, managers/supervisors and teams.
- Management buying-in, support and ownership are critical to PM implementation, so appropriate training and preparation for managers are important.

In addition to the above principles, Awases et al. (2013) recommend the following for addressing the performance challenges in the healthcare sector in Africa. These are:

- Knowledge and competence building through continued professional development and training and clinical specialisation.
- Development of formal performance appraisal systems.
- Development of performance standards.
- Development of leadership and management capacity.

13.6 EMPLOYEE WELLNESS PROGRAMS

Work-related stress and other health problems are prevalent amongst healthcare employees taking into consideration the emotional, physical and stressful nature of healthcare work. This has a consequence on employee healthcare cost, quality of life, job satisfaction, absenteeism, turnover, morale and per-formance, as well as organisational performance (Lerner et al., 2010; Berry et al., 2010). To minimise these, employee wellness programs have been suggested. The phrase refers to any program imple-mented by employers to enhance their employees' health and organisational performance. Since such programs have gained popularity, over 90 per cent of companies in developed countries have invested millions of dollars in them, and it is estimated that, for every dollar spent, a \$2.71 return is yielded (Aldana et al., 2005; Berry et al., 2010). In addition, their implementation in the South African public sector saw a significant relationship between wellness programmes and work–life balance strategies.

Employee wellness programs can be offered on-site and/or off-site for the sponsored healthcare organisations and can be classified into three main types: fitness-oriented, education-oriented and comprehensive wellness programs. Fitness-oriented programs focus on aerobic, nonaerobic and weight training activities. Education-oriented programs focus on workshops on stress relief and stress reduction strategies and other health-related issues, whilst comprehensive programs focus on both fitness- and education-oriented wellness programs (Parks and Steelman, 2008). In the South African context, Abe et al. (2016) identified the following as employee wellness programs available in the public sector: life programmes (stress management, domestic relationship counselling, substance/alcohol abuse counselling, HIV/AIDS counselling and financial/debt counselling); and work programmes (work from home, job sharing, compressed workweek, telecommuting and career break).

For successful planning and implementing of a wellness program amongst healthcare employees, Berry et al. (2010) suggest the following:

- It should be comprehensive and broad in scope to include health-related issues relevant to individual employees.
- It should be offered at employees' convenience (both on-site and off-site) and at low or no cost to employees.
- It should foster employee pride, involvement and fun, whilst at the same time emphasising high standards.
- The work environment should be integrated into wellness programs by offering stretch breaks and the provision of healthy and affordable foods at the work cafeteria, amongst other things.
- It should be offered to all employees without any discrimination.

13.7 CONCLUSIONS

Healthcare employees personify the visible and invisible hands in the delivery of superior and holistic healthcare to patients, and they are a source of competitive advantage for healthcare organisations. By leveraging healthcare employees' privileged position in the healthcare delivery process and managing them strategically, healthcare organisations can get the best out of their employees and build customer-driven and successful healthcare organisations through the application of HRM practices.

However, the application of HRM practices in the African healthcare sector faces several challenges, including the centralisation of the recruitment and selection process; unclear and inaccessible policies and procedures; inadequacy of training and development opportunities; inadequacy of performance appraisal; poor reward systems and management; long working hours; and poor working conditions. Overcoming these challenges calls for the strategic and careful recruitment and selection of employees; the development of clear and accessible policies and procedures; the socialisation, training and development of employees; and the implementation of appropriate reward management and systems. It also calls for the empowerment of employees in addressing the complexity of patient needs as well as the establishment and strengthening of healthcare teams in the delivery of holistic, seamless, multidisciplinary and interconnected healthcare to patients.

Further, considering the poor performance of most African healthcare institutions, employee performance management is critical to the management of healthcare employees and necessitates a paradigm shift from the traditional carrot and stick approach to PM towards the management and development of employees with emphases on efficiency, effectiveness and outcome-based measures. Finally, the adoption of employee wellness programs in relieving employees from the stressful nature of healthcare work is another HRM practice for enhancing employee and organisational performance and healthcare outcomes.

In conclusion, healthcare managers in their quest to deliver superior and holistic healthcare to patients and to build competitive advantage and customer-driven organisations should leverage healthcare employees' privileged position in the healthcare delivery process and manage employees strategically through the application of HRM practices.

Note

1. Some of these challenges and issues emerged from informal interviews conducted with healthcare professionals in Ghana between June and July 2018.

REFERENCES

Abe, E. N., Fields, Z., and Abe, I. I. (2016). The efficacy of wellness programmes as work-life balance strategies in the South African public services. *Journal of Economics and Behavioral Studies, 8*(6), 52–67.

Adu-Gyamerah, E., and Ali, B. M. (2018). No more direct posting – Health Service Director General announces. Retrieved from: www.graphic.com.gh/news/general-news/no-more-direct-posting-health-service-director-general-announces.html.

Aguinis, H. (2005). *Performance management*, Upper Saddle River, NJ: Pearson Education.

Aldana, S. G., Merrill, R. M., Price, K., Hardy, A., and Hager, R. (2005). Financial impact of a comprehensive multisite workplace health promotion program. *Preventive Medicine, 4*, 31–137.

Ali, E. M., and Aameed, S. A. (2016). HRM issues and challenges in healthcare. *International Journal of Management, 7*(2), 166–176.

Aluttis, C., Bishaw, T., and Frank, M. W. (2014). The workforce for health in a globalized context: Global shortages and international migration. *Global Health Action, 7*. doi: http://doi.org/10.3402/gha.v7.23611.

Alvarez, G., and Coiera, E. (2006). Interdisciplinary communication: An uncharted source of medical error? *Journal of Critical Care, 21*, 236–242.

Andalón, M., and Fields, G. (2011). *A labor market approach to the crisis of health care professionals in Africa.* Discussion Paper No. 5483 February 2011, IZA DP No. 548. Bonn: Institute for the Study of Labor.

Armstrong, M. (2014). *Handbook of human resource management practice* (13th ed.). London, England: Kogan Page Limited.

Audit Commission (1992). *Homeward bound: A new course for community health.* London: HMSO.

Awases, M. H., Bezuidenhout, M. C. and; Roos, J. H. (2013). Factors affecting the performance of professional nurses in Namibia. *Curationis, 36*(1). doi:10.4102/curationis.v36i1.108.

Baker, D. P., Amodeo, A. M., Krokos, K. J., Slonim, A., and Herrera, H. (2010). Assessing teamwork attitudes in healthcare: Development of the TeamSTEPPS teamwork attitudes questionnaire. *Quality & Safety in Health Care, 19*(6) doi:10.1136/qshc.2009.036129. Epub August 10, 2010.

Barnett, C. C., Minis, H. P., and VanSant, J. (1997). *Democratic decentralization.* United States Agency for International Development.

Bauer, T. N., and Erdogan, B. (2012). *Organizational socialization outcomes: Now and into the future.* In C. Wanberg (Ed.), *The Oxford handbook of organizational socialization.* Oxford, UK: Oxford University Press.

Berry, L. L., Mirabito, A. M., and Baun, W. B. (2010). What's the hard return on employee wellness programs? *Harvard Business Review, 12*, 1–17.

Borrill, C., Carletta, J. C., Carter, A., Dawson, J. F., Garrod, S., Rees, A., Richards, A., Shapiro, D., and West, M. (2001). *Team working and effectiveness in health care: Findings from the Health Care Team Effectiveness Project.* Aston Centre for Health Service Organisation Research, Aston: Aston University Press.

Bowen, D. E. (2016). The changing role of employees in service theory and practice: An interdisciplinary view. *Human Resource Management Review, 26*(1), 4–13.

Bratton, J., and Gold, J. (2017). *Human resource management: Theory and practice* (6th ed.). Basingstoke: Palgrave Macmillan.

Carter, A. J. W., and West, M. (1999). Sharing the burden: Teamwork in health care settings. In J. Firth-Cozens, & R. L. Payne (Eds.), *Stress in health professionals: Psychological and organisational causes and interventions* (pp. 191–202). Chichester: John Wiley and Sons.

Clemens, M. A., and Pettersson, G. (2008, January 10). New data on African health professionals abroad. *Human Resource Health, 6*(1). doi:10.1186/1478-4491-6-1.

De la Porte, A. (2016). Spirituality and healthcare: Towards holistic people centred healthcare in South Africa. *HTS Teologiese Studies/Theological Studies, 72*(4), a3127. doi:10.4102/hts.v72i4.3127.

English, M., Irimu, G., Nyamai, R., Were, F., Garner, P., and Opiyp, N. (2017). Developing guidelines in low-income and middle-income countries: Lessons from Kenya. *Archives of Disease in Childhood, 102,* 846–851.

Falola, H. O., Osibanjo, A. O., and Ojo, S. I. (2014). Effectiveness of training and development on employees' performance and organization competitiveness in the Nigerian banking industry. *Bulletin of the Transilvania University of Brasov Series V: Economic Science, 7*(1), 161–170.

Gates, D. M., Gillespie, G. L., and Succop, P. (2011). Violence against nurses and its impact on stress and productivity. *Nursing Economics, 29,* 59–66.

Hasenan, H. (2010). *The effect of decentralization towards affective commitment among Universiti Sains Malaysia administrative employees.* Thailand: Universiti Sains Malaysia.

Hollnagel, E., Braithwaite, J., and Wears, R. L. (2014). *Resilient health care.* Surrey, England: Ashgate.

Irving, A. V. (2014). Policies and procedures for healthcare organizations: A risk management perspective [online]. Retrieved from: www.psqh.com/analysis/policies-and-procedures-for-healthcare-organizations-a-risk-management-perspective/.

Kamati, S. K., Cassim, N., and Karodia, A. M. (2014). An evaluation of the factors influencing the performance of registered nurses at the National Referral Hospital in Namibia. *Australian Journal of Business and Management Research, 4*(2): 47–62.

Keers, R. N., Williams, S. D., Cooke, J., and Ashcroft, D. M. (2013). Causes of medication administration errors in hospitals: A systematic review of quantitative and qualitative evidence. *Drug Safety, 36*(11), 1045–1067. doi:10.1007/s40264-013-0090-2.

Kinfu, Y., Poz, M. R. D, Mercer, H., and Evans, D. B. (2009). The health worker shortage in Africa: Are enough physicians and nurses being trained? *Bulletin of the World Health Organization, 87,* 225–230. doi:10.2471/BLT.08.051599.

Koinis, A., Giannou, V., Drantaki, V., Angelaina, S., Stratou, E., and Saridi, M. (2015). The impact of healthcare workers job environment on their mental-emotional health. Coping strategies: The case of a local general hospital. *Health Psychology Research, 3*(1), 2–17.

Kotler, P., and Keller, K. (2012). *Marketing management* (14th ed.). Upper Saddle River, NJ: Prentice Hall.

Kurth, A. E., Jacob, S., Squires, A. P., Sliney, A., Davis, S., Stalls, S., and Portillo, C. J. (2016). Investing in nurses is a prerequisite for ensuring universal health coverage, *Journal of the Association of Nurses in AIDS Care, 27*(3), 344–354. doi:10.1016/j.jana.2016.02.016.

Kwamie, A., Asiamah, M., Schaaf, M., and Agyepong, I. A. (2017). Postings and transfers in the Ghanaian health system: A study of health workforce governance. *International Journal of Equity Health, 16.* doi:10.1186/s12939-017-0583-1.

Lerner, D., Adler, D. A, Rogers, W. H., Chang, H., Lapitsky, L. McLaughlin, T., and Reed, J. (2010). Work performance of employees with depression: The impact of work stressors. *American Journal of Health Promotion, 24,* 205–213.

Liu, J. X., Goryakin, Y., Maeda, A., Bruckner, T., and Scheffler, R. (2017). Global health workforce labor market projections for 2030. *Human Resources for Health, 15*(11). doi:10.1186/s12960-017-0187-2.

Luthans, F., Avey, J. B., Avolio, B. J., and Peterson, S. J. (2010). The development and resulting performance impact of positive psychological capital. *Human Resource Development Quarterly, 21*(1), 41–67.

Lutwama, G. W., Roos, J. H., and Dolamo, B. L. (2013). Assessing the implementation of performance management of health care workers in Uganda. *BMC Health Services Research, 13,* 355. doi:10.1186/1472-6963-13-355.

Makua, M. G. (2015). Transition from student nurse to professional nurse: Induction and professional development support of newly qualified professional nurses. Session at 43rd Biennial Convention, the Honor Society of Nursing, Vegas, Nevada. Retrieved from: http://hdl.handle.net/10755/603126.

Manus, T. M., and Graham, M. D. (2003). *Creating a total rewards strategy.* New York: American Management Association.

McHugh, M. D., Kutney-Lee, A., Cimiotti, J. P., Sloane, D. M., and Aiken, L. H. (2011). Nurses' widespread job dissatisfaction, burnout, and frustration with health benefits signal problems for patient care. *Health Affairs (Project Hope), 30*(2), 202–210.

McNamara, C. (2008). Employee training and development: Reasons and benefits [online]. Retrieved from: www.managementhelp.org/index.html.

Njovu, F. (2013). *Experience of decentralized and centralized recruitment systems in local government authorities of Tanzania: A case study of two local government authorities in Morogoro Region.* The Hague, The Netherlands: Institute of Social Studies.

O'Donnell, O. (2007). Access to health care in developing countries: Breaking down demand side barriers. *Cadernos de Saúde Pública, 23*(12), doi:10.1590/S0102-311X2007001200003.

O'Meara, B., and Petzall, S. (2013). *Strategic recruitment and selection: A system approach.* Bingley, UK: Emerald Group Publishing Limited.

Osei-Frimpong, K., and Owusu-Frimpong, N. (2017). Value co-creation in healthcare: A phenomenological examination of the doctor–patient encounter. *Journal of Nonprofit & Public Sector Marketing, 29,* 365–384. doi:10.1080/10495142.2017.1326356.

Parks, K. M., and Steelman, L. A. (2008). Organizational wellness programs: A meta-analysis. *Journal of Occupational Health Psychology, 13*(1), 58–68.

Prud'homme, R. (1994). *On the dangers of decentralization.* World Bank Policy Research Working Paper 1252. Washington: World Bank.

Salas, E, Cooke, N. J., and Rosen, M. A. (2008). On teams, teamwork, and team performance: Discoveries and developments. *Journal of Human Factors, 50,* 540–547.

Sekhon, H. S., Yalley, A. A., Kumar, R. S., and Shergill, G. (2016). A cross-country study of service productivity. *The Service Industry Journal, 36*(5/6), 223–238.

Sharma, A. E., Knox, M., Mleczko, V. L., and Olayiwola, J. N. (2017). The impact of patient advisors on healthcare outcomes: A systematic review. *BMC Health Services Research, 17*(693), 1–14.

Shayo, E. H., Våga, B. B., Moland, K. M., Kamuzora, P., and Blystad, A. (2014). Challenges of disseminating clinical practice guidelines in a weak health system: The case of HIV and infant feeding recommendations in Tanzania. *International Breastfeeding Journal, 9*(1), 188. doi:10.1186/s13006-014-0024-3.

Shields, J. (2007). *Managing employee performance and reward.* Cambridge: Cambridge University Press.

Soucat, A., Scheffler, R., and Ghebreyesus, T. A. (2013). *The labor market for health workers in Africa: A new look at the crisis.* World Bank Human Development Report 82557. Washington, DC: World Bank [online]. Retrieved from: https://openknowledge.worldbank.org/bitstream/handle/10986/13824/82557.pdf;sequence=5.

St.Pierre, M., Hofinger, G., and Buerschaper, C. (2008). *Crisis management in acute care settings: Human factors and team psychology in a high stakes environment.* Berlin: Springer.

Taormina, R. J. (2004). Convergent validation of two measures of organizational socialization. *International Journal of Human Resource Management, 15,* 76–94.

Tessema, M. T., Soeters, J. L., and Ngoma, A. (2009). Decentralization of human resource function: Functions lessons from the Singapore Civil Service. *Review of Public Personnel Administration, 29*(2), 168–188.

Thomas, E. J. (2011). Improving teamwork in healthcare: Current approaches and the path forward. *BMJ Quality & Safety* 2011, *20*(8), 647e650. doi:10.1136/bmjqs-2011-000117.

Tuckman, B. W. (1965). Development sequence in small groups. *Psychological Bulletin, 63*(6), 384–399.

Weller, J., Boyd, M., and Cumin, D. (2014). Teams, tribes and patient safety: Overcoming barriers to effective teamwork in healthcare. *Postgraduate Medical Journal, 90,* 149–154.

World Health Organization. (2016). *Health workforce requirements for universal health coverage and the Sustainable Development Goals.* Human Resources for Health Observer Series No 17. Geneva: World Health Organization. [online]. Retrieved from: http://apps.who.int/iris/bitstream/handle/10665/250330/9789241511407-eng.pdf;jsessionid=D68608ED7491B96E6CFD499C4106B681?sequence=1.

World Health Organization. (2000). *The world health report 2000. Health systems: Improving performance.* Geneva: World Health Organization.

Wu, Y., Fujita, S., Seto, K., Ito, S., Matsumoto, K., Huang, C., and Hasegaw, T. (2013). The impact of nurse working hours on patient safety culture: A cross-national survey including Japan, the United States and Chinese Taiwan using the Hospital Survey on Patient Safety Culture. *BMC Health Services Research.* doi:10.1186/1472-6963-13-394.

Yalley, A. A., and Agyapong, G. K. (2017). Measuring service quality in Ghana: A crossvergence cultural perspective. *Journal of Financial Services Marketing, 22*(2), 43–53.

Yalley, A. A., and Sekhon, H. S. (2014). Service production process: Implications for service productivity. *International Journal of Productivity and Performance Management, 63*(8), 1012–1030.

14 Physical Evidence and Healthcare Service Quality Management

Robert Ebo Hinson and Michael Nkrumah

14.1 INTRODUCTION

Healthcare quality improvement is one of the key priorities of health systems worldwide (Escribano-Ferrer, Cluzeau, Cutler, Akufo, & Chalkidou, 2016; Chassin, 2013). Influenced by the developments in quality management in the manufacturing industry, continuous quality improvement also became a major area of concern in the healthcare sector from the 1980s (Boaden & Walshe, 2006). A quality conscious healthcare industry can directly benefit overall society because a better healthcare system can lower mortality, diminish illness severity, reduce in-patient stays, and increase life expectancy (Blackstone & Fuhr, 2016; Butt & de Run, 2010). As a result, the healthcare sector is adopting different approaches to management. One of the approaches touted to be of extreme importance to the healthcare sector is the application of service quality.

Understanding service quality is indispensable for health service providers aspiring to attract and retain consumers (Butt & de Run, 2010). This is because the healthcare sector is a business, which needs to have enough financial resources in order to be sustainable. Service quality has therefore become a matter of concern for public and private healthcare institutions across the world. The past few years have seen a concerted effort directed towards improving service quality in healthcare management systems across the world (Anabila, 2019; Mannion & Braithwaite, 2017; Yavas et al., 2016; Gumede, Green, & Dlamini, 2015).

Within the context of healthcare, service quality is described by some as referring to a multiphase interactive action carried out by staff in service situations, the dimensions of which are assurance of competence, activeness, dissemination of information, polite manners by staff, and flexible helpfulness, all of which add valuable meaning to healthcare experiences (Gumede, Green, & Dlamini, 2015).

In the past, literature on healthcare service quality only concentrated on the allocation of resources and infrastructure to patients (Weheba, Cure, & Toy, 2018). However, healthcare consumers, in keeping with current consumer trends, have become more sophisticated and forceful in demanding value for money in their health seeking behaviours (Anabila, 2019) to the extent that service quality has emerged as a key factor shaping their choice criteria. Consequently, patients' views and attitudes have become significant drivers of healthcare marketing strategy, thereby making it necessary for competing healthcare providers to strive to achieve their goals without compromising on quality (Tenkorang, 2016; Anabila, 2019). That notwithstanding, challenges still abound as to how hospital employees, managers, and patients should use the available resources and correct attitude to receive and provide the expected service quality.

The objective of the chapter is to explore and summarize the available pool of knowledge in order to understand what comprises healthcare service quality, how patients assess healthcare service quality, and the key variables that aid such assessment. Consequently, the final sections of the chapter will shed light on the challenges in assessing healthcare service quality and highlight some emergent methodologies that have been appropriated from other disciplines such as business management to help remedy the situation.

14.2 SERVICE QUALITY

The service sector is increasing at a fast pace, leading to intense competition (Akter et al., 2008). Service has been characterized as "any activity or benefit that one party can offer to another, which is basically intangible and does not bring about the ownership of anything" (Kotler & Keller, 2009, p. 789). It may also be characterized as a more intangible activity, or series of activities, which takes the form of an interaction between the customer, the service provider, and systems in an attempt to satisfy the customer (Hinson, 2012). Quality has become an increasingly predominant part of our lives. The desire for quality has caused managers throughout the world to consider quality as a strategic goal to achieve competitive advantage.

In the service industry, quality definitions tend to focus on meeting customer requirements and how well service providers meet their expectations (Lewis & Booms, 1983) – this is usually through an encounter between the customer and service contact person. There is no generally accepted definition of service quality. It is defined as a consumer's evaluative judgement or impression regarding the overall performance and excellence of the service provider during the service encounter (see also Cronin & Taylor, 1992). Grönroos (1984) proposes service quality as a comparison between customer expectations and perceived service. He identifies two dimensions that define service quality: technical quality, which is the outcome of the service encounter (service result); and functional quality, which is the process through which the service, including perceptions of interactions (service process), is delivered.

Service quality has become an important issue and many organizations, including healthcare organizations, have adopted new and innovative means to improve their service quality (Zeithaml, Parasuraman, & Berry, 1990). Healthcare service quality is described as a discrepancy between patients' or patient's attendants' perceptions of services and their expectations about that hospital offering such services (Aagja & Garg, 2010). For instance, Mosadeghrad (2013) believes that healthcare service quality is the provision of

> the right healthcare services in a right way in the right place at the right time by the right provider to the right individual for the right price to get the right results. Hence, the right result is about satisfying the (see Kodom, Owusu, & Kodom, 2019)

With this background, the next section examines in more detail the concept of service quality in healthcare delivery.

14.3 SERVICE QUALITY IN HEALTHCARE DELIVERY

Recent developments reflecting the commercialization of the healthcare industry emphasize the importance of attracting patients and providing them with memorable experiences in order to "create" satisfied and loyal customers. Interestingly, patient satisfaction has also been treated as a surrogate measure for the quality of care from a patient's perspective (Zgierska, Rabago, & Miller, 2014).

The health service sector presents the delivery of differentiated offerings that focus on general hospital services, diagnostic services, consultations, and professional specialist functions, among others (Akter et al., 2008). Although healthcare is described as a service, it is considered to be notably different from other industries in the service sector. This is because healthcare is a credence service, which makes clinical quality often difficult for customers to judge even after the service is performed. This can be due to that fact that:

1. Customers have some combination of illness, pain, uncertainty, fear, and perceived lack of control.
2. Customers may be reluctant co-producers because healthcare is a service that they need, but they may not want.
3. Customers relish privacy physically, emotionally, and spiritually.
4. Customers need whole person service.
5. Customers are at risk of being harmed.
6. Clinicians are stressed physically and emotionally.

Research suggests that assessing service quality can also be controversial in "experiential" services such as healthcare when expertise is required (Upadhyai, Jain, Roy, & Pant, 2019). Consequently, what this means is that service quality evaluation differs for healthcare professionals and patients. While professionals weigh the design and delivery aspect of service, receivers evaluate service on their overall perception of the service. Thus, it is evident that the concept of quality of care means different things to different stakeholders involved in the healthcare system (Pai & Chary, 2016).

Numerous studies within the healthcare literature highlight how perceptions of quality of healthcare services significantly influence patients' behaviours (Agyapong, Afi & Kwateng, 2017; Aliman & Mohamad, 2016). Although many researchers argue that the "real" quality of a service cannot be accurately portrayed in a patient's perceptions, patients will always draw their own conclusions about the quality of a service. Within the domain of healthcare management, patient perception is reality, and is the perceived quality, as opposed to the actual or absolute quality which requires critical management (Agyapong et al., 2017; Aliman & Mohamad, 2016). In this regard, Abdallah (2014) asserted that healthcare managers are faced with constant pressure to deliver quality healthcare.

The nature of human health is very important in the development and success of a country. This can be accomplished if the nature of healthcare services provided to the general population is both effective and a good representation of the expectations of the people. Along these lines, quality patient care ought to be a fundamental guideline of a country's wellbeing system since there are increasing expectations from patients on matters concerning healthcare (Duggirala, Rajendran, & Anantharaman, 2008). In Ghana, and most African countries, for instance, there are key challenges and hurdles inherent in the quality delivery of maternal health services. These include lack of deployment of skilled health workers, inadequate supply of medical equipment for birth and post care, logistics, staff within the medical centres, lack of transportation for women, and an insufficient number of ambulance services and trained emergency response technicians. These barriers threaten the delivery of quality and safe maternal healthcare and amplify the inherent issues related to the quality of services within the healthcare domain (Ghana National Healthcare Strategy, 2016).

14.4 ISSUES OF QUALITY IN HEALTHCARE SERVICES

Substantial evidence indicates that the quality of healthcare that people receive, whether in Ghana or abroad is not ideal, although there may exist contextual differences (Duku, Nketiah-Amponsah, Janssens, & Pradhan, 2018; Atinga, Abekah-Nkrumah & Domfeh, 2011). What makes this evidence especially troublesome is the scant information on what constitutes quality of care and who does and does not provide high quality care, either across the board or for specific health conditions. The utilization of healthcare is found to be sensitive to quality of care such that households limit their demand when services are of poor quality and others bypass low quality health facilities in search of high quality ones (Duku et al., 2018). Studies indicate that quality is uneven throughout the industry with few health institutions free from medical errors, which can often have serious consequences for patients.

Issues of quality in healthcare pertaining to procedures, tests, and therapies are most often the norm although issues exist. Baker, Akgü and Al Assaf (2008) offered a two-way approach to understanding issues of quality in healthcare using dimensions of service quality in healthcare. They distinguished between clinical quality and service quality. The former refers to activities of the healthcare process such as surgical skill, sufficient drugs, logistics, and other factors that translate into better outcome. The latter on the other hand denotes the multifactorial indicators of patients' experiences such as hospital comfort, support from providers, waiting time, appointment and visits, and the physical environment of the facility (see Atinga et al., 2011).

In Ghana, for instance, Duku et al. (2018) found that insured patients who experience long delays and are served with generic drugs perceive the quality of care they receive to be low whilst the uninsured who pay cash for branded drugs and spend less time for service delivery perceive the quality of the care they receive to be relatively higher. In light of the issues raised above regarding quality in healthcare, there is a critical need for evaluation and improvement of quality of care provided to the patients in daily clinical practice, health policy planning, and financing. Consumer or patient opinion yields valuable information about the functioning of the healthcare system, which should be considered while assessing the quality of hospital services. The prime function of the hospital is patient care and to know the quality of hospital services, it is imperative to know what impressions the patients have about the hospital. Hence, to assess the quality of services in the hospitals, there is a need to measure the perceptions of customers regarding the quality and delivery of services and their overall satisfaction. This, then can be used as feedback to enhance the quality of the services.

14.5 ASSESSING HEALTHCARE SERVICE QUALITY

Critical to assessing healthcare service quality is the need to understand the dimensions of service quality in healthcare. The most widely used dimensions of service quality are derived from the original SERVQUAL scale, which was designed to measure service quality using both the gap concept and the service quality dimensions (Weheba, Cure, & Toy, 2018; Asubonteng, McCleary, & Swan, 1996; Arunasalam, Paulson, & Wallace, 2003). From the original scale, five service quality dimensions were drawn. These variables are important to furnishing an understanding of the factors that are critical to assessing healthcare service quality from a patient's perspective, which managers of healthcare organizations should seriously consider.

14.5.1 TANGIBLES

Tangibles refer to the physical evidence such as the quality of the equipment, attractiveness of facilities, physical environment, cleanliness, and associated atmospherics – ambience, comfort, noise, all of which have an impact on both healthcare employees and patients.

14.5.1.1 Managing the Physical Evidence

The physical environment refers to tangible cues including quality service (Zeithaml, Bitner, & Gremler, 2009), the environment in which the service is delivered, and any tangible goods that facilitate the performance and communication of the service (Bitner, 1992). Kotler (1973) was the first to draw our attention to the potential impact of the physical environment and to use the term "atmospherics," defined as "the effort to design buying environments to produce specific emotional effects in the buyer that enhance his purchase probability" (see Kotler & Armstrong, 2013). The healthcare service environment is acknowledged to be an important healthcare quality component. Patients prefer a clean and homelike environment. Although a hospital is a place for treating diseases, there is always a possibility of getting contaminated with infectious diseases. Contamination fears make patients worry during their hospital stay. It should be emphasized that employing proper sanitary practices and having clean facilities not only affect patient perceptions, but also create a synergistic effect on the morale of staff (Gotlieb, 2000), who appreciate working in a clean and attractive environment. Research suggests that in the high involvement healthcare industry, where patients and employees make frequent and protracted medical transactions, there is the possibility that the environment itself can impact on patients' evaluations of service quality (Swain & Kar, 2017; Prabhu & Iyer, 2018).

14.5.1.2 Managing the Service Atmosphere in Healthcare

To create satisfying customer experiences, there is increasing emphasis on adapting atmospheric elements in the shopping environment into the healthcare sector. The elements include, but are not limited to, ambient conditions such as music, scent, colour, space and layout, and symbols and artifacts (Van Rompay & Tanja-Dijkstra, 2010; Van Rompay, Galetzka, Pruyn, & Garcia, 2008).

a Music

Service encounters in healthcare situations, like other retail situations, are often characterized by lengthy waits in waiting areas, underscoring the importance of studying the effects of music in the waiting environments of healthcare settings. To account for such effects, Van Rompay & Tanja-Dijkstra (2010) proposed that music in a service environment creates positive affect, which in turn decreases perceived waiting time. Therapeutic applications of music have been shown to reduce anxiety during normal care delivery, calm patients before surgeries, decrease postoperative pain, reduce feelings of stress and anxiety, and increase the perceived attractiveness and professional quality of the waiting room (see Van Rompay & Tanja-Dijkstra, 2010). On the other hand, noise is also recognized as a distraction and stressor for staff, with reported emotional exhaustion or burnout among critical care nurses.

b Ambient scent

Within the healthcare context, the effects of ambient scent have received limited attention. The study by Lehrner, Eckersberger, Walla, Pötsch, and Deecke (2000) demonstrated that exposure to an ambient orange-flavoured scent has a relaxing effect; women experienced a lower level of anxiety, a more positive mood, and higher levels of calmness. Another study by Lehrner, Marwinski, Lehr, Johren, and Deecke (2005) compared the effects of two scents (i.e., orange and lavender) to a music condition and a control condition. Both scent conditions resulted in improved mood and less anxiety. These studies clearly demonstrate that the use of ambient scent can also be of interest in a healthcare context and may be useful in masking the typical "antiseptic hospital smell" (see Van Rompay & Tanja-Dijkstra, 2010). Finally, the traditional smell of hospitals as a consequence of outmoded organizational arrangements for managing chemicals and waste reduces the hospital's reputation and attractiveness for both professionals and patrons.

c Symbols and Artifacts

The use of light, windows, and art have been demonstrated to promote healing (Mallak, Lyth, Olson, Ulshafer, & Sardone, 2003). A study by Ulrich in 1984 found that patients in rooms with windows facing a natural scene used less pain relief medication and had shorter lengths of stay compared to similar patients with windows facing a brick building wall (see Mallak et al., 2003). Signs displayed on the exterior and interior of a structure are examples of explicit communicators. They can be used to convey rules of behaviour and play an important part in communicating firm image. Quality materials used in construction, artwork, the presence of certificates and photographs on walls, floor coverings, and personal objects displayed in the environment can all disclose symbolic meaning and create an overall aesthetic impression. Moreover, signage is important not only to patients and visitors, but also to staff, both to help them find their own way around the hospital and to avoid wasting time. In particular, signs, symbols, and artefacts communicate the strategy and core values of an organization. Thus, hospitals that aim at reducing their impact on the environment might use this lever to promote and facilitate both patients' and professionals' engagement in environment-oriented behaviours.

d Space and layout

Similar to retail settings, Van Rompay & Tanja-Dijkstra (2010) suggest that healthcare environments are social venues where patient density in waiting rooms or reception areas is often high. In addition to crowded conditions during visits of relatively short duration, patients may also face intrusions of privacy in shared patient rooms during longer periods of hospitalization. Hence, on a managerial level, care should be taken to reduce perceptions of crowding in functional units such as reception areas as much as possible. Although strategies aimed at breaking up larger spaces into smaller subunits are not feasible in certain circumstances, research suggests that the informed use of atmospheric variables such as colour and lighting may attenuate crowding effects. Spatial layout refers to the ways in which machinery, equipment, and furnishings are arranged, the size and shape of those items, and the spatial relationships among them. On the other hand, functionality refers to the ability of the same items to facilitate performance and the accomplishment of goals. Convenient layout increases professionals' productivity; reduces horizontal and vertical travel time and patient transfers; reduces energy consumption; and reduces costs of future layout modifications. Moreover, an appropriate organization of supplies and equipment saves nurses' time and limits time wasted on useless activities, providing more time for patient care, reducing job stress, and increasing job satisfaction.

14.5.2 RELIABILITY

Reliability refers to the ability for hospital staff to perform the promised service dependably and accurately. Thus, patients expect that information related to the nature of their illness, the clinical and diagnostic procedures, their outcomes, and finances should be treated dependably. They also expect that the adequate and appropriate clinical and diagnostic procedures should be prescribed for them to undertake per their symptoms (Ramanujam, 2011; Swain & Kar, 2017; Prabhu & Iyer, 2018)

14.5.3 RESPONSIVENESS

Responsiveness refers to the willingness to help customers and provide prompt service. Patients expect healthcare services to be provided within an appropriate interval such that the waiting time for receiving the first treatment, the time to receive diagnostic reports, and the time gap between required service and the instance of service delivery should not be excessive, bearing in mind the discomfort that most patients are typically in (Ramanujam, 2011; Swain & Kar, 2017; Prabhu & Iyer, 2018).

14.5.4 ASSURANCE

Assurance refers to the knowledge and courtesy of employees and their ability to inspire trust and confidence. Research indicates that patients feel more comfortable if service providers respect their privacy during counselling sessions and examinations. Lack of privacy can make it more difficult for patients to participate actively in their treatment plan (Ramanujam, 2011; Swain & Kar, 2017; Prabhu & Iyer, 2018).

14.5.5 EMPATHY

Empathy refers to the caring, individualized attention the hospital provides to its patients. Having supportive and caring staff responsive to individual needs was viewed as essential to providing quality hospital care. Patients expect their caregivers to be more responsible and accountable and provide prompt service. It is important for patients to get emotional support from providers to help reduce their vulnerability and anxiety. Furthermore, patients expect staff to acknowledge and treat them as individuals, and be interested in providing good quality care (Ramanujam, 2011; Swain & Kar, 2017; Prabhu & Iyer, 2018). Research studies in the healthcare field suggested that a doctor's competence can be evaluated based upon the presence or absence of competence cues such as diplomas or scientific books displayed on the wall in the work environment (Verhoeven, Van Rompay, & Pruyn, 2007). Personal belongings, such as family portraits and decorative objects, also trigger evaluations of the physician as more empathic. These findings take on increased significance when realizing that competence and empathy perceptions are most important in patients' evaluations of doctors and physicians (Van Rompay et al., 2008).

14.6 CHALLENGES IN MEASURING SERVICE QUALITY IN HEALTHCARE

Although many healthcare organizations have started service quality measurement programs (Upadhyai et al., 2019), several factors complicate the measurement of service quality in healthcare services in general and hospital services in particular. First, hospital services contain a significant number of "moving parts" as multiple parties administer care. This requires extreme customization and judgement to ensure quality. Second, hospital service consumers, relative to consumers of other types of services, are sick, reluctant to relinquish personal privacy, require holistic service delivery, and are vulnerable. In addition, the patients receive services from healthcare providers who are under tremendous stress. These factors create significant challenges for those who attempt to measure the patient's perceptions of hospital service quality. Further complicating the assessment of service quality in healthcare services is the fact that they are high in credence attributes. As such, there is the need for appropriating other industry methods for measuring and improving healthcare service quality, namely quality audits and benchmarking.

14.7 CONDUCTING A QUALITY AUDIT IN HEALTHCARE

Audits and quality improvement projects are vital aspects of healthcare governance and continual service improvement in medicine. An audit assesses if a certain aspect of healthcare is attaining a recognized standard. This informs healthcare providers and patients about the state of healthcare delivery and the possible areas for improvement. The aim is to achieve quality improvement and improve outcomes for patients. Audits are a quality improvement measure that allows healthcare organizations to continually work toward improving quality of care by showing them where they are falling short and allowing them to implement improvements. A re-audit or a close of the audit cycle will occur if beneficial change has taken place.

From a Total Quality Management perspective, quality in terms of healthcare is dependent on an effective and efficient audit function (Alhatmi, 2010). Thus, an audit monitors and attempts to measure quality. In recent times, the active inclusion of the patients' views as part of healthcare audits has been achieved and is starting to be incorporated into the healthcare auditing process around the world.

14.7.1 TYPES OF QUALITY AUDITS IN HEALTHCARE

There are various types of quality audits that can be undertaken within the healthcare sector. These include the medical audit, clinical audit, professional audit, managerial audit, and consumer audit (Alhatmi, 2010).

14.7.1.1 Medical Audit

A medical audit is defined as being a systematic, critical analysis of the quality of medical care, including the procedures for diagnosis and treatment, the use of resources, and the resulting outcomes and quality of care for the patient.

14.7.1.2 Clinical Audit

Clinical audit, on the other hand, is an audit by providers of professional services, such as nurses, physiotherapists, and other medical practitioners. A clinical audit aims to increase patient care and outcomes via systematic review of care against explicit criteria and the implementation of change.

14.7.1.3 Professional Audit

Professional audit is concerned with areas appertaining to standards that are acceptable for professional practice, for example acceptable standards required for the prescription of medications.

14.7.1.4 Managerial Audit

Managerial audit can be seen as largely concerned with the use of resources in the provision of health care.

14.7.1.5 Consumer Audit

A consumer audit can be said to review the quality of care provided by health services from the patient's point of view, although there is a considerable debate about the appropriateness of the title "consumer" and "customer" to portray a patient in public services. It establishes the patient's quality agenda through a range of observation and interview techniques, identifies and defines standards of service that patients should reasonably expect, measures performance against those standards, and provides indications of where improvement has (or has not) occurred (McLaughlin & Kaluzny, 1999).

14.8 BENCHMARKING IN HEALTHCARE DELIVERY

As an example of another appropriated healthcare service quality measurement model, benchmarking is the search for the industry best practices which will lead to exceptional performance through the implementation of these best practices (Krishnamoorthy & D'Lima, 2014) and includes a focus on patients and healthcare employees, a continuous process, and a system improvement mindset. Although benchmarking was developed for business, it is increasingly being observed in the public sector (Guven-Uslu, 2005). However, empirical research on the use and function of benchmarking in health organizations is still scarce (Wind & van Harten, 2017). That notwithstanding, benchmarking could help close the widening gap between hospitals that deliver exemplary patient service and those that provide lower levels of care (Ettorchi-Tardy, Levif & Michel, 2012).

Benchmarking in the health sector is conceptualized to imply the systematic and continuous process of assessing the products, services, and work which are regarded as best practice for the purpose of improving an organization (Ettorchi-Tardy et al., 2012).

Barnes, Lawton, and Briggs (1994) developed a process for clinical benchmarking and the stages are highlighted below:

1. Focus and assessment. This allows for benchmark criteria to be established through onsite visits and standards from other hospitals.
2. Outcome analysis and comparison. This stage focuses on allowing variances to be detected between the benchmarks and the actual services.
3. Clinical process documentation. This entails data collection actions to solicit input from clients and employees to ascertain reasons for variance.
4. Benchmark process comparison. In the fourth stage, the patient care processes are compared to the benchmark of the hospital. This stage comprises action planning, which has to do with the implementation and monitoring of the benchmark standards.

Thus, benchmarking is a continuous quality improvement process for healthcare organizations striving for best practice to assess their performances with one another in an effort to improve their service quality. Its greatest potential remains as a vehicle for the sharing and transfer of best-practice knowledge, along with its tangible contribution to the development of learning organizations that can analyze, reflect, learn, and change based on experience.

14.9 CONCLUSION

It is evident that an increased focus on patient-centred care has led to several pieces of research exploring what determines service quality and how it can be measured. Not only that, healthcare service quality has become a defining element shaping the choice criteria of healthcare consumers (Bamfo & Dogbe, 2017). Managers of healthcare organizations must take proactive steps to manage the challenges that are fraught in high credence services by employing continuous improvement tools such as audits and benchmarking to both mitigate service failures and improve overall service quality. Measuring healthcare service quality provides an objective guide for managers and policy makers to improve their services and patient satisfaction. Consequently, the purpose of this chapter has been to highlight some key healthcare service quality factors that impact customer perceptions of the level of service rendered.

This chapter has elaborated on the need to give attention to customer perception variables as well as leverage their rich insights to create models of continuous improvement in quality healthcare delivery. This is against the backdrop that in healthcare sectors, customers are the patients and their perceptions are considered to be the main indicator when assessing the service quality (Otani, Herrmann, & Kurz, 2011). Various dimensions have been used in the measurement of service quality in relation to quality healthcare delivery. All of these dimensions must be weighed as good predictors of service quality in the healthcare industry on the basis of their contribution to defining patient satisfaction with quality healthcare delivery.

REFERENCES

Aagja, J. P., & Garg, R. (2010). Measuring perceived service quality for public hospitals (PubHosQual) in the Indian context. *International Journal of Pharmaceutical and Healthcare Marketing, 4*(1), 60–83.

Abdallah, A. (2014). Implementing quality initiatives in healthcare organizations: Drivers and challenges. *International Journal of Health Care Quality Assurance, 27*(3), 166–181.

Agyapong, A., Afi, J. D., & Kwateng, K. O. (2017). Examining the effect of perceived service quality of health care delivery in Ghana on behavioural intentions of patients: The mediating role of customer satisfaction. *International Journal of Healthcare Management, 11*(4), 276–288.

Akter, R., Hasan, S. R., Siddiqua, S. A., Majumder, M. M., Hossain, M. M., Alam, M. A., & Ghani, A. (2008). Evaluation of analgesic and antioxidant potential of the leaves of Curcuma alismatifolia Gagnep. *Stamford Journal of Pharmaceutical Sciences, 1*(1), 3–9.

Alhatmi, Y. S. (2010). Quality audit experience for excellence in healthcare. *Clinical Governance: An International Journal, 15*(2), 113–127. doi:10.1108/14777271011036364.

Aliman, N. K., & Mohamad, W. (2016). Linking service quality, patients' satisfaction and behavioral intentions: An investigation on private healthcare in Malaysia. *Procedia – Social and Behavioral Sciences, 224*, 141–148.

Anabila, P. (2019). Service quality: A subliminal pathway to service differentiation and competitive advantage in private healthcare marketing in Ghana. *Health Marketing Quarterly, 36*(2), 136–151. doi:10.1080/07 359683.2019.1575062.

Arunasalam, M., Paulson, A., & Wallace, W. (2003). Service quality assessment of workers' compensation health care delivery programs in New York State using SERVQUAL. *Health Marketing Quarterly, 21*(1/2), 29–64. doi:10.1300/J026v21n01_03.

Asubonteng, P., McCleary, K. J., & Swan, J. E. (1996). SERVQUAL revisited: A critical review of service quality. *Journal of Services Marketing, 10*(6), 62–81. doi:10.1108/08876049610148602.

Atinga, R. A., Abekah-Nkrumah, G., & Domfeh, K. A. (2011). Managing healthcare quality in Ghana: A necessity of patient satisfaction. *International Journal of Health Care Quality Assurance, 24*(7): 548–563.

Baker, C., Akgü, N. H. S., & Al Assaf, A. F. (2008). The role of expectations in patient assessments of hospital care: An example from a university hospital network, Turkey. *International Journal of Health Care Quality Assurance, 21*(4), 343–355. doi:10.1108/09526860810880144.

Bamfo, B. A., & Dogbe, C. S. K. (2017). Factors affecting the choice of private hospitals in Ghana. *International Journal of Pharmaceutical and Healthcare Marketing, 11*(1), 80–96. doi:10.1108/IJPHM-11-2015-0054.

Barnes, R. V., & Lawton, L., & Briggs, D. (1994). Clinical benchmarking improves clinical paths: Experience with coronary artery bypass grafting. *The Joint Commission Journal on Quality Improvement, 20,* 267–276. doi:10.1016/S1070-3241(16)30071-2.

Bitner, M. J. (1992). Servicescapes: The impact of physical surroundings on customers and employees. *Journal of Marketing, 56*(2), 57–71. doi:10.1177/002224299205600205.

Blackstone, E. A., & Fuhr, J. P. Jr. (2016). The economics of Medicare accountable care organizations. *American Health Drug Benefits, 9*(1), 11–19.

Boaden, R., & Walshe, K. (Ed.) (2006). The quality management contribution to patient safety. In *Patient safety: Research into practice* (pp. 41–65). Maidenhead: Open University Press.

Butt, M. M., & de Run, E. C. (2010). Private healthcare quality: Applying a SERVQUAL model. *International Journal of Health Care Quality Assurance, 23*(7), 658–673.

Chassin, M. R. (2013). Improving the quality of health care: What's taking so long? *Health Affairs, 32*(10), 1761–1765.

Cronin, J. J., & Taylor, S. A. (1992). Measuring service quality: A re-examination and extensions. *Journal of Marketing, 56*(July), 55–68.

Duggirala, M., Rajendran, C., & Anantharaman, R. N. (2008). Patient-perceived dimensions of total quality service in healthcare. *Benchmarking: An International Journal, 15*(5), 560–583.

Duku, S. K. O., Nketiah-Amponsah, E., Janssens, W., and Pradhan, W. (2018). Perceptions of healthcare quality in Ghana: Does health insurance status matter? *PLoS One, 13*(1). doi:10.1371/journal.pone.0190911.

Escribano-Ferrer, B., Cluzeau, F., Cutler, D., Akufo, C., & Chalkidou, K. (2016). Quality of health care in Ghana: Mapping of interventions and the way forward. *Ghana Medical Journal, 50*(4): 238–247.

Ettorchi-Tardy, A., Levif, M., & Michel, P. (2012). Benchmarking: A method for continuous quality improvement in health. *Healthcare Policy/Politiques de Santé, 7,* e101–19. doi:10.12927/hcpol.2012.22872.

Ghana National Healthcare Strategy (2016). Retrieved on December 28, 2017, from www.moh.gov.gh/wpcontent/uploads/2017/06/National20Quality20Strategy20Ghana.pdf.

Gotlieb, J. B. (2000). Understanding the effects of nurses, patients' hospital rooms, and patients' perception of control on the perceived quality of a hospital. *Health Marketing Quarterly, 18*(1/2), 1–14.

Grönroos, C. (1984). A service quality model and its marketing implications. *European Journal of Marketing, 18*(4), 36–44.

Gumede, P., Green, P., & Dlamini, B. (2015). Evaluation of healthcare services: Cross-sectional case in KwaZulu-Natal, South Africa. *Journal of Human Ecology, 52*(1/2), 32–38.

Guven-Uslu, P. (2005). Benchmarking in health services. *Benchmarking: An International Journal, 12*(4), 293–309.

Hinson, R. E. (2012). *Service marketing excellence with a twist of corporate social responsibility* (1st ed.). Accra: Sedco Publishing Limited.

Kodom, M., Owusu, A. Y., & Kodom, P. N. B. (2019). Quality healthcare service assessment under Ghana's National Health Insurance Scheme. *Journal of Asian and African Studies, 54*(4), 569–587. doi:10.1177/0021909619827331.

Kotler, P. (1973). Atmospherics as a marketing tool. *Journal of Retailing, 49,* 48–64.

Kotler, P., & Armstrong, G. (2013). *Principles of marketing* (16th global ed.). Harlow, UK. Pearson Education Limited.

Kotler, P., & Keller, K. L. (2009). *Marketing management* (13th ed.). New Jersey: Pearson Prentice Hall.

Krishnamoorthy, B., & D'Lima, C. (2014). Benchmarking as a measure of competitiveness. *International Journal of Process Management and Benchmarking, 4*(3),342–359. doi:10.1504/IJPMB.2014.063240.

Lehrner, J., Eckersberger, C., Walla, P., Pötsch, G., & Deecke, L. (2000). Ambient odor of orange in a dental office reduces anxiety and improves mood in female patients. *Physiology & Behavior, 71,* 83–86. doi:10.1016/S0031-9384(00)00308-5.

Lehrner, J., Marwinski, G., Lehr, S., Johren, P. and Deecke, L. (2005). Ambient odors of orange and lavender reduce anxiety and improve mood in a dental office. *Physiology & Behavior, 86*(1–2), 92–95.

Lewis, R. C., & Booms, H. (1983). The marketing of service quality. In L. L. Berry, G. L. Shostack, & G. D. Upah (Eds.), *Emerging perspectives on service marketing* (pp. 99–107). Chicago: American Marketing Association.

Mallak, L. A., Lyth, D. M., Olson, S. D., Ulshafer, S. M. and Sardone, F. J. (2003). Culture, the built environment and healthcare organizational performance. *Managing Service Quality, 13*(1), 27–38.

Mannion, R., & Braithwaite, J. (2017). False dawns and new horizons in patient safety research and practice. *International Journal of Health Policy and Management, 6*(12), 685–689.

McLaughlin, C. P., & Kaluzny, A. D. (1999). Defining quality improvement: Past, present, and future. In *Continuous quality improvement in health care: Theory, implementation, and applications* (2nd ed.) (p. 10). Sudbury, MA: Jones and Bartlett Publishers, Inc.

Mosadeghrad, A. M. (2013). Healthcare service quality: Towards a broad definition. *International Journal of Health Care Quality Assurance, 26*(3), 203–219.

Otani, K., Herrmann, P. A., & Kurz, R. S. (2011). Improving patient satisfaction in hospital care settings. *Health Services Management Research, 24*(4), 163–169.

Pai, Y. P., & Chary, S. T. (2016). Measuring patient-perceived hospital service quality: A conceptual framework. *International Journal of Health Care Quality Assurance, 29*(3), 300–323.

Prabhu, A. M., & Iyer, L. S. (2018). Assessment of SERVQUAL model in hospitals located in tier II cities of India. *Journal of Health Management, 20*(1), 28–37.

Ramanujam, P. G. (2011). Service quality in health care organisations: A study of corporate hospitals in Hyderabad. *Journal of Health Management, 13*(2), 177–202.

Swain, S., & Kar, N. C. (2017). A holistic framework for conceptualizing hospital service quality. *Journal of Health Management, 19*(1), 84–96.

Tenkorang, E. Y. (2016). Health provider characteristics and choice of healthcare facility among Ghanaian health seekers. *Health System & Reforms, 2*(2), 160–170. doi:10.1080/23288604.2016.1171282.

Ulrich, R. S. (1984). View through a window may influence recovery from surgery. *Science, 224*, 420–421.

Upadhyai, R., Jain, A. K., Roy, K., & Pant, V. (2019). A review of healthcare service quality dimensions and their measurement. *Journal of Health Management, 21*(1), 102–127. doi:10.1177/0972063418822583.

Van Rompay, T. J. L., & Tanja-Dijkstra, K. (2010). Directions in healthcare research: Pointers from retailing and services marketing. *Health Environments Research & Design, 3*(3), 87–100.

Van Rompay, T. J. L, Galetzka, M., Pruyn, T. H., & Garcia, J. M. (2008). Human and spatial dimensions of retail density: Revisiting the role of perceived control. *Psychology and Marketing, 3*(4), 319–335. doi:10.1002/mar.20211.

Verhoeven, J. M. W., Van Rompay, T. J. L., & Pruyn, T. H. (2007). Let your workspace speak for itself: The impact of material objects on impression formation and service quality perception. *Advances in Consumer Research, 34*.

Weheba, G., Cure, L., & Toy, S. (2018). Perceived dimensions of healthcare quality in published research. *International Journal of Healthcare Management*. doi:10.1080/20479700.2018.1548156.

Wind, A., & van Harten, W. H. (2017). Benchmarking specialty hospitals: A scoping review on theory and practice. *BMC Health Services Research, 17*, 245. doi:10.1186/s12913-017-2154-y.

Yavas, U., Babakus, E., Westbrook, K. W., Grant, C. C., Deitz, G. D., & Rafalski, E. (2016). An investigation of service quality: Willingness to recommend relationship across patient and hospital characteristics. *Journal of Health Management, 18*(1), 49–69.

Zeithaml, V. A., Bitner, M. J., & Gremler, D. D. (2009). *Service marketing: Integrating customer focus across the firm* (5th ed.). New York, NY: McGraw-Hill.

Zeithaml, V. A., Parasuraman, A., & Berry, L. L. (1990). *Delivering quality service: Balancing customer perceptions and expectations*. New York, NY: The Free Press.

Zgierska, A., Rabago, D., & Miller, M. M. (2014). Impact of patient satisfaction ratings on physicians and clinical care. *Patient Prefer Adherence, 8*, 437–446.

15 Developing Customer Loyalty in Healthcare

Kofi Osei-Frimpong, Kumiwaa Asante,
Michael Nkrumah, Nana Owusu-Frimpong

15.1 INTRODUCTION

Characterized by organizational complexity, the healthcare service consists of various interdependent professionals, working together towards the improvement of the welfare of the patient (customer). Berry and Bendapudi (2007) consider it as one of the most personal and essential services consumers buy, as it has the capacity to improve quality of life, thereby positively impacting the global economy. As a result, patient participation is encouraged as it has been found to improve medical status, psychological well-being and doctor–patient satisfaction (McColl-Kennedy, Hogan, Witell, & Snyder, 2017; Osei-Frimpong, 2017), which reiterates the significance of understanding value co-creating activities within the healthcare service in developing customer loyalty. Hence, this chapter seeks to provide deeper insights into how customers could be managed and be encouraged to actively participate in healthcare service delivery, leading to developing customer loyalty.

In recent times, despite constraints and inadequacies in the healthcare industry in developing countries, such as insufficient hospital beds and the limited number of highly qualified doctors, a high growth rate has been recorded in the industry, thereby increasing the level of competition (Meesala & Paul, 2018). Unfortunately, in developing countries, such as Ghana, discrepancies in customer experience may exist in reference to both the public and private health sectors. Additionally, service quality in private hospitals tends to be better than in public hospitals, which results in higher customer satisfaction and customer loyalty (Anabila, Kumi, & Anome, 2019; Kwateng, Lumor, & Acheampong, 2018). Whereas the service encounter may be somehow rushed, inadequate, and dissatisfying in public hospitals, certain doctors (who may be resident in public hospitals) tend to encourage participation among patients they may attend to in the private hospitals. Several factors may account for the lack of engagement in the public sector, however, and these may include large patient numbers and inadequate health personnel, which adversely affect consultation time and, consequently, participation and satisfaction. Moreover, the perception of service quality has been linked to behavioural intentions of patients while satisfaction has been found to mediate this relationship (Agyapong, Afi, & Kwateng, 2018).

In this vein, the importance of customer satisfaction and loyalty cannot be undermined, as they are tied to service profitability and play a key role in defining the strength of a customer's relationship with an organization (Lonial & Raju, 2015). Hence, the implementation of the patient-centredness approach in the delivery of high-quality service as well as the development of patient loyalty must be viewed as central to the sustenance of healthcare delivery in Africa.

Though healthcare service encounters are gradually changing from the paternalistic (doctor-led) approach to the patient-centric approach (McColl-Kennedy, Vargo, Dagger, Sweeney, & van Kasteren, 2012; Osei-Frimpong, Wilson, & Lemke, 2018), value co-creation by patients is fast gaining prominence in this regard (Lusch & Vargo, 2014). This suggests a need for healthcare providers to collaborate with customers, create the enabling environment to impact positive experiences, and build relationships with customers. Recently, consumers of healthcare have assumed a consumer-ist attitude that demonstrates a need to be satisfied and a right to demand service. For instance, Nettleton (2006) argued that healthcare is ultimately about the "rights of the consumer" and not about the "collective authority of the professionals and the participation of the patient". Lilley (2000) also noted the emergence of individuals becoming more "consumerist", with the right to make choices, attributing this practice to increased access to information which seeks to bridge the provider–consumer knowledge asymmetry.

Extant literature shows that the behaviour of patients tends to be dynamic in that they assume diverse interaction styles in consultations; and this behaviour is usually influenced by the social context, as well as the availability of resources (Engström & Elg, 2015; Osei-Frimpong, Wilson, & Owusu-Frimpong, 2015). These changing behaviours on the part of the healthcare consumer suggest a need for providers to reorient and manage relationships that could result in positive out-comes. In essence, there is an obligation for healthcare customers to completely partake in sharing information as well as making clear their preferences for treatment (Crawford et al., 2002; Elwyn et al., 2010). Yet, research illustrates the existence of different levels of patient participation in healthcare services (Cegala, Street, & Clinch, 2007), particularly in developing countries, which is viewed as a shortfall in customer healthcare co-creation and loyalty building. In contributing to the services literature, this chapter deepens our understanding of customer relationship management techniques and practices in healthcare, with particular interest in outlining strategies to be adopted by healthcare providers to enhance customer participation and improve customer satisfaction and experience.

15.2 CUSTOMER RELATIONSHIP MANAGEMENT

Defined as a combination of processes, people, and technology that seeks to understand the cus-tomers of a company by Vaish, Vaish, Vaisha, & Bhawal (2016), customer relationship management (CRM) strategies are beneficial for the attainment, development, and maintenance of relationships with customers. Additionally, for a successful CRM process to be achieved, Goldsmith (2010) sug-gests that CRM consists of "five inter-linked specific proximate goals that coordinate specific stra-tegic initiatives" that correspond with a categorization of three stages, namely, pre-consumption, consumption, and post-consumption. The goals are "acquire, retain, develop, consult, and convert customers" and should not be seen as separate stages but rather as a process whereby the next stage builds on the preceding stage. In the following section, a brief explanation of the goals of CRM as postulated by Goldsmith (2010) is presented.

15.2.1 Customer Acquisition

As the first goal of CRM, according to Goldsmith (2010), acquisition refers to efforts by a firm geared towards the attraction of customers to an offering. They may include direct marketing, integrated marketing communications, and various pricing strategies. Moreover, the CRM matrix suggests that all the subsequent goals aid in customer acquisition. For instance, a healthcare institu-tion may obtain information from its *retained* customers which may be useful as a tool in customer segmentation and consequently targeting potentially profitable customers. This institution may also *develop* its customers by encouraging customers to buy equivalent higher end products or ser-vices than the one in question (up selling) and/or by cross selling, whereby customers are invited to buy products or services which may be complementary or related. Next, in *consulting* or engaging with their customers, healthcare institutions will be able to identify customer needs and wants in order to create satisfaction and loyalty, which may then most likely result in the *conversion* of a customer to an advocate. Finally, while acquisition sets the stage for CRM, it is also an outcome of a successful implementation of the other goals. Yet, without a successful retention of customers, the institution will lose out on their acquired customers.

15.2.2 Customer Retention

After health institutions have successfully acquired customers, they need to engage in strategies which will help in retaining them. They must also build relationships with customers by getting to understand them, and segmenting them based on their profitability, which will then enable the firm to come up with different strategies to maximize the profitability of the different targets. Also, the use of loyalty and reward programmes (such as Discovery Vitality which will be discussed later on in the chapter) may encourage retention as well as loyalty and positive word-of-mouth, whether in person or electronically, via social media. After customer retention is attained, customer development is key.

15.2.3 Customer Development

The term "customer development" refers to the institution's attempt at creating customer profitability from newly established relationships with customers. Healthcare institutions must garner as much information about customers as possible, whether manually or through information technology, so as to be able to provide valuable offerings, thereby increasing profitability. Also, customer information may serve as a means to predicting customer behaviours, thereby encouraging favourable ones and discouraging those which may be damaging to the institution.

15.2.4 Customer Consultation

In order to provide exceptional value to customers, the institution must remain in constant communication with the customer. In listening, dialoguing, and consulting with customers, while the views and opinions of customers are heard, the firm, based on that information, is able to provide services which are likely to render value to their customers. Institutions are able to gain competitive advantage in their service to their customers by: monitoring consumer activities with regard to the institution as well as their competitors both online and offline; assessing customer feedback, concerns, complaints, and suggestions; and encouraging the customer's role as a co-creator of value. This competitive advantage will most likely result in customer loyalty. More often than not, satisfied and loyal customers end up becoming advocates of a particular brand whereby they spread positive word-of-mouth about the brand and its qualities. Hence, healthcare institutions need to pay attention to the views and opinions of their customers as well as the firm's own goals in order to yield profitable value-laden relationships with their customers.

15.2.5 Customer Conversion

Finally, stemming from the health institution's ability to consult with customers, thereby providing value and creating loyalty, the customer may spread positive word-of-mouth which has the potential of increasing profitability and market share. In some cases, some customers actively promote the brand by telling others about it and encouraging them to become users. Firms need to identify these customers and partner with them in their promotion endeavours. In some cases, the firm may even convert these loyal consumers into "brand enthusiasts" who will work with the firm and convince others to become consumers. In consultation with these advocates, firms are able to learn how their brands can be relevant to customers, and then subsequently create a platform where these customers can actively participate in creating this relevance, enabling them to promote the brand to others (Goldsmith, 2010).

15.3 THE CUSTOMER RELATIONSHIP MANAGEMENT PROCESS IN HEALTHCARE

Customer relationship management is gaining traction in the healthcare sector; it generally includes strategies in line with the management of patient interactions and the healthcare interface, and is usually centred around the patient's needs (Vaish et al., 2016). Further, marketing practices have evolved from transactions to a relationship focus, hence defining the customer as a partner to the service provision (Hoffman & Bateson, 2016). In other words, the consumer–provider partnership has the potential to improve the performance of the healthcare system in offering high-quality and cost effective care. Bruhn and Georgi (2006) note the relevance of building relationships in service provision as this contributes to the perceived value from the perspectives of both the customer and provider. In this instance, service providers (medical doctors, nurses, pharmacists, etc.) should build relationships with healthcare customers, which relationship building is likely to influence: (1) customer participation in the engagement; (2) customer learning; (3) customer collaboration; and (4) overall customer experience. Osei-Frimpong et al. (2015) found that the overall customer experience in the consultation process, which is influenced by the nature of engagement and relationship between the customer and the healthcare service provider, affects the healing process of the customer either positively or negatively depending on the nature of the experience (whether favourable or unfavourable).

Given that customer-centred care and shared decision-making have gained traction in healthcare practice, the doctor–patient (customer) relationship becomes increasingly important. The doctor–patient relationship sheds light on the fact that each party has a role to play in communication and decision-making (Diamond-Brown, 2016), which is critical in the service encounter. In this case, it is required that there is a mutual understanding between the actors as well as an elucidation of their roles and responsibilities. According to Austin and Seitanidi (2012), the underpinnings of the value creation process are modified as the relationship between partners changes, which calls for a need for adaptability in responsibilities of the actors aside their "limiting predefined" roles, particularly on the part of the healthcare customer. While the doctor–customer relationship is encouraged, this also allows for active participation or involvement and orientation of the actors in the consultation process. This approach brings mutuality in control whereby the patient's competences and ideas are explored and integrated into the management plan (Aveling & Martin, 2013; Moeller, Ciuchita, Mahr, Odekerken-Schröder, & Fassnacht, 2013).

Recently, consumers of healthcare have adopted consumerist patterns of behaviour, and some of them make certain requests, particularly in the decision-making process (Laing, Fischbacher, Hogg, & Smith, 2002; Osei-Frimpong et al., 2018). This approach is encouraged in order to enhance the quality of care delivery, and healthcare professionals should reorient to embrace these changes, especially when patient-centred care is promoted across the African healthcare system. Building relationships among the involved actors is considered as a complete approach to the consultation. The value creation perspective usually takes centre-stage in co-creation research as the focal point of expected value creation, whereby importance is placed on the engagement processes between the provider and healthcare customer. This proposes the need for effective collaboration between the involved actors (Taylor, 2009), given the critical importance of the dynamics of the doctor–patient relationship. According to Aveling and Martin (2013), this approach or practice offers an avenue in the enhancement in healthcare delivery while overcoming the aforementioned "inflexibility and directiveness". Hence, via actor involvement, cooperation, and empowerment, the doctor–patient relationship aids in improving the efficiency of health systems and interventions (Gill, White, & Cameron, 2011; McColl-Kennedy et al., 2012). In one instance, Britten, Stevenson, Barry, Barber, and Bradley (2000) found that non-participation by patients in the decision-making process could lead to misunderstandings in prescription decisions. These behaviours could be overcome by building mutual relationships among the actors.

Primarily, healthcare services are dependent on interpersonal interactions between actors, whose roles are the patient (customer) and the professional (Laing et al., 2002). This requires a chain of two-way interactions between the actors in the exchange/encounter process. Liljander and Strandvik (1995) discuss a number of bonds that strengthen the relationship between the service provider and the customer, which in essence project the level of commitment of the actors in the relationship. These are briefly explained in Table 15.1. The assumption is that doctor–customer relationships tied by these bonds are likely to result in mutually beneficial outcomes to both parties. For instance, such relationships build trust (whether implicit or explicit), therefore affording the healthcare customer the opportunity to share detailed information with the medical doctor, and, in turn, enhance participation in the engagement or consultation process. Nevertheless, these relationships are not infallible, as challenges arising from miscommunication may occur in instances where the customer's views are overlooked without any better alternatives or deliberations (Edwards, Davies, & Edwards, 2009). To forestall future challenges that may occur in the relationship, it is pertinent to undertake a thorough provider–patient orientation for a better and well-defined comprehension of their individual views and goals. While it is possible that outcomes of the power-shift (patient autonomy) may result in a tense encounter, a clearer understanding of the roles and responsibilities of each actor could mitigate this problem.

More and more, healthcare customers are gradually changing from mere recipients of care to well-informed, enlightened and active consumers with the confidence to take control of their

TABLE 15.1

Types of bonds between service provider and customer

Type of bond	Illustration
Social bond	Social bonds allow patients to know their doctors on a personal level that builds mutual trust, which also affords them the opportunity to openly talk about their condition and related symptoms.
Cultural bond	Customers may identify themselves with the cultural norms within specific subcultures of the healthcare system.
Knowledge bond	The customer may have an established relationship with a doctor who knows the customer's medical history. This enhances their relationship and, in most cases, healthcare customers define the provider as their family doctor, whom they trust.
Ideological bond	Customers may be inclined to prefer some doctors because of their approach to delivery of care and certain peculiar behaviours they may have in common.
Time bond	The service provider may have flexible service times favourable to the patient. In addition, both parties invest in the relationship over time, and therefore, do not want to switch or part ways.
Psychological bond	The healthcare customer believes in the doctor's abilities to deliver care that will result in positive outcomes.
Technological bond	The healthcare facility has up to data equipment or diagnostics that also give the patient some level of confidence in the facility. In addition, the patient and the doctor are able to share information easily as a result of advancements in technology.
Geographical bond	There are limited possibilities of changing doctors or healthcare facilities because of distance and/or lack of transportation.
Legal bond	The level of confidentiality in relation to patient records. Doctors owe healthcare customers the duty of keeping their medical records/history in strict confidence
Economic bond	Lack of resources may force the customer to consider another service provider where the cost involved meets their budget.

Source: Adapted from Liljander and Strandvik (1995).

various health situations, which is well noted by Berwick (2009, p. 560) as "*nothing about me without me*". Therefore, superior orientation between actors facilitates good relationships which may serve as a bedrock for effective cooperation between healthcare customers and doctors, irrespective of the dissimilarities that may exist between them with regard to knowledge and power.

15.4 UNDERSTANDING THE CHANGING ROLES OF HEALTHCARE CUSTOMERS

Healthcare consumption is characterized by customer satisfaction needs and service demand rights; hence, as healthcare access is a right for every human being, it is also a customer (patient) right. Nettleton (1995) argued that, first and foremost, while healthcare incorporates the collective authority of the healthcare professional as well as the participation of the patient, the rights of the consumer are a singular priority.

The increasing availability of information accessible to healthcare consumers accounts for the rise in "consumerism" among individuals as they harness their rights to make choices in healthcare service delivery. The marketing concept considers the consumer as the central focus of the exchange and this practice has encouraged consumerist patterns among healthcare customers. In essence, service customers' role in the service delivery process can influence both the quality and quantity of production (Wilson, Zeithaml, Bitner, & Gremler, 2016).

The twenty-first century consumer tends to apply the same behaviours as in other social contexts (e.g., retail business) to healthcare provision – which requires that providers orient themselves to understand the changing nature of customers in order to provider quality care that meet the customers' needs (Laing et al., 2002). The Institute of Medicine defines patient-centredness as care that is "respectful and responsive to individual patient preferences, needs and values in clinical decision-making" (Institute of Medicine, 2001, p. 3). This in effect gives healthcare customers the right to take full control of their healthcare decisions. As noted by Nettleton (1995, p. 249):

> Consumerism has come to mean the maximization of patient choice; the provision of adequate information; raising the standards of healthcare; ensuring the quality of services by taking into account the views of consumers; carrying out surveys to ensure consumer satisfaction; developing tools for the assessment of needs; reducing waiting times for treatment; and encouraging consumers to complain if they are not satisfied with the service they receive.

Furthermore, consumerism may serve as a theoretical window into understanding reasons behind consumer healthcare use and the control of their health issues (Laine & Davidoff, 1996). Hence, Thompson (2007) posits the "professional-as-agent" as an outcome of consumerism in healthcare delivery, whereby the preferences and expectations of patients serve as the baseline for the decision-making process. Over time, this trend has brought a number of issues to the fore among healthcare providers. However, research reveals that patients' active involvement in their condition management, including communication with the professional and participation in the decision-making, positively enhances the outcomes of decisions (Osei-Frimpong, 2017). Lupton (1997) contends that the consumerist approach of the patient drives their instinct to a more active role in contrast to the traditionally passive and dependent role in the past. This gives them the edge to take control of their health by independently taking interest in researching diagnosis and treatment information (Cline, 2003), which enhances their communication with the consultant in a more authoritative manner. However, there is increased perceived professional resentment of healthcare consumers' adoption of a more active role in the consultation process including the decision-making process within the African healthcare delivery.

There are instances in which doctors become upset as a result of patients making certain requests as well as increasing their level of involvement in the service encounter (Osei-Frimpong et al., 2015). Healthcare customers on the other side engage in consumerist behaviours not to undermine the competence, expertise, or professional judgement of the doctor, but rather to take full control and ownership of their health condition (Laing et al., 2002). However, given the advancement in information and communications technology (ICT), healthcare consumers seem to have bridged the knowledge asymmetry gap between the healthcare professional and the patient. For instance, recent adoption of online communities (Nambisan & Nambisan, 2009), hospital websites providing information and serving as an interactive platform with patients (Ayers & Kronenfeld, 2007; Chou & Chou, 2002), amongst other social media platforms, have contributed to empowering patients, which also reflects in increased participation in healthcare delivery (Osei-Frimpong et al., 2018).

In addition to online resources for seeking healthcare information, customers engage in other social interactions with family, friends, and healthcare professionals to share ideas on other health related issues. This is highlighted in Payne, Storbacka, and Frow's (2008) claim that access to information, resources, individual knowledge and skills (competence), need assessments, and cognitive behaviours are some of the attributes assisting the patient to create value. In this case, healthcare customers seek information for clarification purposes that allows them to satisfy their cognitive needs. Fundamentally, patients need information on healthcare to improve their performance during clinical encounters including the performance of their responsibilities as value co-creators.

Further, the modern patient has a wealth of meanings, and Gabriel and Lang (2006) debate the healthcare consumer in nine "faces" to include "the consumer as a chooser, communicator, explorer, identity-seeker, hedonist, or artist, victim, rebel, activist and as a citizen" (these faces are briefly explained in Table 15.2). Nevertheless, they note the multifaceted nature of the concept of consumerism, which is used and applied differently depending on the context. As noted, the proliferation of information has largely accounted for these consumerist behaviours, which are changing the face of healthcare delivery in Africa. In effect, the doctor-led approach, which was mainly a question and answer session, is gradually changing to the patient-centred approach. For instance, the Ghana Health Service has recently launched the Patients' Charter that sets out patient rights, in the quest to empower healthcare customers.

Furthermore, the Patients' Charter, as proposed by the Ghana Health Service and created for all Ghanaians living in Ghana, indicates that teamwork or collaboration (by health workers, patients, and society) is paramount in the attainment of optimal and quality healthcare (Ghana Health Service, 2017). In the Charter, the rights and responsibilities of patients have been outlined. Should the roles of all parties be adequately adhered to, patients are most likely to participate in the service encounter and experience overall satisfaction and loyalty. A summary of the patients' rights and responsibilities is given as follows:

- The Right of the individual to an easily accessible, equitable and comprehensive healthcare of the highest quality within the resources of the country.
- Respect for the patient as an individual with a right of choice in the decision of his/her healthcare plans.
- The Right to protection from discrimination based on culture, ethnicity, language, religion, gender, age and type of illness or disability.
- The responsibility of the patient/client for personal and communal health through preventive, promotive and simple curative strategies.

Nevertheless, according to the Patients' Charter, for minors and individuals who may be unable to make decisions for themselves, their rights and responsibilities may be implemented by "accredited and recognized" representatives.

Despite these developments, some doctors and other healthcare professionals are yet to embrace and accept these behaviours (Osei-Frimpong et al., 2015). It is worth noting that consumers have become more critical in the handling of their health issues. In effect, Robinson and Ginsburg (2009) contend that consumer driven healthcare is highly necessary for reasons of efficiency and ethics.

TABLE 15.2
The nine faces of the consumer

Faces of consumer	Brief explanation in relation to healthcare
Chooser	The consumer is presented with a number of options to choose from regarding the choice of a GP or health facility, as well as having the opportunity to make a choice from available treatment options. However, this is also dependent on access to objective information on which to base a rational choice of healthcare services.
Communicator	Consumers communicate and share information with others. In reference to healthcare, consumers' success in managing their condition through their active participation in a shared decision making process would be shared with others.
Explorer	Consumers explore to experience new opportunities, which also provide avenues to bargain. Consumers have the luxury to explore other alternative means to medicine and seek value for money.
Identity seeker	Identity and status of humans in a society are not ascribed but achieved. Consumers build trust in their relationship with healthcare professionals and keep themselves abreast of information.
Hedonist or artist	The emotional experiences of consumers to the healthcare delivered can either make them satisfied or not.
Victim	The flipside of the consumer being sovereign is becoming a victim. A number of errors or negligence on the part of healthcare professionals have resulted in injuring, deforming, causing pain to and sometimes the death of the consumer.
Rebel	Rebellious consumers could take different forms and the outcome has been bizarre. In healthcare delivery, the rebellious consumer may be attributed to the non-compliant patient.
Activist	The era of promoting consumerism in healthcare, in which patients or consumers are encouraged to be informed, play an active role in the decision making process and take control of their condition. Consumer activism is also driven by pressure groups and social movements to champion the consumer cause.
Citizen	The consumer as a citizen has the right of choice and the right to freedom, amongst other things. Access to healthcare is a right for the citizen and a right for the consumer as well.

Source: Table reproduced from Osei-Frimpong (2015, p. 76).

Though consumerism is devoid of any theoretical justification (McClimans, Dunn, & Slowther, 2011), it continues to be an issue of concern in healthcare provision, perhaps as a result of the informed and enlightened customer driven by knowledge acquisition. Today, consumers are beginning to manage the provision of healthcare as rational and sovereign thinkers (just as they behave in relation to other service sectors), in pursuing their interest of choice (Laing et al., 2002). Nevertheless, the supremacy of consumerism is somehow limited by the level of the professional–consumer relationship, which affects the co-creation of value from both perspectives in the context of healthcare. The consumerist approach to healthcare depicts the patient's autonomy in clinical encounters (Taylor, 2009); however, Osei-Frimpong et al. (2015) report that while some patients prefer to engage actively with the doctor in the consultation process, others prefer the doctor to take full control, which leaves the consultation as a mere question and answer session.

The application of consumerism to healthcare is not without criticism. According to Wiles and Higgins (1996), the rising trend of healthcare consumerism is rather challenging, bearing in mind the fact that consumers are not experts and have to rely on the practitioner for treatment. If healthcare is modelled as a "supermarket" where consumers prepare their "wish list" and decide what to buy or not, then to some extent, consumerism will negatively affect the quality of healthcare delivered (Nettleton, 2006).

To address this concern, healthcare professionals in Africa should first recognize, understand, and accept the consumerist behaviours of healthcare customers that result in clinical encounters. In light of this, Osei-Frimpong and Owusu-Frimpong (2017) suggest a need for service providers or doctors to understand the patient and not just limit their role to the provision of information in relation to reporting symptoms. Healthcare professionals (e.g., medical doctors, nurses, etc.) should do the following:

- Adopt an effective communication approach to address these behaviours so as not to negatively affect patient experiences in consultations.
- Create an encounter environment that encourages actor orientation and empowerment.
- Build relationships with healthcare customers to better understand them and enhance the provider–customer orientation.
- Ensure a friendly engagement with the patient, which is, effectively, more likely to generate positive experiences which could positively affect their healing process.

15.5 ENHANCING CUSTOMER PARTICIPATION IN HEALTHCARE SERVICE CO-CREATION AND DELIVERY

Primarily, roles, whether formal or informal, are chosen by individuals by drawing from the roles of other actors and this may create sociological challenges in human encounters such as healthcare service co-creation (Guirguis & Chewning, 2005). Healthcare service co-creation requires the co-operative efforts of the actors involved in the service exchange (i.e., the healthcare professional and the customer) (Lusch & Vargo, 2014). This signifies an interdependence of the actors involved in the service co-creation process which relies on the competences and resources accessible to the actors (provider and consumer). Moreover, the healthcare system's resources may comprise professional expertise, equipment, technology, defined processes, and relational capabilities. The ability of the healthcare facility to utilize these resources to co-create the service with the customer is critical in the service delivery process. As a result, the service co-creation process involves a series of interactions between the involved actors. Consequently, Broderick (1998, p. 352) identified three properties in relation to the degree of interaction between the provider and the customer to include: "(a) the degree of contact intensity, (b) the extent of reciprocity involved in exchange patterns and (c) the level of co-operative behaviour adopted". These offer the foundation of comprehending the actors involved in the nested activities, including their behaviours in the exchange, which aids in the course of engagement.

The dyadic role of the healthcare provider and the customer is very important in the service co-creation process, as roles provide actors with a composite set of identities, which become the basis of individual explanations of social situations. Grönroos and Voima (2013) place emphasis on the criticality of the customers' sphere in co-creating service leading to the realization or achievement of value. This suggests the important role of the healthcare customer in co-creating healthcare service delivery; hence, both the healthcare provider and the customer assume the responsibility of carrying out their respective roles in such a manner as to create the anticipated value.

While healthcare service encounters have seen a number of transformations, moving away from the paternalistic (doctor-led) approach to patient-centric approach (McColl-Kennedy et al., 2017), more emphasis is placed on the healthcare customer as a co-creator of value (Lusch & Vargo, 2014). In this vein, the level of participation of the healthcare customer in the service delivery is important. Customer participation in healthcare service delivery has gained traction in both research and practice partly due to its perceived importance in enhancing management decisions and outcomes including: improved well-being, increased commitment to compliance, value attainment, and enhancing the relational bond between patients and service providers. Participation could be viewed as increased patient information sharing or inputs, as involvement in decision-making, and as a behavioural construct (Osei-Frimpong, 2017).

Patient (customer) participation is defined as a "behavioural construct that measures the extent to which patients provide/share information, make suggestions, and become involved in decision making" (Chan, Yim, & Lam, 2010, p. 49). Following this definition, patients' active participation could be influenced by the relational exchange between the service provider and the patient. In this vein, Engström and Elg (2015) note that motivations associated with participation in such encounters are highly individualistic and relative to individuals' psychological resources. This requires effort on the part of the healthcare provider and customers, in particular by providing an enabling environment and motivation for actors to co-create the service delivery. These clinical encounters tend to provide a means for engagement between the actors, which could be initiated by the provider, patient or both (Osei-Frimpong, 2016; Payne et al., 2008). There is therefore a need to consider the role played by the respective actors in the encounter, which takes into account the different role-related behaviours including participation, perceptions, emotions and compliance (Markham, Ward, Aiman-Smith, & Kingon, 2010).

Likewise, for patients to retain positive affect and engage in participatory behaviours, they need to be well-equipped and motivated (Gallan, Jarvis, Brown, & Bitner, 2013). This indicates that service outcomes, together with increased commitment to compliance and overall realization of value, depend on what transpires in the consulting room throughout the encounter process. Noteworthy is the fact that patients' behavioural intentions are improved (Aveling & Martin, 2013), with patients also becoming more responsible and committed to compliance as a result of their participation in clinical consultations. Customer participation does not end in the consulting room: it goes beyond that. Apart from the service encounter as well as engagement with healthcare professionals, Osei-Frimpong (2017) posits that customer participation in the post-encounter activities is also important. Here, the patient is compelled to comply with medical instructions and the plan of action with regard to their treatment. Importantly, it should be noted that patient participatory behaviours such as complying behaviours toward professional advice may create satisfaction and the attainment of value (Dellande, Gilly, & Graham, 2004; Pinho, Beirão, Patrício, & Fisk, 2014).

Still, patient compliance to professional advice may be compromised due to certain factors such as unawareness, a lack of funds, and a lack of motivation – which may eventually affect patient outcomes. Again, it has been found that with reference to patient loyalty programmes, the adaptability and the well-being of a healthcare service ecosystem may be strengthened (Gambarov, Sarno, Hysa, Calabrese, & Bilotta, 2017). For this reason, certain hospitals in Africa, as well as the rest of the world, have partnered with medical health insurance firms in an attempt to bridge treatment gaps and ever increasing medical costs of patients. An example is the Discovery Medical Health Scheme in South Africa: "an independent non-profit entity governed by the Medical Schemes Act, and regulated by the Council for Medical Schemes" which exists "to care for [their] members' health and wellness by engaging the brightest minds and innovative solutions to provide access to affordable, equitable, and quality, value-based healthcare that meets their needs now and sustainably into the future" (Discovery Medical Health Scheme, 2019). Also, to promote healthier lifestyles, Discovery motivates its members through its rewards programme called Vitality. With Discovery Vitality, members are encouraged and rewarded for living more healthily, and for driving well (through the Vitality Drive programme). Specifically, through the Vitality Health programme, members are rewarded points for eating healthily, exercising, and undergoing their health checks and assessments. Furthermore, this programme comprises of five status levels ranging from Blue, Bronze, Silver, Gold, up to Diamond, with Blue being the most basic. Members begin with a Blue status and based on their lifestyle choices they earn points, which when accumulated up to a certain amount aid in the progression to the next status. Vitality points are reset to zero at the end of every year. Nonetheless, to attain the Diamond status, one must reach Gold for three consecutive years (Discovery, 2019). Vitality points may be redeemed for benefits such as "savings on local and international flights, holiday accommodation, car rental, movies, and gym, as well as cash back at a wide range of partner stores such as VirginActive, British Airways, PicknPay, Woolworths, Bosch Services, DisChem Pharmacies, and Total Fitness".

With loyalty and reward programmes such as these, client participation is enhanced, not only during the service encounter, but even afterwards via healthy post-encounter activities as some reward is sought.

Given the importance of customer participation in the co-creation of healthcare service, service providers must understand a participant's needs and motivation during the service encounter. It is also important to note that customer participation in healthcare service delivery is influenced by both intrinsic and extrinsic motivations (Osei-Frimpong, 2017). In effect, patients' active participation in clinical encounters is not only driven by autonomous regulation, but also influenced by external or controlled regulation. This suggests that healthcare professionals should adopt the delivery approaches in clinical encounters which are essential to enhancing patients' participation (Laing et al., 2002).

Wilson et al. (2016) highlight instances where service providers could enhance customer participation in service co-creation. For instance, healthcare professionals should:

- Provide a conducive environment and employ their communication and interpersonal skills to encourage patient participation in consultations that could result in value outcomes of the service.
- Clearly define customers' roles and understand the implications for productivity, quality, and satisfaction.
- Educate healthcare customers for their roles and provide reasons to participate in the service co-creation process.
- Understand that service encounters, furthermore, require optimal cooperation from both the healthcare professional and the customer, which is can then be seen in the active participation of the customer.
- Take a holistic view of the service delivery in clinical encounters to allow customers an active participatory role. In this case, healthcare professionals should employ a customer-centric approach in clinical encounters to stimulate active participation on the part of the healthcare customer.

15.6 CUSTOMER SATISFACTION IN THE HEALTHCARE SERVICES

The preceding sections have discussed the changing healthcare customer and the need for healthcare providers to better understand their needs and engage them in a way that will result in positive service outcomes. These outcomes as highlighted above include satisfying the healthcare customer. Kotler and Keller (2016, p. 153) define customer satisfaction as, "a person's feelings of pleasure or disappointment that results from comparing a product or service's perceived performance or outcome to expectations". Hence, satisfaction is achieved when the performance of the healthcare system and provider meets or exceeds a consumer's expectation. In recent times, customer satisfaction has become of keen interest to researchers and marketers as satisfying customers is linked to the co-creation of service value to both the provider and customer.

Moreover, Anderson, Fornell, and Lehmann (1994) in their study posit two distinct conceptualizations of customer satisfaction, namely: transaction-specific and cumulative perspectives. Whereas customer satisfaction from a transaction-specific perspective may be regarded as a post-experience evaluation of the customer's one-time purchase of a service, the cumulative view takes into account the overall purchase and consumption experience of a service over a period of time. While healthcare consumption could be a one-off experience (in the case of acute conditions), in most instances, hospital visits are repeated (in the case of chronic conditions) over a period of time. In this instance, customer satisfaction, be it from the transaction-specific or the cumulative perspective, should be a concern of the service provider and the healthcare system as a whole. In effect, healthcare customer satisfaction is known to lead to the overall quality of outpatient services for patients, and has also been linked with immense benefits for the hospital, such as its success and profitability (Alkuwaiti, Maruthamuthu, & Akgun, 2018; Meesala & Paul, 2018). Additionally, while the extant literature posits a number of factors affecting customer satisfaction, in this chapter a three tier classification of key factors will be outlined, namely, *individual*, *interpersonal*, and *structural* factors. It is important to note that these factors may favourably or unfavourably affect healthcare customer satisfaction.

- *Individual Factors*: Individual factors of customer satisfaction refer to aspects of an individual which are exclusively personal and have the capacity to affect one's customer satisfaction outcome. Examples of such factors include attitudes, personality, motivation, and one's overall health. Other important factors to consider are ethnicity and culture (Hopkins, Nie, & Hopkins, 2009); and demographics, specifically gender, residence, education and occupation (Kamra, Singh, & Kumar De, 2016).
- *Interpersonal Factors*: In relation to interpersonal factors, these have been identified as elements of the service encounter pertaining to personal attributes of both the service provider and the service receiver, which have the capacity to affect the ensuing relationship as well as customer satisfaction. In a healthcare setting, examples include "effective communication between patients and caregivers, as well as the relationship between the supervisor overseeing their care" (Forbes & Nolan, 2018). Additionally, Rahmatnejad et al. (2018) highlight the importance of "fulfilment of clinical requirements, nursing and staff care, general behaviour of doctors, and professional behaviour of doctors". Further, the facilities at reception and outpatient department areas also influence healthcare customer's satisfaction. Relatedly, the healthcare professionals' communication skills, their ability to spend enough time with the customer, listening skills, and delivery approach, also contribute to customers' overall satisfaction with the service (Osei-Frimpong, 2016; Rahmatnejad et al., 2018).
- *Structural Factors*: The characteristics or features of a firm, as well as how it is run, which have the capacity to influence customer satisfaction, either positively or negatively, may be viewed as structural factors. These may include the ability to schedule appointments early, prompt response to phone calls, as well as the perception of a shorter waiting time. They may also include physician-related services, and the waiting time for getting test reports; affordability and convenience, fulfilment of clinical requirements. In addition, nursing and staff care, registration and administrative procedures, infrastructure and amenities, and health insurance. Finally, they may include billing accuracy, proper communications about the time of service delivery, promptness of services, and the willingness of employees to help each other (Alkuwaiti et al., 2018; Kamra et al., 2016; Meesala & Paul, 2018). All these influence the healthcare customer's level of satisfaction. This also suggests a need to improve on healthcare structures and facilities in order to satisfy the factors enumerated above.

Customer satisfaction and loyalty are often linked and studied together, and it is believed that loyalty subsequently leads to a service organization's performance (Bowen & Chen McCain, 2015). For instance, healthcare customers often use the phrase "my doctor" to denote their level of satisfaction and trust of the healthcare professional. Such customers easily refer other prospective customers (be it private or public healthcare facility) to such healthcare professionals. A case in point is pregnant women sharing their experiences (both positive and negative) with their friends regarding some healthcare facilities. Unfortunately, the public healthcare facilities in developing African countries tend to be at the centre of discussions of negative experiences, leading to customer dissatisfaction. In an interview, some healthcare professionals alluded to these occurrences being a result of the increased number of customers they attend to on a daily basis. However much they would like to spend quality time with the healthcare customer, they are rather in a hurry to provide care to the long queue of customers at the outpatient department. It is argued that by "efficient operations, employee engagement and service quality", hospitals may be able to improve upon customer satisfaction and loyalty (Lee, Lee, & Kang, 2012). Here, this may result in the occurrence of a chain reaction where employee response and service quality are stimulated, which may then increase the scope and frequency of the relationship between a customer and service provider, and may consequently lead to the recommendation of the service provider to potential customers.

15.7 THE CUSTOMER LOYALTY PYRAMID AND HEALTHCARE SERVICES

Creating and maintaining customer loyalty has been deemed to help organizations develop long-term, mutually beneficial relationships with customers (Pan, Sheng, & Xie, 2012). Given the growing competition in healthcare services, particularly the private healthcare sector in developing African countries, the success of these facilities does not only rely on good technical skills and provision of quality services, but also relies on the provider's ability to satisfy and motivate customers to return to the practice (Zhou, Wan, Liu, Feng, & Shang, 2017). Three schools of thought have emerged that have sought to define loyalty. One school of thought opines that loyalty should be viewed as a behaviour (Hallowell, 1996), another believes that it should be viewed as an attitude (Bandyopadhyay & Martell, 2007), and a third advocates that it should be viewed as emotional attachment (Baloglu, 2002; Mattila, 2001). Aaker (1991) defines brand loyalty as a measure of the attachment that a customer has to a brand. Further, Pan et al. (2012, p. 151) define loyalty as the "strength of a customer's dispositional attachment to a brand (or a service provider) and his/her intent to rebuy the brand (or re-patronize the service provider) consistently in the future". This attachment reflects how likely a customer will be to switch to another brand, especially when that brand makes a change, either in price or in product features (Evanschitzky et al., 2012).

15.7.1 CUSTOMER LOYALTY PYRAMID

Taking into account Aaker's (1991) measure of attachment, whether that is the behavioural, attitudinal, or emotional measure, its end goal should be to capture customer commitment, trust, or bonds. Ensuing from the discussion on loyalty is what has now become widely known as the customer loyalty pyramid. The loyalty pyramid is a tool that facilitates the organization in accomplishing an increase in customer profitability by making use of the existing variances in customer profitability. Organizations apply this tool to make the link between service quality and profitability stronger, as well as to define the best distribution of limited resources.

Aaker's (1991) brand loyalty pyramid describes five types of consumer behaviour on the brand loyalty scale (see Figure 15.1), ranging from not loyal to very loyal (the lowest level is depicted at the bottom of the pyramid). He describes the customer behaviour for each level as:

1. Switchers: These are consumers who are not loyal to the healthcare facility or service provider in question. This kind of consumer does not consider the facility at all in his/her service patronage.
2. Satisfied/habitual buyer: These are consumers that patronize a healthcare facility out of habit. These tend to be reasonably satisfied customers, who basically do not perceive any reason to change their purchase behaviour and hence do not search out alternatives.
3. Satisfied buyer with switching costs: These are satisfied consumers that are reluctant to switch to another healthcare facility due to existing switching costs (unless it is a referral from their trusted facility).
4. Brand likers: These consumers can be classified as true brand enthusiasts. Their brand preference is mostly caused by an experience of emotional benefits alongside more rational benefits, such as price, time, and quality.
5. Committed buyer: These are the proud consumers, in whose (daily) lives the healthcare facility in question actually plays an important role. Committed consumers patronize the service because it ties in with their personal values.

FIGURE 15.1   The Loyalty Pyramid. (Source: Adapted from Aaker (1991)).

15.7.2 Customer Loyalty in Healthcare Services

Customer loyalty is regarded as a high priority in industries such as such as retail or business-to-business services where consumers are spoilt for choice, and hence can easily switch brands (Pan et al., 2012). In these industries, firms develop robust customer service programmes in order to stay competitive, but this may not be the same reality for most healthcare organizations. When it comes to healthcare, doubts lurk with regard to the efficiency and effectiveness of customer loyalty programmes, because from a consumer perspective, medical decisions involve sensitivity and trust in choosing healthcare providers, or treatment options which could also be limited by insurance programmes, geographic locations, or access to resources.

Despite this, customer loyalty is extremely important in healthcare organizations, and should not be underestimated in its power to improve organizations. This is because, despite some consumers being limited by factors beyond their control, most consumers do have a choice in their healthcare providers and will gladly seek out a better experience, if necessary. In essence, customer loyalty is driven by satisfaction, which in turn is driven by perceptions of the quality of the service offered by the healthcare organization (Fisk, Grove, & John, 2014). This makes bad reports easier to deliver and mix-ups and errors easier to understand, and it makes for a smoother overall medical experience. Furthermore, high levels of loyalty mean more referrals. Thus, when a consumer has a good experience, he/she is likely to engage in word-of-mouth referrals, which means more patients to the healthcare facility. Furthermore, key elements of customer loyalty include "hospital brand image, trust, organizational citizenship behaviour and customer complaints" (Zhou et al., 2017).

15.7.3 Improving Customer Loyalty in Healthcare

It is essential for healthcare organizations to establish the patient/customer relationship early with consumers, when they are relatively healthy and may have an everyday, health related question that does not require a hospital visit (Steinwachs & Hughes, 2008). With this in mind, it is advocated that these organizations should work to deliver a superior holistic customer experience by:

1. Developing and executing a social media strategy that will encourage patients/consumers to have meaningful engagement with the healthcare organization's brand. This will make the healthcare organization's brand seem more personal, will lock in "committed buyers" or "brand likers", and will afford the organization the opportunity to address patient complaints proactively (Dixon-Fyle & Kowallik, 2010).
2. Expediting the speed of service whenever possible without compromising the quality of that service.
3. Providing more information to their patients because patient behaviour may be characterized by scepticism, confusion or feelings of neglect, in situations in which they believe information is being withheld from them (Samuel, Dheensa, Farsides, Fenwick, & Lucassen, 2017).
4. Facilitating personal experiences so that patients/consumers feel heard and seen as individuals and engage with service providers on a personal level when discussing their problems.
5. Increasing commitment to privacy and handling delicate or even standard medical topics with a greater degree of understanding and privacy, which will make consumers feel more comfortable and more respected.

15.8 CONCLUSION

It is evident that today's healthcare organizations need to move towards building brand loyalty. Customer loyalty should be a major consideration for all healthcare organizations in Africa. Despite the changes in the healthcare customer's behaviour in relation to participation and demand request, among other things, it is imperative that healthcare facilities, whether public or private, deliver quality service to satisfy their customers. Although technological advances have created an impersonal environment in some aspects of healthcare, and will likely continue to do so, healthcare organizations which prioritize meaningful customer relationships are bound to be the most successful in future. Healthcare service providers should reorient to understand the changing consumer who is now enlightened and informed. This suggests that the information asymmetry is being bridged compared to the past where these customers remained passive. African healthcare service providers should endeavour to provide an enabling environment to allow for increased participation of the customer.

This chapter has discussed a need to consider the customer's satisfaction as being influenced by personal, interpersonal, and structural factors. In this regard, while customers hold high expectations of the service, it is imperative for the service provider to educate, inform, and encourage customers in their roles and responsibilities. While consumerist behaviours also remain a challenge in today's healthcare delivery, fuelled by increased access to information (both online and offline), healthcare professionals should build and develop their communication skills and level of tolerance. These are critical in order not to upset the enlightened customer who is not passive and naïve. Healthcare systems should also consider and recognize the co-creative role of the customer, and this should be promoted through patient empowerment programmes. There should, therefore, be cooperation between the healthcare professional and the customer, and, hence, the delivery of the service should be holistic enough to result in an overall positive experience. These practices will also promote customer loyalty among African healthcare organizations and ensure future sustainability.

REFERENCES

Aaker, D. A. (1991). *Managing brand equity: Capitalizing on the value of a brand name*. New York: The Free Press.

Agyapong, A., Afi, J. D., & Kwateng, K. O. (2018). Examining the effect of perceived service quality of health care delivery in Ghana on behavioural intentions of patients: The mediating role of customer satisfaction. *International Journal of Healthcare Management, 11*(4), 276–288.

Alkuwaiti, A., Maruthamuthu, T., & Akgun, S. (2018). Factors associated with the quality of outpatient service: The application of factor analysis – A case study. *International Journal of Healthcare Management*, 1–6.

Anabila, P., Kumi, D. K., & Anome, J. (2019). Patients' perceptions of healthcare quality in Ghana: A review of public and private hospitals. *International Journal of Health Care Quality Assurance, 32*(1), 176–190.

Anderson, E. W., Fornell, C., & Lehmann, D. R. (1994). Customer satisfaction, market share, and profitability: Findings from Sweden. *Journal of Marketing, 58*, 53–66.

Austin, J. E., & Seitanidi, M. M. (2012). Collaborative value creation: A review of partnering between non-profits and businesses: Part I. Value creation spectrum and collaboration stages. *Nonprofit and Voluntary Sector Quarterly, 41*, 726–758.

Aveling, E.-L., & Martin, G. (2013). Realising the transformative potential of healthcare partnerships: Insights from divergent literatures and contrasting cases in high- and low-income country contexts. *Social Science & Medicine, 92*, 74–82.

Ayers, S. L., & Kronenfeld, J. J. (2007). Chronic illness and health-seeking information on the Internet. *Health: An Interdisciplinary Journal for the Social Study of Health, Illness and Medicine, 11*, 327–347.

Baloglu, S. (2002). Dimensions of customer loyalty: Separating friends from well wishers. *Cornell Hotel and Restaurant Administration Quarterly, 43*, 47–59.

Bandyopadhyay, S., & Martell, M. (2007). Does attitudinal loyalty influence behavioral loyalty? A theoretical and empirical study. *Journal of Retailing and Consumer Services, 14*, 35–44.

Berry, L. L., & Bendapudi, N. (2007). Health care: A fertile field for service research. *Journal of Service Research, 10*, 111–122.

Berwick, D. M. (2009). What 'patient-centered' should mean: Confessions of an extremist. *Health Affairs, 28*, 555–565.

Bowen, J. T., & Chen McCain, S.-L. (2015). Transitioning loyalty programs: A commentary on "the relationship between customer loyalty and customer satisfaction". *International Journal of Contemporary Hospitality Management, 27*, 415–430.

Britten, N., Stevenson, F. A., Barry, C. A., Barber, N., & Bradley, C. P. (2000). Misunderstandings in general practice prescribing decisions: Qualitative study. *British Medical Journal, 320*, 1246–1250.

Broderick, A. J. (1998). Role theory, role management and service performance. *The Journal of Services Marketing, 12*, 348–361.

Bruhn, M., & Georgi, D. (2006). *Services marketing: Managing the service value chain*. Harlow: Prentice Hall.

Cegala, D. J., Street Jr, R. L., & Clinch, R. C. (2007). The impact of patient participation on physicians' information provision during a primary care medical interview. *Health Communication, 21*, 177–185.

Chan, K. W., Yim, C. K., & Lam, S. S. K. (2010). Is customer participation in value creation a double-edged sword? Evidence from professional financial services across cultures. *Journal of Marketing, 74*, 48–64.

Chou, D. C., & Chou, A. Y. (2002). Healthcare information portal: A web technology for the healthcare community. *Technology in Society, 24*, 317–330.

Cline, R. J. W. (2003). At the intersection of micro and macro: Opportunities and challenges for physician–patient communication research. *Patient Education and Counseling, 50*, 13–16.

Crawford, M. J., Rutter, D., Manley, C., Weaver, T., Bhui, K., Fulop, N., & Tyrer, P. (2002). Systematic review of involving patients in the planning and development of health care. *BMJ, 325*, 1263.

Dellande, S., Gilly, M. C., & Graham, J. J. (2004). Gaining compliance and losing weight: The role of the service provider in health care services. *Journal of Marketing, 68*, 78–91.

Diamond-Brown, L. (2016). The doctor-patient relationship as a toolkit for uncertain clinical decisions. *Social Science & Medicine, 159*, 108–115.

Discovery. (2019). *Discovery Vitality*. Retrieved March 24, 2019, from www.discovery.co.za/vitality/how-vitality-works.

Discovery Medical Health Scheme. (2019). *About Discovery Health Medical Scheme*. Retrieved March 24, 2019, from www.discovery.co.za/medical-aid/about-discovery-health-medical-scheme.

Dixon-Fyle, S., & Kowallik, T. (2010). Engaging consumers to manage health care demand. Retrieved July 24, 2018, from www.mckinsey.com/industries/healthcare-systems-and-services/our-insights/engaging-consumers-to-manage-health-care-demand.

Edwards, M., Davies, M., & Edwards, A. (2009). What are the external influences on information exchange and shared decision-making in healthcare consultations: A meta-synthesis of the literature. *Patient Education and Counseling, 75*, 37–52.

Elwyn, G., Laitner, S., Coulter, A., Walker, E., Watson, P., & Thomson, R. (2010). Implementing shared decision making in the NHS. *BM J, 341*, c5146.

Engström, J., & Elg, M. (2015). A self-determination theory perspective on customer participation in service development. *Journal of Services Marketing, 29*, 511–521.

Evanschitzky, H., Ramaseshan, B., Woisetschläger, D. M., Richelsen, V., Blut, M., & Backhaus, C. (2012). Consequences of customer loyalty to the loyalty program and to the company. *Journal of the Academy of Marketing Science, 40*, 625–638.

Fisk, R. P., Grove, S. J., & John, J. (2014). *Services marketing: An interactive approach.* Boston: Cengage Learning.

Forbes, D. R., & Nolan, D. (2018). Factors associated with patient-satisfaction in student-led physiotherapy clinics: A qualitative study. *Physiotherapy Theory and Practice*, 1–9.

Gabriel, Y., & Lang, T. (2006). *The unmanageable consumer.* London: Sage.

Gallan, A. S., Jarvis, C. B., Brown, S. W., & Bitner, M. J. (2013). Customer positivity and participation in services: An empirical test in a health care context. *Journal of the Academy of Marketing Science, 41*, 338–356.

Gambarov, V., Sarno, D., Hysa, X., Calabrese, M., & Bilotta, A. (2017). The role of loyalty programs in health-care service ecosystems. *The TQM Journal, 29*(6), 899–919.

Ghana Health Service. (2017). *The Patients Charter.* Retrieved March 24, 2019, from www.ghanahealthservice.org/ghs-subcategory.php?cid=&scid=46.

Gill, L., White, L., & Cameron, I. D. (2011). Service co-creation in community-based aged healthcare. *Managing Service Quality, 21*, 152–177.

Goldsmith, R. E. (2010). The goals of customer relationship management. *International Journal of Customer Relationship Marketing and Management, 1*(1), 16–27.

Grönroos, C., & Voima, P. (2013). Critical service logic: Making sense of value creation and co-creation. *Journal of the Academy of Marketing Science, 41*, 133–150.

Guirguis, L. M., & Chewning, B. A. (2005). Role theory: Literature review and implications for patient-pharmacist interactions. *Research in Social and Administrative Pharmacy, 1*, 483–507.

Hallowell, R. (1996). The relationships of customer satisfaction, customer loyalty, and profitability: An empirical study. *International Journal of Service Industry Management, 7*, 27–42.

Hoffman, D. K., & Bateson, J. E. G. (2016). *Services Marketing: Concepts, strategies, and cases.* Boston: Cengage.

Hopkins, S. A., Nie, W., & Hopkins, W. (2009). Cultural effects on customer satisfaction with service encounters. *Journal of Service Science, 2*(1), 45–56.

Institute of Medicine. (2001). Crossing the quality chasm: A new health system for the 21st century. Retrieved from www.iom.edu/~/media/Files/ReportFiles/2001/Crossing-the-Quality-Chasm/Quality Chasm 2001 report brief.pdf.

Kamra, V., Singh, H., & Kumar De, K. (2016). Factors affecting patient satisfaction: An exploratory study for quality management in the health-care sector. *Total Quality Management & Business Excellence, 27*, 1013–1027.

Kotler, P., & Keller, K. L. (2016). *Marketing management* (15th ed.). Upper Saddle River, NJ: Pearson.

Kwateng, K. O., Lumor, R., & Acheampong, F. O. (2018). Service quality in public and private hospitals: A comparative study on patient satisfaction. *International Journal of Healthcare Management.*

Laine, C., & Davidoff, F. (1996). Patient-centered medicine: A professional evolution. *Journal of the Academy of Marketing Science, 275*, 152–156.

Laing, A., Fischbacher, M., Hogg, G., & Smith, A. (2002). *Managing and marketing health services.* Cornwall: Thomson.

Lee, S. M., Lee, D., & Kang, C.-Y. (2012). The impact of high-performance work systems in the health-care industry: Employee reactions, service quality, customer satisfaction, and customer loyalty. *The Service Industries Journal, 32*, 17–36.

Liljander, V., & Strandvik, T. (1995). The nature of customer relationships in services. *Advances in Services Marketing and Management, 4*, 67.

Lilley, P. (2000). *Patient Power: Choice for a better NHS.* Demos.

Lonial, S., & Raju, P. (2015). Impact of service attributes on customer satisfaction and loyalty in a healthcare context. *Leadership in Health Services, 28*, 149–166.

Lupton, D. (1997). Consumerism, reflexivity and the medical encounter. *Social Science & Medicine, 45*, 373–381.

Lusch, R. F., & Vargo, S. L. (2014). *Service-dominant logic: Premises, perspectives, possibilities*. Cambridge: Cambridge University Press.

Markham, S. K., Ward, S. J., Aiman-Smith, L., & Kingon, A. I. (2010). The valley of death as context for role theory in product innovation. *Journal of Product Innovation Management, 27,* 402–417.

Mattila, A. S. (2001). Emotional bonding and restaurant loyalty. *Cornell Hotel and Restaurant Administration Quarterly, 42,* 73–79.

McClimans, L. M., Dunn, M., & Slowther, A. M. (2011). Health policy, patient-centred care and clinical ethics. *Journal of Evaluation in Clinical Practice, 17,* 913–919.

McColl-Kennedy, J. R., Hogan, S. J., Witell, L., & Snyder, H. (2017). Cocreative customer practices: Effects of health care customer value cocreation practices on well-being. *Journal of Business Research, 70,* 55–66.

McColl-Kennedy, J. R., Vargo, S. L., Dagger, T. S., Sweeney, J. C., & van Kasteren, Y. (2012). Health care customer value cocreation practice styles. *Journal of Service Research, 15,* 370–389.

Meesala, A., & Paul, J. (2018). Service quality, consumer satisfaction and loyalty in hospitals: Thinking for the future. *Journal of Retailing and Consumer Services, 40,* 261–269.

Moeller, S., Ciuchita, R., Mahr, D., Odekerken-Schröder, G., & Fassnacht, M. (2013). Uncovering collaborative value creation patterns and establishing corresponding customer roles. *Journal of Service Research, 16,* 471–487.

Nambisan, P., & Nambisan, S. (2009). Models of consumer value cocreation in health care. *Health Care Management Review, 34,* 344–354.

Nettleton, S. (1995). *The sociology of health and illness*. Cambridge: Polity Press.

Nettleton, S. (2006). *The sociology of health and illness*. Polity.

Osei-Frimpong, K. (2015). *An examination of value co-creation at the micro level in a healthcare setting: A dyadic approach* (Doctoral dissertation, University of Strathclyde).

Osei-Frimpong, K. (2016). Examining the effects of patient characteristics and prior value needs on the patient-doctor encounter process in healthcare service delivery. *International Journal of Pharmaceutical and Healthcare Marketing, 10,* 192–213.

Osei-Frimpong, K. (2017). Patient participatory behaviours in healthcare service delivery: Self-determination theory (SDT) perspective. *Journal of Service Theory and Practice, 27,* 453–474. doi:10.1108/JSTP-02-2016-0038.

Osei-Frimpong, K., & Owusu-Frimpong, N. (2017). Value co-creation in healthcare: A phenomenological examination of the doctor-patient encounter. *Journal of Nonprofit & Public Sector Marketing, 29,* 365–384. doi:10.1080/10495142.2017.1326356.

Osei-Frimpong, K., Wilson, A., & Lemke, F. (2018). Patient co-creation activities in healthcare service delivery at the micro level: The influence of online access to healthcare information. *Technological Forecasting & Social Change, 126,* 14–27.

Osei-Frimpong, K., Wilson, A., & Owusu-Frimpong, N. (2015). Service experiences and dyadic value co-creation in healthcare service delivery: A CIT approach. *Journal of Service Theory and Practice, 25,* 443–462.

Pan, Y., Sheng, S., & Xie, F. T. (2012). Antecedents of customer loyalty: An empirical synthesis and reexamination. *Journal of Retailing and Consumer Services, 19,* 150–158.

Payne, A. F., Storbacka, K., & Frow, P. (2008). Managing the co-creation of value. *Journal of the Academy of Marketing Science, 36,* 83–96.

Pinho, N., Beirão, G., Patrício, L., & Fisk, R. P. (2014). Understanding value co-creation in complex services with many actors. *Journal of Service Management, 25,* 470–493.

Rahmatnejad, K., Myers, J. S., Falls, M. E., Myers, S. R., Waisbourd, M., & Hark, L. A. (2018). *Factors associated with patient satisfaction in an outpatient glaucoma population*. Paper presented at the Seminars in Ophthalmology.

Robinson, J. C., & Ginsburg, P. B. (2009). Consumer-driven health care: Promise and performance. *Health Affairs, 28,* 272–281.

Samuel, G. N., Dheensa, S., Farsides, B., Fenwick, A., & Lucassen, A. (2017). Healthcare professionals' and patients' perspectives on consent to clinical genetic testing: Moving towards a more relational approach. *BMC Medical Ethics, 18,* 47.

Steinwachs, D. M., & Hughes, R. G. (2008). Health services research: Scope and significance. In R. G. Hughes (Ed.), *Patient safety and quality: An evidence-based handbook for nurses* (pp. 163–177). Rockville, MD: Agency for Healthcare Research and Quality.

Taylor, K. (2009). Paternalism, participation and partnership: The evolution of patient centeredness in the consultation. *Patient Education and Counseling, 74,* 150–155.

Thompson, A. (2007). The meaning of patient involvement and participation in healthcare consultations: A taxonomy. In S. Collins, N. Britten, J. Ruusuvuori, & A. Thompson (Eds.), *Patient participation in health care consultations: Qualitative perspectives* (pp. 43–64). New York: Open University Press.

Vaish, A., Vaish, A., Vaisha, R., & Bhawal, S. (2016). Customer relationship management (CRM) towards service orientation in hospitals: A review. *Apollo Medicine*.

Wiles, R., & Higgins, J. (1996). Doctor-patient relationships in the private sector: Patients' perceptions. *Sociology of Health & Illness, 18*, 341–356.

Wilson, A., Zeithaml, V., Bitner, M. J., & Gremler, D. (2016). *Services marketing: Integrating customer focus across the firm* (3rd European ed.). Berkshire: McGraw Hill.

Zhou, W.-J., Wan, Q.-Q., Liu, C.-Y., Feng, X.-L., & Shang, S.-M. (2017). Determinants of patient loyalty to healthcare providers: An integrative review. *International Journal for Quality in Health Care, 29*, 442–449.

16 Financing Healthcare and Health Insurance

Anita Asiwome Adzo Baku

16.1 INTRODUCTION

Financing healthcare and health insurance is undoubtedly an interesting, practical and management oriented topic that helps in administering the financial resources of a healthcare organisation. The rising cost of healthcare has necessitated another look at how governments and organisations finance healthcare. Health insurance, in its various forms, has been identified as one of the sustainable means of financing healthcare. The method of financing healthcare has implications for the marketing of the service as well as the satisfaction healthcare customers derive from the service. Managing the finances of a healthcare organisation demands some strategic decisions and innovative actions. These are thoroughly discussed in the various sections of this chapter. The financing mechanisms of some sub-Saharan African (SSA) countries have also been established. The main object of this chapter is to discuss the various financing mechanisms and financial management practices of healthcare organisations and also to determine how these decisions affect the marketing of healthcare services and the satisfaction customers derive from the utilisation of these services. The section headings include discussions on financing options in healthcare; national and private health insurance schemes; challenges of implementing health insurance schemes; what constitutes and how to prepare healthcare budgets; managing overhead costs; what the details are in the purchasing, receipts and issuing of stocks; the importance of and how to prepare financial statements; risk management; and healthcare financing and health services marketing.

16.2 FINANCING OPTIONS IN HEALTHCARE

There are various financing options available to nations as well as at the healthcare facility level. Financing healthcare could have a market or capitalist orientation, as the United States of America's system is usually said to operate. There are also the mainly state funded systems like that of the United Kingdom (Kennedy, 2015). Where the state is in charge of financing healthcare, a social insurance system is usually practised, with the state providing support to the social insurance system. An observation by Kennedy (2015) indicates that an average of 70 per cent of healthcare financing in the Organisation for Economic Co-operation and Development (OECD) economies is borne by the governments of these countries. According to the World Health Organization (WHO) (2016), public expenditure for health for African countries averaged 10 per cent of total public spending in 2014, with the highest being Swaziland, spending 17 per cent, and the lowest being Cameroon, spending 4 per cent. Ghana spent about 7 per cent on health (WHO, 2016).

At national levels, governments have the choice of funding healthcare from the state coffers; engaging in what can be referred to as state funded schemes; engaging in social health insurance schemes, community based health insurance schemes or private health insurance schemes; and having healthcare consumers pay out-of-pocket (Bennett & Gilson, 2001). At the healthcare facility level, healthcare organisations choose between having individuals pay at the point of service or engaging with various health insurance organisations or employers in the provision of the service. This section discusses these broad approaches and options available to nations and organisations in financing healthcare.

In state funded schemes, government attempts to provide healthcare services to all citizens through its ministry of health or a national health service system. Funding for such services is achieved through taxes, levies, fines, penalties and donor support (Bennett & Gilson, 2001). Services are provided in public healthcare facilities. However, government may contract non-governmental, private or faith-based healthcare facilities to provide service to the citizenry. In Ghana, for instance, government pays the workers of faith-based healthcare facilities to support them in providing healthcare to Ghanaians (Ministry of Health, 2006). Healthcare services under the state funded system of financing may be free or consumers may be asked to pay a token amount for use of the services (Smithson, Asamoa-Baah & Mills, 1997; Agyepong, 1999). Where there is the requirement for a token sum to be paid, the possibility that some people may not be able to pay exists. Sometimes, governments may target the vulnerable and provide services to them. An example is Gabon, which introduced a non-contributory scheme for its economically vulnerable (persons earning income below US$152) known as *Gabonais Economiquement Faibles* in 2007. It includes the dependants of these persons, pupils, students and refugees. Coverage under the scheme was 90 per cent of the target population in 2015 (WHO, 2016).

Social health insurance scheme is a financing mechanism that relies on the contribution of its members to finance healthcare (Bennett & Gilson, 2001). The contributions are usually mandatory and benefits are linked to the contributions made. The scheme could be limited to a small group of people or extended to cover a whole population. An example of such a scheme, which covers the whole population, is the National Health Insurance Scheme in Ghana. Other African countries with social health insurance schemes include Kenya and Tanzania (Fenny, Yates & Thompson, 2018). Of the total populations in the countries, Ghana topped the list with 38 per cent enrolment in 2015, with the least being Kenya with 11 per cent enrolment (Fenny et al., 2018).

The social insurance could be independent of government involvement. Where it covers the whole population, the contributions of members may not be adequate in financing healthcare, so taxes may be included. Coverage under social health insurance also tends to exclude those who are unable to pay the required contributions (Wouters, 1991). Where government is involved in the scheme, management becomes a complex interaction between government, enrolees, scheme managers and service providers.

Community based health insurance (CBHI) schemes are a financing mechanism for a group of people living in a particular community. They are usually not-for-profit and membership is voluntary for members in the community (Bennett, Gamble, Brant, Raj & Salamat, 2004). Members choose their scheme managers, who collect premiums and contract the services of healthcare providers. These community health insurance schemes attempt to cover the very poor or those usually excluded from social or private health insurance schemes (Dror & Jacquier, 1999). In Ghana, before the introduction of the NHIS, there were the Nkoranza, Dodowa and Gonja West community based health insurance schemes (Baku & Sakyi, 2014). These schemes usually complement the efforts of government in providing healthcare because their income is usually limited to the communities in which they operate (Baku, 2007). According to Fenny et al. (2018), Rwanda has the largest number of number of CBHI schemes and these covered 80 per cent of the total population in 2016. Kenya had the least coverage, at 1.3 per cent of the total population.

Private or voluntary health insurance schemes are voluntary ways individuals and organisations pay for healthcare. Individuals or groups may buy health insurance policies from private insurance companies, and when they become unwell, the insurance pays for the cost of their treatment. These schemes complement social or public health insurance policies as not all ailments may be covered under these schemes. The schemes have been accused of covering only those who can afford to pay premiums. On the flipside, private health insurance schemes stand the risk of suffering from adverse selection. Adverse selection is when only people who are sick or anticipate they may be sick insure (Dror & Preker, 2002). According to McIntyre, Obse, Barasa and Ataguba (2018), private or voluntary health insurance in SSA is minimal except in South Africa and Botswana, which have 47 per cent and 33 per cent of their healthcare expenditure being accounted for by such insurance.

The last method is out-of-pocket payments. Under this system healthcare consumers pay for services from their own resources, at the point of service. The disadvantage of this type of payment is that some people wait until their sickness reaches a deplorable stage before consuming healthcare. This may lead to them making more payments than if they had sought treatment earlier. Out-of-pocket payments exist alongside insurance schemes that may be practised in any country. According to McIntyre et al. (2018) out-of-pocket payment is the most common form of financing healthcare in SSA. Although most SSA countries have attempted to remove user fees, Ghana, Kenya, Senegal and Uganda have been pointed out as still having healthcare users pay user fees through informal means (McIntyre et al., 2018).

At the healthcare facility level, financing for the hospital's activities may come from internally generated funds (IGFs), from donors and/or from government (Ackon, 2003; Agyepong, 1999). IGFs are monies hospitals make through the services they provide. These services include their core and peripheral activities such as operating a restaurant, fee parking, renting of space. Some healthcare facilities also get donor funding from countries or from charitable organisations. Some of this funding may be earmarked for specific projects and some may be to support the budget of the facility. Governments sometimes provide healthcare facilities with some monetary support through the ministry of health. In Ghana, this support to public healthcare facilities has ceased. However, government continues to pay healthcare workers (even for some faith-based healthcare facilities) and invest in the capital projects of some healthcare facilities in the country.

16.3 NATIONAL AND PRIVATE HEALTHCARE INSURANCE SCHEMES

Health insurance operates on the concept of pooling of the health risks of a group of people, through premium payment. In the event of ill health, the contributions of the many contributors would be used to pay for the few who may be sick within the period of the insurance (Dror & Preker, 2002). Insurance generally operates on the assumption that not all insured persons would suffer losses at the same time. National health insurance schemes are social health insurance schemes that attempt to provide coverage for all citizens. Depending on whether a scheme is mandatory for all citizens or not, it may exclude some people who may not be able to afford premiums or those who may be covered by other health insurance schemes or provided for by an employer.

A national health insurance scheme may be managed by government, a private organisation or a combination of both. National health insurance schemes are usually established by legislation and may be financed by taxes or contributions from the members of the scheme or both. Some countries that run a national health insurance scheme include Ghana, the United Kingdom, Australia, South Korea, Germany and many others. Private health insurance schemes also exist. These are privately managed health insurance schemes that require voluntary enrolment. A contract of what is covered and not covered as well as premiums to be paid are issued to the person subscribing to the private health insurance.

Some differences exist between national health insurance schemes and private health insurance schemes. All countries have some form of private health insurance policies. Private health insurance schemes require the payment of premiums by the subscribers. These premiums are usually commercial rates for the policies that they cover, whilst national health insurance scheme enrolees make contributions. The contributions are usually subsidised by government. National health insurance schemes tend to cover some minimum level of basic care for their members whilst private health insurance schemes cover a lot of services as long as subscribers can pay the premium for those services. Whilst some private health insurance schemes may not cover pregnancy (as it is not considered a disease), or elective cosmetic surgeries, national health insurance schemes, like the Ghanaian one, cover pregnancy. The private health insurance schemes tend to complement national health insurance schemes. Citizens who can afford to pay commercial premiums enrol in private health insurance schemes to cover illnesses that are not covered under national health insurance schemes.

16.4 CHALLENGES OF IMPLEMENTING HEALTHCARE INSURANCE SCHEMES

The implementation of a social health insurance scheme for a nation may be wreathed in challenges. The challenges for most governments include issues such as generating funds to finance the scheme, administration of the scheme, and other issues that make the sustainability of the scheme an issue. Most governments attempt to provide universal coverage for healthcare. This means providing access to promotive, preventive, curative and rehabilitative healthcare services for all citizens when required. This is usually achieved through the principles of revenue collection, pooling and purchasing of healthcare services. Whilst the NHIS in Ghana is attempting to reach a point of universal healthcare for its citizens, some factors threaten this possibility.

Generation of funds for the running of the scheme can be problematic if not thought through well at the initial planning stages. In Ghana, for instance, funding for the NHIS is through tax levies, premiums from those in the informal sector and contributions from people on the social security system, as well as donations. These funds, according to Alhassan, Nketiah-Amponsah and Arhinful (2016), are threatened by the existence of a large exemption group. Membership of the scheme is free for children under the age of 18 years, pregnant women and the elderly above the age of 70 years. Of this group of exempt persons, children form the majority. About 60 per cent of the members of the scheme are in the exempt category. This means that contributions to the scheme are reduced greatly. In addition, Ghana has a large informal sector; enrolment for informal sector workers is voluntary and the proportion of those enrolled from that sector is relatively low. Thus, there are not even very many people paying premiums on the scheme.

Some researchers have cited inadequate knowledge amongst managers of the scheme as a problem (Dror & Preker, 2002; Bennett et al., 2004; Alhassan et al., 2016; Fusheini, Marnoch & Gray, 2017). The arguments have been that managers usually have little technical knowledge of scheme management or of issues of insurance. This, it has been argued, greatly limits their ability to efficiently manage the schemes. In Ghana, for instance, researchers have cited political interference as one of the challenges that threaten the scheme. The Chief Executive Officer of the scheme is appointed by government. This implies that there could easily be political manipulation of the scheme. For instance, Fusheini et al. (2017) argue that most of the schemes they surveyed in the northern and southern parts of Ghana did not have qualified personnel managing the schemes. Another administration issue identified was delayed disbursement of claims made to the scheme. Most healthcare facilities complain of delayed claims payment. This delay may be attributed to how the funds are pooled. The funds are first pooled into the consolidated funds of the government, and then disbursed to the NHIS. There have been allegations of government "borrowing" the monies for some periods so that there are not enough funds to reimburse healthcare facilities.

Another cause of delayed claims payment, according to Alhassan et al. (2016) and Fusheini et al. (2017), is the un-automated and cumbersome process of claims verification. Claims made are verified manually, by a group of professionals who sit periodically to do the assessment. This delays processing of claims and subsequent payment of same. As a result, most healthcare facilities tell their clients that some services are not covered under the scheme, so patients pay for the provision of those services to enable them to run the healthcare facility.

At the healthcare facility level, enrolees of the scheme perceive the service provision under the scheme as poor (Baku, 2007). Members usually indicate that those paying for service are treated first, that the nurses display a poor attitude towards NHIS card holders and that medication given under the policies is considered to be of low quality. These challenges notwithstanding, some authors have proffered solutions that would improve the operation of the scheme and, thus, increase the prospects for the scheme's sustainability. Some of these solutions include actuarial calculations of premiums so that premium payers pay more realistic premiums, a review of the exemption policy, automation of claims processing and increase in the insurance levy (Alhassan et al., 2016; Fusheini et al., 2017).

16.5 HEALTHCARE BUDGETS

The budget of a healthcare organisation indicates the revenues expected to be made and cost estimates. Different types of budget can be prepared by a healthcare facility. These include the revenue budget, expense budget, operating budget and cash budget (Gapenski, 2007). A revenue budget provides information on revenues expected from health insurance and out-of-pocket payments. Other revenues such as interest income, return of investments and lease incomes are all included. An expense budget provides information on the cost of providing service – such as salaries and associated labour expenses and non-labour expenses such as administrative costs, utilities, depreciation of assets and medical supplies. The operating budget provides information on both revenues and expenses expected to occur within a period. The cash budget provides information on the actual cash flow situation of the facility, thus presenting managers with information on whether to expect excess revenue or a shortfall.

In the public sector of Ghana, budgeting for public healthcare facilities begins with a call from the Ministry of Finance and Economic Planning (MoFEP) to the Ministry of Health (MoH). The call contains a guide on items that are to be contained in the budget. These items are personal emolument, administration, service and investment (Abekah-Nkrumah, Dinklo & Abor, 2009). Personal emolument is the salaries of all employed in the public health sector of Ghana and those employed under the Christian Health Association of Ghana (CHAG). Administration is all the activities that go into providing healthcare services all over the country. Services includes all items that are used in providing healthcare services; these are made up of consumable and non-consumable medical items. The investment item is made up of all capital and infrastructure expenditures: new acquisitions or maintenance. The call places a ceiling on the items. The MoH informs all its agencies of the process of developing a budget based on the guidelines provided. These agencies also include development partners who provide funding for the health sector. The ministry and its agencies agree on priorities for the year with information on expected inflows from development partners.

According to Ackon (2003), budgets are then prepared from all the levels (community, district and regional level) in Ghana, which the MoH coordinates in providing healthcare. The budgeted items usually focus on administration and services, as government is in charge of emoluments and investments. However, most healthcare facilities use part of their internally generated funds (IGF) to take care of maintenance. The various budgets are aggregated at the MoH for budget hearings organised by the MoFEP. The budget hearings are used by the MoFEP to determine whether the budget guidelines given have been followed, and the ministries, agencies and departments use the opportunity to defend their budgets. When the budgets from the various units are accepted, the items are added to the national budget and presented to the parliament of Ghana for approval.

Funding of the budgeted items usually comes from government, IGFs and development partners. Government funding for the budgeted items is usually channelled through the MoH and the ministry disburses it to the various regions for onward transfer to districts and communities. Development partners also channel their monies through the MoH for onward transfer to the requisite project or institution or programme. Reports on the use of the monies are made through the same channels by which they were received.

16.6 MANAGING OVERHEAD COSTS

According to Huijben, Geurtsen and van Helden (2014), overheads can be defined as all the functions of an organisation directed at helping employees achieve the objectives of the organisation. Every organisation incurs cost in an attempt to achieve its objectives. In relation to healthcare organisations, the objective is to provide patient care. There are costs that are directly associated with providing patient care and costs that are indirectly associated with providing patient care. Those that are indirectly associated with providing patient care are known as overhead costs. There are two types of overheads: generic and specific (Huijben et al., 2014). Generic overheads are those functions that are needed by all organisations, irrespective of the industry in which they sit. Examples of some generic overheads are administrative work, human resource services, information technology services, finance services, security services, legal services and maintenance services. Specific overheads are those support services that are peculiar to a specific sector. For instance, a healthcare organisation or facility may have housekeeping, waste disposal and laundry services as overheads specific to them.

Managing overhead costs falls in the domain of cost accounting. Effectively identifying and allocating the overhead cost to the appropriate unit or department producing the cost will ultimately assist in knowing how to manage the cost. Whilst various methods of cost allocation exist, the grouping of costs into pools and drivers helps in cost allocation (Gapenski, 2007). A cost pool is the grouping of costs that must be allocated and a cost driver is the criterion used to allocate the cost. An example of a cost pool is housekeeping services. A cost driver in relation to housekeeping services could be the physical space occupied by each department providing direct services to patients. A division of the cost pool by the cost driver gives an overhead allocation rate for housekeeping. Thus, to determine the amount of cost to be allocated to the out patients department (OPD) of the organisation, the total housekeeping cost of the organisation is divided by the total square metres of space used by OPD. The result is the overhead that must be allocated to OPD.

Gapenski (2007) indicates there are three main methods of cost allocation: the direct, the reciprocal and the step-down methods. The direct method of cost allocation is when costs from the supporting departments are allocated directly to the patient service departments. Although support departments also incur overheads, charging those overheads on the support units is ignored. The reciprocal method recognises the interdependence of the support units and allocates cost to those support units as well. The step-down method is best explained with an example. Assume that a healthcare facility has three support departments, namely the housekeeping, administration and human resources departments, as well as patient services departments. In the allocation process, the direct costs of housekeeping are allocated to both the patient services departments and the remaining support services departments. Next, administration costs, which now consist of both direct and indirect costs (the allocation from housekeeping), are allocated to the patient services departments and human resources, which is the remaining support department. Finally, the direct and indirect costs of human resources are allocated to the patient services departments. The final allocation from human resources includes housekeeping and administration costs because a portion of each of these support costs has been "stepped down" to human resources. The significant distinction between the step-down and reciprocal methods is that after each allocation is made in the step-down method, a support department is removed from the process. Even though administration and human resources provide support services back to housekeeping, these indirect costs are not recognised because housekeeping is removed from the allocation process after the initial allocation. Such costs are recognised in the reciprocal method.

Gapenski (2007) suggests some ways of managing overhead costs. These include precise identification and recording of overhead costs. The accurate identification should be followed by a meticulous assignment to the appropriate main unit responsible for incurring the cost. Inability to accurately identify and allocate overhead cost prevents the institution of appropriate interventions to reduce the cost. Another means of managing overhead cost is to cut out costs that do not contribute directly to improving the quality of service provided. He suggests outsourcing of the automation of some services such as information technology, human resources and food services. Outsourcing of some functions that are not related directly to the core business of the healthcare facility results in reduction in some costs such as providing medical care for employees who provide those services. Ensuring efficiency by replacing defective and spoilt items of the healthcare facility helps in reducing costs also.

Another suggestion is that extensive investment in and use of technology in managing patient records reduces time and the process of using paperwork. The use of electronic processing of data also saves a lot of cost and space in healthcare facilities. An automated system also reduces time and costs associated with wrong diagnosis and wrongly dispensed medication as hand written medication may be wrongly interpreted. Finally, involving staff in cost cutting initiatives that the healthcare facility may undertake helps them buy into strategies for improved healthcare and reduces the stress and fears of layoffs as a result of cost cutting activities.

16.7 PURCHASING, RECEIPTS AND ISSUING OF STOCKS

Stock is conceptualised as the value and quantity of items kept for use when required. Stocks in a healthcare organisation are made up of consumable and non-consumable medical items. Consumable medical supplies are non-durable supplies that are used and disposed of. Examples of consumable items are antibacterial wipes, bio-hazard bags, patient care gloves, sanitisers, disinfectants, gauzes, bandages, cotton balls, alcohol prep pads, adhesives, catheters and many others. Non-consumable items are durable medical supplies such as medical equipment and spare parts of equipment. Stock management is an important component of hospital management. Dealing with human lives requires that at all times, there are medical supplies available.

The Ghana Health Service (2010) provides the process of procurement for public healthcare facilities in Ghana. According to the process, procurement or purchasing of consumable and non-consumable medical supplies in public healthcare institutions begins with the annual forecast plan by the procurement officer based on consumption patterns in the healthcare facility and requests from user departments. These annual requests are then reduced to quarterly requests and procurement is done at the Central Medical Stores through the Regional Medical Stores. Ghana has a Central Medical Stores that stocks drugs and non-drug consumables for purchase by public healthcare facilities in the country. There are Regional Medical Stores that stock supplies from the Central Medical Stores for healthcare facilities in the various regions to have easy access. However, where the Central Medical Stores and the Regional do not have the items needed by a healthcare facility, the facility can purchase the item on the open market through a tendering process. By law (the Public Procurement Act, Act 663, 2003), every public institution is supposed to have a Tender Evaluation Panel that evaluates bids from various suppliers of goods to the facility. Payments to suppliers of the stocks needed by public healthcare facilities are made after goods have been received and verified by the supply officer, internal auditor and the head of administration. This is a requirement of the Public Procurement Act of 2003.

Each healthcare facility has a supplies officer who receives stocks, stores them and issues them to the department based on requisitions made. Requisitions are supposed to be made on a weekly basis and departments have mini stores in which they keep their requisitions. Emergency situations arise for requisitions to be made on an ad hoc basis. Most public healthcare facilities practise First to Expire, First Out (FEFO). This is a concept of ensuring that consumables that have early expiry dates are used first. Sometimes, public healthcare facilities may run out of stock as a result of the user departments not putting in requests on time, or increased usage of stock as a result of unexpected increased attendance, emergency situations or delayed payment of suppliers of previous stocks. In such situations, the purchasing officer makes ad hoc purchases, though these are discouraged by the Procurement Act.

There are different types of stock management (Mentzer et al., 2001) used by different healthcare facilities all over the world. Some of them include stockless inventory, where the supplier provides stock in small pieces as and when needed and not in bulk to be stored by the healthcare facility. Requisitions for stock are made by the healthcare facility. Thus, the facility does not control inventory. There is also the vendor managed inventory, where the supplier is in charge of managing the inventory levels of the healthcare facility and supplying as and when stocks are getting low. Usually, the supplier is in charge of stock at the healthcare facility. This appears to be a form of outsourcing of the procurement process. Another type of stock management is the automated point of use system. This is a device, kept in the various departments of the healthcare facility, which authorised persons use to indicate any time something is used. The device thus tracks inventory use and determines when restocking should take place.

The main challenges of stock management in Ghanaian public healthcare facilities, as indicated by Maloreh-Nyamekye (2005), are inability to pay suppliers on time, and the possibility of the Central Medical Stores not having stocks so that the healthcare facility may have to purchase from the open market. The inability to pay suppliers on time has been linked to the National Health Insurance Scheme's delayed reimbursement of claims made by healthcare facilities in Ghana.

16.8 FINANCIAL STATEMENTS

Healthcare organisations in Ghana, whether publicly owned or privately owned, prepare financial statements on an annual basis. The financial statements include a balance sheet, income statement and cash flow statement. The statements communicate in monetary terms the economic events and financial status, as well as the performance, of the healthcare facility. Financial statements are important to a healthcare organisation's stakeholders such as its owners, creditors, suppliers, donors (countries and organisations that make financial contributions may require the preparation of a receipt and expenditure accounts), managers of the healthcare facility and employees (Gapenski, 2007).

The owners, creditors and suppliers invest in the healthcare facility and are interested in knowing the financial state of the facility. Suppliers are interested in knowing if the healthcare facility would be able to honour its debt. The management of the healthcare facility require the information for planning, budgeting, allocation and taking other important financial decisions for the facility. Employees are interested in these statements to project their employment status as well as to be able to bargain conditions of service. These statements help private healthcare facilities determine the corporate taxes they have to pay to government and also assist partnerships to know how much each partner is paying in terms of income tax to government.

The preparation of the financial statement must follow some basic accounting principles and standards (Wood & Sangster, 2005). In Ghana, all financial reports must use the International Financial Reporting Standard (IFRS). The use of the IFRS ensures comparison of healthcare facilities across borders and easy understanding and interpretation of reports, so that local healthcare facilities can gain access to international funding; and information provided in financial reports using the IFRS is considered reliable. The accounting concept usually applied in reporting accounting information of the organisation is the accruals method (Wood & Sangster, 2005). Under this method, income and revenues are recognised in the period within which they occur.

In Ghana, public healthcare facilities are required to prepare financial statements for onward transmission to the Ministry of Health and then to the Ministry of Finance and Economic Planning (Abekah-Nkrumah et al., 2009). Although government no longer supports public healthcare facilities with money for service provision, government still pays healthcare workers, and continues to incur capital expenditures such as healthcare infrastructure and some equipment.

16.9 RISK MANAGEMENT IN THE HEALTHCARE SERVICE

The risks that healthcare facilities face cut across all aspects of the work they are engaged in. There are risks associated with patients, medical staff, employees, property, financial risks and many others. The management of such risks is very important for the sustainability of the healthcare organisation. Medical error appear to be one of the main causes of patient related risk. It has been defined as either the use of a wrong plan to achieve a result or the failure of a plan to achieve a result (Carroll, 2009). Thus, medical errors include drug related mishap, diagnosis mishap, therapy mishap, wound infections, communication and equipment failure, and treatment errors which may occur during operations. According to Sternberg (2016), medical errors account for about 10 per cent of all health related deaths in the United States. Other patient related risks include abuse and neglect from other patients, visitors and staff, loss of or damage to patient valuables, use of experimental drugs on patients and inappropriate use of medical information of patients. The risks that medical staff pose to the healthcare organisation include issues of qualification and credibility, dealing with medical staff who pose a threat to patients, financial arrangements with clinicians that are laced with fraud, and the role of clinicians as gatekeepers to various health insurance schemes.

In Ghana, physicians serve as the gatekeepers in the general referral system, as well as referral systems under the national health insurance scheme (Nyonator, Awoonor-Williams, Phillips, Jones & Miller, 2005). Occupational safety and health issues are the main risk concerns for a healthcare organisation's employees. Issues of discrimination in promotion and sexual harassment are risks that the healthcare employee is exposed to. The properties belonging to healthcare organisations are exposed to disasters such as floods and fire, and accidents in the case of vehicles. The loss of patient records (paper or electronic) also poses a risk. The loss of cash by staff who handle it also results in property loss. Financial risks are manifested in the form of legal suits against the healthcare facility or its employees and losses as a result of health insurance plans for which revenues may not be properly determined such as those based on capitation as a payment mechanism.

Carroll (2009) explains that risk management follows a five step process. The steps are: risk identification and an analysis of the losses the organisation is exposed to; a consideration of risk technique alternatives; selection of an appropriate risk management technique or a combination of techniques; implementation of the choice; and, finally, evaluation and improvement of the process. Risk identification and analysis is the process by which the risk manager is made aware of the risk exposures of the healthcare organisation. Information sources include: incident reporting, patient complaints and satisfaction survey reports, prior data on liability claims against the organisation and its employees, information on nosocomial infections and informal discussions with staff. Risk analysis is the process of determining the probability of a loss occurring and the severity of the loss. Risk analysis is an art born out of experience, instinct and training. Various alternatives exist for managing risks that have been identified.

The second step in the risk management process offers two main ways of treating the risks. These are risk control and risk financing. Risk control techniques include risk avoidance, loss prevention, loss reduction and non-insurance transfers of risk such as transferring losses through contract agreements or leases. Risk financing involves either retaining the risk but paying for it as and when loss occurs, or transferring the financial obligations under the risk to a third party such as an insurance company. The risk manager of the healthcare organisation selects the best risk management technique or a combination of techniques based on the effects the techniques may have on the organisation's finances as well as its ability to achieve its goals. The implementation of the chosen technique(s) is very important as it involves people and the use of finances. In case a healthcare organisation decides to avoid a risk, involving the necessary persons is paramount. The final step is an evaluation of the process. Evaluation of the process may be done using previous risk management reports of the organisation and using the practices of similar organisations as a benchmark. The effects of the technique(s) used can also be used to determine their continued use.

16.10 HEALTHCARE FINANCING, HEALTH INSURANCE AND MARKETING OF HEALTH SERVICES

Efficient management of the financial resources of a healthcare organisation would place it in a position to provide quality healthcare services that attract and retain customers. The WHO (2010) identifies some factors as inefficiencies in financial management evident in SSA countries. These factors include medical errors and suboptimal quality of care, the oversupply and over use of medical equipment, inappropriate and costly staff mix, leakages, corruption, waste, fraud, and inappropriate and ineffective use of medicine. The customers of healthcare organisations are varied and all require the attention of the healthcare organisation. A healthcare marketer must be able to identify these customers and establish long lasting relationships with them for marketing purposes. These customers include healthcare consumers, potential purchasers of healthcare services, enrolees of a health insurance scheme, employers, health insurance companies and governments.

Provision of healthcare quality comes at a cost. Donabedian (1966) suggests a quality assurance model for healthcare organisations to ensure that quality is provided and improved upon at all times. In the model, Donabedian (1966) suggests that having a structure and a process should lead to a desirable outcome. The structure includes having facilities, equipment and appropriate staffing; staff must have the necessary licences and the healthcare facility must be accredited. Accreditation ensures that, at least, a minimum level of standard is attained before service provision is rolled out. The process according to Donabedian (1966) involves technical as well as interpersonal care. The technical care includes screening, prevention, diagnosis treatment and follow up care. Aspects of interpersonal care, by which most healthcare consumers measure quality, are respect, communication, provision of knowledge and information, and empathy for the service providers. The combination of these is expected to result in recovery, restoration of function, survival and efficiency.

The provision of an appropriate structure is costly (Donabedian, Wheeler & Wyszewianski, 1982) but it can be done through appropriate financial management and good financing schemes that are able to generate money and balance the need for affordability of care. Ensuring that interpersonal care is maximised also requires the training of employees on how to effectively relate with customers so that the service experience for customers is optimised. This training comes at a cost. Just training employees will not suffice on its own. In addition to training, motivating employees, intrinsically and extrinsically as suggested by Hertzberg, Mausner and Snyderman (1959), requires money. In addition to prudent financial management, which occurs at the facility level, health insurance schemes (in their various forms) help provide healthcare facilities with the requisite money to manage their facilities. However, the management of the schemes, particularly the national ones as discussed in previous sections, has led to facilities not having trust in the early payment of claims that are made. Private health insurance schemes may not have issues with claims payment. Increased consumption of healthcare and early detection and treatment of diseases are some of the advantages to healthcare consumers who use health insurance schemes. A downside to increased consumption is that minor ailments are sent to healthcare facilities. However, health insurance policies have some contractual provisions such as deductibles, coinsurance and co-payments that are meant to discourage such abuse of the system.

16.11 CONCLUSIONS

Healthcare financing and the managing of the financial resources of healthcare organisations have been the main discourse of this chapter. Health insurance, social or private, appears to be the best way of improving financial access for most people, whether in developed or developing countries. However, health insurance comes with its own challenges. The challenge of efficient management for social insurance schemes and issues of adverse selection, information asymmetry and cream skimming for private health insurance schemes are real. A healthcare manager should be able to negotiate health insurance contracts with social insurance managers as well as with private ones on reimbursement arrangements, discounts that the managers of the schemes may seek. Having adequate financial knowledge helps in such negotiations.

Financial knowledge also prepares the healthcare manager to understand budgets, purchasing and procurement issues, managing stocks and managing overhead costs. Inability to prepare realistic budgets, having stocks of consumable and non-consumable medical items and not managing overhead costs can lead to the liquidation of healthcare facilities. Ensuring healthcare quality which attracts and retains the healthcare consumer comes at a cost. Technical and functional quality can be achieved if financing of healthcare is adequate. Thus, the work of the healthcare marketer is made easy when consumers are satisfied in the use of healthcare services.

Research on the subject matter discussed in this chapter could focus on empirical evidence of how healthcare organisations are cutting costs and yet are still providing quality healthcare services to consumers. Public healthcare facilities in Ghana no longer receive funding for services from government, so an investigation into how these healthcare facilities are able to manage their internally generated funds and remain in business would be worth undertaking. Lessons from the relationship between private health insurance companies and healthcare facilities could be explored and suggestions for adoption and adaption made to the National Health Insurance Authority in Ghana; these are ways of improving the health financing goals of nations and healthcare facilities in particular.

REFERENCES

Abekah-Nkrumah, G., Dinklo, T., & Abor, J. (2009). Financing the health sector in Ghana: A review of the budgetary process. *European Journal of Economics, Finance and Administrative Sciences, 17*, 45–59.

Ackon, E. K. (2003). *Management of healthcare organizations in developing countries*. Accra-North, Ghana: Bel-Team Publications Ltd.

Agyepong, I. A. (1999). Reforming health service delivery at district level in Ghana: The perspective of a district medical officer. *Health Policy and Planning, 14*(1), 59–69.

Alhassan, R. K., Nketiah-Amponsah, E., & Arhinful, D. K. (2016). A review of the National Health Insurance Scheme in Ghana: What are the sustainability threats and prospects? *PloS One, 11*(11), e0165151.

Baku, A. A. (2007). *Subscriber perception of quality of health care services under the new Juabeng and Ketu District mutual health insurance schemes in Ghana* (Thesis presented to the University of Ghana in partial fulfilment of the award of a master of Philosophy in Health Services Management). Unpublished document.

Baku, A. A., & Sakyi, E. K. (2014). *In-kind premium payment as an alternative to cash premium payment under health insurance schemes in Ghana: Views from residents of the Dangme West District*. Health Services Management: Readings from Ghana, Business Series Vol. 3, University of Ghana Readers. Tema: Digibooks Ghana Ltd.

Bennett, S., & Gilson, L. (2001). *Health financing: Designing and implementing pro-poor policies*. London: DFID.

Bennett, S., Gamble, K., Brant, S., Raj, G., & Salamat, L. (2004). *21 questions about community-based health insurance schemes*. The Partners for Health Reformplus Project. Abt Association Inc. Retrieved August 3, 2006, from www.goolesearch.com.

Carroll, R. (2009). Risk management handbook for healthcare organisations. San Francisco, CA: Jossey-Bass, Wiley Imprint.

Donabedian, A. (1966). Evaluating the quality of medical care. *The Milbank Memorial Fund Quarterly, 44*(3), 166–206.

Donabedian, A., Wheeler, J. R., & Wyszewianski, L. (1982). Quality, cost, and health: An integrative model. *Medical Care, 20*(10), 975–992.

Dror, D., & Jacquier, C. (1999). Micro insurance: Extending health insurance to the excluded. *International Social Security Review, 52*(1) 5–15. Retrieved September 12, 2006, from www.blackwell-synergy.com.

Dror, D., & Preker, A. (2002). *Social reinsurance: A new approach to sustainable community health financing*. World Bank, International Labour Office, Geneva.

Fenny, A. P, Yates, R., & Thompson, R. (2018). Social health insurance schemes in Africa leave out the poor. *International Health, 10*(1), 1–3. doi:10.1093/inthealth/ihx046.

Fusheini, A., Marnoch, G., & Gray, A. M. (2017). Implementation challenges of the National Health Insurance Scheme in selected districts in Ghana: Evidence from the field. *International Journal of Public Administration, 40*(5), 416–426. doi:10.1080/01900692.2015.1127963.

Gapenski, L. C. (2007). *Healthcare finance: An introduction to accounting and financial management* (4th ed.). Aupha Hap.

Ghana Health Service (2010). *Logistics management of public sector health commodities in Ghana. Standard operating procedures manual: Regional medical stores to service delivery points.* Accra: Ghana Health Service.

Hertzberg, F., Mausner, B., & Snyderman, B. (1959). *The motivation to work.* New York, NY: Wiley.

Huijben, M., Geurtsen, A., & van Helden, J. (2014). Managing overhead in public sector organizations through benchmarking. *Public Money & Management, 34*(1), 27–34.

Kennedy, P. (2015). The contradictions of capitalist healthcare systems. *Critique, 43*(2), 211–231. doi:10.1080?03017605.2015.1051780.

Maloreh-Nyamekye, T. (2005). *A critical analysis of past and current purchasing strategies of Ministry of Health, Ghana: A focus on sector-wide approaches and purchasing product portfolio models* (Dissertation Submitted in Partial Fulfilment of the Requirement of MSc Purchasing and Supply Chain Management. Aberdeen Business School, The Robert Gordon University, Aberdeen, UK).

McIntyre, D., Obse, G. A., Barasa, E. W., & Ataguba, J. E. (2018). Challenges in financing universal health coverage in Sub-Saharan Africa. *Oxford Research Encyclopedia of Economics and Finance.* doi:10.1093/acrefore/9780190625979.013.28.

Mentzer, J. T., Dewitt, W., Keebler, J. S., Min, S., Nix, N. W., Smith, C., & Zacharia, Z. G. (2001). Defining supply chain management. *Journal of Business Logistics, 22*(2), 1–25.

Ministry of Health. (2006). Christian Health Association of Ghana (CHAG), Memorandum of Understanding and Administrative Instructions.

Nyonator, F. K., Awoonor-Williams, J. K., Phillips, J. F., Jones, T. C., & Miller, R. A. (2005). The Ghana Community-based Health Planning and Services Initiative for scaling up service delivery innovation. *Health Policy and Planning, 20*(1), 25–34.

Smithson, P., Asamoa-Baah, A., & Mills, A. (1997). *The role of government in adjusting economies. Paper 26. The case of the health sector in Ghana.* Development Administration Group, University of Birmingham.

Sternberg, S. (2016). Medical errors are third leading cause of death in the U.S. Retrieved May 26, 2019, from www.usnews.com/news/articles/2016-05-03/medical-errors-are-third-leading-cause-of-death-in-the-us.

Wood, F., & Sangster, A. (2005). *Business accounting 1* (10th ed.). Prentice Hall.

World Health Organization. (2016). *Public financing for health in Africa: From Abuja to the SDGs.* Geneva, Switzerland: WHO Document Production Services.

World Health Organization. (2010). *World health report, 2010: Health systems financing the path to universal coverage.* World Health Organisation.

Wouters, A. V. (1991). Essential national health research in developing countries: Health care financing and the quality of care. *International Journal of Health Planning and Management, 6,* 253–271.

17 Managing Healthcare Logistics

Obinna S. Muogboh and Jimoh G. Fatoki

17.1 INTRODUCTION

Effective healthcare management is a critical requirement for any modern economy. In sub-Saharan Africa, the performance story of the healthcare system is not a very exciting one. There is a significant proportion of the population that is not able to access basic healthcare services. For most countries in sub-Saharan Africa, the morbidity and mortality rates are still at very high, unacceptable rates. Consequently, to advance the quality of healthcare delivery in the sub-region, the impediments to quality healthcare need to be identified and resolved.

In sub-Saharan Africa, the healthcare sector is faced with numerous challenges. Some of these challenges can be traced to poor logistics infrastructure available in the region. Some operational issues, such as the availability of a reliable source of power, potable water and means of transportation, that are taken for granted in other climes are not readily achievable in the sub-region. Provision of these basic amenities must be incorporated into any healthcare service delivery plan if it is to succeed in Africa. The role of logistics in achieving quality health outcomes is undeniable. Logistics may be considered as the cornerstone of an efficient and integrated national healthcare system.

Logistics is a critical component of supply chain management in the healthcare service industry. It cuts across the management of supplies, inventory, operation, communication, warehousing, transportation and distribution activities with the aims of meeting customers' requirements and reducing the cost of sales of organizations. In other words, management of logistics helps an organization in integrating activities towards coordinating the flow of services, materials and other related information in and out of the organization (Pokharel, 2005). Healthcare services involve the maintenance and improvement of health conditions of human beings. The industry is believed to be operationally different from other service-providing businesses because one cannot, at any point in time, correctly assume patients' mix as well as their supply consumption (Jarrett, 1998).

In most of sub-Saharan Africa, the provision of health services still relies heavily on governments and some international aid organizations. There is also significant involvement of the private sector in some countries in the sub-region. Presently, service delivery in the public healthcare sector is not only patient-centered, in that the focus is on the individual seeking medical care due to illness or sickness of some kind, but also people-centered, covering all clinical and health-related interests of people in a community (World Health Organization [WHO], 2018). Healthcare-seeking people are constantly demanding and expecting high-quality services together with more sophisticated treatments and healthcare provision at low cost (Organisation for Economic Co-operation and Development, 2015). Providing healthcare for patients is becoming increasingly expensive around the world. Furthermore, hospitals and other healthcare players need to plan for the likely occurrence of disaster events and consequently provide timely and life-saving services in such cases, making the handling of healthcare provision and services highly unpredictable, complicated and complex (Glouberman & Mintzberg, 2001). To address this complexity and criticality, healthcare organizations around the world have undergone all-inclusive transformations through improvement in their logistics and distribution processes (Speed, 2016).

When efficient logistic practices are put in place in a hospital, Poulin (2007) and Feibert, Andersen and Jacobsen (2017) note that about half of the 30 to 46 percent of the budget usually allocated to logistic activities could be saved. The business environment in Africa is very demanding, and organizations are still faced with basic developmental challenges and lack of basic operating infrastructure. Consequently, healthcare logistics management in Africa needs to be agile, innovative and responsive to be able to cope with the unique challenges in Africa.

This chapter provides details of how healthcare service providers in sub-Saharan Africa utilize and integrate human resources, facilities and equipment in the best possible way to meet the needs of achieving the physical, mental, emotional and social wellbeing of their customers (patients). It further discusses the management of crucial logistic activities in sub-Saharan African healthcare industries as well as the organization and maintenance of healthcare facilities and equipment. Finally, insights are provided into the recent innovative concepts used in stock control and storage of supplies, and modern information systems used in healthcare delivery.

The chapter is structured into nine sections. The second section provides details of the management of logistics in healthcare industries. Organizing and maintenance of healthcare facilities and equipment are discussed in Sections 3 and 4 respectively. Section 5 is on stock control management while the sixth section presents the principles used in storage and control of supplies in healthcare industries. Section 7 looks at the healthcare transport, while the penultimate section discusses current information systems used in healthcare logistics. The chapter ends with a concluding section providing information on how to efficiently improve logistic systems in healthcare industries.

17.2 HEALTHCARE LOGISTICS MANAGEMENT

The healthcare sector provides services and products to meet the healthcare needs of people and contribute significantly to the economy of a nation. In the past, these services were mostly hospital-based, but complexity in healthcare industries has extended the service to multi-state hospital systems, ancillary care agencies, and external stakeholders in primary, secondary, tertiary, quaternary, home and community (public) healthcare industries (VanVactor, 2012). Therefore, healthcare practitioners are concerned with how best to reduce their operating costs without compromising the quality of healthcare services while also ensuring accountability to patients, employees and communities (Reilly & Markenson, 2011; Toner et al., 2009).

The healthcare sector in Africa is confronted with many challenges. These challenges include stock-outs of essential medicines, lower quality (or fake) drugs, transportation and power infrastructure, non-compliant storage facilities, lack of reliable information systems, cold chain inconsistencies and lack of financial resources for procurement (Silve & Ouedraogo, 2013). The health system is burdened with issues such as unreliable logistics and poor management information systems, inadequate capacity management, lengthy procurement procedures, paucity of funds for procurement of essential medical kits and consumables, and challenging coordination of the health product supply chain (Silve & Ouedraogo, 2013). Since public health institutions provide a significant proportion of the healthcare needs in sub-Saharan Africa, the system also suffers from considerable weakness in the regulatory framework and sluggish government bureaucracies.

With logistics activities accounting for more than 30 percent of hospital costs (Feibert, Jacobsen & Wallin, 2017), it has been shown that adoption of best practices can eliminate about 50 percent of this logistics cost and ensure that healthcare organizations continue to provide adequate care for their patients within the budgeted fiscal limits (Goldschmitt & Bonvino, 2009). In sub-Saharan Africa, many rural communities are effectively excluded from access to modern healthcare systems because of poor logistics infrastructure, such as good road networks.

Logistics management, as defined by the Council of Supply Chain Management Professionals (2016) (see Mangan, Lalwani & Lalwani, 2016), is that part of supply chain management (SCM) that plans, organizes, implements and controls both the forward and reverse flow and the storage of products, services and associated information between the point of origin (source) and the point of utilization in order to meet customers' needs. In healthcare industries, logistics does not just support stock purchasing, storage and pharmacy, but also covers all levels of operations including care units and operating rooms, with a larger number of support departments and personnel (Poulin, 2007). According to Gutierrez, Gutiérrez & Vidal (2013), management of logistics in healthcare organizations broadly entails managing facilities, staff, transportation and inventory.

Feibert, Jacobsen and Wallin (2017) identified some core healthcare logistics activities as bed logistics, drug distribution, managing blood supply chain, sample transport, patient transport, cleaning, laundry services, food distribution, managing surgical tools, managing medical aids, waste management and mail services. For each logistics activity, scarce resources and personnel are allocated such that the healthcare needs of patients are strategically met in a timely, sufficient, reliable, and sustainable manner, and at acceptable cost (Pan & Pokharel, 2007).

In sub-Saharan Africa, the logistics activities are poorly developed. For instance, the medicine supply chain is often poorly integrated and implemented through the participation of some poorly regulated private sector operators. This is probably one of the reasons why the prevalence of fake or sub-standard drugs is still a major concern in the sub-region. The unreliable power infrastructure also makes the operation and maintenance of cold chain facilities for pharmaceutical products difficult and very expensive.

For efficient logistics practices, resources and operations involved in fragmented activities should be linked in a proactive and dynamic way to address the inherent unpredictability in healthcare services. Activities are integrated together by prioritizing flow of intangible materials and processes as organized by the operational concepts and design adopted by the healthcare industries. This will help to conduct operations effectively, anticipate supplies requirements at any given operational period, and synchronize support personnel and limited resources in an efficient way while lowering superfluous redundancies and competition for scarce resources (VanVactor, 2012). Logistics activities are usually designed to be integrated cross-functionally, yet be autonomous enough on an operational scale to function on their own with measurable outcomes.

In sub-Saharan Africa, given the paucity of funds in comparison to the enormity of the task to be accomplished, it is essential that the quality of healthcare logistics is improved to help deliver health services efficiently and effectively. The healthcare logistics managers must be able to identify and implement best practices by creatively adapting their approach to any given context as circumstances change with time (Silve & Ouedraogo, 2013). The experience of the recent Ebola disease breakout and many other epidemics in sub-Saharan Africa have shown the need for the healthcare logistics systems to be proactive and prepared for any health emergencies, take relevant precautionary measures, and collaborate with other functional areas involved in the health system (Silve & Ouedraogo, 2013).

17.3 ORGANIZING AND MAINTAINING HEALTHCARE FACILITIES

Organization and maintenance of healthcare facilities are critical in ensuring the continuous operation of healthcare services in a cost-effective way. An all-inclusive maintenance regime improves the performance of buildings, maximizes workforce safety, minimizes operating cost, reduces environmental threat, and lessens the risk of material damage or wastage (Oladejo, Umeh & Egolum, 2015). Daskin and Dean (2005) stated that the negative effects of facilities-associated problems go far beyond higher healthcare delivery cost or customer dissatisfaction, as the utilization of too few facilities or adequate facilities that are not well located and organized can lead to increases in mortality and morbidity rates. In a more condensed, congested and concentrated urban healthcare space, maintenance of facilities in the most effective way is a key logistics function that ensures that the industry serves the purpose of providing healthcare services to its patients and visitors at all times (Oyekale, 2017; Yousefli, Nasiri & Moselhi, 2017).

In sub-Saharan Africa, the lack of good maintenance culture is endemic and often visible in healthcare facilities across the region. This affects the quality of healthcare services available in the sub-region. Healthcare institutions and practitioners in the sub-region must be proactive and make extra effort to ensure availability of good and functional facilities.

Shohet and Lavy (2004) identified five elements of healthcare facility management: maintenance management, performance management, risk management, supply services management and development. To attain high service performance in the healthcare industry through effective facility maintenance, Loosemore and Hsin (2001) advocated a holistic maintenance program that will cover key areas such as plant and equipment, building, infrastructure and landscape in hospitals. As a core area of facility management in healthcare organizations, three approaches are usually used for maintenance of facilities based on maintenance cost, complexity of components' repair or replacement, and criticality of facility failure (Horner, El-Haram & Munns, 1997). They are:

i.   *Corrective approach*: This involves the repair of components or replacement of parts of facilities that are no longer functioning to make them serviceable. This reactive strategy generally leads to service delays, reworks, service disruptions, and higher maintenance cost (Higgins, Mobley & Smith, 2002). In most sub-Saharan African healthcare systems, this corrective approach is the predominant approach, leading to observed poor facility performances.

ii. *Preventive approach*: This is a planned strategy carried out periodically to repair or replace facility components at regular time intervals. These time intervals are chosen based on historic operating information or prior experience of the breakdown pattern of a particular facility. This periodic scheduling of maintenance activities has been shown to be particularly appealing to all users of healthcare facilities (Rani, Baharum, Akbar & Nawawi, 2015). It is recommended that sub-Saharan African healthcare institutions begin to adopt a preventive approach in order to get the best out of their existing healthcare facilities.

iii. *Proactive approach*: This is a predictive strategy used to monitor the possibility of failure in a facility and subsequently provide adequate interventions well in advance of the actual facility breakdown. It is especially used in cases where facility breakdown would critically affect the service functionality of the healthcare center. When the proactive approach is used in conjunction with a preventive approach, a healthcare facility can attain its optimum level of performance. Though this is the zenith of facility maintenance, cultural and bureaucratic obstacles would need to be overcome in many sub-Saharan African healthcare institutions before the adoption of this proactive approach.

17.4 ORGANIZING HEALTHCARE EQUIPMENT

Equipment, medical supplies and drugs account for high healthcare budgets and significantly impact on the quality of healthcare services delivered to patients (Kaur & Hall, 2001). Healthcare equipment includes medical instruments, drug delivery systems, cardiovascular devices, orthopedic devices, radiology equipment and other diagnostic equipment. Equipment varies from one healthcare facility to another depending on the type of health services provided, as some equipment used in district and provincial hospitals is uncommon in specialized hospitals. Organizing equipment refers to the process of systematically arranging equipment in such a way that it can be easily retrieved in the most efficient way. In any healthcare system, poor organization of the equipment reduces the overall efficiency of operation by increasing the "search time" for equipment, thereby wasting a considerable amount of time required for direct healthcare provision (Ward, Spencer & Soo, 2015).

One prime objective of healthcare institutions is ensuring the availability of functional diagnostic equipment for proper and quality healthcare management. Unfortunately, quality performance of medical equipment is hindered by numerous challenges such as poor infrastructure (especially, power and water supply), inadequate security, poor maintenance culture and lack of competent operators. A recent experience narrated by an equipment donor to a major public healthcare institution showed a general lack of motivation and commitment to properly operate already installed diagnostic equipment. This often led to situations in which very expensive diagnostic equipment was left idle or unused because of poor maintenance or some other flimsy reason such as inability to renew service agreements with original equipment manufacturers.

The following should be considered when systematically arranging and organizing equipment in healthcare buildings:

1. The management of the healthcare services should determine the type of strategy they want to employ in organizing and storing their equipment. They may decide to establish a central clinical equipment repository in the healthcare building and roll out equipment trolleys to units and rooms where they are needed at any point in time, or they may decide to build an equipment room in every unit/department where equipment can be easily retrieved. However, heavy equipment should be stationed permanently where it is needed. The particular approach adopted should depend on the peculiar challenges facing the healthcare institution.
2. In the equipment room, items should be sorted and arranged in such a way that the more often needed equipment is easily accessible with wide spaces between adjacent items of equipment to facilitate staff movement to all areas of the storage room. Also, of great importance is the need for proper ventilation and aeration of the facility housing diagnostic equipment.
3. Equipment should be positioned in a designated place or location within the equipment room and there should be a way of making sure that when the equipment is in use, another piece of equipment being returned is not set down in its place. Hung signs and labels can be used to designate equipment locations.
4. The equipment room should always be kept clean and neat. Procedures for housekeeping should be developed and duties assigned to workers to maintain all equipment in good condition at all times.

Given the observed poor management in many public healthcare facilities, an interesting model that seem to be gaining ground in some sub-Saharan African public healthcare institutions is the outsourcing of the management and operation of medical equipment. This arrangement means that the provision of medical services requiring use of expensive laboratory equipment is the responsibility of a competent private sector operator, driven by the profit incentive. Such private entities are usually able to keep the equipment functional with a higher level of utilization.

As in the case of facility maintenance, equipment maintenance should adopt the proactive and preventive approach. Wherever possible, service or maintenance agreements should be signed with suppliers of such equipment. This is particularly important as newly installed equipment is bound to have some initial adaptation challenges before it becomes optimally operational.

17.5 STOCK CONTROL MANAGEMENT

One of the core functions of logistics systems is the planning, ordering, storing, moving and accounting for stock in any organization (Kiisler, 2014). Healthcare stock includes, among other things, clinical consumption materials that constitute about 31 percent of the total cost of most hospital budgets (Nabais, 2009). Inadequate hospital materials can impact negatively on the operation, reducing quality of services to patients and causing dissatisfaction to staff and patients. Thus, without reducing the level of healthcare service, stock needs to be available and used in the right way to save cost. That is why Narkotey (2012) stated that in healthcare systems, inventory management involves the movement of supplies (healthcare consumables) to places where they are needed, in a time- and cost-effective manner.

The primary objective of stock control management is to "ensure that the right medical consumables (including medicines) are kept in the right quantities and are available at the right time" (Management Sciences for Health [MSH], 2012a, p. 1). With appropriate management of stock, drugs are delivered promptly, supplies are replenished at a scheduled interval, stock-outs are prevented, transportation and distribution times are significantly reduced, patients are more satisfied, staff are more efficient and the overall operating costs are minimized.

At the facility level, the aims of stock control (MSH, 2012a) are to:

- Prepare effective orders and maintain sufficient safety levels within the limits of the health-care budget.
- Maintain records of supplies in line with requirements or needs.
- Constantly adjust stock levels to take into account the new trends in healthcare delivery and changes in guidelines for standard treatments.
- Store medicines and supplies in a safe and secure manner and ensure they are used during their useful shelf life.

A good storage facility in sub-Saharan Africa must have systems in place to address some of the challenges facing healthcare administration in Africa. For instance, the system must guarantee the integrity of the supply chain through which the drugs are sourced and distributed. It is also important that medical consumables are managed in such a way that they are used during their recommended shelf life. However, in sub-Saharan Africa, the discovery of expired drugs in the supply chain is not uncommon. Such discoveries are an obvious indication of a poorly managed healthcare logistics system. The frequent and indiscriminate sale of prescription drugs over-the-counter is now one of the leading causes of drug abuse in sub-Saharan Africa. Also, the storage facility must be adequately secured to minimize theft. Cold rooms used in the cold chain must have a proper backup power supply to avoid the possible disruption of the power supply from utility companies.

17.6 GENERAL PRINCIPLES REGARDING THE STORAGE AND CONTROL OF SUPPLIES

Storage and control of material supplies in healthcare centers require careful planning and management. The general principles involved are as follows:

1. The building facility housing supplies should be located in a dry and well-ventilated environment that is free from inclement weather conditions. Controlled conditions of temperature and humidity should be maintained at standard limits within the storage store.
2. The size of the store should be estimated based on the levels of stocking desirable, lead times during service delivery, and the range of services rendered by the healthcare organization. As a rule, one square meter per hospital bed should be used for initial planning and costing in cases where supplies are received on a monthly basis (MSH, 2012a).
3. Storage space should be large enough to handle the volume of medicines and treatment kits to be stored during emergence of new diseases or times of emergency. Supplies should not be arranged in corridors, walkways, landings or work areas of healthcare buildings.
4. Adjustable shelves of good quality and proper handling equipment should be used to organize and store supplies in an accessible way with an aisle for workers to move through the storage premises.
5. A weather-protected area should be designated as a receiving bay and be linked to the store to facilitate easy unloading of supplies from delivery vans.

6. For storage conditions, medical and pharmaceutical supplies should be stored at temperature and humidity conditions recommended by manufacturers. In cases where no information is provided for condition of storage, supplies should be stored at normal storage condition of +15 to +25°C depending on the climatic conditions of the storage environment. Table 17.1 shows the special conditions required for the storage of some medical supplies.

17.6.1 STOCK ORGANIZATION AND MONITORING

Supplies in healthcare organizations are organized and monitored in order to reduce customer lead time and hedge against drugs supply and demand uncertainties (McGuire, 2011). Supplies should be stored in such a way that ordered items can be easily picked, periodic inventory taken can be done efficiently and general control of stock can be carried out effortlessly.

Some practical storage methods used in physically classifying stock, as stated in MSH (2012b) are:

- *Therapeutic categorization (pharmacological class):* This is a way of organizing supplies based on types and/or purposes. This method is particularly used in small stores in dispensing small clinical items and cannot be adopted in larger stores.
- *Alphabetical order:* Items are stored alphabetically using their generic names. The method has a disadvantage of reorganizing medicines in stores whenever there is a change in the level-of-use list and the stock administrative system of the healthcare organization. This method cannot be used in stores receiving and dispensing lots of drugs
- *Dosage form:* This method uses the forms in which items exist to stock them, whether they are in solid, liquid, semi-liquid or gaseous forms. For instance, tablets and capsules

TABLE 17.1
Special storage conditions required for different categories of supplies

Product type	Condition of storage	Example
Heat-sensitive	Frozen or refrigerated condition, with storage temperature below freezing point.	Vaccines and blood sera.
Temperature-sensitive	Controlled conditions of temperature and humidity using mechanical ventilators or air-conditioning systems.	Some injectable products (e.g. adrenaline), some suspension products (e.g. ARV stavudine), some creams and ointments, intravenous fluids, X-ray films, chemicals.
Inflammable	Storage in a separate outdoor store with marked labels and provision of firefighting equipment.	Alcohols, kerosene, acetone.
Corrosive	Storage in separate steel shelves or cabinets away from inflammable substances; and industrial gloves or mittens should be used when handling these products.	Aqueous ammonia, glacial acid, sodium hydroxide pellets, silver nitrate.
Attractive	These are drugs or items prone to theft, abuse or misuse. Special security doors and regular independent stock taking/auditing.	Narcotics, expensive medicines.

Source: Adapted from MSHa.

are stored together, while liquids, injections, creams and ointments are stored in a separate storage space. The advantage of this categorization method is that after items have been organized based on their forms, other methods of classification can also be applied to each group created. In addition, items are quickly recognized by their forms and easily stored in designated areas, thereby optimizing storage space.

- *Random bin:* This system uses unique codes to identify storage spaces or bins. As an illustration, in shelving of items, each shelf cell can be coded as A-1, A-2, A-3, etc. with the alphabet A, B, C, ... representing the row label while the number 1, 2, 3, ... represents the column label. Once a bin has been coded, items placed in the bin can further be classified based on other methods earlier discussed. For instance, items within A-1 bin can be stored alphabetically while the ones in B-2 bin can be organized based on dosage form, depending on the method best suited for the supply's arrangement.

17.6.2 STOCK CONTROL AND MANAGEMENT

In managing healthcare stock effectively, procedures to order supplies, receive them, and store, record and account for them must be well written and followed by concerned staff. In a sub-Saharan country, it was reported that the uncoordinated supply of medicines and inability of healthcare centers to optimize accessibility to essential medical and pharmaceutical supplies led to redundancy of workers and wastage of healthcare resources, resulting in a high mortality rate of 12.4 percent as against the 0.5 percent recorded in the United Kingdom in 2011 (Schopperle, 2013; The World Bank, 2013).

Inventory system in hospitals can either be done *perpetually* by continually updating records and accounts for items received, picked, moved to another location or scrapped, or *periodically* by physically counting items at the beginning and ending of a specified duration of time to track inventory levels (Pontius, 2019). Periodic tracking of inventory is usually fraught with errors and the inability to detect inventory discrepancies on time until the point at which records are taken. As technology becomes prevalent in sub-Saharan Africa, hospitals are expected to take advantage of continuous tracking of inventory items using barcode technology. This involves scanning items using a barcode scanner which immediately and automatically updates inventory levels, a process that is more accurate and efficient than the manual process of record keeping. In addition, incorporating radio-frequency identification (RFID) technology to monitor and track healthcare inventory levels by reading "item tags" attached to supplies and products will input information about them into the inventory management software, from which records can be quickly retrieved and in which they can be easily managed (Coustasse et al., 2015).

The following principles are recommended by MSH (2012b) for stock management in health centers:

1. Stocks of food and clothing materials should be separated from medical and pharmaceutical supplies to maintain hygiene standards.
2. While small healthcare organizations may require few staff or even one member of staff who may function in different capacities within the store, large facilities require greater management systems with a large workforce.
3. Records should be kept in duplicated stock cards or ledgers which must contain important information about the item or stock, such as item description, stock number, unit of issue/measurement (for instance ml, gram and tablet), shelf life and date of expiry (if applicable). Big healthcare organizations are advised to use computerized systems for their stock management.
4. Stocks should be ordered based on item usage as determined by storekeeping personnel based on monthly consumption of each item. Several ways are used to calculate quantity of order and safety stocks. Common methods used in healthcare organizations are

requisitioning systems (for large facilities) and a simple imprest or "topping up" system (for small facilities).

5. To prevent wastage of stock through expiry, the First-Expiry-First-Out (FEFO) rule should be adopted whereby stocks with the longest shelf life are situated at the far end of the shelves during stocking while stocks are issued from the front of the shelves. Stocks should be checked regularly for their expiry date, with proper records made in their stock ledger. On no account should stocks nearing their expiry date be accepted into the store unless they will be used immediately. All expired stocks should be removed from the store and disposed of according to recommended standards in the local area.

Table 17.2 provides some basic tips on the management of stocks in a pharmaceutical storeroom.

17.7 HEALTHCARE TRANSPORT SYSTEM

Hospitals in sub-Saharan Africa, especially those in rural areas and semi-urban centers, often pay little attention to transportation activities involving deliveries of health services, transfer of patients, collection and deliveries of drugs/supplies, and other administrative/support services. The expensive, unsafe and sometimes unavailable public transport in some low-income countries of Africa makes patients walk long distances to seek medical attention (Kagee et al., 2011), a situation requiring considerable effort, such as to make them further unwell and prevent them from going for subsequent medical appointments. In some cases, patients in rural communities having hospitals far away from them may deliberately reduce the dosage of drugs prescribed to them because of the difficulties in transportation. According to Hall, du Plessis & McCoy (2003), inter- and

---

TABLE 17.2

Basic tips for managing stocks in pharmaceutical storeroom

Goal to achieve	Management tips
Security against theft	Use double doors/locks on the entrance door of the storeroom. Use burglary-proof windows, wire mesh, latch and padlock. Employ the services of watch guards and extra precaution for "attractive items".
Bulk storage	Store bulk off the floor using pallets or storage racks and limit the height of the stack to prevent crashing during storage. Allow cross air circulation and ventilation within the storeroom.
Orderly arrangement	Avoid overcrowding by providing adequate shelving for ordered items. Use a system of organisation of stocks that is best suited for the supplies. Arrange items neatly on the shelves with correct labels. Arrange lightweight items higher up the shelf, and heavy stocks and fragile items lower down the shelf to avoid spoilage especially during item retrieval.
Accountability	Restrict access to unauthorised persons and check stock frequently to keep track of item on the shelf. If possible, use a stock card for each item: keep stock cards next to items and fasten them to shelves.
Rotation of stock	Items stored in containers should be placed on a shelf according to their expiry date when receiving orders: later ones at the back and earlier ones at the front. When issuing items out of the storeroom, send containers with the earliest expiry dates out first before others.

Source: Adapted from MSH (2012a).

intra-hospital delays in transporting pregnant women from their homes to healthcare institutions have resulted in significant numbers of casualties, with transport-related problems in South Africa being the direct cause of peri-natal deaths.

For increased efficiency in healthcare delivery, safe and quality transport systems for both emergency and non-emergency processes must be provided through effective communication, reduction in delays and waiting times, and appropriate transfer of transport resources, personnel and equipment (Hains et al., 2010). Internally, a centralized hospital-wide patient transportation system can be used to coordinate, dispatch and deliver efficient patient movement from one unit/facility to another so as to decrease delays in care processes, and increase overall service capacity (McCullough, 2015). Facility flow optimization can be adopted for equipment such as wheelchairs, trolley beds and hoists to reduce queues and unavailability of equipment during rush hours and emergency periods. Management of transport systems for healthcare services should be decentralized to allow local government healthcare officers and district healthcare service managers who understand the peculiarities of the needs of people to handle the problem. With improved infrastructure, hospitals and healthcare units should apply information systems to design frameworks that will support communication and collaboration of care processes within the healthcare sector.

17.8 INFORMATION SYSTEMS IN HEALTHCARE LOGISTICS

The health information system is a critical component of any sound healthcare system. It is used at the primary, secondary and tertiary health institutions to manage patients' wellbeing and analyze and guide important healthcare decisions. Reliable healthcare information is also necessary for public health administration by governments and the international aid organizations frequently present in many African countries.

In most advanced countries, healthcare information is computerized, making healthcare decisions easy and more reliable. However, in most sub-Saharan African countries, healthcare information in most public health facilities is predominantly maintained using manual paper filing systems. This system is less efficient and prone to errors and issues of misplaced or lost patient records. In addition, the manual information system is not amenable to integration with other healthcare management software applications.

Improved information systems that are proactive and responsive to health needs of people are essential to enhance health services in African countries (WHO, 2005). The traditional paper-based approach used by health workers to store, obtain, gather and verify a patient's health information comes with errors that impact negatively on the efficiency of healthcare delivery by weakening the chains for supplying data in a timely manner (Mutale et al., 2013). Some sub-Saharan medical institutions still use paper to record surgical procedures, observations and prescriptions, just as some medical practitioners and physicians still handwrite patients' health information using a pen and a notepad (Csiszar, 2011). The challenges of the paper-based method include, among others, the complexity involved in retrieving medical records or files of patients after long timeframes between treatment periods, the inability of patients to transfer their files from one hospital to another, and unavailability of previous medical records of patients, especially during an emergency. This makes it difficult to measure the performance and monitor the progress of health-related activities and objectives, especially in public healthcare institutions, where healthcare service systems are highly fragmented such that exchanges of information within and among healthcare organizations to meet patient/business needs are limited (Abayomi-Alli et al., 2014).

The deployment of electronic health record systems in Africa, though increasing, is slow due to high initial capital investment and subsequent maintenance cost (Abayomi-Alli et al., 2014; Boyinbode & Toriola, 2015). In their study of management of information systems in 46 member states of the WHO African region, Mbondji et al. (2014) noted that only few countries in the region have civil registration systems that generate data required for adequate tracking of mortality rates and causes of death. Thus, to move towards reaching the health-related Millennium Development

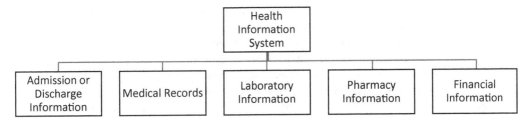

FIGURE 17.1 Organisation Structure of Simple Healthcare Information Systems. (Source: Adapted from Lin (1993)).

Goals of Africa, it is important to adequately assess, measure and monitor health systems performance through strong health information systems (Mutale et al., 2013).

An information system (IS) is an automated computer system that records, manipulates, stores, recovers and disseminates data or information (Health Informatics Forum, 2018). The information system stores and organizes data and analyzes resulting information for users to comprehend and act upon in the most effective and efficient way. At both individual and population levels of healthcare delivery, the information system plays a crucial role in capturing, storing, processing and communicating accurate and timely information to healthcare managers, stakeholders and decision makers to better improve their control, organization and coordination of healthcare facilities, equipment and supplies (Fichman, Kohli, & Krishnan, 2011). It offers improvement in quality of care and reduction in healthcare cost (Kolodner, Cohn & Friedman, 2008) by improving clinical and diagnostic processes, identifying potential unfavorable events in an individual patient and providing insights into possible causes of disease complications.

In the past, the healthcare industry did not show significant interest in IS, but the last few years have led to hospitals investing heavily in information technology (IT) due to increasing levels of diversity in patient characteristics, healthcare professions, treatment options, healthcare delivery processes and interests of various stakeholders (Kettelhut, 1992; Menon, Lee & Eldenburg, 2000). In healthcare logistics, management of information and technology helps in easing the use of input stocks, identifying medical product and bulk movement, tracking distribution of stocks efficiently, and providing logistics information accurately. The operational efficiency of healthcare organizations rests in a major way on how they are able to identify the flows of their logistics processes and eliminate possible barriers using well-structured IS (Protil, Duclos & Moreira, 2002). Advancement in technology in the 2000s led to increased integration of logistics activities using cloud computing, warehousing and big data analytics solutions. Figure 17.1 shows a simple organization structure for healthcare information systems.

17.8.1 Categories of Healthcare Information Systems

In a broad sense, information system (IS) can be categorized into three types:

- Transaction processing system (TPS) that is involved in processing and completion of all transactions within an organization,
- Management information system (MIS) that is involved in organizing, evaluating and supporting information systems, and
- Decision support system (DSS) that is involved in providing data support systems using visual and analytical tools to improve healthcare decision making processes.

In the healthcare industry, Beaumont (2011) has identified the following systems to be critically influenced by IS.

1. *Operational, tactical and strategic:* These systems are used for easy identification and processing of information regarding the day-to-day running of clinical and administrative activities (operations or transactions), the periodic summary or auditing of health-care activities towards effective management at departmental levels (tactics or feeder systems), and the entire organization abstracted summary supporting top hierarchy managers for decision making (strategy). In a typical healthcare industry, for instance, the operational system records the status of an HIV infected patient, the tactical system presents information about the number of such cases diagnosed in a week or a month, and the strategic system provides information on the number of HIV-diagnosed individuals in previous years.

2. *Clinical and administrative:* The clinical system provides information about diagnosis, procedures and medical outcomes of patients, while the administrative system helps in coordinating and managing such clinical and medical information. These two systems work together to generate "care records" of any patient for departments within the health-care center and even organizations outside it (for example, the ministry of health of a country or WHO).

3. *Electronic health/patient records (EHR/EPR):* These are task-based systems used for tracking the records of patients at both individual and population levels. They capture and document clinical knowledge about patients in a structured way, providing health-care observations, evaluations, instructions and actions from all clinical events. This electronic document may also contain attendant data of patients such as protocol, method of measurement and earlier related events. For example, the EHR/EPR record can contain information about the temperature of a patient, height, age, blood pressure, blood sugar level, previous healthcare history, risk of diseases based of paternal or maternal healthcare records, etc.

4. *Financial:* This system supports the business functions of the healthcare organizations, where patient cost is reached based on the information recorded in the clinical system. Patients costing is usually carried out on an estimated basis through retrospective apportioning of total costs or past years' cost of healthcare delivery.

5. *Decision support system (DSS):* This system processes data or facts and converts them into clinically relevant and meaningful information useful for decision making. Three levels of support are usually provided: sorting and classifying of data, and presenting information in a way useful for cognitive processing (for example, presenting a list of drugs used for malaria treatment); providing results of data manipulation (for example, presenting a list of drugs useful for treating malaria in children between the ages of 5 and 15 years); and carrying out appropriate actions using information from data manipulation (for example, prescribing appropriate drugs and possibly arranging the next time of a patient's appointment).

6. *Telemedicine, telematics and eHealth:* These systems use complex data (image, audio and video files) and transfer them from one place to another. They are virtual ways of delivering healthcare, finding uses in teleconferences, tele-dentistry and tele-consultation. eHealth systems are health-related activities that take place on the web, facilitated by medical experts.

7. *Computer simulations:* These are relatively new software systems that allow the creation and manipulation of healthcare models using supercomputers or virtual networking to mimic what is happening in reality. Simulation systems are built to solve some identified problems or improve delivery in a timely manner in healthcare organizations. For example, modeling of cost benefits of Influenza vaccinations, Hypertension or smoking on populations.

17.9 CONCLUSIONS

In this chapter, we have described the role of logistics in healthcare service delivery and highlighted some infrastructural challenges facing healthcare logistics in sub-Saharan Africa. The medical supply chain is often a "hidden" element within healthcare systems – the elaborate pathway between a medicine leaving the manufacturer and being dispensed to the patient. Inefficient or expensive distribution systems increase the final price of drugs to the patient, reducing volume sales and hurting family finances in the largely out-of-pocket private market for medicines (Ajepe, 2015). For the huge investments in clinical medicine to achieve the desired goal of improved quality healthcare outcomes, the supporting healthcare logistics system must incorporate a functional logistics system that will promote adoption of best practices and innovative ideas to overcome some of the peculiar challenges facing the sub-Saharan region.

REFERENCES

Abayomi-Alli, A. A., Ikuomola, A. J., Robert, I. S., & Abayomi-Alli, O. O. (2014). An enterprise cloud-based electronic health records system. *Journal of Computer Science, 2*(2), 21–36.

Ajepe, B. (2015). *The opportunities and challenges for pharmaceutical supply chain in Nigeria/Africa*. OMICS International Conference Series, Pharma Middle East. November 02–04, Dubai, UAE. doi:10.4172/2167-065X.C1.012.

Beaumont, R. (2011). Types of health information systems (IS). Retrieved June 1, 2018, from www.floppy-bunny.org/robin/web/virtualclassroom/chap12/s2/systems1.pdf.

Boyinbode, O., & Toriola, G. (2015). CloudeMR: A cloud based electronic medical record system. *International Journal of Hybrid Information Technology, 8*(4), 201–212.

Coustasse, A., Cunningham, B., Deslich, S., Willson, E., & Meadows, P. (2015). Benefits and barriers of implementation and utilization of radio-frequency identification (RFID) systems in transfusion medicine. *Perspectives in Health Information Management, 12*(Summer).

Csiszar, J. (2011). Paper-based medical records vs. electronic medical records. Retrieved November 7, 2018, from https://smallbusiness.chron.com/paper-vs-electronic-medical-records-40354.html.

Daskin, M. S., & Dean, L. K. (2005). Location of healthcare facilities. In M. L. Brandeau, F. Sainfort & W. P. Pierskalla (Eds.), *Operations research and healthcare: A handbook of methods and applications* (pp. 43–75). Kluwer Academic Publishers.

Feibert, D. C., Andersen, B., & Jacobsen, P. (2017). Benchmarking healthcare logistics processes: A comparative case study of Danish and US hospitals. *Total Quality Management & Business Excellence, 30*(1/2), 108–134.

Feibert, D. C., Jacobsen, P., & Wallin, M. (2017). *Improving healthcare logistics processes*. DTU Management Engineering. Retrieved April 10, 2018, from http://orbit.dtu.dk/files/135020992/Thesis_DCF_FINAL_publish_v.02_ORBIT_combined_v.UPLOAD.pdf.

Fichman, R. G., Kohli, R., & Krishnan, R. (2011). The role of information systems in healthcare: Current research and road ahead. *Information Systems Research, 22*(3), 419–428.

Glouberman, S., & Mintzberg, H. (2001). Managing the care of health and the cure of disease – Part I: Differentiation. *Health Care Management Review, 26*(1), 56–69.

Goldschmitt, D. and Bonvino, R. (2009). *Medical disaster response: A survival guide for hospitals in mass casualty events*. Boca Raton, FL: CRC Press.

Gutierrez, E. V., Gutiérrez. V., & Vidal, C. J. (2013). Home health care logistics management: Framework and research perspectives. *International Journal of Industrial Engineering and Management (IJIEM), 4*(3), 173–182.

Hains, I. M., Marks, A., Georgiou, A., & Westbrook, J. I. (2010). Non-emergency patient transport: What are the quality and safety issues? A systematic review. *International Journal for Quality in Health Care, 23*(1), 68–75.

Hall, W., du Plessis, D., & McCoy, D. (2003). Transport for health care delivery. In *South African Health Review 2002* (pp. 353–372). Health Systems Trust. Retrieved March 14, 2019, from http://siteresources.worldbank.org/INTTSR/Resources/SASR2002REview_chapter18.pdf.

Health Informatics Forum. (2018). *Introduction to IT systems*. Retrieved June 1, 2018, from www.healthinformaticsforum.com/courses/6-health-management-information-systems/unit-2-health-information-systems-overview.

Higgins, L. R., Mobley, R. K., & Smith, R. (2002). Maintenance engineering handbook. New York, NY: McGraw-Hill.

Horner, R. M. W., El-Haram, M. A., & Munns, A. K. (1997). Building maintenance strategy: A new management approach. *Journal of Quality in Maintenance Engineering, 3*(4), 273–280.

Jarrett, P. G. (1998). Logistics in the health care industry. *International Journal of Physical Distribution & Logistics Management, 28*(9/10), 741–772.

Kagee, A., Remien, R. H., Berkman, A., Hoffman, S., Campos, L., & Swartz, L. (2011). Structural barriers to ART adherence in Southern Africa: Challenges and potential ways forward. *Global Public Health, 6*(1), 83–97.

Kaur, M., & Hall, S. (2001). *Medical supplies and equipment for primary healthcare: A practical resource for procurement and management.* Attawell, K. (Ed.). ECHO International Health Services, UK: Dunns. Retrieved June 5, 2018, from http://apps.who.int/medicinedocs/documents/s20282en/s20282en.pdf.

Kettelhut, M. C. (1992). Strategic requirements for IS in the turbulent healthcare environment. *Journal of Systems Management, 43*(6), 6–9.

Kiisler, A. (2014). Inventory management: Basic concepts. Retrieved May 28, 2018, from www.vkok.ee/logontrain/wp-content/uploads/2014/03/Riga-3-july-2014.pdf.

Kolodner, R. M., Cohn, S. P., & Friedman, C. P. (2008). Health information technology: Strategic initiatives, real progress. *Health Affairs, 27*(5), 391–395.

Loosemore, M. N., & Hsin, Y. (2001). Customer focused benchmarking for facilities management. *Facilities, 19*(13/14).

Management Sciences for Health. (2012a). Chapter 46: Pharmaceutical management for health facilities. Retrieved May 26, 2018, from www.msh.org/sites/msh.org/files/mds3-ch46-facilitiespharmacymgmt-mar2012.pdf.

Management Sciences for Health. (2012b). Chapter 44: Medical stores management. Retrieved May 28, 2018, from http://apps.who.int/medicinedocs/documents/s19621en/s19621en.pdf.

Mangan, J., Lalwani, C., & Lalwani, C. L. (2016). *Global logistics and supply chain management.* Hoboken, NJ: John Wiley & Sons.

Mbondji, P. E., Kebede, D., Soumbey-Alley, E. W., Zielinski, C., Kouvividila, W., & Lusamba-Dikassa, P. S. (2014). Health information systems in Africa: Descriptive analysis of data sources, information products and health statistics. *Journal of the Royal Society of Medicine, 107*(1_suppl), 34–45.

McCullough, D. (2015). Internal patient transportation: A critical link to patient flow optimization. Retrieved March 14, 2019, from www.midwestmedicaledition.com/2015/08/21/83284/internal-patient-transportation-a-critical-link-to-patient-flow-optimization.

McGuire, G. (2011). Handbook of humanitarian health care logistics (2nd ed.). Retrieved May 25, 2018, from www.google.com.ng/search?q=handbook-of-humanitarian-health-care-logistics-may-2011%2520(1).pdf&oq=handbook-of-humanitarian-health-care-logistics-may-2011%2520(1).pdf&aqs=chrome.69i57.1143j0j9&sourceid=chrome&ie=UTF-8#.

Menon, N. M., Lee, B., & Eldenburg, L. (2000). Productivity of information systems in the healthcare industry. *Information Systems Research, 11*(1), 83–92.

Mutale, W., Chintu, N., Amoroso, C., Awoonor-Williams, K., Phillips, J., … Baynes, C. (2013). Improving health information systems for decision making across five sub-Saharan African countries: Implementation strategies from the African Health Initiative. *BMC Health Services Research, 13*(Suppl. 2), S9. doi:10.1186/1472-6963-13-s2-s9.

Nabais, J. I. B. (2009). Inventory management for the health sector: ABC analysis approach. Retrieved May 28, 2018, from https://run.unl.pt/bitstream/10362/10278/1/Nabais_2010.pdf.

Narkotey, A. M. (2012). Inventory management in the Ghana health service and its role in healthcare delivery: A case study of health facilities in HO municipality. Retrieved May 26, 2018, from http://ir.knust.edu.gh/bitstream/123456789/4823/1/Annor%20Michael%20Narkotey.pdf.

Oladejo, E. I., Umeh, O. L., & Egolum, C. C. (2015). The challenges of healthcare facilities maintenance in tertiary hospitals in South East Nigeria. *International Journal of Civil Engineering Construction and Estate Management, 3*(2), 1–6.

Organisation for Economic Co-operation and Development. (2015). *Health at a glance 2015: OECD indicators.* Paris: OECD Publishing. Retrieved June 3, 2018, from http://dx.doi.org/10.1787/health_glance-2015-en.

Oyekale, A. S. (2017). Assessment of primary health care facilities' service readiness in Nigeria. *BMC Health Services Research, 17*(1), 172–183.

Pan, Z. X., & Pokharel, S. (2007). Logistics in hospitals: A case study of some Singapore hospitals. *Leadership in Health Services, 20*(3), 1751–1879. doi:10.1108/17511870710764041.

Pokharel, S. (2005). Perception on information and communication technology perspectives in logistics: A study of transportation and warehouses sectors in Singapore. *Journal of Enterprise Information Management*, *18*(2), 136–149.

Pontius, N. (2019, Jan.). 4 types of inventory control systems: Perpetual vs. periodic inventory control and the inventory management systems that support them. Retrieved March 14, 2019, from www.camcode.com/asset-tags/inventory-control-systems-types/.

Poulin, E. (2007). Benchmarking the hospital logistics process. *Business Logistics & SCM*. Retrieved April 11, 2018, from https://logisticsmanagementandsupplychainmanagement.wordpress.com/2007/03/27/benchmarking-the-hospital-logistics-process/.

Protil, R. M., Duclos, L. C., & Moreira, V. R. (2002). Logistics information systems in hospitals: A case study in Brazil. In M. J. Ferreira de Oliveira (Ed.), *Accessibility and quality of health services. Proceedings of the 28th Meeting of the European Working Group on Operational Research Applied to Health Services (ORAHS), Rio de Janeiro (Brazil), July 28th–August 2nd , 2002* (pp. 241–255).

Rani, N. A. A., Baharum, M. R., Akbar, A. R. N., & Nawawi, A. H. (2015). Perception of maintenance management strategy on healthcare facilities. *Procedia - Social and Behavioral Sciences*, *170*(1), 272–281.

Reilly, M. J., & Markenson, D. S. (2011). *Healthcare emergency management: Principles and practice*. Sudbury, MA: Jones & Bartlett Learning.

Schopperle, A. (2013). *Analysis of challenges of medical supply chains in sub-Saharan Africa regarding inventory management and transport and distribution*. Retrieved May 27, 2018, from http://1i4rh11vccjs3zhs5v8cwkn2.wpengine.netdna-cdn.com/wp-content/uploads/2016/05/Medical-Supply-Chain-Challenges.Masterthesis.ASchoepperle.pdf.

Shohet, I. M., & Lavy, S. (2004). Development of an integrated healthcare facilities management model. *Facilities*, *22*(7/8), 210–220.

Silve, B., & Ouedraogo, A. (2013). Professionalizing health logistics in Burkina Faso: Challenges, implementation and sustainability. *Public Health Research*, *3*(6), 157–161. doi:10.5923/j.phr.20130306.01.

Speed, V. (2016). Healthcare logistics: Filling a new prescription for supply chain improvement. Retrieved April 10, 2018, from www.inboundlogistics.com/cms/article/healthcare-logistics-filling-a-new-prescription-for-supply-chain-improvement/.

The World Bank (2013). Data: Mortality rate, under-5 (per 1,000 live births). Retrieved May 12, 2018, from http://data.worldbank.org/indicator/sh.dyn.mort.

Toner, E., Waldhorn, R., Franco, C., Courtney, B., Rambhia, K., Norwood, A., Inglesby, T. V., & O'Toole, T. (2009). *Hospitals rising to the challenge: The first five years of the US Hospital Preparedness Program and priorities going forward*. Prepared by the Center for Biosecurity of UPMC for the US Department of Health and Human Services.

VanVactor, J. D. (2012). Strategic health care logistics planning in emergency management. *Disaster Prevention and Management*, *21*(3), 299–309.

Ward, J., Spencer, R., & Soo, E. (2015). Standardising the organisation of clinical equipment on surgical wards at North Bristol NHS Trust: A quality improvement initiative. *BMJ Open Quality*, *4*(1). Retrieved June 12, 2018, from http://dx.doi.org/10.1136/bmjquality.u208308.w3441.

World Health Organization. (2005). Health information system reform in South Africa: Developing an essential data set. *Bulletin of the World Health Organisation*. Retrieved November 7, 2018, from www.who.int/bulletin/volumes/83/8/shawabstract0805/en/.

World Health Organization. (2018). Health services. Retrieved April 10, 2018, from www.who.int/topics/health_services/en/.

Yousefli, Z., Nasiri, F., & Moselhi, O. (2017). Healthcare facilities maintenance management: A literature review. *Journal of Facilities Management*, *15*(4), 352–375.

18 Managing Policies and Procedures in Healthcare Management

Philip Afeti Korto

18.1 INTRODUCTION

Empirical studies of policy implementation have received committed attention since the 1970s. Mendes and Aguiar (2017) observed that Wildavsky and Pressman (1973) brought the issue of policy implementation to the forefront and ignited the hot discourse among social scientists since the 1970s. The overarching aim of policy implementation research in the 1970s, according to Mendes and Aguiar (2017), was to critically examine policy implementation theory and find a concrete one. Such implementation theories, including incrementalism, institutionalism, street-level bureaucracy and many others, apply to various policy types, one of which is public sector health policy. Primarily, public health policy is formulated by government or a governmental agency to address health-related problems that affect society (Simon, 2010). For example, high costs for healthcare services can impede access to care and be attended by preventable deaths, especially deaths due to self-medication, and this can ignite the formulation of public policy (Nyonator & Kutzin, 1999; Badasu, 2004; Agyepong, 1999).

Some scholars (Mendes & Aguiar, 2017; Ajulor, 2018) have opined that different policy actors need to be involved in health policy-making and implementation in order to achieve the policy objectives. As such, the health policy of a country emerges as a result of divergent views and conflicts involving various interest groups that make demands. In Africa, however, most public health policies are not well thought through by the various policy actors because the policies originate from political party manifestoes meant for winning an election. In Kenya and Ghana, for example, decentralization and national health insurance policies emanated from political party manifestoes.

Alfond (1975) propounded structural interest in healthcare theory and identified three (3) main categories of participants in public health policy-making in order to analyse the extent to which their respective interests and influences change with the passage of time. These participant categories are:

i **Dominant Structural Interests:** The dominant structural interests are those of the medical profession due to the exclusive and monopolistic nature of the profession. In view of the special knowledge and clinical autonomy doctors have, society depends on them to be healthy and governments would find it extremely difficult to implement public health policies without the involvement of doctors (Ackon, 2003).

ii **Repressed Interests:** The interests of the community. More often than not, the interest groups' access to healthcare is restricted. The interest groups share common interests "in maximizing the responsiveness of health professionals and organizations to their concerns for accessible high quality healthcare" (Alfond, 1975:192).

iii **Challenging Interests:** These are policy-makers, directors and hospital administrators who challenge the dominance of doctors within healthcare institutions. Even though the doctors may be free to diagnose diseases and prescribe relevant medicines, the types and number of cases they treat may be determined by the hospital management.

It is obvious from the foregoing that Alfond's theory of structural interests understandably illustrates the key actors or interest groups in public health policy-making and how these actors influence the health policies of a country. However, if not modified, Alfond's theory would be difficult to apply in most developing countries in Africa as the economic and political climate of the USA (a developed country) where Alfond developed the theory is different from what exists in developing countries. Quite apart from this the public health sector of most developing countries in Africa is led by doctors who are active in the policy arena so it is impossible to challenge their dominance.

Contrary to Alfond's classification, Okoro (2016) opined that there are five (5) categories of policy actors, namely political actors (elected representatives), bureaucratic actors (public administrators), special interests (individuals or organizations in specific areas), general interests (people who represent other interests not related to the policy) and experts (people who have knowledge and experience in the area).

The social problem that a public policy is meant to address would remain unresolved if the policy created as an antidote for the problem was inappropriately implemented or poorly managed to achieve the desired results. Public policy implementation basically involves translating of a formulated and adopted policy into reality by providing authorized operational procedures and resources. This is done through allocation of the varied resources, such as human, material, machine and financial resources, necessary in carrying out the activities earmarked under the policy (Ajulor, 2018).It is important for public sector healthcare managers and health policy students to clearly understand the procedures involved in health policy implementation. This chapter therefore aims at providing a practical understanding of various aspects of health policy.

18.2 POLICY ARTICULATION AND HEALTHCARE DELIVERY

The essence of public policy-making is to ensure its effective implementation to remedy a problem that affects society as a whole or only a cross-section of society (Anderson, 2003; Simon, 2010; Ajulor, 2018). Suffice it to say that every public policy is created to address an identified public problem. For example, Ghana's Free Maternal Healthcare Policy being implemented has been designed to generally improve upon maternal healthcare delivery and to specifically address the problem of the high maternal mortality ratio (MMR) in Ghana which was 319 per 100,000 live births (LBs) in 2015 and the same in 2017.

As such, health policies must be well articulated so that the intended beneficiaries become aware of the existence and contents of the policy. Policy articulation is very important in the dissemination of the policy goals to the policy implementers. Arguably, healthcare delivery, especially in the public sector, thrives on public policy implementation with the strategic aim of solving public problems effectively for the ultimate benefit of society as a whole or only a segment of it (Ajulor, 2018). In using public policy to combat lifestyle diseases such as HIV/AIDS, stroke, obesity, diabetes and liver cirrhosis, for example, the policy must be well articulated to facilitate adherence and effective healthcare delivery (Anand, Phalguna, Kishore & Ingle, 2011: 2).

In Ghana, for example, the Ministry of Health (MOH) observed that non-communicable diseases (NCDs) are noted to be the leading causes of morbidity, disability and mortality, that some of the NCDs are lifestyle-related and that they include, but are not limited to, cardiovascular diseases, cancers, diabetes and chronic respiratory diseases (Ministry of Health, Ghana [MOH], 2012). As such, fighting NCDs or lifestyle diseases calls for formulation and implementation of regulatory public health policies that will encourage certain good lifestyles and discourage others that have detrimental effects on people's health. For example, in its bid to fight NCDs and promote healthy lifestyles in Ghana, the MOH made the Regenerative Health and Nutrition Policy (RHNP) in 2006 which informed the introduction of the Ghana Shared Growth and Development Agenda (GSGDA) from 2010 to 2013.

Mindful of the importance of these two interventions in combating lifestyle diseases in Ghana, the policies were well articulated with numerous advertisements in the media and on billboards throughout the country. The implementation was approached with multi-sectoral collaboration in the area of trade, agriculture, transportation, education and urban planning (MOH, 2012). The idea was to strengthen the entire health system, promote healthy lifestyles and discourage lifestyles that constitute the predisposing causes of NCDs.

It must be emphasized, however, that in most African countries, health policy formulation, implementation, health resource mobilization and allocation as well as health policy monitoring and evaluation are spearheaded by the respective country's ministry responsible for healthcare delivery. In the case of Ghana, for example, Ackon (2003: 154) affirmed this when he said, "Most health policies are made by the MOH in an attempt to solve health problems that communities express as needs or complaints." However, the MOH works with its agencies such as Ghana Health Service (GHS), teaching hospitals (THs) and the regulatory bodies such as the Medical & Dental Council, Nurses and Midwives' Council, Pharmacy Council, Allied Health Professions Council, Pyschology Council and the Food and Drugs Authority. Obviously, the GHS is not only the largest of the MOH agencies in Ghana but it is also the most conspicuous among them (MOH, 2012).

Broadly, the GHS operates in two echelons: at administrative level and at functional level. The functional level relates to the service delivery structure. The five (5) functional levels are national, regional (10 regions), district (254 districts), subdistricts (numerous) and the community. The GHS provides primary, secondary and limited tertiary healthcare services while the THs have the responsibility for tertiary healthcare delivery. Currently, there are five (5) THs located in Accra (Korlebu Teaching Hospital), Cape Coast (Cape Coast Teaching Hospital), Tamale (Tamale Teaching Hospital), Kumasi (Komfo Anokye Teaching Hospital) and Ho (Ho Teaching Hospital). The levels of healthcare delivery by the GHS are pictorially depicted in Figure 18.1.

It has been empirically established without any scintilla of doubt that public policy implementation influences citizens' behaviour to a large extent (Australian Public Service Commission, 2007; Shah, 2011). However, the manner in which public policy is articulated also has the potential to influence human or citizen behaviour. For example, Liberman, Samuels and Ross (2004) observed that if the policy is articulated with prohibition or regulations, it may emphasize a moral obligation or invoke different levels of moral suasion. Public health policy articulation is largely determined by both political actors and popular discourse, especially in the media, thereby making the citizenry understand the policy from various perspectives.

Ineffective policy articulation and failure to monitor policy implementation can lead to street-level bureaucrats using their discretion to make poor choices with attendant negative

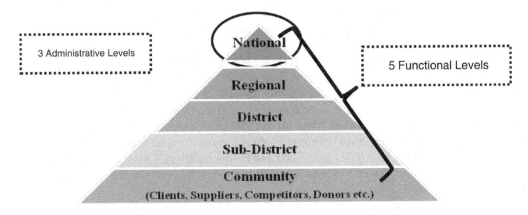

FIGURE 18.1   Structural Levels of the GHS. (Source: Korto (2014)).

effects on the attainment of the desired policy goals. For example, in a study at a GHS facility in Accra (the national capital) to assess the effects of frontline health workers' decisions on the implementation of the Free Maternal Healthcare Policy (FMHP) by the GHS, Korto (2014) reported alarmingly that 53 per cent of 40 frontline health worker informants indicated that the policy-makers' directives were flouted. Even though the directives regarding implementation of the FMHP are that full blood count (FBC) tests should be conducted free for pregnant women, the hospital management authorized the charge of GH¢15.00 (about $4) out of pocket for each FBC test done for pregnant women. The implication is that pregnant women may run FBC repeatedly within the period of pregnancy and may end up paying more or may not be able to afford the test.

The FBC tests help to check the pregnant women's haemoglobin levels so as to determine whether or not they are anaemic. The dangers are that making pregnant women pay for FBC and other tests that are supposed to be free for them can impede financial access to comprehensive maternal healthcare delivery.

Empirical evidence revealed that in the exercise of their discretion during health policy implementation, street-level bureaucrats at the hospital level tend to be more concerned about revenue generation and deny access to patients who are entitled to free services and this often leads to a fall in antenatal attendance at various health facilities (Nyonator & Kutzin, 1999; Badasu, 2004; Agyepong, 1999).

Counter policy directives by street-level bureaucrats at the point of policy implementation tend to deviate the policy from its desired outcomes and objectives. This is attributable to non-inclusion of policy implementers in policy formulation. In keeping with this assertion, Ajulor (2018: 1512) states, "The non-inclusion of the target beneficiaries in the formulation and implementation of the health policies has serious implication on policy failures in Nigeria and Africa in general." Heywood (2007: 436) also submitted that policy outcomes are often different from policy objectives during policy formulation. This is serious, especially in the case of developing countries, because public policy decisions have critical effects on societal development (Agyepong & Adjei, 2008). Therefore, policy must be effectively articulated for the information of the citizenry who are the beneficiaries of policy outcomes.

Ghana's National Health Insurance Policy suffers from such deviations from policy directives periodically due to over delay in the reimbursement of insurance claims to service providers under the scheme. Health facility managers are often compelled under such circumstances to charge fees for services that are supposed to be provided free to the citizenry under the policy.

What tends to be more effective is when policy articulation takes the form of taxes or fines to discourage a given unacceptable lifestyle, say smoking, among the youth. The World Health Organization (WHO) (2008) observed that tobacco use was a significant cause of 100 million preventable mortalities globally in the twentieth century. In Ghana, Government has made various frantic efforts in consonance with the WHO Framework Convention on Tobacco Control (WHO FCTC) to discourage smoking especially at public places. Notable among these tobacco usage regulations is the passage of the Public Health Act (Act 851; see Parliament of Ghana, 2012) and the Tobacco Control Regulations, 2016 (LI 2247; see Parliament of Ghana, 2016).

The two enactments introduced various restrictions on tobacco handling and usage in Ghana. For example, Section 63 of the Public Health Act states that "the manufacture, importation and sale of a tobacco product in Ghana shall be done such that the product shall bear a health warning on its package as the Food and Drugs Authority (FDA) shall determine." Specifically, Section 64 of the same law demands that anyone who sells tobacco must "conspicuously display at the point of sale a health warning determined by the Food and Drugs Authority." Also, the law prohibits the sale of tobacco to children and no one must send children to buy tobacco nor request a child to light tobacco or tobacco products.

In view of the foregoing and other restrictions enshrined in the enactments, a person who flouts the law is liable for prosecution and shall pay a fine of 750 penalty units or be imprisoned for three years or both especially "in the case of a continuing offence to a further fine of ten penalty units for each day during which the offence continues" (Section 77 of Public Health Act, 851; see Parliament of Ghana, 2012).

One may thus submit with a fair margin of certainty that the policies on tobacco use in Ghana articulate financial penalties for cigarette importation with its cascading financial burden on the smoker who is the end user of the product which is established to be harmful to health. However, most ordinary citizens do not know about the law regulating tobacco use in Ghana. It therefore behoves the Ministry of Health to collaborate with the National Commission for Civic Education (NCCE) to carry out public education throughout the country.

Shah (2011:2) opined that whenever some forms of behaviour are penalized or rewarded, policies actually change the costs and benefits of different directions of lifestyle or human behaviour; hence, public education is very important. Policies are "rules of the game of everyday life…. Policies mainly affect the individuals under the jurisdiction of the government that makes and enforces the rules" (Shah, 2011: 2).

Shah (2011) further argued that the rational choice model of public policy, which assumes that people rationally seek to maximize their welfare, helps people to assess choices and make better ones especially for their health. To this end, it is obvious that policy articulation is very vital in healthcare delivery, which thrives on public policy implementation with the ultimate aim of addressing a societal or social problem, say cigarette smoking, in public places and among the youth.

Quite apart from the health policies, public problems must also be articulated especially through media publications and political activist agitations or street demonstrations in order to draw government's attention to them (Ajulor, 2018; Heywood, 2007). For example, the Government of Ghana declared in July 2008 that the maternal mortality ratio (MMR) of 740 per 100,000 live births (LBs) was a national emergency (Ministry of Health, Ghana, 2008). Ghana's MMR figure, however, seems to be quoted differently for even the same period. WHO (2012:40) quoted Ghana's 2008 MMR to be 580 per 100,000 LBs contrary to the 740 per 100,000 LBs recorded by the Ministry of Health, Ghana (2008). Statistical gaps of this nature can make problem definition very difficult.

18.3 CHARACTERISTICS OF EFFECTIVE POLICY

Generally, an effective policy must be one that addresses a given social problem identified at the agenda setting stage of the policy cycle or just identified by a political actor. The policy must be implementable in terms of its application and funding. Specifically, an effective policy must have these features:

- It must be clearly and concisely documented, devoid of unnecessary jargon or verbiage.
- The problem the policy is meant to solve as well as the policy objectives must be clearly spelt out.
- Policy implementation and evaluation methods must be outlined.
- Required resources for policy implementation and the sources of those resources must be determined.
- Policy scope and implementation period must be communicated to the street-level bureaucrats.
- The institution designated for policy implementation must be identified. In most cases, the institution to implement the policy is either in existence already or is newly established for the purpose of implementing a new policy.
- The views of street-level bureaucrats must have been sought during policy-making.
- The policy must not have been just transferred verbatim from another country but, rather, it must have been duly formulated mindful of the local socio-economic environment.
- The policy implementation must not be pushed as a mere partisan political agenda as this affects policy sustainability.

18.4 WAYS OF STATING POLICY

More often than not, public policies are clearly documented and packaged in the form of policy statements. It is the duty of the policy-maker to document the policy and state the policy objectives and the implementation structures while indicating the sources of funding. Usually, a public policy that is not documented with a policy statement tends to fail because the implementation modalities are not documented for ease of reference at the point of implementation.

In summary, therefore, policy statements largely relate to policy documents that guide implementation, monitoring, regulation and evaluation as well as the policy goals to be achieved. In practice, policies may be stated in the form of laws, directives, circulars, procedures and rules. Sometimes, the policy statements come in the form of government white papers. Usually, policies that are stated as laws are enforceable in the courts. For example, devolution of healthcare delivery in Kenya has been enshrined in the national constitution (Oktech & Lelegwe, 2016). Policy statements are not always rational and goal-oriented but they equally have expressive character through which a polity's identity is revealed. However, real-world decision processes do not necessarily follow rational principles (Kornov & Thisen, 2000). Policy statements and policy compilation are closely linked.

18.5 COMPILING AND COMMUNICATING POLICY

Having made a public policy for healthcare delivery, there is the need to compile and effectively communicate the policy or disseminate information about the policy to both the policy implementers and the target beneficiaries (Kornov & Thisen, 2000; Ajulor, 2018).

Generally, a policy document outlines various items, including but not limited to policy title, policy problem, date of policy adoption, the approving authority or polity, policy purpose or rationale, policy objectives, sources of funding policy, policy implementing authority, specified period of policy implementation and evaluation procedures.

The expectation is that an adopted public policy must be clearly compiled and endorsed using a government white paper or any other chosen method. For example, Ghana's Single Spine Pay Policy (SSPP) was adopted using a white paper issued by government in November 2009 (Government of Ghana, 2009). This white paper (WP No.1/2009) became the SSPP document that spells out the implementation modalities. The white paper also indicates what government accepted as the policy content, and what it did not accept, and spells out the policy objectives, one of which is to "place all public sector employees on one vertical structure." Additionally, the SSPP white paper demarcates the policy scope by stating that the SSPP applies to the public sector organizations created by article 190 of Ghana's Fourth Republican (1992) Constitution.

However, certain public policies are also compiled or documented using statutory instruments such as acts of parliament, executive or legislative instruments or court rules which are often referred to as case law. For example, Ghana's National Health Insurance Policy (NHIP) was adopted using an act of parliament (Act 650 of 2003, later replaced with Act 852 of 2012). This law is thus the NHIP document that spells out how the policy should be implemented to achieve the stipulated objectives.

In Ghana, a draft public policy is usually documented and communicated to Cabinet using what is called a cabinet memo under the hand of the sector minister. Having passed an act of parliament to adopt and document a public policy, it is also important that the law making body issues a legislative instrument (LI) to further spell out the implementation processes. Regarding Ghana's fiscal policy (also known as the national budget), it is compiled and communicated to Parliament in the form of an Appropriation Bill in tandem with Article 179 (1) (a) of the 1992 Constitution of Ghana. When passed by Parliament, the Appropriation Bill becomes the Appropriation Act or the national budget. Upon the dictates of the constitutional provision referred to earlier, every fiscal policy of the government is extensively documented and sometimes translated into local languages on the official website of the Ministry of Finance so as to ensure effective policy communication. Aspects of the Appropriation Act relating to healthcare delivery are usually stated.

One may therefore conclude, based on the foregoing, that all legal enactments of a country are public policies but not all public policies are legal instruments. Using the Venn diagram, therefore, public policy is tantamount to the universal set while law is a subset of the universal set (public policy).

It behoves the policy-maker to effectively communicate the adopted policy to the chosen echelons of policy implementation so that the street-level bureaucrats understand the policy contents. The policy contents include, but are not limited to, the policy goals, implementation methods, target beneficiaries and the required resources as well as time and method of evaluation for the policy implementing institution.

In real life situations, however, it is not every public policy that is clearly documented at the point of policy adoption. Very often, public policies in Ghana and other African countries are either contained briefly in a political party's manifesto prior to a general election or are announced by government officials in the media. Prior to the general elections in Ghana in 2016, for example, the Free Senior High School (Free SHS) Policy being implemented in the country was contained in the manifesto of the political party currently in power (New Patriotic Party). Apart from the manifesto, there was no defined policy document before implementation started.

In the case of Ghana's Free Maternal Healthcare Policy (FMHP), its introduction was only in the form of a presidential media declaration in July 2008 by John Agyekum Kufuor – President of Ghana, as he then was (Opoku, 2009; HERA & Health Partners, Ghana [HERA & HPG], 2013). The policy was later placed under the National Health Insurance Scheme (NHIS) and hence its implementation is being funded through the National Health Insurance Fund (NHIF).

The FMHP "was introduced in 2008 in the media as a programme supported by the UK Government … from the general pool of resources of the National Health Insurance Fund, which includes contributions from international partners via health sector budget support" (Hera & HPG, 2013:1). Perhaps in acceptance of such policy declarations, Weihrich, Cannice and Koontz (2010:98) defined policies as "general statements or understandings that guide or channel thinking in decision making."

It is worth noting that the Free Maternal Healthcare Policy is primarily meant to address the problem of high maternal mortality ratios in Ghana in order to attain the erstwhile Millennium Development Goal (MDG) 5 by reducing financial barriers to the utilization of maternal healthcare (Arthur, 2012). This thus necessitated effective implementation of the policy at the institutional level in the health sector to curb the situation in order to ultimately attain the MDG 5 in the country by 2015. Unfortunately, Ghana could not attain the said MDG by the stipulated year and the maternal mortality menace the policy was meant to address still lingers.

For effective public policy implementation to occur, the policy must be effectively communicated between citizens or street-level bureaucrats and the policy-maker or government (Ajulor, 2018; Ahn, 2012). Policy miscommunication or ineffective policy communication and policy failure are correlated. Ahn (2012:8) submitted, "… the effectiveness of public policy communication depends on how well it is adapted to our changing information environment and information behaviours of citizens as deficiency in its communication may increase the likelihood of policy failures."

Dialoke, Ukah and Maduagwuna (2017) asserted that the problem in Africa with regard to public policy is not the policy plan or formulation but rather that Africa has challenges with policy implementation and policy communication. This situation often leads to policy failure which is highly attributable to non-involvement of both the policy implementers and the target beneficiaries in the policy process from the beginning. Also, formulated public policies are not effectively communicated to the citizenry. Ggoobi and Barungi (2016) reported from Uganda that most African public policies fail because of planning without proper management, policy imposition by central governments regardless of the policy's suitability to the needs of the people and failure to clearly communicate the policy objectives to the populace.

Ackon (2003) and Ajulor (2018) opined that health policy failure in Africa is due to the stark reality that the policies do not command sufficient support from those affected by the problem being addressed. This insufficient target beneficiary support for the health policy implementation can equally be blamed on inability of policy-makers to clearly articulate the policies for better understanding among the societal members who ultimately benefit from the policy outcomes. Citizens and policy implementers ought to be well informed about the existence of the policy and policy contents and purposes, through policy communication. Policy success is largely attributable to effective policy communication.

It also behoves policy networks to educate their membership about the existence of a policy, its implementation modalities and its relevance. The policy network relates to policy interests and information sharing by policy actors with mutual or similar interests and it often refers to the patterns of interaction among the policy actors within the policy arena or domain (Rhodes & Marsh, 1992; Heywood, 2007; Denhardt & Denhardt, 2007). Diversity of policy interests tends to create the policy networks. Mostly, the policy networks are used as political pressure tools and information gathering and lobbying tools. Each network has its cynical interests, trying to influence policy decision in its favour.

Rhodes and Marsh (1992) identified five (5) types of policy networks (see Table 18.1). These networks range in a continuum from policy communities, which are highly integrated with protected boundaries, to issue networks, which are loosely integrated with permeable boundaries. Mostly, professional associations or labour unions act as policy networks for the purpose of negotiation with political actors to influence policy decisions (Ajulor, 2018; Ackon, 2003). Table 18.1 depicts the policy network typologies Rhodes and Marsh (1992) identified.

Perhaps in support of Rhodes and Marsh's (1992) policy network typologies, Ackon (2003) identified the Ghana Medical Association (GMA) and the Ghana Registered Nurses' and Midwives' Association (GRNMA) as policy communities in the health policy-making arena of Ghana. The GMA and GRNMA, which are professional associations, influence health policy especially at the adoption and implementation stages of the iterative public policy process (Ackon, 2003). The policy process is depicted in Figure 18.2.

Based on Rhodes and Marsh's (1992) classification of policy networks, one may also describe the GMA and GRNMA as both policy communities and professional networks, or dominant networks in Alfond's (1995) view. Other professional associations in the health sector of Ghana may just be termed as issue networks or as networks with repressed interests as Alfond (1995) described it.

TABLE 18.1
Policy Community and Policy Network

Type of Network	Characteristics of Network
Policy community/ territorial community	Stability, highly restricted membership, community vertical interdependence, limited horizontal articulation
Professional network	Stability, highly restricted membership, vertical interdependence, limited horizontal articulation, serves interests of profession
Intergovernmental network	Limited membership, limited vertical interdependence, extensive horizontal articulation
Producer network	Fluctuating membership, limited vertical interdependence, serves interests of producer
Issue network	Unstable, large number of members, limited vertical interdependence

Source: Rhodes & Marsh (1992:14).

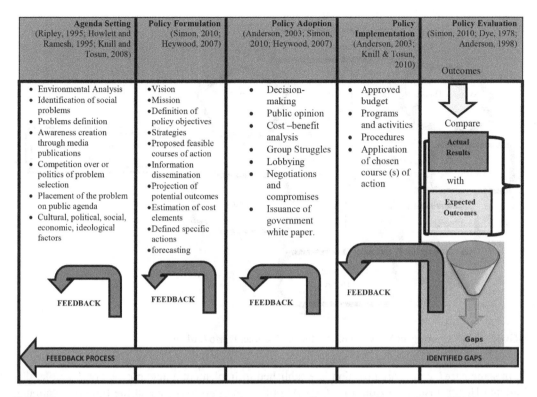

Agenda Setting (Ripley, 1995; Howlett and Ramesh, 1995; Knill and Tosun, 2008)	Policy Formulation (Simon, 2010; Heywood, 2007)	Policy Adoption (Anderson, 2003; Simon, 2010; Heywood, 2007)	Policy Implementation (Anderson, 2003; Knill & Tosun, 2010)	Policy Evaluation (Simon, 2010; Dye, 1978; Anderson, 1998) Outcomes
• Environmental Analysis • Identification of social problems • Problems definition • Awareness creation through media publications • Competition over or politics of problem selection • Placement of the problem on public agenda • Cultural, political, social, economic, ideological factors	• Vision • Mission • Definition of policy objectives • Strategies • Proposed feasible courses of action • Information dissemination • Projection of potential outcomes • Estimation of cost elements • Defined specific actions • forecasting	• Decision-making • Public opinion • Cost –benefit analysis • Group Struggles • Lobbying • Negotiations and compromises • Issuance of government white paper.	• Approved budget • Programs and activities • Procedures • Application of chosen course (s) of action	Compare Actual Results with Expected Outcomes

FEEDBACK   FEEDBACK   FEEDBACK   FEEDBACK   Gaps

FEEEEDBACK PROCESS   IDENTIFIED GAPS

FIGURE 18.2   The Feedback Element within the Iterative Policy Process. (Source: Korto (2014)).

During policy compilation and communication, the institution designated for policy implementation is conspicuously identified. Institution identification for policy implementation is highly linked to the institutional model of policy.

Knill and Tosun (2008) submitted that the institutional model or institutionalism views public policies as institutional outputs. Some thinkers (Anderson, 2003; Simon, 2010) have also observed that institutionalism is a classical and a highly descriptive model of or approach to the study of policy-making. Institutionalism focuses on traditional institutional arrangements (rules, laws, procedures and other matters), organizational structure, job descriptions, functions and mandates that abound with various governmental agencies or organizations (legislatures, executives, courts etc.) and how these collectively influence public policy-making in diverse ways.

Even though institutionalism has been labelled as a descriptive model, its application lies in organizational charts that depict the line of authority, institutional powers and accountability. "The Powers, structures and governing rules of institutions are considered the basis for understanding policy decisions and outcomes" (Simon, 2010: 27). The primary purpose of the institutional approach to policy is the discovery of the nature and form of institutional authority, methods of institutional policy choices and the extent to which different institutions interact with one another (Anderson, 2003; Simon, 2010).

Denhardt and Denhardt (2007) advised that it is the responsibility of the polity (policy-maker) to focus on direct service delivery through either a newly created institution or an existing one so as to forestall diffusion of policy implementation responsibility. For example, whereas Ghana's Free Maternal Healthcare Policy was given to an already existing organization, the Ghana Health Service (GHS), to implement, implementation of the Free SHS Policy was assigned to the Ghana Education Service (GES), an organization which is pre-existent to the Free SHS Policy.

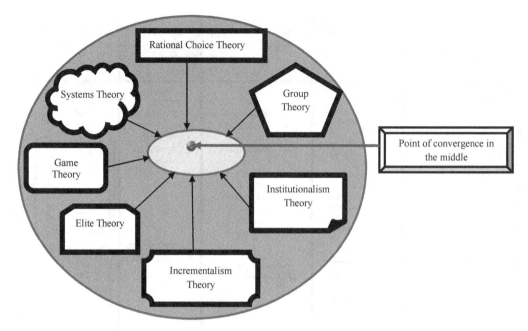

FIGURE 18.3   Convergent View of Policy Models. (Source: Korto (2014)).

In some cases, a new organization is established to implement a new policy. For example, the National Health Insurance Authority (NHIA) only came into existence at the time the National Health Insurance (NHI) Policy was introduced. Apart from the institutional model of public policy, other models such as rational choice, system, game, elite, incremental and group models influence the policy-making process at various stages. However, what is necessary is convergence or an eclectic approach to understanding public policy, because the models are complementary rather than opposing. In support of the convergent approach, which is pictorially depicted in Figure 18.3, Anderson (2003) cautioned against a rigid or dogmatic adherence to only one policy model.

18.6 ADVANTAGES AND DISADVANTAGES OF PROCEDURES IN HEALTHCARE MANAGEMENT

According to Weihrich et al. (2010), procedures are plans that establish a required method of handling future activities. Usually, procedures outline a chronological sequence of actions. For example, the procedure for carrying out a mass burial of unknown dead bodies in the custody of hospital mortuaries is that the hospital management must first announce their custody of such bodies to the general public and later carry out the mass burial subject to approval of a local authority (District Chief Executive) if the bodies are not collected by any family. This is because dead bodies become state property once the bereaved families or relatives cannot be found. Procedures are closely linked to policies. Policy-making itself and for that matter policy implementation in general follow certain procedural processes. Table 18.2 highlights some advantages and disadvantages of procedures in healthcare management.

18.7 HEALTH PROCEDURE MANUALS

Manuals are usually in the form of books or booklets that contain relevant information about procedures for healthcare delivery. Mostly, a healthcare organization's policies, rules, regulations, protocols and standard operating procedures (SOPs) are captured in manuals. For example, Ghana Health Service has various manuals, one of which is, for example, the Malaria in Pregnancy

TABLE 18.2

Advantages and Disadvantages of Procedures in Healthcare Management

A. Advantages of Procedures in Healthcare Management	B. Disadvantages of Procedures in Healthcare Management
• They provide steps for operational activities • They improve work performance • They assure consistency and replication • They support iterative actions • They forestall variation in processes • They establish the purpose for organizational activities • They are used for training employees	• They create bureaucratic steps • They lead to monotonous work activity • They impede creativity and the use of discretion • Strict adherence may sometimes lead to disability or mortality

Manual. Usually, procedure manuals communicate corporate mission and vision (Weihrich et al., 2010). Healthcare procedure manuals help healthcare professionals to standardize daily operational activities. The manuals also provide clarity on what needs to be done at any time. They serve as professional reference materials. In a way, the manuals communicate the desired activities necessary to provide the needed quality healthcare to the patient.

18.8 RULES, REGULATIONS AND STANDARD OPERATING PROCEDURES IN HEALTHCARE DELIVERY

Every organization performs certain activities or undertakes operations that are in tune with its mission or mandate. The organization's mission statement or object thus reflects or depicts its mandatory core business, core values and clients. It is therefore necessary that the organization's employees understand the mission and carry out the organization's operational activities in tune with the mission.

More often than not, a public organization's mission or objects which denote the reason or rationale for establishment are enshrined in the laws that establish those organizations. For example, the objects of the Ghana Health Service (GHS) are clearly stated in the law that established the GHS, the Ghana Health Service and Teaching Hospitals Act (Act 525; see Parliament of Ghana, 1996). These objects are found under Section 3 (1) of the Act and they include:

a. Implement approved national policies for healthcare delivery in the country.
b. Increase access to improved health services.
c. Manage prudently, resources available for provision of health services.

In keeping with these three objects of the GHS, its mission statement reads: "To ensure and *prudently* manage comprehensive and *accessible* health services with special emphasis on primary healthcare at regional, district and sub-district levels in accordance with *approved national policies*." It is obvious that the three objects or reasons for establishing the GHS have informed the mission statement of the organization.

Working in tandem with the mission (why we exist) calls for rules, regulations and standard operating procedures (SOPs). According to Weihrich et al. (2010), rules spell out specific required actions or non-actions within an organization and they allow no use of discretion. For instance a "no smoking" label placed at a hospital is a rule that allows no discretion for a smoker. Suffice it to say that rules reflect a managerial decision regarding actions that are permitted and those that are prohibited. One may define regulations as administrative or policy directives issued for compliance. For instance, the WHO has International Health Regulations that guide healthcare delivery globally.

SOPs are documented or written steps for required healthcare delivery activities that are duly approved by the management of the organization and they serve as a guide for work performance. Intrinsically, SOPs are procedure specific and they regulate actions and therefore reflect functional areas within the healthcare delivery spectrum. Mostly, SOPs outline the expected operational practices that are relevant to the performance of organizational activities within the establishment of quality standards which are simply defined as performance criteria (Weihrich et al., 2010).

In the health sector of Ghana, SOPs come in the form of policies, charters, procedures, manuals, guidelines and legislative instruments called regulations. Generally and sometimes specifically, SOPs are made to:

- Ensure efficiency (judicious use of scarce health resources) and effectiveness (achieving required health outcomes).
- Provide consistency and reliability in healthcare delivery (e.g. adherence to Cholera treatment protocols by health institutions in Ghana).
- Serve as a guide against errors.
- Serve as a guide for ensuring safe working environments.
- Help forestall negligence and its attendant medico-legal suits.
- Serve as a roadmap for dealing with professional deviances or variations from the professional norm.
- Document routine or repetitive operational activities within the organization.

Every organization's SOPs are designed in line with the organization's mission or core mandate, thereby describing both technical and operational elements of the organization's work procedures and processes. In Ghana, both the MOH and its agencies such as the GHS use various SOPs to guide service delivery. Some of these SOPs and their purposes are listed in Table 18.3.

These manuals are reviewed periodically to reflect new trends and their reviews are approached in a consultative manner and using multidisciplinary teams.

18.9 CONCLUSION

One may assert with a significant margin of certainty that regardless of how comprehensive, well-articulated, sound or good an adopted public policy may appear on paper, it is of no use unless the policy is effectively implemented by street-level bureaucrats to solve the societal problem(s) identified. "On paper, policies may appear to make sense yet to the worker in the field they may be of little use in solving a problem to the point of hindering a problem's resolution" (Levesque, 2010: 2). As such, public policies, especially those relating to healthcare delivery, must not just be implemented but the implementation procedures must be well managed to attain policy success.

Saetren (2005: 573, cited in Paudel, 2009) observed that translating policy into practice in most developing countries is a significant and legitimate challenge as several factors, such as poverty, partisan political interference, citizen participation and discretion of public servants (street-level bureaucrats), among other factors, influence the policy process to a large extent. Paudel (2009: 49) explained, "A common assumption is that policy implementers are involved at every stage of the policy-making process, and that they are the most powerful groups in setting the policy agenda." In the public sector of any country, the policy implementers are the public servants, e.g. nurses, doctors, teachers etc. whom Lipsky (1980) termed as "street-level bureaucrats." Undoubtedly, it is perceived that the street-level bureaucrats by the nature of their jobs have better understanding of the needs of clients since they are in constant touch with the people on a daily basis.

In this chapter, we have thoroughly discussed the management of public health policies and procedures in healthcare, with practical examples drawn from the public health sector of Africa in general but with specific focus on Ghana. In particular, however, we have touched on public policies; policy articulation; characteristics of effective polices; ways of stating policy; compilation

TABLE 18.3

Some SOPs in the Public Health Sector of Ghana and Their Purposes

Standard Operating Procedures (SOPs)	Main Purpose
Antimalarial Policy	To provide prompt, safe, effective and appropriate antimalarial treatment to the entire population
Code of Conduct and Disciplinary Procedures	Provide practical and explicit guidance for handling disciplinary and grievance processes for managers, employees and their representatives
Empirical Study Consent Form	Consent form is for the signature or thumb print of the participant. It is an acknowledgement that one has seen the information sheet, read and understood it and has agreed to participate in the study voluntarily
Ghana Viral Load (VL) Scale Up Operational Plan	To guide healthcare providers to deliver high quality, effective and standardized VL testing to monitor patients on antiretroviral therapy (ART) in the country
Malaria Case Management Guidelines	They are the sole recommendations for the management of malaria in Ghana and all who are engaged in managing malaria in Ghana should abide by these guidelines. The guidelines outline malaria treatment regimes in Ghana and therefore guide case management
Guidelines for Public Health Units in Hospitals	To: • strengthen surveillance of all health events in hospitals • assist in the control and prevention of health events of public health importance in the hospital • facilitate the establishment of screening services for non-communicable diseases for staff and general public • strengthen the functional linkage between the hospital and MMDAs • protect health and safety of staff and clients and communities • support hospital research
Guideline for the Establishment of Screening Services in Regional Hospitals	The purpose of this Guideline is to provide broad direction for the establishment of screening services in hospitals for early case detection and treatment of non-communicable diseases. The document defines the kinds of services to provide, identifies what type of health workers are needed to provide the service, equipment requirements, training needs, relevant structures, and roles and responsibilities of all stakeholders

and communication of policy; policy networks; policy models or theories; procedures in healthcare management (merits and demerits) as well as rules, regulations and standard operating procedures (SOPs). We learnt that numerous definitions for public policy have been assembled in literature, so there is no universally accepted definition for public policy. Regardless of how the definitions are phrased, however, each public policy is designed for implementation to address a public problem that affects an entire society or only part of the society.

The chapter has also discussed relevant practical issues in healthcare management with examples mostly from Ghana even though examples from other African countries have been cited. The Ministry of Health (MOH) and Ghana Health Service (GHS) have been largely used as case study organizations to aid the reader's understanding.

It is worth recommending that public policy implementation in Africa should not only be made participatory and consultative by involving the policy implementers and the target beneficiaries but also be made more transparent. Effective and efficient public policy implementation is relevant to sustainable development, and no sustainable developmental agenda is possible and fruitful if the target beneficiaries are not actively involved in the policy process. African governments and for that matter politicians need to move away from imposing public policies that are only meant for vote winning and do not actually address societal problems.

It is also recommended that public policy-makers in Africa must move away from the most common trend of adopting foreign-made solutions for local problems in the name of policy transfer. Such policy transfer actions do not only tend to underestimate local intellectual and physical capacities but also lead to policy failure and further lead to underdevelopment of African countries.

Emphasizing the need for local content in public policy-making and implementation, Ajulor (2018: 1513) states,

> Sustainable development should emanate from the process in which the people participate in all stages of decision-making from problem identification and programme formulation, resources mobilization and implementation, to monitoring and evaluation. Participatory development contributes local knowledge to the process and ensures that the problems addressed are the priorities of the target community-led initiative.

As such, African governments should thoroughly consider various environmental factors in their bid to make and implement public health policies, since those policies impact positively or negatively on the wellbeing of the citizenry. It has been established empirically that a healthy nation is a wealthy nation because good health and the economic development of a nation correlate positively. This is because a largely sick population cannot be actively productive.

REFERENCES

Ackon, E. K. (2003). *Management of Healthcare Organizations in Developing Countries*. Accra: Bel-Team Publications Ltd.

Agyepong, I. A. (1999). Reforming Health Service Delivery at the District Level in Ghana: The Perspective of a District Medical Officer. *Health Policy and Planning, 14*(1), 59–69.

Agyepong, I. A., &. Adjei, S. (2008, February 2). Public Social Policy Development and Implementation: A Case Study of the Ghana National Health Insurance Scheme. *Health Policy and Planning, 23*, 150–160.

Ahn, M. (2012). Effective Public Policy Delivery System in the Age of Information Overload: The Role of Imagery on Citizen Perception and Compliance of Public Policy. *The Korean Social Science Journal, 39*(1), 1–17.

Ajulor, O. V. (2018, February 9). The Challenges of Policy Implementation in Africa and Sustainable Development Goals. *International Journal of Social Sciences, 3*(3), 1497–1518. doi:10.20319/pijss.2018.33.14971518.

Alfond, R. R. (1975). *Health Care Politics: Ideological and Interest Group Barriers to Reform*. Chicago: The University of Chicago Press.

Anand, T., Phalguna, K., Kishore, J., & Ingle, G. K. (2011, July 1). Awareness about Lifestyle Diseases Associated Risk Factors in School Going Children in Delhi. *Journal of Nursing Science & Practice, 1*(1), 1–9.

Anderson, J. E. (2003). *Public Policymaking: An Introduction*. Boston: Houghton Mifflin Company.

Arthur, E. (2012). Wealth and Antenatal Care Use: Implications for Maternal Health Care Utilization in Ghana, Benin and Nigeria. *Health Economics Review, 2*(1), 14.

Australian Public Service Commission. (2007). *Changing Behaviour: A Public Policy Perspective*. Canberra: Australian Government.

Badasu, D. M. (2004). Implementation of Ghana's Health User Fee Policy and the Exemption of the Poor: Problems and Prospect. *African Population Studies Supplement, 19*(290), 285–302.

Denhardt, J. V., & Denhardt, R. B. (2007). *The New Public Service: Serving, Not Steering*. London: M.E. Sharpe.

Dialoke, I., Ukah, F. O., & Maduagwuna, I. V. (2017). Policy Formulation and Implementation in Nigeria: The Bane of Underdevelopment. *International Journal of Capacity Building in Education and Management (ICBM), 3*(2), March.

Dunn, W. N. (1994). *Public Policy Analysis: An Introduction* (2nd ed.). Eaglewood Cliffs, New Jersey: Prince Hall.

Dye, T. R. (1998). *Understanding Public Policy*. Upper Saddle River, New Jersey: Prince Hall.

Ggoobi, R., & Barungi, J. (2016). *Socio-economic effects of Chinese agricultural investments on the environment and local livelihoods in Uganda.* ACODE Policy Research Paper Series No.78. Kampala, Uganda.

Government of Ghana. (2009, November). Government White Paper on the Single Spine Pay Policy. Accra: Cabinet, Government of Ghana.

HERA & Health Partners, Ghana (2013). *Evaluation of the Free Maternal Healthcare Initiative in Ghana.* Accra and Reet, Belgium: HERA–HPG.

Heywood, A. (2007). *Politics* (3rd ed.). Basingstoke and New York: Palgrave Macmillan.

Howlett, M., & Ramesh, M. (1995; 2003). *Studying Public Policy: Policy Cycles and Policy Sub-Systems.* Oxford: Oxford University Press.

Knill, C., & Tosun, J. (2008). *Policy-Making.* In Daniele Caramani (Ed.), *Comparative Politics.* Oxford: Oxford University Press.

Kornov, L. & Thisen, W. A. H. (2000). Rationality in Decision- and Policy-Making: Implications for Strategic Environmental Assessment. *Impact Assessment and Project Appraisal, 18*(3), 191–200. Online Journal. doi:10.3152/147154600781767402.

Korto, P. A. (2014, December 1). *The Effects of Frontline Health Workers' Discretion on the Implementation of the Free Maternal Healthcare Policy by the Ghana Health Service: The Case of La General Hospital, Accra* (Unpublished Master's Thesis submitted to Ghana Institute of Management and Public Administration).

Laxmikanth, M. (2009). *Public Administration for the UPSC and State Civil Service Preliminary Examinations.* New Delhi: Tata McGraw-Hill.

Lee, K. (1982). *Policy Making and Planning in the Health Sector.* London and Sydney: Croom Helm.

Levesque, M. (2010). Build It … If You Can! Discretion, Building Inspectors and Part 8 of Ontario's 2006 Building Code. *Canadian Political Science Association Annual Conference* (pp. 2–42). Montreal, QC: Concordia University.

Liberman, V., Samuels, S. M., & Ross, L. (2004). The Name of the Game: Predictive Power of Reputations versus Situational Labels in Determining Prisoner's Dilemma Game Moves. *Personality and Social Psychology Bulletin, 30*(9), 1175–1185.

Lipsky, M. (1980). *Street-Level Bureaucracy: The Critical Role of Street-Level Bureaucrats.* Michigan: Russell Sage Foundation.

Lowi, T. J. (1972). Four Systems of Policy, Politics and Choice. *Public Administration Review, 34*(4), 298–310.

Mendes, V. L. P. S., & Aguiar, F. C. (2017). Implementation of Public Health Policy and its Challenges in the Digital Age. *Brazilian Journal of Public Administration, 51*(6), 1104–1121.

Ministry of Health, Ghana. (2008). *National Consultative Meeting on The Reduction of Maternal Mortality in Ghana: A Partnership Action*, s.l.: unpublished, pp. 1–43.

Ministry of Health, Ghana. (2012). National Policy for the Prevention and Control of Chronic Non-Communicable Diseases in Ghana. Accra: MOH.

Nyonator, F., & Kutzin, J. (1999). Health for Some? The Effects of User Fees in Volta Region of Ghana. *Health Policy and Planning, 14*(4), 329–341.

Okoro, F. (2016). Actors and roles in decision-making process. Technical report. Retrieved April 23, 2019, from www.researchgate.net/publication/315014371_ACTORS_AND_ROLES_IN_DECISION-MAKING_PROCESS.

Oktech, C. T., & Lelegwe, L. S. (2016). Analysis of Universal Health Coverage and Equity on Health Care in Kenya. *Global Journal of Health Science, 8*(7).

Opoku, E. (2009). *Utilization of Maternal Care Services in Ghana by Region after the Implementation of the Free Maternal Care Policy.* Texas: University of North Texas Health Science Centre.

Parliament of Ghana. (1996, December 30). Ghana Health Service and Teaching Hospitals Act, Act 525 of 1996. Accra: Assembly Press.

Parliament of Ghana. (2012, October 9). Public Health Act, Act 851 of 2012. Accra: Assembly Press.

Parliament of Ghana. (2016, September 19). Tobacco Control Regulation (L.I. 2247 of 2016). Accra: Assembly Press.

Paudel, N. (2009, December). A Critical Account of Policy Implementation Theories: Status and Reconsideration. *Nepalese Journal of Public Policy and Governance, 25*(2), 36–54.

Rhodes, R. A. W., & Marsh, D. (1992). Policy Networks in British Politics: A Critique of Existing Approaches. In D. Marsh & R. A. W. Rhodes (Eds.), *Policy Networks in British Government* (pp. 1–26). Oxford: Clarendon Press.

Ripley, R. B. (1995). *Stages of the Policy Process in Public Policy Theories, Models and Concepts: An Anthology.* (D. C. McCool, Ed.). Eaglewood Cliffs: Prince Hall.

Shah, P. (2011). *Social Change & Public Policy.* New Delhi: Centre for Civil Society.

Simon, C. A. (2010). *Public Policy: Preferences and Outcomes* (2nd ed.). Boston: Longman.

Sunstein, C. R. (1995). On the Expressive Function of Law. Univ. Pa. Law Rev. 144, 2021–2053.

Walt, G. (1994). *Health Policy: An Introduction to Process and Power.* Johannesburg: Witwatersrand University Press; London and New Jersey: Zed Books.

Weihrich, H., Cannice, M. V., & Koontz, H. (2010). *Management: A Global and Entrepreneurial Perspective* (13th ed.). New Delhi: Tata McGraw Hill.

Wildavsky, A., & Pressman, J. (1973). *Implementation.* Berkeley: University of California Press.

World Health Organization. (2008). WHO Report on the Global Tobacco Epidemic, 2008: The MPOWER Package. Geneva, Switzerland: World Health Organization. Retrieved May 18, 2018, from www.who.int/tobacco/mpower/mpower_report_full_2008.pdf.

World Health Organization. (2012). Retrieved August 28, 2014, from www.whqlipdoc.who.int/publications/2010/9789241500265_eng.pdf.

19 Technology and Health Services Marketing in Africa

Kenneth Appiah, Ibelema Sam-Epelle, Ellis L .C. Osabutey

19.1 INTRODUCTION

The quality of medical care has customarily been measured by objective criteria such as mortality and morbidity; more subjective valuations are repeatedly ignored (Dagger, Sweeney, & Johnson, 2007). The healthcare sector has been slow to move beyond a supply-side approach to quality assessment. The changing structure of the industry implies that the role patients play in defining what quality means has become a critical competitive deliberation. Consequently, service providers are struggling to devise meaningful customer-oriented quality assessment measures (Dagger et al., 2007). The need for effective marketing activities in the health services sector cannot be overemphasised. Over the last two decades emerging information and communications technologies have acquired the potential to improve the quality and delivery of health services in Africa; however, the adoption processes remain slow and complex (Ami-Narh & Williams, 2012). Maintaining and delivering quality is one thing, but another important issue in health services is communication between stakeholders. This means that effective marketing communication will need to rely extensively on exploiting opportunities presented by the wide range of information and communications technologies. Consequently, the marketing mix will need to shift to digital as the healthcare market evolves. An implication for marketers is that crystalising customer segments is more important than ever, since they consider educating through content a top priority (Affect, 2018). Today, the proliferation of mobile technologies and the usage of social media provide a low-cost avenue for content dissemination to service users across various sectors of the economy.

Social media has become one of the effective mechanisms used by both the private and public sectors to deliver promotional messages (Narangajavana et al., 2017; Venkatesh, Chan & Thong, 2012). A considerable number of studies have emphasised the increasing use of social media by organisations over the last two decades (Garrido-Moreno, Garcia-Morales, Lockett, & King, 2018; Sigala & Chalkiti, 2015). Through social media, people maintain contact with others; hence it can provide a means of communication between medical institutions and their stakeholders. Additionally, it can be used in advertising and promoting strategies, by posting information about discounts, offers and advantages of accessing the products provided by service providers (Radu et al., 2017). The GSMA (2019) emphasises the growing access to and use of mobile phones in the world. These developments have enabled wider personal and organisational uses. As a result, providers and staff members in the medical sector now use mobiles for social networking, continuing education, transferring patient records, and managing physician referral networks with applications (Hammer, 2017).

19.2 HEALTHCARE SERVICES IN AFRICA: SOME CHALLENGES

There is very limited investment in healthcare services across Africa; the investment shortage is estimated at $25–$30 billion according to experts (Atieno, 2017). Additionally, there is a shortage of skilled and experienced doctors in Africa (Atieno, 2017; Naicker, Plange-Rhule, Tutt, & Eastwood, 2009).

For instance, although sub-Saharan Africa is inhabited by 13 per cent of the world's population it has 24 per cent of the global disease burden, yet only possesses 2 per cent of doctors worldwide (Atieno, 2017). In addition, the health sector in Africa has been characterised by congestion in hospitals, long distances to health facilities, shortage of health personnel, reliance on paper-based records, and inefficient operations. These have given rise to an urgent need for digital innovations in the African healthcare services sector (Hempel, 2018b). Although technology makes it possible for a single doctor to reach many patients conveniently, there is still need for further investments in augmenting the training of health professionals, especially doctors, whose skills development requires practical exposure. Some of the exposure needs to explore the use of new and emerging technologies (Atieno, 2017).

To a large extent, regulatory and legal challenges also hinder optimal healthcare services in Africa (Hempel, 2018d, 2018c). Given that governments fall short with respect to the needed investment in healthcare provision, service providers must rely on foreign investments and buy-ins. Despite this need, the healthcare industry is immersed in complex regulations that present hurdles for entrepreneurs. Moreover, healthcare start-ups have the challenge of dealing with access to personal data; however, there are limited safeguards towards dealing with data protection issues. An outlier to the issues within the continent appears to be South Africa (SA), indicated by the significant level of health tourism. The country is regarded as the centre for the application of modern technologies and innovation in healthcare delivery. It is also the testing ground for entrepreneurship, having the largest life sciences market on the continent; government-sponsored schemes to promote start-ups; a large number of investors entering the market; and huge human capital and talented youth (Hempel, 2018b).

19.3 INFORMATION TECHNOLOGY AND HEALTHCARE SERVICES IN AFRICA

Information and communication technology (ICT) has seen an upsurge with wider access to people across both developed and developing countries. The ubiquitous ICT presence is having significant impact on businesses and other socio-cultural dynamics (Ami-Narh & Williams, 2012). Over the last three decades African government initiatives have given much needed attention to policy initiatives to broaden ICT access, to leverage opportunities to urban and rural populations as well as increase productivity and innovation in both the private and public sectors (International Telecommunications Union, 2006). Kwankam (2008) observes that adopting wider use in health services in developing countries can bring about extensive benefits to reducing the problems in the sector. He notes that through ICT, practitioners can offer services beyond their physical reach. Which means services could be provided to areas where doctors and other medical staff have no presence but can co-ordinate medical provision from a distance. This can enable less experienced practitioners to remotely access help from experts to improve service delivery. Wider ICT access can also enable healthcare consumers to actively participate in shaping the quality of healthcare services delivery (Kwankam, 2008).

In 2017, the World Health Organization Regional Office for Africa and the International Telecommunication Union (ITU) signed a Cooperation Agreement, on using digital services to save lives and improve people's health in the region. The initiative will establish the platforms in countries to deliver digital health services such as mHealth, e-learning, health information systems, and telemedicine, among others. It is anticipated that all countries in the African region will benefit from this initiative over the 2018–2030 period, over a span of four 3-year phases. The partnership focuses on building a capable workforce to effectively use ICT as well as addressing the need for multi-stakeholder partnership models that can bring about the sustainable adoption of digital health. Moreover, the new Agreement intends to merge existing efforts and resources towards making available ICT foundations and platforms that are a requirement for providing and scaling up digital health services in the region (World Health Organization, 2017).

Africa is currently undergoing a digital revolution. For instance, most countries across sub-Saharan Africa have a high level of mobile penetration (85 per cent), while internet penetration is rising (Atieno, 2017; Poushter, 2016). Already some African countries have come up with innovative ways they can leverage mobile technologies to mitigate shortages in the healthcare service delivery.

Nonetheless, partly influenced by the challenges discussed above, low-cost solutions have been the most viable sort of innovations. For instance, in Malawi, there have been hotline innovations such as 'Chipatala Cha Pa Foni', which facilitates citizens' toll free calls regarding pregnancy and paediatric health advice, using an mHealth platform to provide access to hospital information via mobile phones. The wireless heart diagnostic system invented by Sanga Kathema, 'IHMMS', which is built from discarded electronics, represents another low-cost solution – which aids in circumventing the lack of cardiologists, as it can be easily employed by nurses and other health personnel. Similarly, in Togo, innovators like Kodio Afate Gnikou have taken the problem of e-waste created by first-world countries and deposited in the third world, and are transforming these leftover parts into a 3D printer which tackles forecasted potential health challenges. In Uganda, Brian Gitta and six student friends developed 'Matibabu' ('medical centre' in Swahili) – a low-cost, reusable device that can test for malaria quickly and accurately, without drawing blood. It clips on to the patient's finger and shines a red beam of light onto the skin, detecting changes in the shape, colour, and concentration of red blood cells, all of which are affected by malaria (Hempel, 2018a).

In the following, several cases of healthcare innovations across Africa are presented, pointing to cases in Rwanda, Malawi, Tanzania, South Africa, Kenya, Uganda, Ghana, and Nigeria. The cases are far from exhaustive; however, they shed light on the diversity of healthcare innovations, expand on the prominence of low-cost solutions, and illuminate the contribution of entrepreneurial efforts to healthcare across the African continent.

19.3.1 RWANDA

The exponential growth of the health sector in Rwanda is partly driven by the innovative use of mobile technologies in areas like telemedicine, and drone services for health packages and products movement (Atieno, 2017; Hempel, 2018d). Such initiatives have improved Rwanda's status in reducing child mortality, which is one of the most critical parameters of a country's healthcare system (Hempel, 2018a). In conjunction with the Rwandan government ministries of health, youth, and ICT, Babylon, a British telemedicine firm, launched a mobile-based healthcare scheme in 2016, focusing on quick and easy access to live medical doctors and professionals through mobile devices. In the same year, Zipline (a Silicon Valley company), kick-started its operations in Rwanda, employing drones in the delivery of health packages and products (e.g. blood needed for transfusions and vaccines) – to mitigate unavailability issues in communities due to logistical challenges such as bad roads. Additionally, they offer benefits such as a decrease in stock-outs and efficient delivery at affordable prices. Over twenty health centres and clinics in Rwanda have access to the drone service, and the initiative serves over two million of its populace who lack access to primary healthcare (Hempel, 2018d). A similar initiative is evident in Malawi where local start-ups like 'Micromek' are taking advantage of the drone corridor introduced in the country to explore the use of the cutting-edge technology to render quick delivery and transportation options for medical supplies in the hard to reach areas of the country (Hempel, 2018c). Besides drones, other logistical solutions can be seen in other parts of Africa such as Ghana. For instance, 'SnooCODE RED', a logistics app, significantly reduces emergency response times of ambulances, through a custom-made mapping system that aids better navigation through dense urban areas (Hempel, 2018a).

Other benefits of technology initiatives in Rwandan healthcare extend to hospitals, particularly nurses. One case in point is IV Drip Alert – a device that enables nurses to more easily manage intravenous fluids through a wireless alert system, hence reducing patients' risks of complications due to empty IV bags. This system is more accurate and efficient than manual systems, due to an automatic monitoring device. The solution circumvents serious problems like air embolisms which can occur if the observer forgets to change the IV at the correct time (Hempel, 2018a).

19.3.2 SOUTH AFRICA

South Africa champions the continent's largest healthcare market, valued at approximately US$28.1 billion, and there are 101 mHealth services across the country, of which 83 are live. As South Africa ventures into numerous digital health sectors such as telemedicine, mHealth, wearables, and medical devices, the Department of Science and Technology in the country notes that there is need to develop its health innovation system using a model that brings together government, academia, industry, and civil society, which will benefit from manufacturing capability, research and academia, and the regulatory environment (Hempel, 2018b). The country is experiencing the growth of digital health accelerators, aimed at supporting digital health innovation; concurrently the government is fast-tracking the implementation of a National Health Insurance Scheme to cover its citizens. In the interim, on the demand side, digital innovations like 'hello doctor' are available to connect patients with doctors; mHealth implementations like MomConnect have achieved over 460,000 service adopters in the country. Conversely, innovations like 'EMGuidance' assist health personnel in their work; and novelties such as 'Stock Visibility Solutions (SVS)' by Vodacom, aid the capturing of drug stock levels daily on the supply side (Hempel, 2018e, 2018b).

In addition, the country's manufacturing capabilities and knowledge, with highly competitive and innovative firms, distinguishes it from other African economies (Hempel, 2018b). In the country, telemedicine start-ups are innovating in healthcare services, particularly individuals' health tracking. While platforms such as 'connectmed' are championing the space, start-ups like 'Vitls' are producing wearable health trackers which allow medical teams to remotely monitor a patient's vital signs. Later start-ups to the game, such as 'HearX' have recently secured funds for a hearing-focused digital health initiative. Others such as 'OculusID' have developed biometric solutions with impairment detection through the application of non-invasive, hygienic and cost-effective innovations. 'CapeRay' is another healthcare start-up intending to develop an innovative means for doctors to diagnose breast cancer, through combining X-ray and ultrasound breast screening equipment.

19.3.3 MALAWI

There is a clear shortage of doctors in Malawi, quantified at one doctor for every 88,300 people in the country. To mediate such challenges, Malawian entrepreneurs are elevating the healthcare sector through e-health and mHealth technologies (Hempel, 2018c). Start-ups like 'IMOSYS', which is being funded by the World Bank in its five-year project, are implementing a national tuberculosis control project to provide care interventions that aim to reduce diagnostic and treatment delays for the ailment (Hempel, 2018c, 2018a). Alongside, major Malawian healthcare players like 'Baobab Health' are developing low-cost power backup systems, touchscreen-based user interfaces designed for users with limited experience, and low-cost information appliances that are significantly more robust in harsh environments than traditional computers – in order to provide low-cost diagnostic tools and communication devices for health personnel, especially in the rural areas, where more than 83 per cent of the populace lack access to healthcare tools (Hempel, 2018c).

19.3.4 TANZANIA

Tanzanian healthcare entrepreneurs are contributing reasonably to the overall innovation in the country. The 'Be a lady' initiative is a good example which is led by Lulu Said Ameir and focuses on healthcare and hygiene for adolescent girls in secondary schools by installing sanitary pad vending machines. The information from the use of these vending machines is fed back to compare school attendance rates and make recommendations on ways to reduce school absenteeism (Hempel, 2018a). The initiative has also been able to impact low-income earners, by supplying their adolescent girls with access to good quality, affordable sanitary pads.

Another Tanzanian case is that of 'Jamii' – a micro-health insurance start-up using low-end mobile technology (USSD App) to launch insurance policies from as low as US$1 per month for the low-income populace. Founder and chief executive officer (CEO) of the initiative, Lilian Makoi, projected that it will have helped impact the lives of 720,000 people by 2018 as the service expands across Africa (Hempel, 2018a). Healthcare entrepreneurial efforts are also impacting Tanzanian hospital networks. 'Okoa', meaning 'to save', is one such effort, a web-based monitoring software designed to combat the theft of medical supplies across the networks of hospitals in the country. It achieves this by monitoring medicine inventories at the national medical store and in hospitals, and reporting discrepancies to the Ministry of Health. As a result, it helps to cut healthcare costs and ensure medicines are available to those who need them (Hempel, 2018a).

19.3.5 UGANDA

In Uganda, inaccurate diagnosis and treatment of ailments has influenced Brian Turyabagye to create 'Mama-Ope' – a biomedical smart jacket that helps doctors identify pneumonia faster and more accurately. It measures temperature and breathing rate and compares it to a database of parameters. The team behind the initiative aim to reduce the margin for human error and help doctors make faster, more accurate diagnoses (Hempel, 2018a). 'Ask without Shame' is another entrepreneurial healthcare initiative in Uganda; it provides emergency sex education via mobiles through an android app, Whatsapp, calls, and SMS. Medical experts and counsellors are always available to assist users with the right information regarding sexuality.

19.3.6 KENYA

In Kenya, the E-Con wheelchair is a culmination of various solutions proposed by entrepreneurial effort. It is a 4×4 wheelchair that can go off-road, climb stairs, allow the user to stand upright, and automatically navigate familiar terrain, all while keeping its passenger perfectly level. The country is also home to Mensa Healthcare, an initiative that enables patients to accurately communicate their prescription history with a tracking tool more efficient than memory, through a personal portable health records system (Hempel, 2018a).

19.3.7 NIGERIA

According to the World Health Organization (WHO), birth asphyxia is one of the three major causes of new-born deaths;,accounting for 23 per cent of death worldwide. In Nigeria, 'Ubenwa Intelligence Solutions' is developing a machine learning system that can input the cry of a baby, analyse its amplitude and frequency patterns, and give an instant diagnosis of the condition; hence, the condition can now be detected without medical expertise or use of clinical methods (Hempel, 2018a).

19.4 HEALTHCARE MARKETING

The purpose of healthcare marketing is to study and recognise the requirements and desires of potential patients, in order to meet those necessities at peak standards (Radu et al., 2017). According to the Centres for Disease Control and Prevention (CDC), health marketing involves creating, communicating, and delivering health information and interventions, using customer-centred and science-based strategies to protect and promote the health of diverse populations. The complexity of health marketing can be seen through the diversity of perspectives regarding the term, including (Centers for Disease Control and Prevention, 2011):

- A multidisciplinary practice that promotes the use of marketing research to educate, motivate, and inform the public on health messages.
- An integration of the traditional marketing field with public health research, theory, and practice.
- A complex framework that provides guidance for designing health interventions, campaigns, communications, and research projects.
- A broad range of strategies and techniques that can be used to create synergy among public health research, communication messages, and health behaviours.

In this vein, Health Marketing is a multidisciplinary area of public health practice, which draws from fields such as marketing, communication, and public health promotion to provide a framework of theories, strategies and techniques that can be used to guide work in public health research, interventions, and communication campaigns (Bernhardt, 2006; Centers for Disease Control and Prevention, 2011). In recent years across Africa there has been a proliferation of private healthcare facilities that are competing with and in some instances complementing the provision by the public sector. These private healthcare organisations also need to make even more effort at marketing communication to reveal how they stand out from private providers as well as how they can complement public sector healthcare provision. Therefore, the marketing function has assumed a very important role in the health delivery sector. In meeting the new priorities for healthcare marketing, five essentials are proposed for marketing plans, in order to capitalise on emerging opportunities. These include: advanced social media, targeted content and promotion, creative media relations, emerging tech campaigns, and business-oriented metrics (Affect, 2018). The measurement challenge is highlighted in a subsequent section.

19.5 DIGITIZING AND MOBILISING HEALTH: MHEALTH

Globally, there is a growing number of mobile device users; this even more the case in Africa. Recently, there has been a flood of mobile devices on the market, including smartphones, tablets, and wearables. The proliferation of these personal effect technologies is making it easier for people to adopt their use for health service. Mobile technologies and the internet easily solve the problems of geographical barriers and low resources, thereby taking healthcare services to the millions who would have otherwise lacked medical attention (Atieno, 2017).

Digital health initiatives help ensure fairness in service delivery and thereby stimulate progress in public health, in addition to making the system work for the whole population. Such initiatives have already demonstrated the significant potential of ICT to empower healthcare workers and the beneficiary population by providing them with the right information at the right time and place (World Health Organization, 2017).

The concept of mHealth is one of the key technological domains resulting from the advances in remote healthcare and e-health systems which is bringing together major academic research and industry disciplines worldwide to achieve innovative solutions to healthcare delivery, exploiting the introduction of new wireless standards and network systems with true mobile broadband and fast internet access (Istepanian & Zhang, 2012).

There is no standard definition for mHealth; its complexity is evident in the perspectives taken by scholars, practitioners, and even world institutions. Definitions of mHealth have focused on either the 'technological' or 'functional' dimension (Nunes & Simões-Marques, 2015) (see Table 19.1).

mHhealth services were predicted to be a twenty-six-billion-dollar market globally by 2017; Asia-Pacific is the fastest growing mHealth market, only surpassed by the USA (Hammer, 2017)

TABLE 19.1
Dimensions of M-health

Technological dimension	• M-health comprises mobile computing, medical sensor, and communications technologies for healthcare (Istepanian, Jovanov, & Zhang, 2004).
Functional dimension	• M-health involves medical and public health practice supported by mobile devices, such as mobile phones, patient monitoring devices, personal digital assistants (PDAs), and other wireless devices (Hempel, 2017; World Health Organization, 2012).

– as North America dominates the global digital health market, which is expected to exceed US$379 billion by 2024 (Hempel, 2017). In Africa, these services are also enjoying growth in countries like South Africa, Rwanda, Nigeria, Kenya, and Malawi. Other African countries would need to learn lessons from countries that have implemented the integration of mHealth services into healthcare provision.

19.6 HEALTHCARE MOBILE USAGE

The rise in smartphone ownership in Africa means that people are increasingly going online to find information via the mobile route. For instance, a significant proportion of smartphone users gather information about a specific medical problem or procedure, or diet, nutrition, and fitness-related information on their smartphones (cf. Hammer, 2017).

Healthcare providers are also turning to mobiles as professionals in the industry use smartphones and medical apps to facilitate mHealth. Compliance and IT security regulations that made it a challenge for the healthcare industry to adopt mobile devices in the past are continually being resolved; hence, more organisations are finding adoption acceptable (Hammer, 2017). Research also demonstrates the need for digital methods of promoting medical care services in order to expand a business, and the important role of social networking sites in marketing communications has been emphasised by many scholars (Radu et al., 2017).

Additionally, there are benefits of mHealth apps for improving patient care. These apps can be broken down into 'wellness' and 'medical' app categories. In app stores, a significant proportion (85 per cent) are wellness apps and medical apps make up the remainder – most of these are free to use or get started. The former is typically used by patients, while the latter is designed to be primarily used by physicians (Duffy, 2011; Hammer, 2017). Health apps are becoming more secure as they are being developed with HIPAA-compliance[1] in mind, hence the wider adoption in healthcare organisations (Hammer, 2017).

19.7 THE MEASUREMENT CHALLENGES

Despite all the opportunities provided by the mHealth solutions, challenges lie ahead as well, such as globally accepted policies, guidelines, and standardised metrics (Hempel, 2017).

Though measurement has been continually contemplated by marketing and PR executives, execution still suffers. The evolving health marketing landscape has resulted in linking PR and marketing efforts more closely to business/financial metrics, as a top priority for marketers. The development of metrics aids in measuring the real value of marketing activities to the business, and can aid in strategic decisions (Affect, 2018). Regarding social media, there are communication platforms that can promote certain behaviours, thus influencing decision-making (Radu et al., 2017). Table 19.2 provides suggested metrics across marketing and overall business metrics.

TABLE 19.2
Metrics for measuring healthcare business

PR/MARKETING METRICS	BUSINESS METRICS
• Share of Voice	• Market Penetration
• Customer/Patient Engagement	• Market Leadership
• Traffic to Website	• Market Share
• Downloads	• Sales/Revenue
• Registrations	• Cost Savings
• Lead Generation	• Brand Loyalty

Source: Adapted from Affect (2018).

19.8 HEALTH SERVICE QUALITY

Service quality has become an important corporate strategy for healthcare organisations, just as quality in healthcare is currently at the forefront of professional, political, and managerial attention, primarily because it is being seen as a means for achieving increased patronage, competitive advantage, long-term profitability; it is also being used as an approach to achieving better health outcomes for consumers (cf. Dagger & Sweeney, 2006; Dagger et al., 2007).

Conceptually, the definition of service quality is mainly specified at an abstract level, via either a 'formative' or a 'reflective' approach. In the former, the dimensions of the construct give rise to or cause the overall construct, whereas in the latter, dimensions are viewed as reflective indicators of their higher order construct (Dagger et al., 2007).

Scholarship has also understood service quality in terms of dimensionality. For instance, the SERVQUAL scale which is predominantly employed in understanding service quality encompasses five dimensions: reliability, empathy, tangibles, responsiveness, and assurance (Parasuraman, Zeithaml, & Berry, 1985, 1988). However, researchers have found the scale to be unidimensional (e.g. Brown, Churchill, & Peter, 1993).

The dimensional structure of service quality perceptions has raised replication problems (Dagger et al., 2007). For instance, Buttle's (1996) critique of the widely applied SERVQUAL scale is partly based on the difficulty of reproducing its dimensions across diverse service contexts. The construct is also predominantly expressed as a second-order factor (e.g. Grönroos, 1993; Parasuraman et al., 1988) and, more recently, as a third-order factor (e.g. Brady & Cronin, 2001). In this regard, Dagger et al. (2007) opine that:

> This structure suggests that service quality comprises several primary dimensions, which in turn share a common theme represented by the higher order global perceived service quality construct ... these dimensions have subdimensions that combine related attributes into subgroups.
>
> (p. 124)

The scholars contend that representing perceptions of overall service quality as third-order factors to the subdimensions recognises that the evaluation of the construct may be more complex than previously conceptualised. Their study findings were drawn from developing and empirically testing a multidimensional hierarchical scale for measuring health service quality and investigating the scale's ability to predict important service outcomes: service satisfaction and behavioural intentions. Results suggest that customers evaluate service quality at an overall level, a dimensional level, and at sub-dimensional level and that each level drives perceptions at the level above.

Dagger et al.'s (2007) approach contrasts conceptualisations of service quality perceptions wherein assessment is based on an expectation (dis)confirmation approach – i.e. the construct is defined as a consumer's judgement of, or impression about, an entity's total excellence or superiority (Parasuraman et al., 1985, 1988). In this context, judgements that shape perceptions of service quality are often described in terms of the incongruity between consumers' hopes of service and definite service performance (Grönroos, 1993; Parasuraman et al., 1985). Although commonly applied, this approach has been the subject of substantial criticism and debate (see Dagger et al., 2007).

19.9 CONCLUSION

An ageing population, mounting competitive pressures, increasing consumerism, and emerging treatments and technologies all partly influence the growth in healthcare; hence, it is one of the fastest growing sectors in the service economy (Andaleeb, 2001; Dagger et al., 2007). Technological developments impact changes in healthcare. The provision of healthcare services can go a long way, via digital technology adoption and mediation, to significantly reducing costs. Affect's (2018) recent study indicates that technology enablement is the most crucial concern for healthcare marketers in 2018. In this regard, social media is a key component included in the mix in order to meet the needs of target audiences. The targeting fitness of electronic media has led to its usage by marketing managers in medical institutions as means of advertisement when they advance marketing campaigns (Radu et al., 2017). Nonetheless, while emerging technologies (e.g. new drugs and treatments, new devices, new social media support for healthcare) will drive innovation, the human factor will remain one of the stable limitations of breakthroughs (Thimbleby, 2013).

In Africa, digital solutions can bolster healthcare access and services across the continent at a fraction of the cost of traditional solutions (Atieno, 2017). Rapid improvement in IT infrastructure coupled with growing demand for cost-effective technologies in healthcare such as mHealth (mobile health) will boost the digital health market over the coming years. Already the ubiquitous nature of mobile technologies influences pervasive usage in the healthcare industry, as the nature of the job often requires physicians to be accessible always. These users have perpetual information needs that mobile devices meet. While access to the internet and proliferation of internet-enabled devices has gone a long way in mitigating the problems faced by the health sector in the region, these systems are only as good as the quality of health practitioners using them to reach the patients (Atieno, 2017). Therefore, the development and use of digital technologies will not improve service quality on their own. However, with good health infrastructure and competent health professionals, digital telecommunications could enhance health service provision significantly.

For healthcare marketers to stay competitive, adopting immersive technology such as artificial intelligence and augmented reality and implementing metrics and measurement becomes critical to improving service quality; it has a significant impact on service satisfaction and behavioural intentions, and also mediates the relationship between the dimensions and intentions. The nine subdimensions (*interaction, relationship, outcome, expertise, atmosphere, tangibles, timeliness, operation, and support*) drive four primary dimensions (*interpersonal quality, technical quality, environment quality, and administrative quality*), which in turn drive service quality perceptions.

Note

1. The Health Insurance Portability and Accountability Act (HIPAA) sets the standard for sensitive patient data protection. Companies that deal with protected health information must have physical, network, and process security measures in place and follow them to ensure HIPAA Compliance. Covered entities (anyone providing treatment, payment, and operations in healthcare) and business associates (anyone who has access to patient information and provides support in treatment, payment, or operations) must meet HIPAA Compliance. Other entities, such as subcontractors and any other related business associates, must also comply (De Groot, 2018).

REFERENCES

Affect. (2018). *Healthcare marketing 2018: Guide to meeting new priorities in a shifting environment.* Retrieved from www.affect.com/wp-content/uploads/2017/11/Affect_Healthcare_White_Paper.pdf.

Ami-Narh, J. T., & Williams, P. A. (2012). A revised UTAUT model to investigate E-health acceptance of health professionals in Africa. *Journal of Emerging Trends in Computing and Information Sciences, 3*(10), 1383–1391.

Andaleeb, S. S. (2001). Service quality perceptions and patient satisfaction: A study of hospitals in a developing country. *Social Science & Medicine, 52,* 1359–1370.

Atieno, M. (2017). How technology can improve healthcare in sub-Saharan Africa. Retrieved November 22, 2018, from http://innov8tiv.com/technology-can-improve-healthcare-sub-saharan-africa/.

Bernhardt, J. M. (2006). Improving health through health marketing. *Preventing Chronic Disease Public Health Research, Practice, and Policy, 3*(3), 1–3. Retrieved from www.cdc.gov/pcd/issues/2006/jul/pdf/05_0238.pdf.

Brady, M. K., & Cronin, J. J. (2001). Some new thoughts on conceptualizing perceived service quality: A hierarchical approach. *Journal of Marketing, 65*(3), 34–49.

Brown, T. J., Churchill, G. A., & Peter, J. P. (1993). Improving the measurement of service quality. *Journal of Retailing, 69*(1), 127–139.

Buttle, F. (1996). SERVQUAL: Review, critique, research agenda. *European Journal of Marketing, 30*(1), 8–32.

Centers for Disease Control and Prevention. (2011). What is health marketing? Retrieved November 20, 2018, from www.cdc.gov/healthcommunication/toolstemplates/whatishm.html.

Dagger, T. S., & Sweeney, J. C. (2006). The effect of service evaluations on behavioral intentions and quality of life. *Journal of Service Research, 9*(1), 3–18.

Dagger, T. S., Sweeney, J. C., & Johnson, L. W. (2007). A hierarchical model of health service quality: Scale development and investigation of an integrated model. *Journal of Service Research, 10*(2), 123–142.

De Groot, J. (2018). What is HIPAA compliance? Retrieved November 22, 2018, from https://digitalguardian.com/blog/what-hipaa-compliance.

Duffy, M. J. (2011). Smartphones in the Arab Spring. *IPI Report: Media and money,* 53–56.

Garrido-Moreno, A., Garcia-Morales, V. J., Lockett, N., & King, S. (2018). The missing link: Creating value with social media use in hotels. *International Journal of Hospitality Management, 75,* 94–104.

Grönroos, C. (1993). A service quality model and its marketing implications. *European Journal of Marketing, 18*(4), 36–44.

GSMA. (2017). *State of the industry report on mobile money.*

Hammer, R. (2017). 30 amazing mobile health technology statistics for today's physician. Retrieved November 21, 2018, from https://getreferralmd.com/2015/08/mobile-healthcare-technology-statistics/.

Hempel, V. (2017). Future possibilities of mobile health in the African context. Retrieved November 22, 2018, from www.dr-hempel-network.com/digital-health-technolgy/mobile-health-in-africa-mhealth/.

Hempel, V. (2018a). 16 Young digital health: Healthcare innovators in Africa who are changing the face of healthcare in sub-Saharan region. Retrieved March 11, 2019, from www.dr-hempel-network.com/digital-health-startups/16-young-digital-health-healthcare-innovators-in-africa/.

Hempel, V. (2018b). 5 Reasons why South Africa is the centre for technology healthcare innovation. Retrieved November 22, 2018, from www.dr-hempel-network.com/growth-of-digital-health-market/5-reasons-why-south-africa-is-the-centre-for-technology-healthcare-innovation/.

Hempel, V. (2018c). Digital healthcare in Malawi: Challenges faced by the African country. Retrieved November 22, 2018, from www.dr-hempel-network.com/health-policies-in-india/digital-healthcare-in-malawi/.

Hempel, V. (2018d). Is Rwanda the testing market for latest digital health technology? Digital health sector in Rwanda. Retrieved November 22, 2018, from www.dr-hempel-network.com/health-policies-in-india/digital-health-sector-in-rwanda/.

Hempel, V. (2018e). How to finance your digital health startup in Southern Africa region? Retrieved March 11, 2019, from www.dr-hempel-network.com/digital-health-startups/finance-your-digital-health-startup-in-southern-africa/.

International Telecommunication Union. (2006). ICT and telecommunications in least developed countries: Mid-term review for the decade 2001-2010. Geneva: ITU. Retrieved June 21, 2019, from www.itu.int/ITU-D/ldc/pdf/ICTand%20TELinLDC-e.pdf.

Istepanian, R. S. H., & Zhang, Y. T. (2012). Guest editorial introduction to the special section: 4G health – The long-term evolution of m-health. *IEEE Transactions on Information Technology in Biomedicine, 16*(1), 1–5. doi:10.1109/TITB.2012.2183269.

Istepanian, R., Jovanov, E., & Zhang, Y. T. (2004). Introduction to the special section on m-health: Beyond seamless mobility and global wireless health-care connectivity. *IEEE Transactions on Information Technology in Biomedicine, 8*(4), 405–414. Retrieved from www.ncbi.nlm.nih.gov/pubmed/15615031.

Kwankam, S. Y. (2008). eHealth for service delivery: Special considerations for resource-challenged health systems. *Studies in Health Technology and Informatics, 134*, 97–106.

Naicker, S., Plange-Rhule, J., Tutt, R. C., & Eastwood, J. B. (2009). Shortage of healthcare workers in developing countries – Africa. *Ethnicity & Disease, 1*, 60–64.

Narangajavana, Y., Fiol, L. J. C., Tena, M. Á. M., Artola, R. M. R., & García, J. S. (2017). The influence of social media in creating expectations: An empirical study for a tourist destination. *Annals of Tourism Research, 65*, 60–70.

Nunes, I. L., & Simões-Marques, M. J. (2015). Exploiting the potential and facing the challenges of mobile devices: Application examples. *Procedia Manufacturing, 3*(AHFE), 807–814.

Parasuraman, A., Zeithaml, V. A., & Berry, L. L. (1985). A conceptual model of service quality and its implications for future research. *Journal of Marketing, 49*(4), 41–50.

Parasuraman, A., Zeithaml, V. A., & Berry, L. L. (1988). SERVQUAL: A multiple-item scale for measuring consumer perceptions of service quality. *Journal of Retailing, 64*(1), 12–40.

Poushter, J. (2016). Smartphone ownership and internet usage continues to climb in emerging economies. Retrieved from www.pewresearch.org.

Radu, G., Solomon, M., Gheorghe, C. M., Hostiuc, M., Bulescu, I. A., & Purcarea, V. L. (2017). The adaptation of health care marketing to the digital era. *Journal of Medicine and Life, 10*(1), 44–46. Retrieved from www.ncbi.nlm.nih.gov/pubmed/28255375.

Sigala, M., & Chalkiti, K. (2015). Knowledge management, social media and employee creativity. *International Journal of Hospitality Management, 45*, 44–58.

Thimbleby, H. (2013). Technology and the future of healthcare. *Journal of Public Health Research, 2*(3), e28.

Venkatesh, V., Chan, F. K., & Thong, J. Y. (2012). Designing e-government services: Key service attributes and citizens' preference structures. *Journal of Operations Management, 30*(1–2), 116–133.

World Health Organization. (2012). *mHealth new horizons for health through mobile technologies*. Retrieved from www.who.int/about/.

World Health Organization. (2017). WHO and ITU to use digital technology to strengthen public health services in Africa. Retrieved November 21, 2018, from https://afro.who.int/news/who-and-itu-use-digital-technology-strengthen-public-health-services-africa.

20 Application of Technology in Healthcare Delivery in Africa

Ernest Yaw Tweneboah-Koduah and Deli Dotse Gli

20.1 INTRODUCTION

In the advanced economies, there is demonstrable evidence of the game changing role of technology in the delivery of healthcare service. Generally, technology has been responsible for decreasing the cost of goods and services provided and for increasing productivity. With specific reference to the healthcare sector, technology is often mentioned as the main reason for decreased cost of delivery of services and also increasing quality in terms of both services provided and the clinical outcomes achieved. Kern and Jaron (2003) opine that information technology has tremendous potential for enhancing quality and safety as well as for reducing costs and creating service innovations. Take for instance, the electronic medical record (EMR) innovation which many developed economies have implemented and which has been celebrated for massively reducing medication errors and adverse drug events and also lessening the communication gap between a healthcare giver and the receiver (Gao, Li & Luo, 2015). In light of the above benefits, key social advocacy groups and political actors in Sub-Sahara Africa have argued for an increased use of health technology in order to improve the quality of healthcare and to lower delivery costs. Thus, much can be said of South Africa, Rwanda and Ghana where a chunk of their annual national budget is dedicated to the health sector through investment in cutting edge technologies.

The population of Africa is increasing rapidly. In 2016, the population of Africa was estimated to be 1.2 billion people and as such Africa was labelled as the second largest and second most populous continent on earth (United Nations [UN], 2017). A 2013 report by the World Health Organization suggests that, although the population of Africa is estimated to grow from 1.2 billion to 2.6 billion by 2050, the continent has the lowest health workforce capacity of 3 per cent and healthcare expenditure of 1 per cent globally, which has contributed to the region's highest burden of communicable diseases (25 per cent of global) such as malaria, HIV/AIDS and tuberculosis. It is also the case that about 58 per cent of the African population lives in highly inaccessible or rural areas (UN, 2017), typically sparsely populated with little or no access to medical care due to lack of medical facilities and professionals, at a time when 55 per cent of the world population lives in urban areas with 53 per cent of the world digitally connected and having advanced healthcare (World Health Organization [WHO], 2013). Notwithstanding the fact that sustainable urbanization is regarded as essential to sustainable development as the world continues to urbanize, sustainable development largely depends on successful management of urban growth, particularly in low-income and lower-middle-income countries like Ghana (KPMG, 2012). The United Nations (2017) indicates that policies to improve the lives of both rural and urban dwellers are critical to guarantee access to infrastructure and services such as healthcare for all. Leveraging technology is becoming vital to healthcare delivery as it has the potential to deliver quality medical care to not just inaccessible rural dwellers but also urban folks; and, when the right investment is made and implemented correctly, it can be a cost-effective way of expanding access to excellent medical care. After studying this chapter, you should be able to

- describe the various type of technological innovations shaping healthcare delivery in Sub-Sahara Africa
- describe the exact challenges technological innovation addresses in the healthcare sector
- understand the factors impeding technological adoption in healthcare delivery
- appreciate some technological innovations enhancing delivery of healthcare in Africa
- appreciate the differences between direct marketing and online communication

20.2 DIGITAL TECHNOLOGIES FOR IMPROVED HEALTHCARE

The United NationsDevelopment Programme (2013) states that, the financial investment required in healthcare assets only in order to match the growing population of Sub-Sahara Africa is estimated to be $45–$60 billion. However, leveraging mobile and digital technology alone can substantially reduce this figure (Cilliers, Viljoen & Chinyamurindi, 2018). This is because many countries in Sub-Sahara Africa have already achieved a high level of mobile penetration (85 per cent) and internet penetration is also on the rise – mobile devices have become increasingly common and have been adopted in some countries in Sub-Sahara Africa as a force for delivering better healthcare. The benefits of mobile technologies lie in access. Barriers like geographical distance and low resources, which have long prevented millions of people from getting the care they need, are much easier to overcome in the digital age. In fact, there are innumerable ways in which mobile technology can be deployed to improve healthcare access and delivery.

For example, in Uganda, about 27,000 government healthcare givers use a mobile health system called mTRAC to report on medicine stocks across the country (O'Donovan et al., 2018). Another example is the Ebola crises that wrecked West Africa countries like Guinea, Liberia and Sierra Leone in 2014/2015; a WhatsApp system was very instrumental in saving more lives. According to Eilu and Pettersson (2018), the WhatsApp system allowed the BBC to use its platform to share lifesaving health information with people in rural and quarantined areas, as well as ask questions and share stories and local solutions. Additionally, Novartis, a global healthcare company with inroads in Africa has been working on a mobile healthcare (mHealthcare) pilot project in Nairobi and Mombasa to better understand the supply chain cycle and build capabilities to ensure medicines reach those patients in need (Dimitrov, 2016). This system only requires pharmacists to register their patients for survey via SMS. The survey results will assist in mapping out where patients are located in order to redistribute medicines to areas where they are most needed.

20.3 FACTORS INHIBITING THE USE OF DIGITAL TECHNOLOGY IN HEALTHCARE DELIVERY IN AFRICA

Although digital technologies improve the quality of healthcare delivery, eagerness for digital technological innovation among policy-makers, health officials and even healthcare seekers has not matched the uptake and utilization of digital technologies in practice (Kuerbis et al., 2017). Lack of public–private partnership and professional resistance to new technologies are cited as the major barriers to digital technological innovation adoption in healthcare delivery on the African continent (Balfour et al., 2009). Implementing and embedding new technologies of any kind involves complex processes of change at the micro level for professionals and patients and at the meso level for healthcare organizations themselves (Ross et al., 2016). However, in recent times, the principal impediment in adopting digital technological innovation for delivering healthcare in Sub-Sahara Africa is the language barrier. According to Gewald et al. (2017), many digital technologies are programmed in languages not understood by African users. With a holistic understanding and incorporation of the language requirements of Africans, mobile phone applications or digital technologies can accelerate universal health coverage on the continent (Kolltveit et al., 2016). The United Nations defines universal health coverage as all people and communities being able to receive the quality health services they need while also not being exposed by the use of such services to financial hardships.

20.4 THE SPECIFIC CHALLENGES TECHNOLOGY CAN REMEDY

There is much scope for advancement in Africa's healthcare sector. In particular, innovations in mobile and information and communication technology can address many of the challenges that affect excellent healthcare coverage and delivery, such as the following as suggested by Okoroafor et al. (2017):

- Limited availability and unavailability of human resources and the lack of access to health services in rural areas and areas that are termed "hard to reach"
- Poor access to information on prevention practices and lifestyles diseases
- A lack of capacity for training sufficient healthcare practitioners
- Duplication of diagnostic tests
- Lack of coordination between players in the healthcare sector

The above-mentioned innovative scenario may well be the way in which leveraging mobile technology can work to improve the efficiency of healthcare resources and services in Africa (Cunningham, & Cunningham, 2018). More importantly, such advances will reduce the transaction costs (in money and in time) of seeking healthcare interventions (Hannah et al., 2018). This could radically change the balance between demand and supply of the continent's healthcare resources.

20.5 TOP TECHNOLOGICAL TRENDS ADVANCING EFFICIENT HEALTHCARE IN AFRICA

With Africa currently undergoing a digital revolution and with the healthcare sector witnessing unprecedented transformation by virtue of technology (WHO, 2013), areas like telemedicine, drones for delivery healthcare supplies, virtual reality and mobile financial services will continue to shape the future direction of technology in healthcare delivery in Africa. The following sections will discuss these areas and others in detail.

20.5.1 TELEMEDICINE

The World Health Organization (2013) considers telemedicine as the use of telecommunications and information technology, also known as the use of information and communications technology (ICT), to extend access to quality medical care and to provide improved healthcare using remote diagnosis, treatment and health information to underserved isolated rural areas by removing distance and cost barriers. Basically, telemedicine offers healthcare seekers and practitioners an avenue for accessing healthcare that was previously nonexistent (Hannah et al., 2018). Telemedicine technology offers healthcare seekers in inaccessible areas a way to receive the highest quality care, provided they have an internet connection and a smartphone. Telemedicine can save both time and money. With the financial and technical support of Microsoft, Botswana was the first country in Sub-Sahara Africa to launch a telemedicine service (Okoroafor et al., 2017). By this service, healthcare seekers in remote or rural areas where there are no healthcare facilities can receive medical help or consultation through Skype. Doctors can also access high-resolution pictures on the cloud, meaning they can "examine" the patient in real-time, regardless of where the patient is, and make a diagnosis and prescribe treatment straight away (Kolltveit et al., 2016).

Another form of telemedicine is the Bisa technology in Ghana. Bisa is a mobile application that connects a healthcare seeker to a healthcare practitioner (Amankwaa, Abass & Gyasi, 2018). All that is needed is for the healthcare seeker to have a phone with internet connectivity. With Bisa, there are dedicated healthcare practitioners on standby to assist the healthcare seeker (Hannah et al., 2018). This is an advantage to people who need healthcare but are constrained by factors such as poverty, long queues at medical facilities, stigmatization, especially for people who have symptoms of sexually transmitted disease (STDs). Users of the Bisa platform have the option to send health related questions to doctors. In addition, users can send images and audio or video messages about affected areas to doctors and, within a maximum of two hours, feedback is received (Amankwaa, Abass & Gyasi, 2018). The mobile application does not only address the problem of access to medical attention from qualified doctors, but also helps in the prevention and spread of diseases by providing up-to-date healthcare information on the epidemiology and pathogenesis of common diseases (Zainul, Nasrul, & Hafid, 2018). Further, in Ghana, the Novartis Foundation and its partners developed a telemedicine system to expand the reach of medical expertise (Dimitrov, 2016). The system connects frontline health workers with a simple phone call to consultation centres in referral hospitals several hours away, where doctors and specialists with the right expertise are available around-the-clock.

20.5.2 VIRTUAL REALITY

In recent times, virtual reality has been playing a phenomenal role in healthcare (Mantovani et al., 2003). Conventionally, virtual reality is known for gaming and watching videos (Donker et al., 2019). Healthcare organizations can use virtual reality for various purposes including helping healthcare seekers who are in serious pain (Khanal, Gupta & Smith, 2016). It can also help people tolerate medical procedures that are usually very painful. Virtual reality can be used to track body movements, allowing patients to use the movements of their therapy exercises as interactions in a virtual reality game (Gold & Mahrer, 2017). For healthcare professionals, virtual reality can be a teaching tool. It can be used to learn anatomy, practise operations and teach infection control (Donker et al., 2019). The innovation is so important that Facebook has a division for virtual reality. In 2017, Facebook partnered with the Children's Hospital in Los Angeles to build a virtual reality simulation that places medical students and staff in rare trauma situations where split-second decisions determine whether a patient lives or dies (Oculus, 2017). Virtual reality can reproduce training scenarios in true-to-life fashion (Mantovani et al., 2003). These visceral, interactive exercises up the stakes compared to traditional educational tools like non-VR simulations and mannequins (Khanal, Gupta & Smith, 2016). These virtual scenarios based on the case studies from the Children's Hospital in Los Angeles let doctors and students practise and learn in realistic workplace conditions (Oculus, 2017). Healthcare facilities in Africa must invest in virtual reality because of the enormous benefit in improving healthcare delivery.

20.5.3 MOBILE FINANCIAL SERVICE

Lack of financial services is an impediment to the delivery of excellent healthcare (Nisha et al., 2015). The poor are those who suffer the most as lack of access to financial services restricts their ability to save and invest and engage in formal insurance mechanisms (Johnson & Nino-Zarazua, 2011). This situation makes poor households rely on informal risk sharing mechanisms during times of distress (Gertler, Levine & Moretti, 2006). According to Munyegera and Matsumoto (2016) mobile money transfer technology (MMT) has the potential to improve risk sharing in the presence of income shocks, as it allows the mobile phone to store monetary value on the system. This value can be sent or received simply by text (SMS) messages, thus reducing the transaction costs associated with borrowing and lending (Jack & Suri, 2014). Knowing that effective and accessible healthcare has been recognized as important in uplifting living conditions and reducing poverty in Sub-Sahara Africa, credit constraints and the high cost of health services contribute to keeping more than a billion people in low- and middle-income countries from using recommended healthcare (Mobarak & Rosenzweig, 2013). Also, considering the fact that borrowing within informal networks is the main insurance mechanism among the poorer unbanked households, mobile money technology can help them overcome these credit constraints by making it easier to borrow money from family and friends.

20.5.4 Cloud

According to Hossain and Muhammad (2016), by 2020, 75 per cent of communications and engagements with healthcare facilities will occur by mobile devices. Already mobile devices are making massive inroads in the delivery of effective healthcare services in Africa (Hossain & Muhammad, 2016). Examples are the Bisa application software in Ghana and telemedicine in Botswana. In fact, the cloud is taking over and in no time the entire healthcare ecosystem, especially hospitals, will have forgotten the days when a doctor's assistant would have to search a file to access the medical records of a client (Amankwaa, Abass & Gyasi, 2018). Hospitals, healthcare institutions and doctor's offices are now storing patients' medical records in the cloud, with patients able to access test results online at any time (Muhammad et al., 2017). Cloud technology has accelerated the way the healthcare industry in Africa can use or share information across a network.

20.5.5 Internet of Things

The Internet of Things (IOT) is another technological innovation taking the healthcare industry by storm (Muhammad et al., 2017). The Internet of Things is changing all industries and healthcare is no exception (Islam et al., 2015). Internet of Things enabled devices can provide remote data from equipment such as fetal monitors. When information such as temperature, heart rate and glucose level is automatically transmitted in real-time via wearable devices, it enables hospitals to operate more efficiently and patients receive better care. The Internet of Things has already made its mark in the healthcare industry in Sub-Sahara Africa (Bhatt, Dey & Ashour, 2017). For instance, in Nigeria, Vodacom recently partnered with Kaduna State Government to launch a mobile technology based healthcare programme, SMS for Life 2.0, in the state (Dimitrov, 2016). It aims to increase the availability of essential medication by monitoring drug stock levels, improving the delivery of healthcare for citizens who access public health services. The telecoms company concluded the training and deployment of SMS for Life 2.0 in Kaduna, with over 250 facilities using the platform to date. Because of the effectiveness of the initiative in effective healthcare delivery, it is planned to roll out in all 36 states.

20.5.6 Drones for Delivering Healthcare Supplies

In most parts of Africa, it is a herculean task to transport medical supplies such as medicines, blood products and vaccinations from central storage facilities to hospitals and health centres in rural areas where they are needed (Scott & Scott, 2017). This makes handling emergency situations very difficult. Indeed, lack of medical equipment and supplies has often complicated the health delivery challenges confronting the continent. The future of overcoming this problem almost certainly lies with drone innovation (Scott & Scott, 2019). Evidently, Rwanda has a good story to tell as the first country in Sub-Sahara Africa to successfully commercialize drone delivery services to help distribute medical supplies to remote areas. The project was in partnership with US Company Zipline Technology and it was aimed at cutting the delivery time of medical supplies to minutes instead of hours and days. Three years after its successful operation in Rwanda, Ghana followed suit, but on a larger scale. According to Scott and Scott (2017), the drone technology is a significant opportunity for changing the health delivery needs of people in emerging economies. In other words, drone technology is saving lives of people who may have otherwise lost their lives through childbirth, snake bites, accidents and other life-threatening emergencies. In Malawi, drones deliver HIV test kits to the remotest parts of the country.

20.5.7 COUNTERFEIT DRUG DETECTOR

Counterfeit medications claim thousands of lives each year. A 2016 World Health Organization report suggests that between 64,000 and 154,000 people die per year in Sub-Sahara Africa from taking fake anti-malaria medications alone, and other counterfeit drugs claim about 300,000 more lives annually. According to Lehmann, Katerere and Dressman (2018) the human toll of the illicit or counterfeit drug market is staggering. It is estimated that the counterfeit drug trade is a $30 billion operation in Sub-Sahara Africa (WHO, 2016). The rise of counterfeit drugs is attributable to the growth of the pharmaceutical industry over the past few decades making suppliers to flood markets with cheap fake drugs – which may contain improper doses, incorrect or entirely absent active ingredients, or may have been warehoused or stored in substandard conditions and expired (Lartey et al., 2018). In Nigeria, for instance, the rise of fake drugs is closely tied to national crises and associated global trends towards market liberalization and the commodification of health (Klantschnig & Huang, 2018). Drawn by lower prices, pharmacists often purchase and sell substandard drugs without knowing their origin or contents. Data suggest that around one in every ten drugs sold in Sub-Sahara Africa is counterfeit (Klantschnig, & Huang, 2018).

Accordingly, counterfeit or fake pharmaceutical drugs are of great policy importance to international organizations. The World Health Organization set up a programme on poor quality drugs in 2006 and it has focused particularly on Sub-Sahara Africa (International Medical Products Anti-Counterfeiting Taskforce [IMPACT], 2011). In 2010 the UN Office on Drugs and Crime (UNODC) followed suit and highlighted counterfeit drugs for the first time as a major threat in its *Global Crime Threat Assessment*, alongside cocaine trafficking, maritime piracy and human trafficking (UNODC, 2010). Interpol also joined these efforts three years later by signing a pioneering agreement with pharmaceutical corporations to extend its campaign against so-called pharmaceutical crime (Interpol, 2014). Within the last decade, the fight against fake and counterfeit drugs has become a technology issue. Indeed, technological innovation is regarded as the panacea in the fight against counterfeit drugs in Sub-Sahara Africa (Roth et al., 2018). Consequently, there are some remarkable technological innovations that have emerged such as the RxAll app and mPedigree goldkey.

The RxAll app is a scanner that can detect fake drugs in 20 seconds to protect people from this growing issue. The app was developed by a Nigerian who was a victim of fake drug consumption (Evans et al., 2017). The app was built by the application of artificial intelligence to verify the legitimacy of medicines on the market. Along with the nanoscanner, RxAll is linked to a central database that contains the spectral profile of hundreds of drugs. With the handheld nanoscanner, anyone can scan a drug to detect its chemical makeup and feed that data into RxAll's cloud-based platform (Jacobson, Lin & McEwen, 2017). The algorithm embedded in the platform analyzes the drug's spectral profile and cross-checks it against the known profile for the legitimate version of the drug. Once the algorithm has determined if the drug is real or fake – a process that takes just around 20 seconds – the result is sent to the RxAll app. According to the company, the nanoscanner works at a 96.7 per cent accuracy rate.

Presently, RxAll has deployed over 70 devices to the food and drug administration agencies of five countries in Africa, as well as 200 pharmacies across Nigeria and Kenya, where they have detected and prevented the sale of over 60,000 substandard drugs (Icheku, Onianwah & Nwulia, 2018). Whilst the RxAll app is mainly for use by firms, mPedigree's goldkey is for use by both customers and firms. mPedigree employs mobile and web technologies in securing pharmaceutical products against faking, counterfeiting and diversion. The services of mPedigree are deployed by standard authorities in countries such as Nigeria, Kenya, Tanzania, South Africa, Bangladesh, Uganda and many others. The effectiveness of the system is underscored by the fact that mPedigree codes appear on over 500 million drug packets from clients such as AstraZeneca, Roche and Sanofi.

20.5.8 AI Doctor

One of the technologies used is "Artificial Intelligence" (AI), known in the healthcare sector as "AI doctor", which shows great promise for the future of healthcare in Africa. The solution delivered by AI doctor is called CareAi – an AI-powered computing system, anchored on blockchain, that can diagnose infectious diseases, such as malaria, typhoid fever and tuberculosis, within seconds (Roth et al., 2018). The platform is engineered to serve displaced refugees, poor people and those unregistered within traditional healthcare systems. By bringing AI and blockchain together, CareAi uses an anonymous distributed healthcare architecture to deliver health services to patients anonymously (Wahl et al., 2018). If AI systems could handle some of the minor healthcare issues, the available healthcare professionals could focus on the most difficult issues. Indeed, technology could bring parity, removing the need for so many healthcare professionals, and establish functioning service equilibrium in the healthcare sector in Africa.

20.6 DIRECT MARKETING AND ONLINE COMMUNICATIONS

Direct marketing is one of the foremost marketing communication methods and is regarded as highly effective in informing people about products and services as well as building relationships with the target market and potential customers (Park, Paudel & Sene, 2018). It is a tool ideal for contacting both potential and existing customers directly to resolve their unique needs, instead of employing indirect media between the company and the public, such as magazine ads or billboards that are seen by the general public. Direct marketing is different from mass advertising, which is presented to everyone; instead, it is presented only to people who are suspected of having an interest in or need for the company's product, based on information gathered about them.

Direct marketing tools include: telephone calls, catalogues, fliers, newsletters, post cards, text messages, targeted online display ads, emails, coupons and brochures. The sole goal of direct marketing in the healthcare sector is to persuade the public in the direction of the organization's offering (Camilleri, 2018). Notwithstanding the fact that a sale is the ultimate goal, some customers will not be in a position to make a purchase decision instantaneously. But they might make a call for detailed information, visit the company's website, return a postcard requesting a quote, and enter their name and other personal information.

Cell phones have become very important as tools of direct marketing in recent years in healthcare delivery in Sub-Sahara Africa. This claim is behind the fact that over the last decade, cell phone subscription in Africa has surpassed landlines and it is unparalleled how people on the continent have embraced this technology. In most African countries, but especially Rwanda and Ghana, cell phones are changing how healthcare is delivered by providing real-time information on who is dying and from what illness, who is sick and where clusters of diseases are occurring (Patrick et al., 2008). Cell phones are also making it possible for parents to very easily register the birth of their child, thereby reducing the number of children that end up slipping through the net, and allowing governments to more accurately plan interventions, such as vaccination schedules (Mars, 2013).

20.6.1 Reasons Direct Marketing Is Successful

For a direct marketing communication campaign to yield the desired response in the healthcare sector, personalization of the message is paramount. Without a tailor made message, your audience will not fully take it on board and may not understand what you are offering. Even if they do, they may not be moved enough to act upon it. It is therefore important to maximize your return on investment in your direct marketing campaigns by leveraging tailor made messages. Selvakumar, Parkavi, Suganya and Abirami (2019) outline the general reasons direct marketing is more successful:

1. Drafting personalized or tailor made messages makes the recipient feel the message is meant just for them, leading to the feeling of self-importance.
2. It makes economic sense (it is cost-effective) to market to audiences who have been identified as potential customers.
3. Direct marketing contributes to higher return on investment (ROI), considering the fact that the chance of making a sale to a targeted customer list is higher to begin with.
4. It is easy to measure direct marketing activities, since direct marketing uses a number of built-in ways to track the success of each campaign, allowing you to improve with each mail or email cycle.

Three ways to make direct marketing effective in healthcare delivery are:

1. **The "Shiny Objects" condition** – A successful direct marketing initiative includes targeted mailings, personal selling, telemarketing, catalogues and customized offers. These five elements are known as the "shiny objects" (Zarei & Maleki, 2019). Their effectiveness in influencing health behaviour is based on a thorough understanding of your target audience's needs. The "shiny object" mostly attracts the older generations who are not social media freaks.
2. **Content driven online marketing** – The nature of healthcare delivery means that, without a clear-cut message on customer need and benefit, the public will not show interest in your offering (Zarei & Maleki, 2019). When a healthcare institution is known for communicating value (rich content) in its blog, informational webinars, white papers and through direct emails, the public holds its members in high esteem as experts and thought leaders. Online marketing has become powerful at influencing health behaviour largely because of the emergence of social media tools such as Facebook, Instagram, Twitter, LinkedIn and many others. Facebook, Twitter, Instagram and LinkedIn have a global active followership of over 3.5 billion people and are key to enhancing healthy living through online health information engagement (Benetoli, Chen & Aslani, 2018)
3. **Blending Digital and Direct Marketing which guarantees desirable outcomes** – The relevance of today's healthcare institutions would be nil without their ability to integrate the strength of both online and offline marketing campaigns (Andreasen, Goodstein & Wilson, 2005). Content in traditional media (offline), such as the newspapers, is seen by audiences as more credible and they often seek it out to confirm or reinforce what they have seen on digital media (online). Customer engagement and loyalty are at the core of a healthcare institution's ability to use both digital and direct marketing techniques. With both techniques, one can be assured of effectively reaching out to the socially adept and information-driven prospects.

20.6.2 ONLINE COMMUNICATION

Online communication is here to stay and should form an integral part of any communication plan, most especially deployed together with a direct marketing communication plan (Dixon, 2010). Online communication is defined as the ways in which people, as well as computers, can communicate with each other over a computer network, such as the Internet. These ways embrace posting comments on websites, such as blogs, social networking sites, filling out online forms, forums, instant messaging (IM), chat rooms, and email.

The online communication tool most widely employed by companies, government agencies and protected areas are specialized apps, Facebook, Twitter, YouTube, blogs and texting. These examples are collectively called social media (Kaplan & Haenlein, 2010). Social media, however, in the healthcare sector can be challenging and, like any communication tool, its use requires careful planning. In this scenario, it is relevant to keep in mind that not all online communication tools should be used just because they are fashionable. Among the advantages of online communication, however, are real-time communication and the facts that the response time is less and it represents savings in management.

Using online communication based technologies such as secure messaging, videoconferencing, and remote physiological monitoring is critical in improving the patient–provider relationship and the quality of healthcare (Dixon, 2010). Evidence in Sub-Sahara Africa suggests that patients and practitioners are using online communication tools to deliver stupendous primary healthcare but success is most often impeded by difficulties in integrating electronic health records and payment models that support implementation and growth (Watkins et al., 2018).

Notwithstanding these challenges, patients are committed to using technology to work together with healthcare practitioners online. Providing financial and institutional support for the use of these technologies will incite healthcare providers to embrace them more rapidly, leading to the delivery of efficient healthcare services in Sub-Sahara Africa (van Rensburg, Bhugra & Saxena, 2018).

A practical example of how online communication technologies are improving primary healthcare in Sub-Sahara Africa is the aforementioned Bisa app in Ghana. As presented on the company's website,

> Bisa is a mobile application that allows users with an android, Iphone or Windows phone to directly interact with medical practitioners without being physically present at the hospital. This is an advantage to people who need medical care and advice but are not able to visit the hospital for various reasons like poverty, long queues at the hospital, the fear of stigmatization, especially for people who have symptoms of STDs makes them embarrassed to seek the needed treatment.

20.7 CONCLUSIONS

Currently, healthcare in Sub-Sahara Africa is inefficient, logistically constrained, bedevilled with social infrastructure issues, error-prone and of variable quality. Information technology has the potential to significantly improve healthcare delivery by bringing decision support to the point of care, by providing vital links and closing "open loop" systems, and by allowing routine quality measurement to become reality. Achieving this potential will be a herculean task, and success is far from guaranteed, but it is possible with a clear-cut, inclusive partnership strategy. If it is to occur, a public–private partnership is needed to bring the required investment to galvanize this change, possibly in large part from central government, with development of a national health information infrastructure representing the most fundamental strategy.

REFERENCES

Amankwaa, G., Abass, K., & Gyasi, R. M. (2018). In-school adolescents' knowledge, access to and use of sexual and reproductive health services in Metropolitan Kumasi, Ghana. *Journal of Public Health, 26*(4), 443–451.

Andreasen, A. R., Goodstein, R. C., & Wilson, J. W. (2005). Transferring "marketing knowledge" to the nonprofit sector. *California Management Review, 47*(4), 46–67.

Balfour, D. C., Evans, S., Januska, J., Lee, H. Y., Lewis, S. J., Nolan, S. R., ... & Thapar, K. (2009). Health information technology: Results from a roundtable discussion. *Journal of Managed Care Pharmacy, 15*(1 Supp A), 10–17.

Benetoli, A., Chen, T. F., & Aslani, P. (2018). Consumer perceptions of using social media for health purposes: Benefits and drawbacks. *Health Informatics Journal*, 1460458218796664.

Bhatt, C., Dey, N., & Ashour, A. S. (Eds.). (2017). *Internet of things and big data technologies for next generation healthcare*. Springer.

Camilleri, M. A. (2018). *Travel marketing, tourism economics and the airline product: An introduction to theory and practice*. Springer.

Cilliers, L., Viljoen, K. L. A., & Chinyamurindi, W. T. (2018). A study on students' acceptance of mobile phone use to seek health information in South Africa. *Health Information Management Journal, 47*(2), 59–69.

Cunningham, P., & Cunningham, M. (2018). mHealth4Afrika: Challenges when co-designing a cross-border primary healthcare solution. In *2018 IEEE International Symposium on Technology and Society (ISTAS)* (pp. 32–36). IEEE.

Dimitrov, D. V. (2016). Medical internet of things and big data in healthcare. *Healthcare Informatics Research, 22*(3), 156–163.

Dixon, R. F. (2010). Enhancing primary care through online communication. *Health Affairs, 29*(7), 1364–1369.

Donker, T., Cornelisz, I., van Klaveren, C., van Straten, A., Carlbring, P., Cuijpers, P., & van Gelder, J. L. (2019). Effectiveness of self-guided app-based virtual reality cognitive behavior therapy for acrophobia: A randomized clinical trial. *JAMA Psychiatry.*

Eilu, E., & Pettersson, J. S. (2018). Mobile social media for preventing the Ebola virus disease spread in Liberia. In S. Paiva (Ed.), *Mobile solutions and their usefulness in everyday life* (pp. 173–188). Springer.

Gao, Y., Li, H., & Luo, Y. (2015). An empirical study of wearable technology acceptance in healthcare. *Industrial Management & Data Systems, 115*(9), 1704–1723.

Gertler, P., Levine, D. I., & Moretti, E. (2006). Is social capital the capital of the poor? The role of family and community in helping insure living standards against health shocks. *CESifo Economic Studies, 52*(3), 455–499.

Gold, J. I., & Mahrer, N. E. (2017). Is virtual reality ready for prime time in the medical space? A randomized control trial of pediatric virtual reality for acute procedural pain management. *Journal of Pediatric Psychology, 43*(3), 266–275.

Hannah, C. E., Freese, M. J., Beebout, S., Kakale, Y., & Wanat, K. A. (2018). Recommendations for the use of telemedicine in severely under-resourced settings: Results from a pilot study in Niamey, Niger. *International Journal of Dermatology, 57*(12), e151–e153.

Hossain, M. S., & Muhammad, G. (2016). Cloud-assisted industrial internet of things (iiot): Enabled framework for health monitoring. *Computer Networks, 101*, 192–202.

Icheku, V., Onianwah, I. F., & Nwulia, A. (2018). Comparative cross-sectional quantitative study of health status among consumers of bitter kola in Igbuzor community living in Oshilmili North Local Government area of Delta state. *Universal Journal of Food and Nutrition Science, 6*(1), 28–40.

International Medical Products Anti-Counterfeiting Taskforce (IMPACT). 2011. *Facts, activities, documents developed by the Assembly and the working groups of IMPACT, 2006–2010*. Rome: Italian Medicines Agency.

Interpol. 2014. *Pharmaceutical crime and organized criminal groups*. Lyon: Interpol.

Islam, S. R., Kwak, D., Kabir, M. H., Hossain, M., & Kwak, K. S. (2015). The internet of things for health care: a comprehensive survey. *IEEE Access, 3*, 678–708.

Jack, W., & Suri, T. (2014). Risk sharing and transactions costs: Evidence from Kenya's mobile money revolution. *American Economic Review, 104*(1), 183–223.

Jacobson, J., Lin, C. Z., & McEwen, R. (2017). Aging with technology: Seniors and mobile connections. *Canadian Journal of Communication, 42*(2).

Johnson, S., & Nino-Zarazua, M. (2011). Financial access and exclusion in Kenya and Uganda. *The Journal of Development Studies, 47*(3), 475–496.

Kaplan, A. M., & Haenlein, M. (2010). Users of the world, unite! The challenges and opportunities of Social Media. *Business Horizons, 53*(1), 59–68.

Kern, S. E., & Jaron, D. (2003). Healthcare technology, economics, and policy: An evolving balance. *IEEE Engineering in Medicine and Biology Magazine: the Quarterly Magazine of the Engineering in Medicine & Biology Society, 22*(1), 16–19.

Khanal, P., Gupta, A., & Smith, M. (2016). Virtual worlds in healthcare. In A. Gupta, V. L. Patel & R. A. Greenes (Eds.), *Advances in Healthcare Informatics and Analytics* (pp. 233–248). Cham, Switzerland: Springer.

Klantschnig, G., & Huang, C. (2018). Fake drugs: Health, wealth and regulation in Nigeria. *Review of African Political Economy*, 1–17.

KPMG. (2012). The state of healthcare in Africa. *The Economist*. www.blog.kpmgafrica.com/state-healthcare-in-africa-report/.

Lartey, P. A., Graham, A. E., Lukulay, P. H., & Ndomondo-Sigonda, M. (2018). Pharmaceutical sector development in Africa: Progress to date. *Pharmaceutical Medicine, 32*(1), 1–11.

Lehmann, A., Katerere, D. R., & Dressman, J. (2018). Drug quality in South Africa: A field test. *Journal of Pharmaceutical Sciences, 107*(10), 2720–2730.

Mantovani, F., Castelnuovo, G., Gaggioli, A., & Riva, G. (2003). Virtual reality training for health-care professionals. *CyberPsychology & Behavior, 6*(4), 389–395.

Mars, M. (2013). Telemedicine and advances in urban and rural healthcare delivery in Africa. *Progress in Cardiovascular Diseases, 56*(3), 326–335.

Mobarak, A. M., & Rosenzweig, M. R. (2013). Informal risk sharing, index insurance, and risk taking in developing countries. *American Economic Review*, *103*(3), 375–380.

Munyegera, G. K., & Matsumoto, T. (2016). Mobile money, remittances, and household welfare: Panel evidence from rural Uganda. *World Development*, *79*, 127–137.

Nisha, N., Iqbal, M., Rifat, A., & Idrish, S. (2015). Mobile health services: A new paradigm for health care systems. *International Journal of Asian Business and Information Management (IJABIM)*, *6*(1), 1–17.

Oculus (2017). VR's healthcare revolution: Transforming medical training. www.oculus.com/blog/vrs-healthcare-revolution-transforming-medical-training/?locale=en_US. Accessed on June 14, 2019.

O'Donovan, J., Kabali, K., Taylor, C., Chukhina, M., Kading, J. C., Fuld, J., & O'Neil, E. (2018). The use of low-cost Android tablets to train community health workers in Mukono, Uganda, in the recognition, treatment and prevention of pneumonia in children under five: A pilot randomised controlled trial. *Human Resources for Health*, *16*(1), 49.

Park, T., Paudel, K., & Sene, S. (2018). Sales impacts of direct marketing choices: Treatment effects with multinomial selectivity. *European Review of Agricultural Economics*, *45*(3), 433–453.

Patrick, K., Griswold, W. G., Raab, F., & Intille, S. S. (2008). Health and the mobile phone. *American Journal of Preventive Medicine*, *35*(2), 177–181.

Ross, J., Stevenson, F., Lau, R., & Murray, E. (2016). Factors that influence the implementation of e-health: A systematic review of systematic reviews (an update). *Implementation Science*, *11*(1), 146.

Roth, L., Nalim, A., Turesson, B., & Krech, L. (2018). Global landscape assessment of screening technologies for medicine quality assurance: Stakeholder perceptions and practices from ten countries. *Globalization and Health*, *14*(1), 43.

Scott, J., & Scott, C. (2017). Drone delivery models for healthcare. In *Proceedings of the 50th Hawaii International Conference on System Sciences*.

Scott, J. E., & Scott, C. H. (2019). Models for drone delivery of medications and other healthcare items. In *Unmanned aerial vehicles: Breakthroughs in research and practice* (pp. 376–392). IGI Global.

Selvakumar, S., Parkavi, R., Suganya, R., & Abirami, A. M. (2019). Big data analytics in healthcare sector. In *Machine learning techniques for improved business analytics* (pp. 94–106). IGI Global.

United Nations. (2017) World population prospects: Key findings and advance tables: The 2017 Revision. Department of Economic and Social Affairs, Population Division, Working Paper No. ESA/P/WP/248. United Nations.

United Nations Development Programme (2013). Impact investment in Africa: Trends, constraints and opportunities. www.undp.org/content/dam/undp/library/corporate/Partnerships/Private%20Sector/Impact%20Investment%20in%20Africa/Impact%20Investment%20in%20Africa_Trends,%20Constraints%20and%20Opportunities.pdf. Accessed on July 4, 2019.

United Nations Office on Drugs and Crime. (2010). *The globalisation of crime: A transnational crime threat assessment*. Vienna: UNODC.

van Rensburg, B. J., Bhugra, D., & Saxena, S. (2018). WPA–WHO Africa Mental Health Forum: Recommendations and position statement. *World Psychiatry*, *17*(1), 116.

Wahl, B., Cossy-Gantner, A., Germann, S., & Schwalbe, N. R. (2018). Artificial intelligence (AI) and global health: How can AI contribute to health in resource-poor settings?. *BMJ Global Health*, *3*(4), e000798.

Watkins, J. O. T. A., Goudge, J., Gómez-Olivé, F. X., & Griffiths, F. (2018). Mobile phone use among patients and health workers to enhance primary healthcare: A qualitative study in rural South Africa. *Social Science & Medicine*, *198*, 139–147.

World Health Organization. (2013). *Utilizing eHealth solutions to improve national health systems in African region*. World Health Organisation, Africa, Report AFR/RC63/9.

World Health Organization (2016). World Health Statistics 2016: Monitoring health for the SDGs. www.who.int/gho/publications/world_health_statistics/2016/en/. Accessed June 14, 2019.

Zainul, Z., Nasrul, N., & Hafid, F. (2018). Monitoring health service satisfaction in hospital via smartphone in central Sulawesi. *Jurnal Kesehatan Prima*, *12*(2), 112–123.

Zarei, A., & Maleki, F. (2019). Asian medical marketing, a review of factors affecting Asian medical tourism development. *Journal of Quality Assurance in Hospitality & Tourism*, *20*(1), 1–15.

21 Technology and Social Media in Healthcare Delivery

Raphael Odoom and Douglas Opoku Agyeman

21.1 INTRODUCTION

I think every healthcare institution should be using social media in their practices. This is how communication is happening right now. As a paediatric provider, you're not just communicating in the exam room, but ideally, you're being involved in your community, making your community a better place for children. It really becomes global with these technologies.

(a paediatrician, cited in Campbell et al., 2016, p. 8)

Technology has progressed enormously in the twenty-first century work environment. Modern technological extensions such as social networking sites, e-communication, emailing systems and websites have advanced rapidly in the last decades. These technologies have evolved rapidly due to their affordability and portability, effective R&D and universal availability. There is also an evolution of the market place to accommodate these technologies owing to high consumer demands and expectations. Thus, technology such as social media, for instance, touches our everyday lives in many different ways: from work-related usage, such as instant messaging with customers, to relaxation activities such as web entertainment and online friendships. As a consequence, technology has become an indispensable tool for individuals and a strategic device for firms that desire to survive, develop and perform well in the competitive business environment (Annam, 2002).

What about the health sector? Like other sectors, the healthcare sector is a dynamic and ever-changing environment. The dynamic nature of the health sector has been occasioned by a revolution in health service technologies necessitating a deeper understanding of customers' expectations, behaviour intentions and service choices. Rising healthcare costs, increased illness complexity, increased number of patient concerns per office visit, and a growing shortage of physicians are contributing factors to the healthcare technology revolution (State Health Access Data Assistance Centre [Shadac], 2011). For instance, a report from the Massachusetts Institute of Technology shows that the technology revolution is creating opportunities in healthcare delivery, the impact of which is not fully understood in the healthcare arena (Halevi et al., 2018).

This has sparked a lot of debate concerning the role of technologies such as social media and other healthcare technologies including telemedicine, e-health records and e-health communication. This discourse is no different in sub-Saharan Africa, where studies show that less than 50 per cent of Africans have access to modern health technologies, arguing that the healthcare sector in sub-Saharan Africa needs to leverage digital technologies (Abegaz, 2018). Advocates perceive that these technologies are creating efficiencies and driving significant innovations in healthcare delivery services. For instance, e-health technologies are used to share information between providers and patients, provide personalised consumer self-management resources, build social support networks for providers and consumers, and deliver personalised and accessible health information to consumers (Baur & Kanaan, 2006). Social media technology, for instance, can also be used to establish contact with patients, or for customer service and support, the provision of news and information, patient education and advertising new services. Patients can also benefit from the use of social media technology through accessing health information, education and tracking personal records.

On the other hand, technological pessimists have labelled the foregoing healthcare technology expressions as hype (Kanter, 2012), citing factors such as dissemination of medical information of poor quality, job losses and abuse of information rights (Kanter, 2012). Such scholars further perceive that social media platforms can be distracting and cannot replace face-to-face interactions when it comes to the truly meaningful actions that build strong relationships between healthcare providers and patients. As a result, many healthcare institutions had previously avoided the use of social media, and even restricted their employees from using it (Bock & Rosen, 2017). Despite these negative perspectives towards technology applications in healthcare service delivery, it may be impossible for healthcare institutions in the twenty-first century to ensure enhanced and effective healthcare delivery while side-lining these technologies.

It is important to note that it is not the technology per se but the way it is being conceptualised against realities in different contexts that is the problem. As Noeleen Hezyer of the UN Development Fund for Women puts it, "there are tremendous opportunities if we know how to shape this technology and if we know how to intervene" (Fuchs, 2003). Hence, healthcare providers and organisations are increasingly realising that healthcare technologies such as mobile health, telehealth and social media applications provide specific opportunities to serve the public, patients and physicians by providing healthcare information to patients in distant places. These technologies also benefit the health provider through awareness creation and brand enhancement. Despite doubts in generalising this claim (Lim, 2016) in particular, there is a need to examine how the power of healthcare technologies is appropriately leveraged by the healthcare providers for their personal benefit as well as for contributing to the national and global healthcare needs. As modern societies adapt to the presence of internet enabled technologies such as social media platforms and become increasingly connected through them, their use in healthcare delivery and consumption is expected (Halevi et al., 2018).

The proliferation of technologies in the last decades has influenced the healthcare environment, but to date authors have suggested that there is a lack of understanding of the role of these technologies in the healthcare industry (Kumar, 2017). Healthcare technologies have not been consistently adapted to drive reorganisation and reform of healthcare delivery. Compared to other sectors, the healthcare system is far from taking full advantage of the latest trends and advancements in technology to deliver health services, education, and research (Alshakhs & Alanzi, 2018). In sub-Saharan Africa (SSA), there are many sites on the web providing health information to seekers, and even organisations providing online health services. For instance, in Kenya, the African Medical and Research Foundation has developed computers and internet systems in local communities where local healthcare professionals can provide healthcare services (Abegaz, 2018). However, very few healthcare organisations integrate healthcare technologies as part of the comprehensive and personalised health experience that health consumers are seeking (Campbell & Craig, 2014).

This chapter discusses the role or opportunities that social media and healthcare technology can offer to the healthcare system, through innovation and improvement. It highlights some types of healthcare technologies that will guide research and development, along with some current examples. Some action steps are suggested to accelerate the adoption of technology into routine health practices in sub-Saharan Africa.

21.2 CONCEPT OF TECHNOLOGY

Technology is generally accepted as science or knowledge put to practical use to solve problems or invent useful tools (Tihanyi & Roath, 2002). Finding what constitutes the best definition of technology is a serious problem due to different paradigms and perspectives. As such, a useful starting point in understanding the concept of technology is to consider it from the context of this chapter, which is the health sector. The World Health Organization explains that technology is the "application of organised knowledge and skills in the form of devices, medicines, vaccines, procedures and systems developed to solve a health problem and improve quality of lives" (Wahab et al., 2012, p. 33). This encompasses pharmaceuticals, organisational systems, procedures and devices used in the healthcare sector, as well as computer- and internet-supported applications and platforms used by both healthcare providers and patients. Significantly, these technologies involve standardised physical objects, as well as traditional and designed social means and methods to treat or care for patients as well as communicating with patients.

In the health sector, it is strongly argued that the concept of technology should not be viewed only in terms of physical constituents or technology that is embodied in the product, but as being also associated with the informational component which comprises clinical procedures, administrative rules, marketing and quality control (Bozeman, 2000). This suggests that if technology is to be considered as information, then it is generally applicable and easy to reproduce and reuse. Similarly, Van De Belt et al. (2010) proposed that health technology is differentiated knowledge about particular applications, tacit, usually uncodified and largely cumulative within health institutions. Thus, health technology is considered as the health institutions' "intangible assets" which form the basis of an institution's competitiveness and will generally discharge under special conditions. Nevertheless, it is important to note that health technology can contain information which is not easily reproducible or transferable. This is because valuable technological knowledge, which is the intangible assets of the firm, is a learning process which needs to be assimilated and internalised. In effect, two essential components can be distinguished from these technology definitions: (1) "knowledge" or strategy; and (2) "getting things done" (Tihanyi & Roath, 2002).

Apart from understanding the concept of technology, the classification of technology is also essential in explaining the various kinds of technologies that are embodied in the product, health delivery process and human capital of the firm. Geisler (1999) in his extensive review of health technology literature classified technology from four different perspectives, namely: technology as artefact, technology as management and information, technology as a process and technology as a dimension of the organisation. With regard to technology as artefact, Geisler proposes that "technology" includes specific tools, solutions and devices (e.g. a syringe, a drug, a diagnostic reagent) used in healthcare delivery. Geisler deliberates on these artefacts as the physical components of health technology. Most analyses of the magnitude or intensity of use of medical technology concentrate on the first perspective (that is, technology as artefact) or a physical perspective on technology. The physical perspective lends itself to measurement, impact analysis and economic evaluation. However, the physical perspective also tends to restrict both the understanding of the nature of technology and the assessment of its effects from a range of different perspectives.

On the other hand, technology as management and information describes information, intelligence, techniques, methods and approaches (e.g. health informatics), and methods for creating knowledge (e.g. clinical trials, systematic reviews of evidence). These help in saving time and cost, as well as improving the efficiency of operations in the health sector. The last two perspectives – technology as a process and technology as a dimension – explain technology as assemblages of machinery, and assemblages of machinery and expertise respectively. This presupposes that technology in the health sector is always associated with achieving certain health-related tasks, resolving certain health problems, completing certain tasks using particular skills, applying knowledge and exploiting assets. Table 21.1 provides a summary of the perspectives of health technology.

21.3 TECHNOLOGICAL INNOVATIONS IN HEALTHCARE DELIVERY

The scope of technological innovation continues to grow and is constantly transforming the global industry. In healthcare, technological innovations are increasingly playing a role in almost all processes: from patient registration to data monitoring; from lab tests to self-care tools. For instance,

TABLE 21.1
Perspectives of Health Technology

Perspective	What Health Technology Contains
Technology as artefact	Tools
	Solutions
	Devices
	Processes
Technology as management and information	Information
	Intelligence
	Techniques
	Methods
	Approaches
Technology as a process	Stages of the innovation process
Technology as a dimension of the organisation	Core competencies
	Basic strengths of the organisation
	Dreams and aspirations

Source: Geisler's four perspectives of health technology (Fett, 2008).

significant technological breakthroughs such as nano technology, brain implants, telemedicine, e-health records, network sensors, are just a few of the potentially transformative developments already under way. In the last decade, the use of social media technology in healthcare has been rapidly increasing. Healthcare institutions, particularly hospitals and other specialised clinics, are using social media to enhance relationships with patients, answer queries about practices, promote health awareness campaigns and perform community outreach services. This section discusses some technological advancements in healthcare that have emerged over the last two decades, as well as the benefits and disadvantages they bring to both health providers and patients.

21.3.1 SOCIAL MEDIA AND HEALTHCARE

While social media sites or applications are not new technologies themselves, they have only recently been introduced into the healthcare delivery systems and setting, augmenting wireless devices such as beepers and overhead pagers. The social media concept consists of a group of applications that facilitate the creation and exchange of user-generated content over the internet. The phenomenon has taken the world by storm, revolutionising the way we communicate as a society, including the medical and healthcare community where the sheer range of medical and healthcare-related information is prominent (Dahl, 2018; Luarn & Chiu, 2015). In fact, these sites are evolving to become the prevalent ways employed by healthcare professionals to reach out to consumers and find new ways to deliver service.

Healthcare professionals often engage social media applications such as LinkedIn and Twitter for professional purposes such as collaborating with other professionals and colleagues. Some sophisticated sites even offer instant chats with nurses and doctors about medical issues and reminders for people to get regularly needed tests and vaccines. Other platforms rising in popularity are Doximity and Sermo, which are designed exclusively for licensed physicians seeking to network and collaborate in a secure and HIPAA-compliant professional setting (HIPAA being Healthcare Insurance Portability and Accountability) (Halevi et al., 2018). Healthcare professionals such as clinicians also use social media applications such as Facebook, Twitter and LinkedIn to create opportunities for networking and collaborations, and to seek peer advice. Hospitals are increasingly using social media networks for promotional purposes and to gauge consumer experiences with their organisations. On the other hand, they have also allowed patients to connect with their clinicians to seek advice and more immediate responses to their health problems, thus changing the dynamics of patient–doctor communications (Halevi et al., 2018).

Further, patients use social media applications to understand medical conditions and make health decisions, including selecting a doctor, researching courses of treatment and finding communities composed of those with similar diagnoses. Health institutions are even now employing social media applications to recruit patients for clinical trials and these have proven to be more effective in terms of their wide reach, cost effectiveness and usability. Consequently, it behoves other healthcare providers to be active on social media and provide accurate and reliable information, connect with patients and implement marketing techniques where applicable.

21.3.2 Electronic Health Records (EHRs)

As the technologies have emerged, the introduction of electronic health records (EHRs) to replace the conventional paper-based approach of recording patient records has been a game changer for the healthcare system (Kabene & Wolf, 2011). For over a decade, the healthcare system had operated disparate systems. For instance, they had one system that examined pharmacy, one that performed orders and one that undertook documentation. Integrating these systems into a single platform, or at least a more structured platform, has allowed more integrated and efficient care for patients and many allied healthcare professionals. The benefits of EHR technology have been categorised to include: lower healthcare costs, enhanced patient care, and ease of work flow (Kabene & Wolf, 2011). For instance, since paper-based records are location specific, patient information contained in one record may differ substantially from records kept by another provider.

The digitalisation of medical records has streamlined the process of accessing information for healthcare providers. They have used electronic health records for scheduling patients' appointments, updating patient records with diagnostic codes, and submitting medical forms. Digitalisation also reduces the risk of errors in patient data and financial details. Accessing patient records digitally can be done in an instant and they can be viewed via portable devices, increasing efficiency and productivity. This contributes to enhanced patient care by bridging the geographic and temporal gaps that exist when several physicians who are geographically dispersed treat the same patient. Thus, it is highly important that all healthcare professionals become cognisant of past and current medical histories when one patient is treated by several healthcare providers.

With regard to lower healthcare costs, a study from the University of Michigan in October 2018, for instance, found that the shift from paper-based records to electronic health records reduces the cost of outpatient treatment by 3 per cent. This is because EHR can automatically alert the treating physician to potential issues, such as allergies to certain medicines, which is extremely useful for doctors in order to enhance patient care. In effect, this ease of access to vital medical information improves the speed and reliability of service delivery, centralisation and efficiency of patient information, and utilisation as a data and population health tool for the future (Kabene & Wolf, 2011). However, in spite of the immense opportunities and efficiencies that EHRs can potentially offer, their implementation into existing healthcare systems poses some potentially deterrent and serious risks, such as confidentiality breaches, technological breakdowns and incompatibilities. Hence, electronic records should not be hastily incorporated into healthcare systems without legitimate precautionary measures.

21.3.3 mHealth

The rapid growth in the use of smartphones has opened a new world of opportunities for use in behavioural healthcare. Mobile health is freeing healthcare devices of wires and cords and enabling physicians and patients alike to check on healthcare processes on the go (Malvey, & Slovensky, 2014). An R&R Market Research report estimates that the global mHealth market will reach $20.7

billion by the close of the year 2019, indicating it is only becoming bigger and more prevalent. Smartphones and tablets allow healthcare providers to more freely access and send information (Jayanthi, 2014). Mobile phone software applications (apps) are also available for a variety of useful tasks to include symptom assessment, psychoeducation, resource location and tracking of treatment progress. Physicians and service providers can also use mHealth tools for orders, documentation and simply to reach more information when not with patients. However, mHealth is not only about wireless connectivity. It has also become a tool that allows patients to become active players in their treatment by connecting communication with biometrics (Malvey, & Slovensky, 2014). Significantly, mHealth has the opportunity to take healthcare monitoring out of the office and out of the lab and basically make it part of your life. In sub-Saharan Africa, use of mobile phone subscription had increased to about 700 million as at 2016. The large population of mobile subscribers presents opportunities for healthcare outfits to employ social media and technology applications to tracking and eliminating some diseases, though these opportunities are not without challenges (Abegaz, 2018).

21.3.4 TELEMEDICINE/TELEHEALTH

Healthcare delivery organisations are advancing efforts to prevent the prevalence of chronic disease among an ageing population (Steventon et al., 2012). Increasingly, telehealth has been employed as one possible approach to this problem. This healthcare technology of "telehealth" involves the remote exchange of data between a patient and healthcare professionals as part of the patient's diagnosis and healthcare management such as monitoring of blood pressure and blood glucose. These technologies allow patients to better understand their health conditions by providing tools for self-monitoring; these encourage better self-management of health problems, and alert professional support if devices signal a problem. As a consequence, telehealth promises better quality and more appropriate care for each patient, as well as more efficient use of healthcare resources by reducing the need for expensive hospital care. The relevance of this technology is justified by its ability to recover the investment, particularly in rural settings where there is no access to the same resources metropolitan areas may have. A large-scale study published in *CHEST* journal shows that patients in an intensive care unit equipped with telehealth services were discharged from the ICU 20 per cent more quickly and saw a 26 per cent lower mortality rate than patients in a regular ICU (Steventon et al., 2012).

In sub-Saharan African countries such as Kenya, Ethiopia, Tanzania or Uganda, several sorts of telemedicine equipment such as digital cameras, e-health scanners and sophisticated computers systems have been provided by Computer Aid International to support healthcare delivery in the region. Adam Higman, vice president of Soyring Consulting in St. Petersburg, asserts that "while telemedicine is not necessarily a new development, it is a growing field, and its scope of possibility is expanding" (Jayanthi, 2014). The cost benefits of telehealth cannot be ignored either. For example, Indianapolis-based health insurer WellPoint rolled out a video consultation programme in February 2013 whereby patients could receive a full assessment through a video chat with a physician. Claims are automatically generated, eliminating time out of office costs for healthcare employers and employees.

Undoubtedly, many healthcare technologies have emerged strongly into the healthcare delivery of developed and some developing nations, especially in SSA. Among these technologies are sensors and wearable technology which could be used to detect and send an alert to a care provider when a patient falls down. Another technology is real-time locating services which are used as tracking systems. They gather data on areas and departments which have high potential for efficiency and utilisation. There is also pharmacogenomics/genome sequencing which is a personalised medical service.

21.4 ROLE OF TECHNOLOGY AND SOCIAL MEDIA IN HEALTHCARE

The contribution of technology to healthcare can be quite subjective, because it is usually diffi-cult to answer the questions of who sets the goals and to whom the outcomes are desirable or not (Heeks, 2002). Having this subjectivity in mind, this chapter does not intend to judge the outright success or failure of health technologies, but to assess their potential to create opportunity, effi-ciency, security and enhanced patient care.

One of the most important, and highly debated, elements of our society is the quality of health-care available to patients. Undeniably, a driving force behind quality healthcare is the adoption of technology that enables healthcare providers to provide better patient care (Thimbleby, 2013). For instance, medical scientists and physicians are constantly conducting research and testing new procedures to help prevent, diagnose and cure diseases, as well as developing new drugs and medi-cines that can lessen symptoms or treat ailments. Thus, through the use of technology in medical research, scientists have been able to examine diseases like malaria and polio on a cellular level and produce antibodies against them. Specifically, technological innovations in the healthcare industry continue to provide healthcare professionals with new ways to improve the quality of care delivered to their patients and improve the state of global healthcare. This is because, through the integration of technology with areas such as disease prevention, surgical procedures, better access to informa-tion, and medical telecommunications, the medical industry and patients around the world continue to benefit.

Improving quality of life is one of the main benefits of integrating these innovations into medi-cine. Medical technologies such as minimally invasive surgeries, better monitoring systems, and more comfortable scanning equipment are allowing patients to spend less time in recovery and more time enjoying a healthy life. Again, the integration of medical equipment technology and tel-ehealth has also created robotic surgeries during which, in some cases, physicians do not even need to be in the operating room with a patient when the surgery is performed. Instead, surgeons can operate out of their "home base", and patients can have the procedure done in a hospital or clinic close their own hometown, eliminating the hassles and stress of health-related travel. With other robotic surgeries, the surgeon is still in the room, operating the robotic devices, but the technology allows for a minimally invasive procedure that leaves patients with less scarring and significantly less recovery time.

A report by Pew Research Centre (2014) showed that 80 per cent of patients used the internet to search for and retrieve medical and healthcare-related information. Other research reports, such as those by Frost and Sullivan and QuantiaMD, highlighted that at least one social media technol-ogy was used by 87–90 per cent of physicians for personal reasons, with a further 67–75 per cent opting for more professional postings (Telecare Services Association, 2012). With the widespread availability of and accessibility to the internet in modern times, social media are now increasingly being utilised as platforms for engaging in and contributing to serious discussion and information retrieval on medical and health issues.

Technology also promotes participatory medicine. Participatory medicine is a movement which allows physicians and patients to digitally connect and take an active role in managing health. The technology-enabled infrastructure is changing the way that physicians and patients engage in med-ical and healthcare. For instance, social media technologies such as participatory medicine allow healthcare givers and patients to connect and interact with other physicians and patients to obtain timely solutions to health problems at lower costs (Eysenbach, 2008). Social media technologies are thus useful resources in searching for, learning and sharing myriad medical and health-related information, which consequently increases the sense of engagement in personal care (Chou et al., 2009). It also offers physicians an ideal platform for real-time collaboration and sharing of new ideas, past experiences, and current medical and healthcare research (Antheunis et al., 2013).

Again, participatory medicine through social media contributes to continuous improvement in patient outcomes because physicians are able to engage in and contribute to real-time knowledge advancement conveniently as well as to facilitate a more rapid adoption of the best and most up-to-date medical and healthcare practices. For patients, social media provides an opportunity to engage in more effective and efficient self-management (Antheunis et al., 2013). For instance, patient networking sites, such as PatientsLikeMe in the USA, Health Unlocked in the UK, and HealthShare in Australia, allow patients with similar medical conditions and healthcare needs to connect and interact with each other, discuss their conditions and needs, make more informed decisions when selecting physicians and medical treatments, and improve self-monitoring.

Technology in healthcare delivery also improves quality of services. Current processes in medical and healthcare are beginning to identify opportunities to include the patient's voice more prominently in quality improvement initiatives (Kivits, 2006). Patients and caregivers maintain a constant presence on social media channels, where they can openly share and discuss issues pertaining to their past and current experiences with medical and healthcare services (Read & Guistini, 2011). Those with and without experiences in a particular health problem often suggest new ways to make patient outcomes and the continuum of care seamless and of higher quality (Fichman et al., 2011). In effect, listening to and learning from their stories and discussions offer tremendous promise for developing a more nuanced understanding of the depth of experiences of other patients (Deitrick et al., 2007).

Thus, the extraordinarily rich and exponentially growing sources of self-reported stories and interactive discussions in social media make it relatively easy to comprehend that people in social media conversations could support and contribute to further improvement in the quality of care in the healthcare sector. For instance, the "How Are You?" portal has been created by NHS East of England and Cambridge Healthcare to allow patients to create personal health records. It prompts them to enter periodic updates on their health status and to securely share their information with medical and healthcare providers, informal caregivers, family and friends. Again, the platform helps patients to track patient updates which allow receivers to monitor a patient's well-being and alert them when the patient may be in need of extra help or additional encouragement.

In many SSA countries, health technology also supports emergency and preparedness. In the era of social media, the way people connect and communicate with others has been altered. Evidence suggests that the use of social media increases tremendously when catastrophes occur because the demand for immediate and in-depth information surges among members of the public, who then give rapt and sustained attention to these media sources (Fraustino et al., 2012). Largely, the success of public health emergency systems often relies on routine attention to preparedness, timeliness in responding to daily problems, and the resilience that promotes rapid recovery. Consequently, social media contributes to placing medical emergency management professionals in a better position to respond to and make informed decisions about emergency medical catastrophes. For example, several researchers collected haemoglobin data from members of TuDiabetes, a social networking site for the international diabetes community, and found that the results for users from the USA mirrored those in a national survey conducted by the US Center for Disease Control and Prevention. By this, social media becomes an efficient platform for collecting data and disease surveillance (Weitzman et al., 2011). Thus, the immediate and widespread reach and connectivity offered by social media improve all component efforts before, during and after disasters, including disseminating, sharing, communicating and gathering information on emergency plans, and establishing and participating in emergency networks.

The foregoing significant roles of technology and social media in healthcare delivery have not emerged without negative effect. First, despite various empirical evidence that links virtual health information to positive health-related outcomes, there are serious concerns regarding information provided through this medium. One of the significant issues about the role of technology in healthcare delivery is defamation, which can have negative impacts on the reputation of another person or institution. Largely, engagement and conversation on social media are not only accessible to a wider audience but also remain for a longer period of time than conventional dialogues and traditional media. Even though technology systems help patients to tell stories, share experiences and receive advice, negative information about patients' health has the potential to reflect poorly on patients, physicians and medical institutions and can also be difficult to control when it gets out of hand. According to Butt (2012), frivolous comments may be entertaining at an individual level, but may be captured and disseminated to the public and thus tarnish the image of the physician or the medical institution. In other words, social media activities have the potential to cause unwanted defamation, which can consequently lead to loss of employment, the filing of civil claims, and placing public confidence in the profession at risk (Mansfield et al., 2011).

21.5 ACCELERATING THE ADOPTION OF TECHNOLOGY INTO HEALTHCARE

In an age of disruptive innovation, there are a lot of great technological ideas to transform the healthcare system, yet it can be tremendously difficult to accelerate the adoption of these technologies into routine healthcare practices (Arshoff, 2010). For instance, these health technologies can help secure accumulation and exchange of vast amounts of health data about patients. They also have the potential to empower individuals, increase transparency, enhance the ability to study healthcare delivery and payment systems, and ultimately improve healthcare. However, technologies such as social media, electronic health records (EHRs), telehealth devices, remote monitoring technologies and mobile health applications are remarkably underutilised, especially in sub-Saharan Africa. For instance, in 2010, just 25 per cent of physician offices and 15 per cent of acute care hospitals took advantage of EHRs. Even fewer used social media, remote monitoring and telehealth technologies.

Quite surprisingly, one would realise that while many consumers access their banking information online daily, only 7 per cent have used the web to access their personal health information. This begs the question as to what could be the possible reason for the slow adoption. In an answer to this, Kanter (2012) cites factors such as competence, level of complexity, cost of product, loss of control, real threats – changed responsibilities, lost jobs and increased uncertainty – as some of the contributing factors. For the purposes of this discussion, and considering the nature of the industry, we consider the PEPP model by Lalla and Arshoff (2013) to explore how healthcare systems can accelerate the adoption of technologies into routine health practices. We summarise the current model into four stages, namely: Prepare, Engage, Plan and Proceed.

21.5.1 PREPARE

The first stage in the integration is the preparation stage. Effective preparation begins with starting the planning and introduction process early, with a major focus on understanding the possible reasons for accepting and/or resisting adoption. This understanding often changes how innovation is introduced (Lalla & Arshoff, 2013). Favourable reasons will mean that the organisation can continue with the process to integrate technologies. In the event that there are objections, it means that the organisation must revisit the reasons for integration and improve on the specifics. In the preparation process, it is also important to identify and recruit the best quality personnel for the innovation's adoption process. Experience shows that a business may often need more than one champion at a site and the champions should be a mix of physicians and healthcare professionals to be able to fully integrate the system.

This implies that both clinical and economic data on benefit outcomes should be defined by healthcare professionals and providers and the benefits explained and aligned with hospital's objectives, strategies, plans and quality improvement plans (QIPs). Also, there should be a link to hospital metrics such as cost savings due to reduced adverse events, shorter length of stay and/or fewer readmissions. The preparatory stage also includes providing financial incentive payments for the adoption and meaningful use of certified technology. Another important consideration in this stage is that materials and plans that address issues and support hospital objectives and QIPs should help build support for the innovation and its adoption.

21.5.2 ENGAGE

The second step in the integration process is the engagement. Engagement of all individuals who benefit directly or indirectly from the innovation needs to be highlighted. Being inclusive is important. Here, it is important for the lead persons in the integration to include the obvious and non-obvious stakeholders as well as front line employees in the process. This stage is essential because any person who matters in the integration process and is not integrated can slow any aspect of the implementation process (Lalla & Arshoff, 2013). Further, it is essential to support the development of a trained workforce to implement and use health IT technologies. This could be a government or donor initiative to help equip the health system with necessary innovations to enhance patient care. For example, to meet the anticipated growth in demand for health IT professionals, HITECH made available $118 million to support the training and development of more than 50,000 new health IT workers. It has been suggested that the future for healthcare in rural areas in Africa depends on investment in technology. In most SSA countries, lack of funding has slowed investment in healthcare, creating an avenue for a state–private partnership. For instance, in Nigeria, Vodacom recently partnered Kaduna State government to launch a mobile technology based healthcare programme, "SMS for life 2.0", to support healthcare delivery in Nigeria and the SSA region (Abegaz, 2018).

Further to the process of engagement, healthcare institutions need to gather information about what is currently being done by interviewing all the identified stakeholders. Use the information to map the current process (including timelines). Identify strengths, weaknesses, challenges and other areas that need improvement. Share information about innovation (including benefit rationale for its use, as well as hospital objectives and plans) during interviews. Finally, in this process, lead implementers must ask stakeholders where they think the innovation fits relative to their responsibilities, patient care challenges and hospital plans. This is important to help identify emerging challenges to the implementation process and how it can be resolved.

21.5.3 PLAN

At this stage, the lead implementers consolidate findings and information to develop a map of current processes showing strengths, weaknesses, timelines and any learning. It is important to note that the health system must develop a strawman for the proposed implementation adoption plan. This stage is very essential in the integration process by which the technology is actually implemented (Lalla & Arshoff, 2013). It is a key step to gaining support for the technology. This stage also allows stakeholders to collectively review, analyse and enhance the proposed plan of implementation. After the meeting, which should be based on learning and suggestions, the institution needs to amalgamate the findings into a single document adoption/implementation plan. This document becomes the final roadmap to support healthcare providers' adoption, implementation and use of certified technology.

For instance, The Regional Extension Centre (REC) Program in the USA, established through the HITECH Act with more than $720 million in grants over a four-year project period, has set up 62 centres across the nation with staff and resources dedicated to helping providers implement and become meaningful users of certified EHR technology (ONC, 2011). Support is provided by the Health Information Technology Research Centre (HITRC), which will work to gather relevant information on effective practices and help the RECs collaborate with one another and with relevant stakeholders to identify and share best practices in EHR adoption, meaningful use and provider support.

Moreover, to accelerate EHR adoption, the US system has provided financial incentives to doctors and hospitals and relied on private companies to compete to sell EHR systems to them. The UK purchased and deployed new EHR systems centrally for primary care from four main providers (ensuring discounts and centralised procurement), while secondary care was purchased from private companies, through local budgets, with funding available centrally for the most digitally mature hospitals to act as exemplars. Also, the healthcare institutions should encourage the inclusion of meaningful use in professional certification and medical education (ONC, 2011).

21.5.4 PROCEED

The last step in the integration process is the actual integration of the technology into the systems of the organisation. After the plan is completed and there is engagement with enough buy-in from stakeholders, the next step would be the launch of the implementation plan. A few steps are also relevant in the process (ONC, 2011). First the lead implementer must conduct meeting(s) with all stakeholders and employees who could be directly or indirectly affected by the adoption of the innovation. Healthcare institutions should remind attendees of the inclusive processes such as the engagement and participation levels. They should share the implementation plan, timelines and launch date and get ready to launch. As the plan gets implemented, it is crucial that the progress be monitored and issues/challenges be addressed as priority. Employees tend to quickly identify challenges so that relevant adjustments made to the plan, and these are critical to ensure engagement, support and a successful adoption. The last process in the implementation is to schedule and conduct status updates. Initially, the updates should be daily, then moved to weekly, monthly, biannually and annually routines. The objective of the updates is to course-correct and optimise. Organisations that plan to introduce technology should allocate sufficient time and resources to successfully adopt innovation.

21.6 CONCLUSIONS AND RECOMMENDATIONS

"If we don't know where we are going, we won't know when we don't get there", says the quotable Yogi Berra. The market will surely figure out a way to make money, and technology will advance in miraculous ways. Instead, we need to figure out a way to have a healthier and happier patient (and not just treating them as individuals), and to do that we have got to focus on integrating technology with the healthcare system.

Undoubtedly, the role of technology applications in healthcare has expanded exponentially, especially in SSA. The ability of a healthcare delivery organisation to employ the most effective one to store, share and analyse health information is important. Healthcare organisations can use healthcare technologies to create and deliver services and help users consume them. The use of technology increases provider capabilities and patient access while improving quality of life for some patients and saving the lives of others. In effect, we are moving into an era in which physicians can see patients remotely and accurately diagnose, even in the most rural areas, through telemedicine. In effect, healthcare delivery has progressed from using technology to improve patient care and the healthcare industry to impacting our society as a whole. In the integration of technology into the operations of health service delivery, lead implementers must prepare, engage, plan and execute. In doing this, all stakeholders must be involved in developing the implementation plan. After implementation, the process should be monitored and adjustments made to the process.

To achieve significant benefits from technology, this chapter recommends, first, that management of health institutions, especially in SSA, should recognise the benefits of instituting technologies in their operations. Second, healthcare providers should identify the department, units or sections of their operation that require technology and the resources required to deploy the needed technologies. The chapter also recommends that management should broaden their effort and view from the physical components of healthcare technologies to non-physical areas such as social media, mobile health, telemedicine and teleHealth, among others. Moreover, as part of the implementation effort, adequate resources should be provided to maintain the facilities to better serve their purpose and the investment in them.

Furthermore, the chapter recommends that, while healthcare providers and institutions are concerned about integrating technology into service delivery, they should be mindful of negative consequences associated with such technologies. Because of this, appropriate security, safety and privacy policies should be developed to check defamation, invasion of privacy and other risks associated with information piracy. The chapter also recommends that health institutions should ensure a controlled system in which clients are screened properly before they are allowed to engage with the official technological applications of institutions. It is expected that, when these are implemented, they will help healthcare organisations to improve their service creation, delivery and consumption systems towards delivering more effective and efficient healthcare for customers. Technology adoption in SSA is on the rise owing to the internet revolution, mobile phone use and social media applications. In view of this, stakeholders around the world, especially in the sub-Saharan region must consider these as opportunities to improve health service delivery.

REFERENCES

Abegaz, S. T. (2018). Marching for 3D printing: Its potential to promoting access to healthcare in Africa. In J. A. Morales-Gonzalez & E. Aguilar Nájera, *Reflections on bioethics* (chapter 7). IntechOpen.

Alshakhs, F., & Alanzi, T. (2018). The evolving role of social media in health-care delivery: Measuring the perception of health-care professionals in eastern Saudi Arabia. *Journal of Multidisciplinary Healthcare*, *11*, 473.

Annam, S. (2002). *ICT as a tool for rural development*. Department of Electrical Engineering, Indian Institute of Technology Kanpur.

Antheunis, M. L., Tates, K., & Nieboer, T. E. (2013). Patients' and health professionals' use of social media in health care: Motives, barriers and expectations. *Patient Education and Counseling*, *92*(3), 426–431.

Arshoff, L. (2010). Assessing innovations: What is the optimal approach for healthcare organizations? *Healthcare Quarterly (Toronto, Ontario)*, *13*(2), 87–89.

Baur, C., & Kanaan, S. B. (2006). *Expanding the reach and impact of consumer e-health tools*. US Department of Health and Human Services.

Bock, B., & Rosen, R. (2017, January). Introduction to social media and healthcare technology minitrack. In *Proceedings of the 50th Hawaii International Conference on System Sciences*.

Bozeman, B. (2000). Technology transfer and public policy: A review of research and theory. *Research Policy*, *29*(4–5), 627–655.

Butt, C. M. (2012). *Patient care and digital spaces: The role of social media within participatory medicine* (Doctoral dissertation, University of Wisconsin–Stout).

Campbell, B. C., & Craig, C. M. (2014). Social media and health: Current and future healthcare provider perspectives. *Journal of Contemporary Medical Education*, *2*(2), 129.

Campbell, L., Evans, Y., Pumper, M., & Moreno, M. A. (2016). Social media use by physicians: A qualitative study of the new frontier of medicine. *BMC Medical Informatics and Decision Making*, *16*(1), 91.

Chou, W. Y. S., Hunt, Y. M., Beckjord, E. B., Moser, R. P., & Hesse, B. W. (2009). Social media use in the United States: Implications for health communication. *Journal of Medical Internet Research*, *11*(4).

Dahl, S. (2018). *Social media marketing: Theories and applications*. Sage.

Deitrick, L. M., Capuano, T. A., Paxton, S. S., Stern, G., Dunleavy, J., & Miller, W. L. (2007). Becoming a leader in patient satisfaction: Changing the culture of care in an academic community hospital. *Health Marketing Quarterly*, *23*(3), 31–57.

Eysenbach, G. (2008). Medicine 2.0: Social networking, collaboration, participation, apomediation, and openness. *Journal of Medical Internet Research*, *10*(3), e22.

Fett, M. (2008). *Technology, health and health care*. Occasional Papers: Health Financing Series, Volume 5.

Fichman, R. G., Kohli, R., & Krishnan, R. (Eds.). (2011). Editorial overview – the role of information systems in healthcare: Current research and future trends. *Information Systems Research*, *22*(3), 419–428.

Fraustino, J. D., Liu, B., & Jin, Y. (2012). *Social media use during disasters: A review of the knowledge base and gaps* (pp. 1–39). National Consortium for the Study of Terrorism and Responses to Terrorism.

Fuchs, R. (2003). DPA report: Information and communication technologies for development; final draft.

Geisler, E. (1999). Multiple-perspectives model of medical technology. *Health Care Management Review*, *24*(3), 55–63.

Halevi, G., Liu, A. C., & Yoon, J. H. (2018). Social media utilization by healthcare leaders. *Journal of Scientific Innovation in Medicine*, *1*(1).

Heeks, R. (2002). i-development not e-development: Special issue on ICTs and development. *Journal of International Development*, *14*(1), 1–11.

Jayanthi, A. (2014, January 28). 10 biggest technological advancements for healthcare in the last decade. Becker's Health IT & CIO Review. Retrieved from www.beckershospitalreview.com/healthcare-information-technology/10-biggest-technological-advancements-for-healthcare-in-the-last-decade.html.

Kabene, S., & Wolfe, M. (2011). Risks and benefits of technology in health care. In *Clinical Technologies: Concepts, Methodologies, Tools and Applications* (pp. 13–24). IGI Global.

Kanter, R. M. (2012, September 25). Ten reasons people resist change. *Harvard Business Review*, *74*.

Kivits, J. (2006). Informed patients and the internet: A mediated context for consultations with health professionals. *Journal of Health Psychology*, *11*(2), 269–282.

Kumar, R. (2017). Paradigm shift: Role of social media and information technology in healthcare advancements. *Journal of Health and Medical Informatics*, *8*, e146.

Lalla, F., & Arshoff, L. (2013, April). A mental health initiative to enhance schizophrenia treatment efficacy. *Healthcare Management Forum*, *26*(1), 46–50.

Lim, W. M. (2016). Social media in medical and health care: Opportunities and challenges. *Marketing Intelligence & Planning*, *34*(7), 964–976.

Luarn, P., & Chiu, Y. P. (2015). Key variables to predict tie strength on social network sites. *Internet Research*, *25*(2), 218–238.

Malvey, D., & Slovensky, D. J. (2014). *mHealth: Transforming healthcare*. Springer.

Mansfield, S. J., Morrison, S. G., Stephens, H. O., Bonning, M. A., Wang, S. H., Withers, A. H., … & Perry, A. W. (2011). Social media and the medical profession. *Medical Journal of Australia*, *194*(12), 642–644.

Office of the National Coordinator for Health Information Technology (ONC). (2011). *Federal health information technology strategic plan, 2011–2015*.

Pew Research Internet Project (2014). Mobile technology fact sheet: Pew Research Center's Internet & American Life Project. Washington, DC: Pew Research Centre. Retrieved from www.pewinternet.org/fact-sheets/mobile-technology-fact-sheet/.

Read, K., & Guistini, D. (2011). Social media for health care managers: Creating a workshop in collaboration with the UBC Centre for Health Care Management. *Journal of the Canadian Health Libraries Association*, *32*(3), 157–164.

State Health Access Data Assistance Centre (Shadac). (2011). Trends in U.S. employer-sponsored health insurance. Retrieved April 15, 2012, from www.shadac.org/publications/trends-in-us-employer-sponsored-healthinsurance.

Steventon, A., Bardsley, M., Billings, J., Dixon, J., Doll, H., Hirani, S., … & Rogers, A. (2012). Effect of telehealth on use of secondary care and mortality: Findings from the Whole System Demonstrator cluster randomised trial. *BMJ*, *344*, e3874.

Telecare Services Association (2012). What is telecare? Retrieved September 10, 2012, from www.telecare.org.uk/consumer-services/what-is-telecare.

Thimbleby, H. (2013). Technology and the future of healthcare. *Journal of Public Health Research*, *2*(3).

Tihanyi, L., & Roath, A. S. (2002). Technology transfer and institutional development in Central and Eastern Europe. *Journal of World Business*, *37*(3), 188–198.

Van De Belt, T. H., Engelen, L. J., Berben, S. A., & Schoonhoven, L. (2010). Definition of Health 2.0 and Medicine 2.0: A systematic review. *Journal of Medical Internet Research*, *12*(2).

Wahab, S. A., Rose, R. C., & Osman, S. I. W. (2012). Defining the concepts of technology and technology transfer: A literature analysis. *International Business Research*, *5*(1), 61–71.

Weitzman, E. R., Cole, E., Kaci, L., & Mandl, K. D. (2011). Social but safe? Quality and safety of diabetes-related online social networks. *Journal of the American Medical Informatics Association*, *18*(3), 292–297.

Index

Page numbers in **bold** refer to tables and those in *italic* refer to figures.